D0554224

SICILY

SICILY

THREE THOUSAND YEARS OF HUMAN HISTORY

SANDRA BENJAMIN

STEERFORTH PRESS
HANOVER, NEW HAMPSHIRE

For information about permission to reproduce
selections from this book, write to:
Steerforth Press L.C., 25 Lebanon Street
Hanover, New Hampshire 03755

Library of Congress Cataloging-in-Publication Data
Benjamin, Sandra.
  Sicily : three thousand years of human history / Sandra Benjamin. —
1st ed.
     p. cm.
Includes bibliographical references and indexes.
ISBN-13: 978-1-58642-101-4 (alk. paper)
ISBN-10: 1-58642-101-8 (alk. paper)
  1. Sicily (Italy) — History. I. Title.

DG866.B46 2006
945'.8–dc22

2006009394

Second Printing

To the new
EUGENE
for helping me
in new ways

CONTENTS

MAPS

ACKNOWLEDGMENTS

When in Sicily during the writing of this book I usually based myself in Mazara, with its ambience conducive to researching, to writing, and to relaxing. There I received scholarly and personal help especially from Arch. Michele Abruzzo; Dott. Aurelio Burgio and his wife, Signora Pina; Baldo Calafato; Prof. Salvatore Ingrassia and his wife,Prof.ssa Rosa; Dott. Maurizio Pantaleo; Dott. Corrado Sansone; and Arch. Mario Tumbiolo. Elsewhere in Trapani province I thank Prof. Giovanni Alagna, Avv. Ignazio Caruso, and Giuseppe DeArcangelo and his wife, Crocetta Benenati.

In Palermo and environs, thanks to Dr.ssa Patricia Ardizzone; Dott. Franco Barna; Dott. Andrea Borruso; Suora Anna Maria Catelani; Prof. Pippo Costanzo; Prof. Giorgio Chinnici and his wife, Nora, and daughter, Valentina; Rosalba Damiata; Dott. Fabrizio D'Avenia; Prof. Giacomo Dentici and his wife, Dott.ssa Rosamaria Buccellato; Ing. Domenico La Cavera; Dott. Vito La Fata; Dott. Gioacchino Lanza Tomasi; Dott. Rosario Lentini; Prof. Giuseppe Carlo Marino, Dott. Romolo Menighetti; Avv. Giuseppe Palmeri; Prof. Francesco Renda; Prof.ssa Patrizia Sardina; Padre Michelangelo Simonato; Prof. Alberto Tulumello; and Prof. Paolo Viola.

In Messina, thanks to Prof.ssa Michela D'Angelo; Dott. Sergio Di Giacomo; Prof.ssa Maria Teresa Di Paola; Prof. Giuseppe Martino and his wife, Prof.ssa Silvana Salandra; and Prof. Rosario Moscheo. In Lipari, Dott.ssa Maria Grazia Vanaria. In Catania and its province, Anna Rita Anguzza; Prof. Sebastiano Favitta; Dott. Andrea Imbrogiano and his family; Prof. Giacomo Pace; Antonino Vasta; and Ercole Vasta. In the province of Enna, Primo David. In the province of Agrigento, Dott.ssa Maria Gerardi Marino. In the province of Siracusa, Saro Cuda and Katherine Magnus.

Farther afield, several people provided hospitality that facilitated my doing research in their cities: In Naples, Pina and Antonia Palladino, and Maria and Vito Salandra. In New York City, Peggy

Earle, Jerry and Eleanor Koffler, Tom McCauley and Marianne Di Palermo McCauley, Evgeny Rivkin and his family, and Sara and Bernie Zagdanski.

To librarians and others who sought material for me in their professional capacity, it goes without saying that without them this book could never have been written. Those known to me by name are Dott. Alberto Costantino in Trapani; Dott. Rino Rocco Russo in Caltagirone; Dr.ssa Cuffaro at the Biblioteca Nazionale in Palermo; and in Naples, Dott.ssa Vera Valitutto (Università degli Studi), Letizia Ragonesi (Istituto Universitario Orientale), Dott. Giovanni Marcello (Biblioteca Nazionale), Antonia Mara (municipal library); Dott.ssa Cristina Liguori and others at the branch St. Elmo; and Tony Salandra. I owe particular thanks to Dott. Rosario Salafia and his friendly staff in Mazara, Dott. Salvatore Pedone in Palermo, Dott. Roberto Foderà and Dott. Riccardo Abbate of ISTAT in Palermo, and Dott.ssa Lucia Marinelli in Naples. It's impossible to express sufficient appreciation of the New York Public Library's collections. I'm indebted to the people at the reference desk in the General Reference Division at 42nd Street not only for help in locating particular items but also for ideas, and to the Belmont branch for its numerous publications on Italian history and its atmosphere of repose.

Regarding the nuts and bolts of constructing a book, I'm grateful to Gene and to mms for coming to my aid in moments of computer distress.

INTRODUCTION

When you hear "Sicily" what's the first thing you think of? If you're like most people, the immediate association is "Mafia." To be sure, the island has suffered, for hundreds of years, the peculiar gangster-government collaboration known now as "Mafia," yet Sicily has a rich history that long antedates that organization.

In the beginning were the Greeks, who dominated Sicily for five hundred years. As it is the classical sites that bring most tourists to Sicily, I have described some of the architecture still visible (after two-thousand-plus years) and the political and economic conditions that gave rise to those temples and fortifications.

The trimillennial drama continued with protagonists from three continents: the Romans from the Italic peninsula occupied Sicily for six hundred years, followed by the Vandals and Goths from northeastern Europe and the Byzantines from westernmost Asia. Then Muslims from North Africa came to Sicily and diffused their advanced culture and agriculture. The Normans from what is today northwestern France introduced the Sicilians to feudalism and to the ideas of parliament and responsible government. A scion of the Normans, Frederick, while king of Sicily was also Holy Roman Emperor and one of Europe's most complex sovereigns ever.

As Europe developed nation-states, Sicily was occupied by the aggrandizing Spanish. The houses of Savoy and of Hapsburg ruled Sicily for brief periods, then the Spanish took over again as the Bourbon dynasty. Giuseppe Garibaldi won Sicily from the Bourbons and made it part of a new Kingdom of Italy. After World War II, Sicily was ruled briefly by the Americans and the British — that was a novelty for the Americans, though the British had been instrumental in running Sicily off and on for centuries.

So had the outlaws, if not for quite so long. This book will consider how the serial foreign occupation helped to create an environment in which the Mafia sprouted.

Many regions of the world, indeed other regions of Italy, experienced similar invasions, resettlement, and foreign rule, without subjecting themselves to Mafia-like domination. So in Sicily additional forces must have been at work. Climate and topography inevitably influence the character of a people, and we shall see how they did so for Sicilians. In a word, wheat. Dry, hilly Sicily supports few crops; wheat was the staple of the classical Mediterranean diet, and Sicilians cultivating their hard wheat needed little initiative or industry. This fostered the poverty and passivity that traditionally characterized the island.

In consequence, the ambitious emigrated. In recent centuries Sicily has been unusual among nations in the high proportion of its residents who moved abroad. Emigration not only took Sicilian practices to other lands, it also significantly changed the lives of people who remained on the island.

These forces, tightly interwoven, go a long way toward explaining Sicily and the Sicilians. Most books on Sicily deal primarily with the fine arts or with religious life, but I have hardly touched on them. I have focused rather on the economic and demographic aspects of Sicily's story. This book is a general history, an account of welfare and warfare. Within it I have highlighted certain threads that run through the centuries: Sicily's particular patterns of land use and landholding, and Sicily's unique relationship with the church. Sicily's character has also been determined by the *lack* of influence from events that affected Europe generally, namely the Crusades and Columbus's discovery of America.

Sicily is known for its Mafia and its emigration. Note the development of banditry and corruption forerunning the modern Mafia, but note too that the problem of the Mafia in today's Sicily is something different from foreigners' common perception. Likewise, the high emigration from Sicily overshadows the importance of its immigration. Besides the several peoples who ruled Sicily — essentially those in this book's chapter titles — other peoples participated in Sicily's story, among them Jews and Ligurians and Albanians. All are ancestors of modern Sicilians. Having found their study fascinating, I invite you to come and meet them.

—ᖶ 1 ᖷ—

LIPARI

Warnings against going to Sicily have been broadcast for a long time. Just listen to Homer, as he talks about the strait that separates Sicily from the mainland:

> On the western side you'll see a big flowering fig tree, below which is the lair of Charybdis. He vomits thrice daily, then gulps down copious amounts of the waters. Don't be caught near Charybdis at those hours, or he'll swallow you and your ship. On the opposite side of the strait, where the banks are higher, you'll see a rock so smooth that it appears polished. In a cave halfway up that rock lives a monster called Scylla with the body of a dog, but with six necks and six heads. Each of its mouths has three rows of overlapping teeth, which it uses to grab six men from every passing ship.

Scylla and Charybdis sound just as frightening as the Mafia. Today's visitor to Sicily may be reassured to know that he is no more likely to be killed by the Mafia than by Homer's monsters.

ᖴᖴ

Homer didn't claim to have seen the beasts himself; he was organizing and telling some stories of his people. The team of Scylla and Charybdis was a fanciful explanation for the very real shipwrecks frequent at the northeast tip of the island. As Homer lived in Asia Minor and narrated these stories around 730 B.C., we know that the accounts of sailings to Sicily were then familiar in ports of the eastern Mediterranean — over a thousand miles distant.

The Greeks called it Trinacria, the three-pointed island. We infer from Homer that the island was known not only to sailors but to a broader population: in his war poem *The Iliad*, he refers casually to the story of Daedalus, in a way that assumes his audience to be familiar with the place. Daedalus — not quite so well known at our time and place — went to Sicily but avoided the straits. Having killed someone in his homeland, Athens, he fled to Crete. There he constructed the Minotaur's labyrinth and generally worked with such originality that the king refused to let him leave. So Daedalus built wings of wax and feathers for himself and his son, Icarus, and they soared away. But the boy flew too close to the sun, his wax melted, and he fell to his death. Daedalus continued to glide, occasionally descending to dip his wings in the water to cool them, until he reached Sicily. So if you are thinking of an escape to Sicily, you aren't the first. Daedalus flew there too.

Sicily became the landing place in that story probably because of its location plunk in the middle of the Mediterranean, which gave the island a central location in the civilized world. At the time of Homer, scaremongers notwithstanding, seamen kept bringing boats safely into Sicily from all around the Mediterranean. Some of their passengers did business in Sicily and then departed, while other passengers remained and developed communities. During the same decades that Homer was becoming the first author in the Western world, Greece was establishing her first colonies on the Sicilian mainland.

✑

Before making our tour of those colonies, though, we'll visit Lipari, a small island off Sicily's north coast. Today you reach Lipari from Messina by taking a train west for an hour to Milazzo and then a boat northwest for an hour. Yet visiting Lipari is less a trip through space than through time. Homer lived some twenty-seven hundred years before us; if we go back twenty-seven hundred years before Homer, we'll find Lipari already flourishing.

Homer heard tales of Lipari that were already ancient. Seafarers told him of this island where the people worked a hard rock to make various kinds of blades. The stone workers claimed to be the island's first inhabitants, having found it empty when they arrived from the Sicilian mainland. But the Greeks who returned from Lipari, recalling how they had shivered there, saw its past differently: here lived and ruled the god of the winds, Aeolus. Homer tells the story of the Ithacan king Odysseus landing on Lipari. When he was about to depart, Aeolus offered him a wine bag of wind to speed his voyage, and Odysseus stowed it in the hold of his ship. Nine uneventful days at sea brought the ship within sight of Ithaca, so close they could see the fires on shore. The crew, meanwhile, had been eyeing that wine bag and speculating about its contents: doubtless some valuable gift from Aeolus that Odysseus didn't intend to share. So the men untied the bag, the winds escaped, and a storm arose that drove their ship all the way back to Aeolus.

The Greeks called the island Aeolia; it's the largest of a group of islands now known as both "Aeolian" and "Lipari." Had Odysseus remained on Aeolia, he would doubtless have joined the men there in working the hard volcanic rock, obsidian.

This obsidian was born of an eruption of the volcano Monte Pelato, in Aeolia's northeast, around 7000 B.C. Generations passed, into the period we call neolithic. On the big island of Sicily people were beginning to plant crops and raise animals, but they still obtained food through gathering and hunting. Those who went to seek food in the mountains behind Sicily's north coast could, in clear weather, see small islands in the distance and doubtless wondered if food might be easier to find on those islands. But for a long long time they couldn't get there to investigate. Eventually, sometime during the fifth millennium B.C., they improved their boats and navigational techniques sufficiently to send out a few of their most intrepid explorers, who discovered some of Lipari's appealing features: it was unpopulated, certain parts were extremely fertile, and in the northeast part of the island large areas were covered by shiny black rocks with edges of greater sharpness than anything they had ever seen before. The explorers decided to fetch their friends.

∾

The neolithic era is the period when humans used stone implements. They used a lot of flint, as it is relatively easy to shape. Although flint is very hard, neolithic persons found that by pressing a stone or a bone against a piece of freshly dug flint they could make its edges flake off and in so doing sharpen an edge for cutting. Obsidian, having natural sharp edges, required less work to make a knife, so the people of Lipari brought it into use alongside flint. The new islanders turned pieces of obsidian into cutting tools and before long (just a few centuries) they had an export industry.

The Lipari craftsmen became skilled in working obsidian, but the demand for their product had less to do with their skill than with the scarcity of the raw material. A few other volcanic Mediterranean islands had small quantities, but Lipari had by far the largest supply. Although obsidian is a product of volcanic eruption, most volcanic eruptions yield no obsidian. Obsidian is that rare lava that cooled very quickly, into a kind of natural glass; usually lava is exploded by hot air, making pumice, a light-colored, lightweight substance for which prehistoric man had no use. But apparently he could use all the obsidian implements he could get, certainly all that Lipari could produce. The location of Lipari in the center of the Mediterranean facilitated the transport of the heavy product. Craftsmen streamed into Lipari — so many that some of the newcomers had to settle and practice their trade on nearby smaller islands. In the Mediterranean basin during the neolithic era, the Aeolian archipelago was a major population center, and Lipari a boom town.

As I type away at my computer, beside it on my desk stands a three-kilo hunk of obsidian. The laptop, matte black, symbolizes international commerce of our time. The obsidian, its shiny black brightened by straight, narrow white lines running irregularly through it, represents international commerce at its very beginning. Neolithic man wanted sharp tools for cutting his animals and his enemies. Obsidian was the sharpest workable material he knew, and most obsidian came from Lipari, so Lipari enjoyed a seller's market. For some seventeen hundred years.

That was around 4500–3000 B.C. But more significant than the *when* is the *where*: notwithstanding the fertility of her lavic soil, Lipari's strong winds precluded the growth of grain sufficient to feed the population. The migrants from the mainland had to spend much of their time fishing, seizing sea-animals and wild birds, gathering wild fruits, and trying to eke what crops they could out of the land.

Of course the obsidian producers added to their alimentary stocks by their trade. The food and drink naturally arrived in containers, most of them ceramic.* Neolithic people used ceramics for pots and drinking cups, for statues and construction elements, and for containers of all kinds — for them ceramic was as multiform and as ubiquitous as plastic is for us.

At a remove of fifty centuries, and despite the fragility of ceramic ware, many thousands of pieces of early pottery can now be examined on Lipari. The archaeologists who study the pieces of pottery know how to read them like words in books — from the form of a piece they usually know how it was used, and from the form and decoration they usually know where it was made and when. The scholars move from provenance to foreign trade, for having determined the kind or kinds of ceramics produced in a given locality, they can attribute the discrepant pieces to foreign production. The foreign pieces indicate either the presence of foreign peoples or commerce with them. Archaeologists collectively can determine the provenance of most pottery pieces. Pottery is therefore important not only as work of art but also as document about the movement of peoples.

The ceramics found on Lipari claim special attention because Lipari produced relatively little pottery. The soil being lava-based, it lacked clay. When the islanders made pottery using just the local

---

* *Pottery* and *ceramics* are synonyms, at least as regards pieces made through the Middle Ages (when pottery generally refers to a simpler earthenware than ceramics).

kaolin soil, the result was poor. They imported clay from the north coast of Sicily to mix with the local kaolin soil and made other pieces more successfully. Lipari residents used a great deal of pottery made by other peoples.

Fragments found on Lipari are among the oldest known from the Mediterranean area. Some pieces have elegantly incised and stamped decorations of a type characteristic of the culture of Stentinello. Stentinello, probably Sicily's earliest agricultural society, had its base in southeast Sicily. The ceramics found on Lipari suggest that the first settlers there originated in Stentinello and drifted up to Sicily's north coast. They would be the first known group of Sicilian migrants.

∾

In the fifth and fourth millennia B.C. — a period about as long as that separating us from Christ — Lipari lived prosperously if not always tranquilly. As Lipari had a corner on a prime material for tools and weapons, foreigners cast envious eyes on her. Typically for seafarers, the Aeolians in Lipari had built their first housing on the coast, but in time they felt threatened enough to move their settlement to a hill in the southern part of the island's east coast, a natural fortress from which they could dominate the best landing places on the island; later the hill would be called "il Castello" (the Castle).

A group is known to have invaded around the start of the fourth millennium, probably from across the Adriatic. The newcomers battled the locals for a long time and seem to have gained hegemony over the island. A lot of obsidian from Lipari has been found along the Dalmatian coast.

Lipari continued to live well. It appears that the new leadership had less concern about defense. Around the middle of the fourth millennium new settlements were begun, one on flatland close to il Castello and others, tiny, on the plateau. Lipari's population increased, so that in the second half of the millennium Lipari, the city on the Aeolian Island of the same name, was one of the greatest in the Mediterranean basin. The obsidian that underlay the island's importance can still be seen in the residual fragments from the era that dot the islands of the Aeolian archipelago.

But all good things come to an end. The distressing chain of events started in the lands to the east, where during the first half of the third millennium Greeks were learning about metals. When they used copper and then bronze (copper alloyed with tin) to make tools and weapons, these gradually replaced obsidian.

Modern economists tell us that the developments causing technological unemployment will give rise to new kinds of work, and so it happened for Lipari. As the Greeks accelerated their travel around the Mediterranean to sell their metal products, Lipari regained importance, since she could control the ships passing through the Strait of Messina. Some mainland Greeks settled on Lipari; they were later given the name Aeolians because they were of the people who told the story about the wind god Aeolus. Quite skilled in navigation, the Aeolians maintained commercial ties with Thessaly and places further north on the Greek mainland as well as with the Aegean islands. The Aeolians took Lipari into the Bronze Age.

Starting around 1800 B.C. the residents of il Castello moved to higher ground, where they built a new kind of housing, round or oval huts with sunken floors. The hilltop was rocky and less comfortable than their coastal sites — they must have moved because near the coast they felt threatened. Other indications of their new insecurity are the increase in the size of the communities in which they grouped themselves on the hilltop, and the construction around their villages of strong stone-and-mud walls.

The Aeolians feared other Greeks. All Greeks were good navigators and were seeking land for expansion. In the wake of new metal products came trade wars that rippled waters around the Mediterranean. The Aeolians on Lipari traded with the different Greek peoples. Throughout the five centuries when Mycenae was one of the world's most advanced civilizations, Lipari traded regularly with her. By the sixteenth century B.C. the Aeolians had returned to il Castello on the coast.

∽

Waves of immigrants broke upon Lipari's shores from time to time. Around 1300–1200 Ausonians came down from the Italian peninsula, lived peacefully with the islanders, yet gained hegemony over them. A large group of Sicels arrived from mainland Sicily and clashed violently with the islanders. And around 900 B.C. some group destroyed Lipari, just destroyed her, interrupting all indications of human life.

Who overthrew Lipari? There are theories, but there's nothing sure. The answer may be discovered someday, perhaps in the cave where King Aeolus kept his winds.

Don't smile — those winds are important. They won't bother you on the streets of Lipari, for modern buildings provide a windbreak. But walking along the seafront you'll feel the winds just as Homer's sailors did twenty-seven hundred years ago. Even there don't lament the winds, for they have been instrumental in preserving Lipari's great legacy of earlier peoples.

Strong winds are usually a destructive force. On Lipari though strong winds lay soft blankets. In the crumbly highlands the winds, blowing mostly from the west, whip up cumuli of dust that they then sweep down to the coastal areas. Along Lipari's east coast new ground builds up with extraordinary speed. The rapid dust cover made a coating between strata, so that the works of successive generations weren't jumbled together. Lipari is rather like an underground multistory garage, with a different civilization on each level.

So many remains of ancient civilizations are scattered around Sicily that archaeologists call it "Europe's museum." Nobody can keep track of all Sicily's ruins. Unique to Lipari is the accessibility in a small area of many excavated strata. It's the best place to see earliest Sicily.

—∽ 2 ∾—

THE GREEK PERIOD

SAILORS AND SETTLERS

Maybe at the time Lipari perished, certainly in the following century, the northeast coast of Sicily was bursting with life. Thither came Greeks and Phoenicians to dominate commerce and piracy. The Phoenicians had travelled much farther than the Greeks, for their homeland lay on the Mediterranean's far eastern shore. Their merchant marine had already been trading around Greece, and the Greeks were so impressed by the easterners' specialty purple dye that they called them "Phoenikes" ("purple").

Around 800 — all dates during the Greek period are of course B.C. — the Phoenicians, in their homeland having trouble with their neighbors, decided to move. On North Africa's north coast, from where they could control traffic between the eastern and the western Mediterranean, they established the city of Carthage and became known as Carthaginians. By then they were familiar with the central Mediterranean and knew the three-cornered island to be the largest island in the entire sea — sailing around it took almost eight days. They were expert at sailing through the Strait of Messina; indeed Scylla and Charybdis are Phoenician names, the first meaning "the rock" and the second "the hole of death."

Phoenicians/Carthaginians plying between their old and new homes encountered Greeks frequently. The Greeks adapted the Phoenician system of writing, in which a symbol represents a sound. When our story of Sicily proper opens with its colonization by the

Greeks, just a few Greeks and Carthaginians know the alphabet; it isn't yet in common use. History is written record; the story of Sicily's colonization is prehistory.

We'll become acquainted with the Carthaginians soon, when Sicily's Greek colonists collide with them.

✎

The Greek islanders arriving in Sicily knew what they wanted in a colony, for Greek city-states had already established hundreds of colonies around the Mediterranean. Colonization for the Greeks had no overtones of exploiting indigenous people (although there would be some of that). Rather, many districts of Greece, finding themselves inundated with refugees and no longer able to feed the people, undertook to develop sites where their own surplus populations could be economically self-sufficient. The great distances involved, relative to the transport available, didn't permit the *metropolis* (mother city) administrative control over its colonies. The metropolis just decided on an approximate site, found volunteers (or undesirables) to settle it, and appointed the leader-founder; then the colonists would create their own independent city-states. Colonization was important enough to the Greeks that they had a particular word for "the founder of a new settlement," *oecist*.

Although in earlier times the Greeks had been satisfied to trade, they now felt obliged to protect their trade around Sicily by having Greeks live there. The Greeks' primary motive though was finding new land to grow grain. They knew that the east coast of this large island had not only suitable fields but also more rainfall than did their home islands, so here the colonists could expect to produce enough grain to feed themselves and to export to their metropolis.

The Greeks understood their adventure to be momentous, for they recorded it in detail. In referring collectively to their colonies in Sicily and their colonies on the Italian peninsula they used the name Magna Graecia (greater Greece). The *oecist* Teocles was the first to lead a group to settle Sicily, in or around 734 B.C. Over the next fifty years Greeks established about twenty Sicilian colonies. The sequence of settlement, down Sicily's east coast and then along the south coast, prompts our itinerary of a circuit clockwise around the island.

Map 1. The Central Mediterranean, 800–300 B.C.

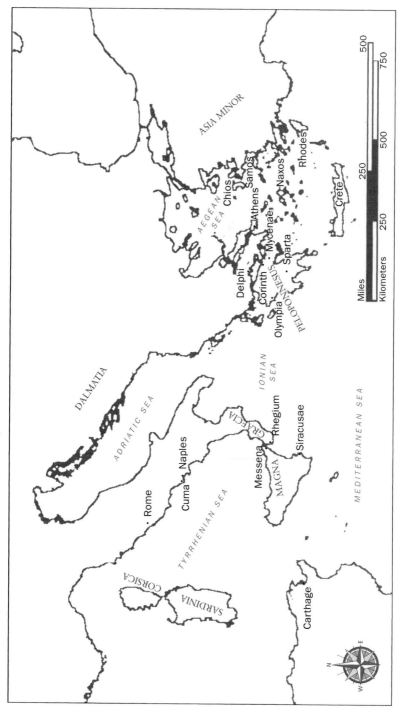

NAXOS*

In Homer's time as well as our own, foreigners travelling to Sicily liked the look of the small mountain rising just north of the huge volcano. The Greeks were familiar with the small mountain because when boats sail to Sicily from the east the main current brings them into a bay at the mountain's foot, not far south of where the sea narrows into the strait; the bay was eminently suitable for landing and for trading. The group of colonists under Teocles settled below the small mountain, which they called Tauro. From its summit their lookout would have a good view up into the strait — very important, as their settlement was bound to attract pirates.

This first group of colonists came mostly from Chalkis, north of Athens on the island of Evvoia; we call them Chalcidians. Some of the group though must have come from Naxos (a small island in the Cyclades southeast of Athens), as they gave the name Naxos to their settlement. The infertility in the immediate vicinity of the new Naxos did not deter the settlers because this first settlement was intended to be a beachhead.

They identified the ground around Naxos as lavic rock, signifying the presence of fertile land nearby. That the fertile soil was already being cultivated was doubtless known to the Chalcidians before they came. On the other hand the inhabitants, although familiar with Greek traders, would not have anticipated these Greeks' intention to live there. When the indigenous Sicels did realize it, fighting broke out, but the Greeks held their ground. The newcomers evidently arranged a division of land with the Sicels that was satisfactory to both, because the evidence indicates that the two groups farmed adjacent territory and gives no indication of further fighting between them. The Sicels are known to the world only through the Greek invasion, for they themselves left nothing to tell us about their activities.

While still negotiating the establishment of their colony, the newcomers to Naxos built an altar to Apollo. As Greeks, they practiced their religion earnestly. According to their belief, the afterlife did not

---

*Each Greek colony mentioned now has an archaeological site. Details on each site can be found in guidebooks specifically about Sicily.

involve eternal rewards or punishments for the deceased's life led on earth, but rather depended on the behavior toward him by the living: an ancestor would be happy in paradise so long as his descendants made food offerings to him regularly, ideally every day. If the offerings ceased, then the departed would become unhappy and possibly vengeful. The religion obliged the faithful to make their offerings at an altar, so Greeks establishing new colonies built altars immediately.

As the Naxos settlers explored the narrow coastal strip, where the land began to rise they found clay of good quality for their pots and containers. They built ovens in scattered spots, placing some near the altars for making objects connected with religious ritual. Gradually the town of Naxos developed to the west of the Apollo altar, between the altar and the narrow river — not right on the river, as it sometimes overflowed its banks, but a fifteen-minute walk from it. Where the short river feeds into the sea the colonists found basalt columns, some of them broken into rocks of regular polygon shapes. The settlers used these massive lavic rocks for their wall. On the western side of their settlement they constructed the wall to serve also as embankment. The Greek colonists were the first people in Sicily to build with stone.

Some of the newer colonies were to grow bigger than Naxos, which remained a little colony by the bay. The colony's clusters of houses never extended as far as a kilometer in any direction, but their fields expanded and glowed with wine grapes. The Chalcidians were the first to plant vines in Sicily. Naxos grew prosperous, thanks to Apollo.

As the son of the Greeks' major god, Zeus, Apollo enjoyed prominence among the gods. Apollo was primary god of the great oracles, where mortals made inquiries about the future and sought counsel. He was master at Delphi, the oracle in the center of the Greek mainland. As the voyage to Sicily was long and risky, and the idea of going to settle in a distant land was perturbing, the Greeks setting out to colonize commonly went to Delphi before sailing for Sicily. Apollo Archegetes, Apollo in his aspect as founder, became patron of Greek colonization in Sicily.

Because Naxos had the first temple to Apollo in Sicily, colonists throughout Sicily deemed Naxos a sacred place. The colony flourished as Greeks departing Sicily for Delphi and elsewhere in Greece stopped first at Naxos to offer sacrifice at Apollo's altar.

KATANE (PRESENT-DAY CATANIA)

Everyone knew about Mount Etna. Hesiod and Homer referred to it in their poems. The Greeks coined its name from their word meaning "I burn." From Tauro's summit looking southward one had a clear view of the volcano, and the Naxos settlers considered it a sacred spot. The Chalcidians took five years to become acquainted with their new land before moving south of the volcano.

Katane they established at the innermost point of a wide gulf, which was also the northeast corner of a fertile plain. The new colony would send out the agricultural produce of the interior and receive crafted goods from overseas. Although the vocation of trader was not quite respectable — seafarers were a disreputable lot — without trade life would be very poor indeed.

The leaders back home considered the traders crucial to maintaining the loyalty of the colonists in general, for only frequent voyages would keep the colonists aware of the developments in Greek politics and culture. Greeks tended to be intensely patriotic toward their native city-state, taking pride in its autonomy. They expected those Greeks now living in Magna Graecia to administer themselves and to feel a similar patriotism toward their own new city-state.

At the same time the sponsoring city-state considered its colonies its creatures, even a century after settlement. By then though the settlers in Sicily could define their differences from the Greeks in the homelands. In Sicily each man had more space than his counterparts in the old country, and he was producing more food. He felt richer and he was less tied to tradition. Yet colonists still felt constrained to administer themselves in accord with the wishes of the few wealthy men ruling the sponsoring metropolis. Even though her commerce with the Greek homeland was in fact flourishing, Katane led the colonies in trying to break away from the motherland's oligarchic form of government.

Toward the end of the seventh century, the philosopher Carondas wrote out some laws for his native Katane, which other colonies of Magna Graecia also adopted. It figures that colonists feel an urgency to address their particular conditions with new laws while old societies maintain old practices. Of Carondas's laws, two interest us today: that participants at assemblies must not carry weapons and that divorced men and women must not marry anyone younger than their former spouse. Apparently Carondas succeeded as legislator in putting some of his ideas into practice, so that for a certain period Katane enjoyed a moderate government halfway between oligarchy and democracy.

Sublimating fears of pirates and volcanic eruptions, the dwellers under Mount Etna lived at peace with the other Chalcidian colonies and with their Sicel neighbors. They prospered from Katane's importation of vases and terra-cottas not only from the homeland of Evvoia and nearby Attica and Corinth, but also from the distant Chios. The resulting preeminence of their city helped her exert cultural influence, and we know of poets and philosophers passing through. Cultural life in the colonies around this time included a lot of epic poetry, such as that of Homer being read to the accompaniment of the lyre.

Leontinoi (present-day Lentini)

Just before settling Katane, a Naxos party went farther south and inland to found the agricultural community of Leontinoi: before establishing their trading community the Greeks wanted to see what they would have for trading.

They tried to establish themselves at a site on the southern edge of the large plain, but on a peripheral hill the Chalcidians were met by the local community of Sicels — met but not welcomed. In times gone by these Sicels had moved to the hilltop from flat fields, probably in reaction to raiding. Now when the group from Naxos arrived, the Sicels fought fiercely to protect their land. (Thucydides wrote a sober account of the battle.)

Before they could settle themselves at Leontinoi, the Chalcidians had another people problem. Some migrants from Megara, west of Athens, had been circulating in the area, trying to find a good site for a colony. When the group of Chalcidians under Teocles at Leontinoi sent off a party to Katane, the Megarans joined the reduced population at Leontinoi. But the Megaran dialect was different from the Ionian dialect of the Chalcidians, and their gods and festivals were different. Before long the ethnic tensions became serious; the Chalcidians kicked out the Megarans, who moved east to the coast.

On the other hand, after the initial skirmish with the Sicels, the Chalcidians established what they considered good relations with them. Sicels, Homer reported, never worked the land themselves, just collected the bounty of wheat, barley, and grapes. Grains were the staple of the Greeks too, of course, but they had to produce much more than their own needs required, so as to have a surplus to send to the metropolis; furthermore, the Greeks wanted a diet more varied than that of the indigenous people. The Greeks expected to produce legumes and grapes, and olives to eat and to make into the oil that would serve for fuel and (instead of soap) for washing. They would eat the meat of sheep, pigs, and goats. They used mules as beasts of burden, though for this purpose oxen were better because the ox could plow and then be slaughtered for food. The rich kept cattle for dairy products and raised horses for military use. A good supply of all these things required work, and the Greeks managed to have the work done by Sicels. Some Sicels avoided forced labor by moving inland; like Native Americans in modern times, the simpler natives of Sicily were driven from their homes by the civilized newcomer.

Within a few decades of their first settlement in Sicily, the Chalcidians had a network of colonies and subcolonies, and Greeks from other city-states also had colonies along the shores of eastern Sicily. Although the Greek colonists included women, it didn't take much longer than nine months before babies were born of relations between a Greek and a Sicel. Willy-nilly the indigenous people were hellenizing.

MAP 2. Early Major Settlements, 734–580 B.C.

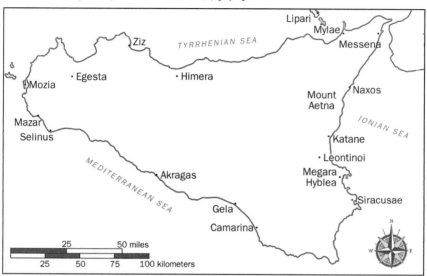

MEGARA HYBLEA

We met a group of Megarans at Leontinoi. Their colonization got off to a bad start, having foundered at another site even before they tried to live with the Chalcidians and failed. From Leontinoi their *oecist,* Lamis, took them east to the coast. (This zone of Sicels had been inhabited since the dawn of time.) There the Megarans stopped, and there Lamis died. Finally King Hyblon of the Sicels invited them to move a bit north into land adjoining his, where the shore curved east into a jagged peninsula. When that worked out, the Megarans showed their appreciation by calling their colony Megara Hyblea.

They began to plan their city, following the Greek pattern, leaving an open area in the center to serve as market and for the eventual civic buildings. The *agora* was of the greatest importance — it was the main square, the grand piazza, the site of the city's commercial, civic, and social affairs. These public activities would be overseen by the gods, for civic buildings were generally sited near shrines or even had their own altars.

By around 650 the people of Megara Hyblea felt rich enough to construct major public works: they built along the sides of the open area, on the south side erecting two small temples and on the north and east sides two covered *stoa* (colonnades) — it was beginning to look like a real *agora*. The fourth side of the square — actually a trapezoid — was left open, in accordance with Greek practice, to facilitate the arrival of the citizenry for rituals or for emergencies. The workers cleared streets to link the *agora* with the residential area. This work was substantially completed in the second half of the century, i.e., 650–600 B.C.

The first colonists at Megara Hyblea lived by the shore, in simple stone dwellings with single square rooms. When the next few generations expanded their houses to two or three rooms, some households were pushed out and had to move elsewhere. The Greeks had always planned their city centers but left their residential areas to grow erratically; now the Megara Hybleans diverged from the Greek practice and laid out their settlement's streets in a grid pattern. To reflect

MAP 3. Greek Sicily: Colonies and Their Subcolonies
with dates of foundation (all dates are B.C.)

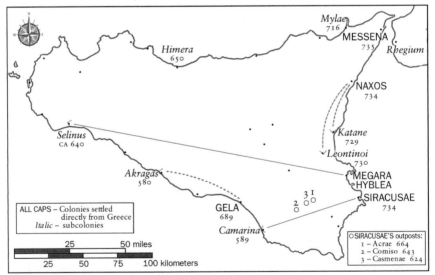

Greek ethos that all the colonists began their Sicilian lives as equals, the Megara Hybleans did their best to plot housing sites of equal size and shape. They integrated a political notion of equality into Greek architectural symmetry, and in the process seem to have distinguished themselves as the Mediterranean world's first urban planners.

SIRACUSAE (PRESENT-DAY SIRACUSA)

The founders of Siracusae came from Corinth, one of the oldest and most powerful city-states of Greece. In the rush to colonize Sicily, Corinth lost to Chalkis by a hair. On the other hand, the Corinthians took the best site: the offshore island of Ortygia ("quail"), with marvelous landing places, very easy access to the mainland, vast fields beyond, and crowds of civilized people. Ortygia had long been famous among the Greeks — Mycenaeans and Cretans came here to trade in the Bronze Age — and now Ortygia flourished as a center of Greek and Carthaginian commerce. From Ortygia the colony quickly expanded onto the mainland and developed into the city called Siracusae (from Syraka, a nearby swamp).

To Siracusae from Greece came more immigrants, including master builders, artisans, and men of letters. The ships also carried men and women charged with establishing other colonies. Chalkis, Naxos, and other metropolises shipped their excess men and women off to a colony so that there they might produce vital grain; then too the metropolises saw colonies as outlets for metropolitan craft products (essentially *keramikos*). Among the metropolises only Corinth had a different perspective: having founded Siracusae, Corinth would never found another colony in Sicily. Corinth chose not to export men to raise grain but instead to conserve her manpower and employ it in the crafting of items to be exchanged with the colonies for grain. For a century after the Greeks began to live in Sicily almost all the ceramics imported into Sicily came from Corinth.

In 689, forty-four years after the founding of the Ortygia-Siracusae colony, Greek colonists arrived on the south shore of Sicily, ninety kilometers west of Siracusae as the quail flies. They came from Crete and Rhodes and, like the Siracusans, spoke the Dorian dialect. The new colony, Gela, would soon be crucial to events in Siracusae.

Feeling commercially challenged by the existence of Gela, and being rich enough to afford it, Siracusae established outposts to facilitate her control of the hinterland to the west and south: among them in 664 Acrae (forty kilometers to the west) and in 644 Casmenae (just a bit west of Acrae).* Now Siracusae had not only dimensions and architecture equivalent to cities in the Greek homeland, she also had her own satellites. From the Syraka swamp came the odor of aggrandizement.

As the Chalcidians dominated the northeast of Sicily, the Dorian speakers dominated the southeast.

GELA

By the time that Crete and Rhodes decided to take part in the colonization of Sicily, it was almost too late. Forty-five years had passed since the Greeks settled Ortygia, and by now the entire Ionian littoral was colonized, obliging the new Dorian-speaking colonists to look further west. They sailed south and west from Siracusae some 160 kilometers before arriving at the spot they would make their home.

They decided where to go, Thucydides tells us, on the advice of the Delphic oracle. Then too, Cretans felt a certain kinship with Daedalus, and they figured that here was the part of Sicily in which he had landed. This stretch of south coast bordered the greatest of Sicily's plains. They selected a site for their city between two rivers, where a narrow plateau forty meters high runs for about four kilometers parallel to the gulf. The rivers would give them access to black fertile soil extending very far, as well as providing water for their crops. The gulf lacked a real harbor, but skilled sailors that they were, the Greeks didn't need a harbor; they beached their boats.

They designated their sacred area at the eastern end of the plateau and began to build a temple to Athena, in Doric style, and their own houses close by. Gradually the Gelans descended from the plateau to

---

* Today, more or less at Palazzolo Acreide and Monte Casale, respectively.

build shrines and to establish farms and villages around the plain. No indigenous peoples were living in the immediate vicinity of Gela, so no one disturbed the colonists as they grew their crops. Quite soon they were exporting grain to Greece, and then Greek products were arriving in Gela, and the colonists started trading them with the Sicels and Sicani who lived in their vast hinterland. Compared to the Sicels in the east, the Greeks thought the Sicani of the wide center to be sparser and friendlier.*

The land was so productive that "the Gelan fields" were soon renowned. And production wasn't limited to cereals — the Gelans found the low rolling hills well suited to raising horses, and horses were in demand for cavalry. It was mostly the breed of Gela that made Sicily famous for its fine horses.

Akragas (present-day Agrigento)

Gela, the last of the Sicilian colonies founded directly from Greece, herself founded Akragas in 580. And Akragas was to prove the last of the major subcolonies. The founding ceremony was attended by at least one envoy from Gela's metropolis, Rhodes.

As the Gelans were settling Akragas for the purpose of developing trade relations with the Carthaginians, they placed the subcolony at the western edge of secure Greek territory, halfway between Gela and the Megarans' western outpost. They found a spot for Akragas suitable also in the north-south direction: three kilometers north of the coast two rivers joined to flow into the sea, and just before they joined they almost encircled two neighboring hills. The colonists,

---

* Modern Italian calls them, respectively, Siculi and Sicani. The termination in "-i" is an Italian-language plural. "Siculi" is accented on the first syllable, "Sicani" on the second: *si*culi, sic*a*ni. To help distinguish visually between these similar names, I've spelled the name of the eastern group as Sicels and that of the western group as Sicani.

The Sicels may not have been indigenous: Thucydides thought it probable that they came to the island of Sicily from the Italian peninsula. In those far-off days the king of the Sicels had a son named Italus, whose name was given to the Italic people.

And now we know the origin of the island's name, "Sicily."

living on a hill, could easily travel farther inland. Along the rivers lay a fertile plain, not so extensive as the one north of Gela but large nonetheless. As well as the excess grain she was bound to produce, Akragas would sell Gela's wheat and characteristic pottery.

Though sure to prove viable economically, the site lay so close to Carthaginian territory that the settlers would be at risk. All the colonists on the south coast lived in constant fear of the Carthaginians, but the hope was that perhaps this site's being inland would discourage Carthaginian raids.

Late in the sequence of settlements, Akragas benefitted from the builders' experience in other colonies, and in fact the city was laid out imposingly right from the beginning.

SELINUS (PRESENT-DAY SELINUNTE)

The Greeks had shrunk from settling in western Sicily because the hardy Carthaginians were determined to monopolize trade in the western seas. Seemingly more restless than the other colonists, the Megarans decided to beard the lion in its den. Their traders paved the way; the Greeks probably had a trading post in Selinus before they settled. The men of Megara Hyblea came together here with men from Megara in Greece, both groups to offer their compatriots' exceptional pottery in exchange for metals and cloth. Here relations between the Greeks and the Carthaginians were good, and in due course the Megarans built their dwellings on the unoccupied hill. The official opening of the subcolony, as similar important occasions, demanded speeches by prominent persons from the metropolis — Megara in Greece sent Pammilus to join representatives of Megara Hyblea for the ceremony.

The small hill where the colonists built their city stood just behind the shore's outermost point, where the shoreline curves as an arc into the sea. Here were the mouths of two rivers (one of them the Selinos, from which the colony took its name); thus the colony was set above marshy delta. The Megarans here weren't giving priority to agriculture, but still they had to eat. Although they were impressed by the *selinon* (wild celery) that grew in the marsh, the wild grasses and fauna of the marsh sufficed only so long. In order to grow any food, they had to cultivate the fertile lands to the north.

The indigenous people who lived to the north were good trading partners of the Carthaginians, and Selinus wanted to remain in the Carthaginians' good graces. There were, to be sure, skirmishes between the Greeks and some indigenous Sicani. A different indigenous people, the Elymi, lived in a large settlement called Egesta about three-quarters of the way north from Selinus to the coast. Although related to the Sicani, the Elymi seemed a prouder people. They didn't want newcomers in their area, but there was trade between Egesta and Selinus, and in time the men of Elymi began to accept some arts and practices from Selinus.

The relationship between the Elymi and the Selinuntans started to deteriorate when some Greeks arrived during the period 580–576 (during the fiftieth Olympiad, according to the Greek calendar). They were Rhodians and Cnidians from the eastern islands, led by Pentathlus. They had been trying to set up a colony well north of Selinus, but the Elymi didn't want them around. So Pentathlus sent for help from the settlers at Selinus. Naturally Selinus gave aid, as it was in the interests of all Greeks to strengthen the Greek presence vis-à-vis the Carthaginians. War broke out; the upshot was the rout of the Greeks and the death of Pentathlus.

Due to her presence in the Carthaginian territory, Selinus assumed an importance beyond that justified by her small size and remote location. Envoys from the east — that is, from the colonies and from Greece — kept coming to Selinus to trade and otherwise deal with the Carthaginians. Despite an occasional setback, Selinus prospered. Crops were being raised in the northern hinterland, and trade with the Carthaginians was bringing profits. The colony's acropolis soon boasted a main road going north-south and a few cross-streets as well as her first temples.

EGESTA (PRESENT-DAY SEGESTA)

From Selinus we make a detour inland, directly north about three-quarters of the way to the coast, to the city the Greeks called Egesta.

Map 4. Distribution of Peoples, 600–300 B.C.

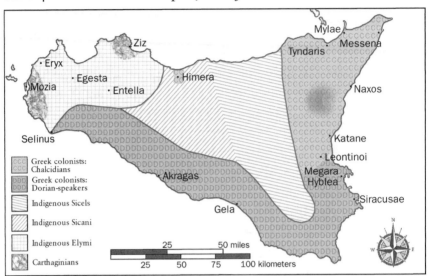

This was the main city of the Elymi people, whose other two localities, Entella to the southeast and Eryx (Erice) to the west, give us an
idea of the extent of their territory.

Very little is known about the Elymi, although the Greeks considered
them an ancient people. The story grew up that the Elymi descended
from people of Troy, whom a storm blew off course to Sicily's western
shore. They were supposed to be refugees from the Trojan War, located
in time between myth and 1200 B.C. Mentioned by Thucydides, this
genealogy would prove of practical importance to Egesta later on.

By 700, when substantial numbers of Carthaginians had come to
the area, the Elymi were all living inland, which in western Sicily
equates with hilly country. They became the allies and trading partners of the uncompromisingly coastal Carthaginians. The Greeks'
settling of Selinus proved crucial for Egesta. The two cities made
some attempts at trading, but after Pentathlus and his group endeavored to settle in the area, Egesta turned into an implacable enemy of
the Greeks and of Selinus.

CROSSING INTO CARTHAGINIAN TERRITORY

At Selinus we crossed from land settled by the Greeks to land controlled by the Carthaginians. Both Greeks and Carthaginians were traders by geographical necessity and industrious by nature. They developed differently in Sicily because they differed in their objectives: the Greeks went to sea in order to find cultivable land, the Carthaginians went to sea in order to trade. With their best ships covering a hundred miles in twenty-four hours, the Carthaginians moved products around as no other people in the ancient world. They established trading ports, hundreds of them, on shores and islets.

Much more than the Greeks, the Phoenicians and their descendants produced goods primarily to sell to other peoples. The Greeks didn't trade west of Sicily, though they happily exchanged their grains for the Carthaginians' foreign merchandise: the glass and the purple dye, which were particularly Phoenician, and perfumes, cloth, papyrus, ivory, and metals (especially silver from Spain). So far, while the Greeks were settling the eastern three-fourths of Sicily, the Carthaginians didn't interfere.

MAZAR (PRESENT-DAY MAZARA)

On the Sicilian shore closest to their North African headland — only 160 kilometers distant — the Carthaginians found a fine landing place, which they called Mazar. From its estuary a river led far into the interior, a big help in trading with the Sicani and the Elymi.

When the Greeks arrived in southwest Sicily about 650, soon to settle Selinus with its marshy shore, they needed a good port. Mazar was close enough and served the Selinuntans as *emporium* — that's a good Greek word, meaning precisely "trading place." In the process of making an emporium for themselves, the Selinuntans made Mazar a Carthaginian emporium too.

MOZIA (ALSO CALLED MOTYA)

Northwest of Mazara twenty-five kilometers, Carthaginians found the island of their dreams. It lay very close to the mainland, in a lagoon, thus it was easy to reach. It was small, a little more than two kilometers in circumference, and almost round, thus it would be easy to defend. The shallow waters made it easy to land boats and made it possible to collect salt. The Carthaginians used the islet as a way station for a while, then around 700 B.C. they started developing it into a permanent settlement, Mozia.

The Carthaginians (like the Greeks) arranged from the first for the local disposition of their deceased. In a place on the shore they buried the ashes of some two hundred people, some of them before 700. The Carthaginians' seaside cemetery may antedate their settlement, the ashes being those of seafarers who had stopped here temporarily or perhaps of some scouts. As the survivors spent much of their time on boats, disposing of their dead at sea would certainly have been simpler. Yet these Carthaginians made the effort to cremate their mates and bury their ashes in a spot dedicated to that purpose.

Modern history books tell us that the Phoenicians studied the heavens, explored the seas, and invented the alphabet. Actually, ordinary Carthaginian men occupied themselves with sailing and fishing. Around Carthage and western Sicily they fished primarily for tuna, which swam so abundantly through the Sicilian channel that the Carthaginians caught far more fish than they could eat or trade before it rotted. The Phoenicians had developed a system of extracting salt from sea water — one of their major contributions to mankind — and they and their descendants were always looking for shallow coastal waters where they could build cribs for the evaporation process. They used the salt to preserve the fish. So fundamental to Carthaginian life was this procedure that it's assumed the work of salt collection and tuna preservation was directed by priests.

To the west of Mozia's seaside cemetery, the settlers marked off a sacred area, dedicated a water well, and gradually erected a sanctuary. In the center of the island they set up their handicraft area, building the furnaces for preparing their world-famous purple dye.

The essential material for the dye came from the Mediterranean sea creature called murex. After breaking open the murex shells, or simply squashing the smaller shells, the Carthaginians used a tool to remove the dye-producing gland. They added the glands to a liquid in a pottery vessel and heated it slowly, slowly. The vessel was not put on or even over flame, rather the heat was directed from a nearby furnace through a hot-air pipe. In due course the mixture became a dye solution, a dye that would not fade from cloth. What was the liquid? Ah, the Carthaginians kept that detail to themselves.

They used the dye to give a purple color to the threads that elsewhere on the island were spun from wool. *Mozia* or *motya* seems to be the Phoenician/Carthaginian word for "spinning mill." The heavy costs of catching and processing the tiny marine snails made the dye very expensive and the wearing of the purple-dyed cloth affordable only for royalty.

Like the Greeks' Siracusae, Mozia by the mid-seventh century grew prosperous through Mediterranean trade. Consequently, she attracted all kinds of people who like markets, including pirates, indigenous people, and Greek colonists. It's thought, because of a statue of Apollo found on Mozia, that a group of Greeks even resided there.

How spirited must have been their discussions. Greeks and Carthaginians would have conversed about ships and seas and Sicani and celery, but not so easily about cemeteries and sanctuaries. Their deepest beliefs clashed. The Greeks knew all about honoring and propitiating the gods, they often offered a ritual meal, food that came from their harvest. The offerings of the Carthaginians, on the other hand, came from their own bodies, namely their children. Although Greek gods and goddesses might eat their own offspring, the divinities never claimed the lives of human babies. The Carthaginian god Ba'al, god of their Phoenician ancestors, and a couple of their other gods too, demanded the life of each man's firstborn son.

In their sanctuary called a *tophet*, on Mozia's northwest shore, the priests strangled the baby boys. Mozia's pottery workshops turned out masks to put into the urns with the boys' ashes, masks depicting faces smiling and sad at the same time, to manifest to the gods the mixed emotions of the sacrificing parents. Near the *tophet* they buried the urns and marked each of them with an upright stone, and when they had used up the space consecrated for the boys' urns, they just started another layer, so that the several hundred upright stones represented only the most recent boys sacrificed to Ba'al.

ZIZ, OR PANORMUS (PRESENT-DAY PALERMO)

Very early in their acquaintance with Sicily, the Carthaginian sea-farers occupied the site on a smallish bay that was to become Palermo. A solitary mountain rose from the coast; otherwise the shore merged into a fertile plain. As lands producing foodstuffs were few and far between in hilly northwest Sicily, the Carthaginians recognized the value of settling here. The two rivers watering the land would serve as routes into the interior. During the eighth century they developed the headland, which they called Ziz, into a port for many peoples — it was one of the few cities the Carthaginians founded. The Greeks called the city "Panormus" ("all-harbor") for its superior qualities in sheltering ships.

HIMERA (ALSO CALLED IMERA)

Across the breadth of Sicily the mountains begin to rise close to the Tyrrhenian, so that northern Sicily lacks the coastal plains of southern. Such topography suited the Carthaginians but not the Greeks, so at first the Greek colonists left this littoral to the Carthaginians.

But once the Greeks had settled themselves down the Ionian coast, they cast eyes on the Tyrrhenian. Slightly west of the center of Sicily's north coast they came upon lands suitable for grain fields. Around 650, three residents of Zancle (Messina) established the colony at Himera. The Greek word *imera* means "day"; perhaps the Greeks thought of themselves bringing light into the Carthaginian territory.

While still very young, the colony became known as the home of an important lyric poet, Stesichorus (born around 640). "Stesichorus" was a nom de plume meaning "maker of choruses"; it was his idea to assemble narrative into couplets and verses of different lengths, to be sung by choruses. He originated the harmonious blending of song, instrumental music, and dance enjoyed by audiences in Katane and other colonies.

MAP 5. Physical map of Sicily

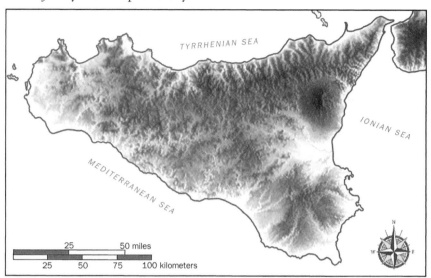

MYLAE (PRESENT-DAY MILAZZO)

Mylae was settled in 716 by a contingent from Zancle, the Chalcidian colony on the Strait of Messina. Opposite the throat of the strait, directly westward overland, lies a narrow peninsula that juts into the Tyrrhenian toward the Aeolian Islands and offers some lands for grain.

If they could win control of this peninsula, the Greeks would dominate the eastern Tyrrhenian in addition to the strait from the south. The peninsula had been populated from time immemorial, and in order to secure it for themselves the Chalcidians had to repulse not just the pirates but groups from as far away as Athens.

Of one commodity there was enough for all: fish. Tuna in abundance swim down from the coast of the Italian peninsula, but their progress southward into the strait is blocked by the strong currents, so they disperse and in the eastern Tyrrhenian provide a feast for the swordfish.

The largest of them measuring, from tail to "sword" tip, about twice the length of a grown man and weighing around five times as much, the swordfish couldn't be caught by a lone fisherman, but only by many men organized as for hunting. The pursuers sailed out in many small boats — Strabo cites Polybius — each boat holding one man who rowed and one other who stood ready with his spear. A single man serving as lookout for the whole fleet could easily see any swordfish in the vicinity, for they swim with a third of their body above water. On the signal, the boats drew close and the fishermen struck. Their spears were made with a barbed head attached loosely to the shaft, to which was also attached a long cord, so that when the barbed head became embedded in the fish, the fisherman was able to recover his shaft. He paid out the cord while the wounded fish thrashed and tired. When the fish died, the men pulled it into the boat if it was not too large; the largest fish they towed to shore.

The turmoil notwithstanding, there was little risk of losing the shaft of the spear. The shafts were made ingeniously of pine and oak; while the heavier oaken end might sink, the lighter pine end stayed afloat and could be retrieved easily. The pursuers faced a greater risk from their prey, whose long, sharp "swords" could cut through the bottom of a boat and sometimes wounded boatmen.

Homer refers to swordfishing near Scylla, and Strabo finds no fault with that, but he does correct Homer regarding Charybdis. Homer said that Charybdis spews forth water "thrice" daily, whereas Strabo (writing seven centuries later) contends it should be "twice." He is however gracious enough to say that the error may have been that of a scribe.

LIPARI (ALSO CALLED AEOLIA)

Those tiny islands northwest of Milazzo — we saw in the introduction how they were named Aeolian after the god of the winds. As to their alternative name Lipari, *lipos* in Greek means "fat" — the Greeks cast approving eyes on this "fat," rich land.

As a Greek colony, Aeolia began late. The group from Rhodes that tried around 580 to settle in Elymi territory near Egesta, only to be driven away by the Seluntans, was heading toward the strait, and home, when it landed at Aeolia — probably with great relief, for

Etruscan pirates were plying the waters aggressively. The few hundred inhabitants on the archipelago's main island lived in constant fear of pirates; on the smaller islands no one lived.

Zancle, or Messena (present-day Messina)

At the throat of the Strait of Messina there's a small peninsula shaped just like a sickle with its curved part to the north. The indigenous people, the Sicels, called their community Zancle. Thucydides explains that the name derived from their word for "curve." Strabo writes that *zancle* was the Sicel word for "port." Either way, we have learned two things: that the Sicels named their community after its seafront, and that an important historian of Magna Graecia lacked familiarity with the native language.

The peninsula's shape makes it easy to land boats right at the strait where navigation is otherwise treacherous. The sickle offered safety for swarms of merchants and pirates, fiercely competitive Carthaginians, Etruscans, Greeks from Greece, and Greeks from Ortygia. Amid them a group of Greeks managed to start a colony four or five years after the Chalcidians had settled at Naxos. Strabo says Zancle was settled by colonists from Naxos. Thucydides says Zancle was settled by Chalcidian pirates who had been living on the Italian mainland up near Naples, joined by some Ionians. The mix of peoples in Zancle, and the mix-up about their origins and about where their loyalties lay, were characteristic of this city from the first.

The colonists began their city at the base of the peninsula. They weren't put off by the poor fertility of the nearby land, given their other economic possibilities. As the overwhelming reason for this settlement was to control traffic through the strait, the colonists didn't waste time before starting to build, on the far shore, the city called Rhegium.*

More than in Magna Graecia's agricultural colonies, the population here was unstable. Zancle lodged seafarers from all the known world — at times a greater number from one region, at times a greater number from another regions as political circumstances

---

* The modern Reggio di Calabria, on the toe-tip of the Italian mainland.

changed. The Greek islands' constant strife displaced many, turning them into boat people. Sixty years or so after the foundation of Zancle, a group arrived from the Peloponnesus, people called Messenes, fleeing Spartan violence. As refugees they didn't bring much with them, but in due course they gave the city a new name.

GREEK-SICILIANS AND CARTHAGINIANS

It's time for another change of name. Akragas and Lipari, the last of the Greek settlements, were not settled directly from Greece, and by the time they were settled around 580, Sicily had housed Greek colonists for a century and a half. They really shouldn't be called colonists any more. They are Greek-Sicilians.

RELATION OF COLONIES TO MOTHERLAND
Very little is known about the colonial period. Nonetheless, the ceramics imported from Corinth and those produced in Sicily — among them the particular beauties crafted in Gela and Megara Hyblea — do tell us that the colonists maintained a little trade among themselves and much more with their metropoli. We know too that the ancient Greeks were great travellers.

Traders had plied the Mediterranean since time immemorial; now the traders' ships took nontrading passengers as well. When the weather was good the trip between the east coast of Sicily and the shores on the eastern side of the Greek mainland needed about twelve days. The first generations of colonists stopping at Apollo's temple in Naxos may well have been going to their hometowns in Greece on family and personal business. Greekness was not diminished by living on Sicily — Greece had always consisted of many islands, and Sicily was just another island, albeit for them a new and bigger one. The primary expression of Greekness was participation in Greek religious rituals, by observing the festivals and visiting the shrines. Consulting the oracle, at Delphi or in other places, was a way of acknowledging the gods' power, thus of paying homage.

The Greek homeland held many festivals, usually semireligious in nature, as entertainment that the poor as well as the rich might enjoy. Dramatic and musical events abounded, but athletics were primary. Around the time that the Greeks were establishing themselves in Sicily, the Olympic Games were expanding from a local to a quadrennial all-Greek competition. Over the years, for the upper classes of Greek-Sicilians, it became *de rigueur* to attend. Soon Naxos would have a native athlete of whom to be proud: in the 560s a certain Tisander won several boxing competitions at Olympia and at Delphi. Reciprocally, a colony's ceremonial occasions were generally attended by a representative from the metropolis.

How close the relations were may well have varied from one colony to another. Some bits of evidence suggest that relations were not all that close between Siracusae and Corinth. For example, as writing came into use among scholars and businessmen, notwithstanding the traffic between the two cities Siracusae and Corinth developed different alphabetic forms. More monumentally, the Greek homeland in the middle of the seventh century witnessed the construction of the first temples of the kind we know. Stone replaced wood as building material, and to beautify the temples their builders settled on particular forms or "orders" of decoration such as the Doric order developed in wealthy Corinth. In Sicily around this time the Greek settlers had a crash program of altar- and temple-building. Sicily did not lack stone, nor did the colonists hesitate to lay out their towns in accord with the traditional metropolitan model. Yet it took several decades before the new building styles in Greece were adopted in Sicily. Even granted that the architects of the period used no blueprints (they had to keep techniques and the image of the final structure in their heads), the delay would seem inordinate if in fact the colonial builders consulted regularly with their homeland counterparts. It was only in the 560s that Siracusae started a Doric-style temple in Ortygia, to be dedicated to Apollo and larger than anything in the Greek homeland.

THE NEW WEALTH SEEKS POWER

On arrival at a new settlement, all colonists received equal parcels of land. Doubtless there were some exceptions to this rule, but certainly Megara Hyblea and several other colonies in Magna Graecia followed the practice. Once the colonists were settled in Sicily, though, official guidelines were shelved as agricultural production determined individual wealth. Colonization further blurred the lines between classes as prosperity from trade distributed wealth beyond the circle of landowning aristocrats. Merchant oligarchies developed, demanding their share of political power. New kinds of rulers rose to power, profiting from new economic circumstances.

Yet local strife in Sicily was aggravated by political developments in Greece. Most of the Greek lands were perpetually at arms, due largely to the pressure of population on food supply. The lands at battle included those with colonies on Sicily, and Sicilians naturally took sides. Athens, with nearby grain lands making her economically healthier than most of Greece, never had any colony in Sicily. But when, in the first half of the fifth century, Athens developed a participatory democracy, Sicilians were watching.

Prosperous Leontinoi was one city that aspired to the Athenian system. The middle classes, wanting a say in the governance of the colony, took up arms, making Leontinoi the first of the Sicilian colonies to experience internal military conflict. A certain Panatius led the populace in a battle against the aristocracy for control of the city. Victorious, Panatius took the title "tyrant," which had come into use in Greece to indicate a ruler who represented the middle classes and had won power by overthrowing the existing government. When Panatius succeeded in maintaining himself as ruler of Leontinoi, power-hungry men in other colonies sought to become tyrants too.

In flourishing Siracusae, land came quickly into the hands of the *gamoroi* (literally "those who share the land"). These rich landowning Siracusans established themselves as Siracusae's rulers. As such they anxiously watched the growth of Gela, flourishing from grain but lacking her own harbor; they worried that Gela would interfere in Siracusan markets. Around the year 590 Siracusae founded a subcolony to mark the frontier between her own territory and Gela's: Camarina, on the coast about two-thirds of the way from Siracusae to Gela. Camarina soon had a life of her own — she dealt with the Sicels of the hinterland, giving them a port, and she traded with Gela as well as with Siracusae. Siracusae tried to restrain Camarina and, in 553, went so far as to demolish her.

At this time when Siracusae's aristocratic *gamoroi* were occupied, the landless, the *killyrioi*, saw a chance to improve their position. They were essentially the indigenous Sicels who had been forced into working the Greeks' land. Although the colonists to the north had made terms more or less acceptable to the Sicels, the Siracusans treated their neighboring Sicels badly and pushed many of them into the swamps of Sicily's far southeast. This was another reason (besides anxiety about Gela) that Siracusae had established military outposts to her west, effectively to keep the Sicels enclosed. The idea of revolt certainly didn't originate with the *killyrioi* in Siracusae — similar episodes having occurred in Greece and in Leontinoi — but these *killyrioi* prevailed; the fighting in Siracusae ended with them chasing their oligarchs out of the city.

In contrast to Siracusae (and like the Chalcidian colonies) Gela had reasonable relations with her indigenous neighbors. As Megara Hyblea had long ago established a subcolony at Selinus in the west, so Gela did so in 580 at Akragas (Agrigento), near the south coast about a third of the way from Licata to Selinus. Akragas would open up new markets. Thus Gela competed in the settlement leapfrog along the south coast. To the east, Gela traded as far as she could until she ran up against Siracusae; but in 589 Siracusae had put a limit to Gela's expansion by establishing the Camarina subcolony twenty-five kilometers to Gela's southeast. This made Gela realize the urgency of defenses, which led her to construct a wall at the northern edge of the plateau, behind the houses and shops, to protect her position and wealth.

Akragas, built from the first as a beautiful city, got off to a bad start politically. Within ten years of her founding, Akragas was ruled by Phalaris. It was said that he gained control by embezzling funds earmarked to build a temple of Zeus and using the funds to create an army for himself. However he had gotten it, he used his army to extend his domination north and west into the territory densely populated by the Sicani. At Himera, on the Tyrrhenian coast directly north of Akragas, the lyric poet Stesichorus, old and blind, warned against Phalaris. Phalaris succeeded in bringing under his control all the inland area that Gela had earlier brought under her control, taking many indigenous prisoners in the process. He proved a cruel man; a story was later told about his taking prisoners, forcing them into a large bronze model of a bull, and roasting them to death.

THE OLYMPIC GAMES AS POLITICAL VEHICLE

More common misfortunes of life included earthquakes, volcanic eruptions, pirates, malaria, and war. But one had to enjoy oneself too. Diversions included visits to Greece and especially, at the appropriate season, to Olympia — for the upper-class Sicilians, of course.

The Olympic Games had far more significance than "games" as pastime. They honored the supreme god Zeus, who held court on Mount Olympus, and they symbolized Greek nationhood. The Greeks dated their calendar from the first Olympics (776 B.C.) as the Christians date theirs from the birth of Christ; events were often reported as having occurred during this or that Olympiad. The Games were so important that when they took place the Greeks even suspended their wars. Meant to foster amity, the Games were conceived as a strong link among the widely dispersed Greeks. (The colonies of Magna Graecia, including Siracusae and Gela, as well as some of their wealthiest citizens, donated enough treasure to Olympia to account for about half the total.)

Once one arrived there, to participate in games such as jumping or javelin throwing was not expensive, but the competitions using horses and carriages cost plenty. Some of the competitors considered their outlay an investment, for victory in the Games opened doors to political advantage. It wasn't just coincidence that the aristocrat Pantare of Gela owned the four-horse chariot that won the race in

512 (or maybe it was 508) and that from 505 to 491 two sons of his ruled Gela. They were the city's first tyrants; from 498 Gela was ruled by the younger and stronger of them, Hippocrates.

If these men didn't have to think about costs, they did have to think about a new form of exchange. During the Greeks' first two centuries in Sicily, most trade was by barter. On those occasions when a seller could find nothing he wanted in exchange for his goods, the trader would give him iron spits that could later be exchanged for practical products. Greeks first saw coins in the eastern Mediterranean about 600, and very soon thereafter Greek rulers began cutting their own metal pieces of identical size and stamping them with characteristic designs to identify them and guarantee their worth. Naxos was the first colony in Sicily to mint her own coins (around 550–530). Practically all Naxos coins showed grapes, a major source of the community's income. By 500, coins were being minted in Katane, signaling the city's importance; her coins had designs representing the river god Amenanos, as befit a city where life flowed smoothly. Around the same time the far-western trade center Selinus issued coins showing the leaves of the *selinon* (wild celery), which had become the city symbol. In Gela, Hippocrates was the first ruler to issue money, and his coins depicted a man on horseback.

GELANS TAKE OVER EASTERN SICILY

The wealthy Gelans' passion for horses may well have evolved as compensation for their city's lack of a port. Conventional wisdom held ships indispensable for warfare, but in lieu of a navy Hippocrates strengthened his cavalry. On horseback and on foot his troops crossed the land between Gela and the east coast, overwhelming Leontinoi and Zancle; he made a foray against Naxos too, but her walls held. Hippocrates sold the many prisoners into slavery, thereby augmenting his income. The prisoners were Sicels and Greeks just like the mercenaries were Sicels and Greeks — Hippocrates didn't discriminate. He paid the mercenaries in coin; that was, in fact, the main use of coin, for agricultural products were bartered.

While Hippocrates was terrorizing the east of Sicily, the west was thriving under him. Gela and her subcolony at Akragas traded profitably with the indigenous people to the north. Ordinary Gelans could feel they were living in a splendid city — their shops were strung out along the city's main street running westward from the sacred precincts. Outside the wall, on the plateau's slopes and down on the surrounding flatland, many shrines served for worshipping local gods. Gelan potters were capable and original, doing work highly valued abroad. Hippocrates strengthened his outposts enough to threaten Siracusae, took over Leontinoi, even rebuilt Siracusae's destroyed subcolony Camarina for his own purposes around 493. Hippocrates' invasion of Siracusae seemed so likely that Corinth sent negotiators. But Siracusae was spared otherwise: in 491 Hippocrates, in the eighth year of his rule, died in battle against the Sicels.

Gelon, the head of Hippocrates' cavalry and his longtime friend, offered himself as protector of the deceased's young children. From that position Gelon sprang to power. In 488 he went off to Greece and won the chariot race at Olympia. Three years later he was to win a much bigger prize, for which he had not competed.

～

About sixty years previously, Siracusae's dispossessed *gamoroi* started trying to rebuild their lives in Siracusae's hill station at Casmenae. The *killyrioi* revolt had given "power to the people," but the *gamoroi* decided that in Siracusae "the people" had not proved themselves as effective governors. The *gamoroi*, seeing in Gelon's strength an opportunity to regain their privileges, in 485 shied themselves off to Gela to implore Gelon to bring order to their city. Gelon jumped at the chance. When he departed with his court a year later, he took with him a large number of Gela's residents, both populace and aristocrats.

En route to Siracusae, Gelon destroyed the Camarina that his predecessor had rebuilt and carried off her residents to Siracusae. From Siracusae he looked north and in 483 invaded Megara Hyblea, damaged and plundered her, expelled her people, and turned her into a bulwark for Siracusae's defense. The Greek historian Herodotus, born about this time, was to write that Gelon sold the populace into slavery, but made Siracusan citizens of "the fat ones."

From a larger populace Gelon could draft a larger army and navy and more workers to strengthen the city's defenses. He needed in fact to extend the city walls, as the newcomers were building their housing outside them, and the increasing importance of the city meant that foreigners would seek to control her. Siracusae was huge — already the dominant political and economic force in Greek Sicily — and she was growing bigger from month to month.

THE GREEK POWERS INVOLVE THE CARTHAGINIANS
The Greek Alliances

Back in the 490s when Hippocrates was overrunning the east, all the Greek-Sicilian towns saw need for a balance of power. Political machinations and shifting alliances involved not only Gela and Siracusae but also refugees from the Greek island Samos, the Sicel territory of Kale Acte, and the two cities on the strait, namely Zancle and Rhegium. Rhegium was now a rich city ruled by Anassila and with a large community of Messenes; Anassila persuaded the arriving Samites to take over Zancle. The Zancle ruler called to Hippocrates for help, but then Hippocrates was killed. Over the next few years Anassila, of Messene origin, replaced the Samites in Zancle with other refugees from Greece and replaced the name Zancle with Messena. Messena and Rhegium were now allied against Gela and Siracusae.

Anassila was, importantly, the son-in-law of Terillus, tyrant of Himera. Himera was a substantial city, the Tyrrhenian coast's westernmost Greek town before the Carthaginian territory. A century had passed since the poet Stesichorus warned Himera about the designs of Akragas; in the meantime, after overthrowing Phalaris, some wealthy men of Akragas established an oligarchy. To Akragas came many new settlers, for the colonies in general were gaining in population and the west held the great attraction of fertile new lands. Akragas flourished through export; her wine grapes and olives soon became known for good quality. General prosperity brought an end in turn to the oligarchic government, when in 488 Theron seized power as tyrant.

On the fast track to becoming the mightiest of cities in the Greek world, Akragas by now dominated a swath of Sicily north to the Tyrrhenian coast. Theron — extremely wealthy, a descendant of one of the men who had ousted Phalaris — had married his daughter to Gelon (the tyrant of Gela who would soon advance to being tyrant of Siracusae). Theron craved power in the Tyrrhenian. As Himera on the Tyrrhenian coast was isolated from the other Greek cities, Theron forced out Himera's tyrant, Terillus. The lineup had expanded to Akragas and Gela and Siracusae (in Sicily's south) against Himera and Messena and Rhegium (in the north).

Accompanied by Rhegium's Anassila, Himera's deposed tyrant Terillus went for help to the Carthaginians. Terillus had a friend in the Carthaginian leader, Hamilcar. Interestingly, if Herodotus was right, Hamilcar had a Carthaginian father but his mother was a Siracusae girl. Whatever his origins, the Carthaginian leader Hamilcar agreed to fight on behalf of Terillus, in effect against Siracusae. Carthaginians considered this a good occasion for halting the expansion of the Greeks into Sicily's west.

The Carthaginians Think of Defense

Traditionally the Carthaginians had gone about their business of fishing and trading without establishing colonies. Even though their capital, Carthage, had always coveted Sicily, she allowed the Carthaginians around Sicily a free hand; and the Greek settlers thriving in Selinus and Akragas were a long way from their home-land politics and weren't inclined to interrupt their good life. Greeks and Carthaginians were never partners, but the symbiosis brought them both prosperity — why rock the boats?

Carthaginians and Greeks followed different policies in respect to the indigenous peoples: the Cathaginians worked out partnerships with their neighbors while the Greeks (especially Siracusans) subju-gated theirs. No problem, until around 580 when the group from Rhodes went wandering through Elymi territory looking for a place to settle. The locals ousted the Rhodians but remained anxious that Greeks would try again to seize land in Sicily's west. So far Mozia's defenses, primarily naval, had deterred invasion of the island, but now the Carthaginians constructed their first wall. They expanded and strengthened the island-city during the rest of the sixth century.

Mozia had more ships than she knew what to do with, literally: in addition to the ships of the Carthaginians themselves, great numbers of merchant vessels called there. To facilitate the unloading, servicing, and reloading of them all, Mozia built a *cothon*, a rectangular flat-bottomed harbor large enough for three or four ships at a time. In the lagoon itself, the Carthaginians built a causeway, twelve meters high, seven meters thick, connecting Mozia's eastern shore to the mainland. Now the Carthaginians could walk back and forth between Mozia and the mainland; on the other hand, it was no longer possible to circumnavigate Mozia.

In the second half of the sixth century the Carthaginians occupied themselves with modernizing Ziz (Palermo), building northward as they expanded. The "new city" walls, surrounding the old and new quarters together, reached to the port with its naval base.

Still, the Carthaginians inhabited just a tiny bit of Sicily, though they clearly considered western Sicily to be within their sphere of influence. For centuries they contented themselves with commercial control and allowed the Greeks to occupy land with impunity, but the Greeks' recent incursions along the Tyrrhenian coast, especially at Himera, had gone too far. Besides, the Carthaginians had always traded all around the Mediterranean without conflict, but in recent years they came upon Siracusans everywhere.

The Battle of Himera, 480
In stemming the Greek tide in the Tyrrhenian, the Carthaginians had thus far had the support of the Etruscans, reflected in commercial treaties between them. Now though the Etruscans had to contend with the rise of the Romans, so the Carthaginians could no longer count on them. Hamilcar looked elsewhere for military support, when the call came from Himera's deposed tyrant: in the next couple of years the

Carthaginians assembled troops from Spain, Sardinia, and Corsica to add to their North Africans. Sources number the Carthaginian forces at three hundred thousand, but we might take that with a grain of salt, seeing that the Carthaginians had so much of it.

Anyhow, the numbers counted less than the logistics. The Carthaginians sent their troops to their main naval base at Ziz, whence some were ordered to proceed to Himera on foot and some by ship. Those marching were met by Greek soldiers on Himera's plateau and engaged in battle; they never had a chance to connect with their waterborne comrades. In the battle, lasting from dawn to dusk, the Carthaginian army was destroyed and General Hamilcar killed. Gelon of Siracusae had the survivors taken prisoner and demanded reparations. From this crucial Battle of Himera (480), Siracusae emerged a great power.

∽

Gelon, the biggest fish in Gela, had moved in midcareer to Siracusae to disport himself in a bigger pond. Now he was lord over the three seas around Sicily. He ruled with the title "tyrant," a word that then had no overtones of cruelty. By stabilizing the government of his adopted city he brought glory to her, which attracted more residents and thus served his policy of increasing the population. The multitude mourned when he died in 478, the most powerful man in Magna Graecia.

Gelon of Siracusae and Theron of Akragas defeated the alliance of Carthaginians, Himera, Messena, and Rhegium. But Rhegium's Anassila, who had fomented the war, suffered not one bit. For reasons unknown he and his men never fought — one wonders if his partici-pation might have brought about a different outcome and spared the Carthaginians. On a later occasion, for whatever it's worth, Anassila won, in the Olympic Games. In a race of chariots pulled by mules, he owned the winning team. He had it depicted on coins in Messena and Rhegium.

Theron of Akragas sent those persons remaining in Himera west-ward along the coast ten kilometers to the thermal baths where they developed the town of Termini Imerese. (Thermal baths are in Greek *thermae,* of which word *termini* is an Italian deformation.) The coins

Theron issued there showed the rooster representing Himera on one side and the crab representing Akragas on the other. Meanwhile, the battle's surviving Carthaginians were led to work in the Greek cities. Those allotted to Akragas were assigned particularly to work on a new temple to mark the victory.

TEMPLES

For a few generations before the recent warfare, the Greek bulwarks against the Carthaginians were Himera and Selinus. Although Selinus was involved in constant border disputes with the indigenous Elymi to the north, she managed to avoid the encroachment of Siracusae and Akragas and the corresponding military expenditures. At the time when the major cities to the east were forming their opposing alliances, Selinus gave her attention to the construction of temples. Her first major temples got under way in the 550s, ten years or so after Siracusae's first temples, in similar Doric style. Thanks to continuing good relations with the Carthaginians, Selinus remained prosperous and therefore had resources enough to build a half-dozen major temples over the next century.

These were major public works, employing new concepts of mathematics and geometry from Greece. Preliminary stages were design (carried out, of course, without benefit of paper or pencil) and the quarrying of the rocks (some of the Selinus columns came from quarries thirteen kilometers distant). Chiseled blocks, some shaped into cylinders, were transported to the construction site using wheels and draft animals. Meanwhile, for parts of the temple that the architects thought would benefit from emphasis, cutters shaped smaller pieces into sculptures, friezes, and moldings, to which painters applied bright colors. In the Greek homeland any large structure, bathed by the intense sun, needed relief from the dazzlingly white marble. Sicily, lacking marble, constructed with limestone, so the golden yellows, vibrant reds, and royal blues were applied out of tradition or in an attempt to divert attention from the inferior material.

Finally the temple could be erected. The raising of columns toward heaven required ramps. Inclines were built of earth, rebuilt as the temple grew skyward. Finally friezes and architraves (the horizontal pieces) were carried to the top on ramps grown immense.

Selinus took the old idea of temples and raised it to a new height, embodying her wealth in temples larger than the ones in the old country.

ᘏᕽ

Akragas, settled about sixty years after Selinus, happened to start building her temples in the 490s, about sixty years after Selinus. Akragas' temple to Olympian Zeus, the biggest structure in the Western world,* began to rise in the 470s to memorialize the Battle of Himera.

Winning a victory brought a man a little closer to the gods, and indeed the community treated him as though he were one. Any man who rendered a service for his city, such as winning a military victory or improving agriculture, might hope later to join the pantheon of the city — albeit as a hero, not as a god. Though sometimes it seemed there was little difference: the gods were anthropomorphic, like human beings with their strengths and foibles. That followed from the attribution of power to all deceased. If the person had been powerful in life, it stood to reason that he would be powerful after his death, so that living beings would try to avoid or appease his anger. Individuals commonly asked help from gods and heroes whom they honored.

The most powerful gods, the gods of the elements, controlled the soil and the weather upon which the Greeks depended, and they received homage from all the citizens. Besides, every city had a particular god or gods, each in due course with a dedicated temple or shrine. Even a minor god had a domain. If the gods smiled, if the fields produced a bounty, then the Greeks would have enough to eat and enough resources left over for temples.

Living generally in a warm, dry climate, the Greeks did not build tem-

---

* Zeus would later be called Jupiter by the Romans. The world's largest Doric temple measures 117 meters long, almost 57 meters wide, and over 30 meters high. Outside it stood an altar with dimensions (54 by 17 meters) of a normal temple, for the simultaneous sacrifice of one hundred oxen.

ples to be houses of assembly. A temple was a house of the god — or of the goddess — whose image they set therein. From his place in the temple the deity could witness the sacrifices being made to him at the altar outside. Temples were built large in part to honor the god but also to provide storage room for the ritual objects and for the offerings.

Even before the temple to Zeus was completed, Akragas undertook to build more temples: during the 460s to the earth-goddess Demetra, and a score of years later to Hera, the wife of Zeus. The goddess Hera protected marriage, and women generally, whether married or not. Hera was resurrected by Zeus; soon after her birth she had been eaten by her father. Gela, watching as Akragas displayed her immense riches, must have felt swallowed by her child.

THE PHILOSOPHER EMPEDOCLES

The prosperous years of temple-building in Akragas coincided with the lifetime of her most famous son. Empedocles, born around 495 of an aristocratic family, spent his life as a philosopher — in that era all men who put forth ideas were called "philosophers." In a place where gods were honored especially through building, Empedocles defined god in geometric terms: "God is a circle whose center is everywhere and whose circumference is nowhere."

The physical world occupied his thoughts. He developed the theory of four elements: earth, air, water, and fire. These were fundamental and indestructable. Things change only due to motion; what seem to be changes in quality and quantity of objects are really changes in the position of basic particles of which the object consists. (This is a fundamental principle of modern physics.) He further postulated that what brings particles together is love, and what separates them is hate.

Empedocles was not only reflective but also practical. When Selinus decided to clear her marshes so that boats could dock near the city, she hired Empedocles from Akragas. He was given responsibility for the project, which he performed in the mid-440s. The continuing gratitude of the local people may have had less to do with the docking of boats than with the great reduction in suffering from malaria.

Atmosphere, Empedocles believed, was a corporeal substance, not a mere void. This belief gave rise to a story about his death. Empedocles wanted to prove his theory, so he went up to Mount Etna and jumped into a crater, convinced that the vapors would have enough body to support him. They didn't. This has the ring of legend. For one thing, Empedocles was a favorite of storytellers. For another, the thinkers of Empedocles' time and place didn't employ empirical method. *He* might have — although others then thinking of making experiments would likely have been discouraged by Empedocles' result. Who knows? Vulcanologists at Mount Etna swear that a long-ago eruption threw up his sandal.

❧

Men of letters were among the visitors who swarmed Akragas and sang and wrote her praises, yet Empedocles had reservations.

He warned the people against their opulence and is said to have commented that the people of Akragas "were building as though they would live forever and were eating as though they would die tomorrow." Empedocles' activities extended to his city's political matters, regarding which (in contrast to physical matter) he believed change to be possible. Certainly Empedocles was living in a time of social upheaval: the perennial struggle of the poorest classes against the oligarchies and the newer conflict in Greek Sicily about gaining independence from the metropoli in Greece.

SOME TYRANTS OF THE EARLY FIFTH CENTURY

Two years after defeating the Carthaginians at Himera, Siracusae's tyrant Gelon died in 478. Gelon had earlier left his brother Hiero (also called Hieron) to rule Gela, and now Hiero succeeded him in Siracusae. Hiero continued his brother's policies, though he did establish a secret police. In 476 he had all the inhabitants of Naxos and Katane deported to Leontinoi. The people of Katane he replaced with some ten thousand men of Dorian origin, and he changed the city's religion to that of Demeter and changed the name of the settlement from Katane to Etna.

Apparently Hiero liked moving around, for he made trips to

Greece during which he competed in the Olympic Games. When in 468 he finally won a chariot race he must have been particularly gratified, as Gelon had won an Olympic chariot race twenty years before.

In Greek Sicily's version of chess, the tyrant as king moved the colonist-pawns around. Virtually all Sicilians depended on their parcels of land, for food of course, but besides that it must have rent their hearts to leave their altars. Yet the tyrants were constantly confiscating the Sicilians' lands and shunting them about. They were taken away when a city was destroyed, taken away to establish a new city or to resurrect an old one, taken away to Siracusae simply to augment her population. Men in the military or the messenger service were sent great distances, often returning only to learn that, by tyrannical order, their old neighborhoods were devastated or desolate. New arrivals in each city were to receive land, but there were so many new arrivals that it was a bureaucratic nightmare.

In Akragas and elsewhere the system of government by tyrant was dying. Since many of the tyrants had behaved like despots, the very meaning of the word had evolved: "tyrant" no longer meant any ruler who had come to power in a particular way, but had assumed the meaning of "despot." When the tyrant Theron of Akragas died, the son who succeeded him, Trasideo, lasted only two years. What occasioned his ouster is not known, although the historian Diodorus Siculus characterized Trasideo as "violent and an assassin." Diodorus used the same words in describing other rulers, so we can't rely on him for a true picture of any individual; on the other hand, the lack of variety in his depictions may reflect a lack of variety in the tyrants' behavior. People in Akragas, in any case, had had enough; after Trasideo, they placed their government in the hands of aristocrats.

SIRACUSAE, ALL-POWERFUL
The Etruscans and the Battle of Cuma, 474
After the battle of Himera subdued the Carthaginians, the Etruscans surfaced. The Etruscans specialized in iron (a product of their home in the Italian peninsula's center), and they were skilled too in the

working of bronze and of gold; their products were much in demand. The Greeks called the Etruscans "Tyrrheni" or "Tyrseni"; the sea between Himera and Naples was for the Greeks the Etruscan Sea.

Etruscan pirates had long coveted Lipari. It was as though the island had been made to order for them: located amid Greek and Carthaginian travel routes and at a comfortable distance from the straits, small enough to be entirely theirs and provide refuge from their hurly-burly world. Mediterranean seafarers of the time generally sailed only during the warmer months, around six months each year, and lay over during the winter. Yet Lipari was the pirates' particular haven in summer, since the archipelago lacked a natural source for drinking water: during the hot summer any invader risked dying of thirst. Lipari's Greeks, themselves pirates, managed to hold their own in the sea battles until shortly after the year 500. The Etruscans seized Lipari, but the islanders managed to get rid of them (a feat that they marked by donating twenty bronze statues of Apollo to his sanctuary in Delphi). Determined to end the piracy, the tyrant of Rhegium took the expensive step of fortifying the straits, but even that proved inadequate.

Siracusae's tyrant Hiero wanted the Tyrrhenian commerce for himself. When the city of Cuma, on the Tyrrhenian coast just north of Naples, called to him for help against the Etruscans, Hiero sent his navy. In the great battle of Cuma, in 474, his forces defeated the Etruscans, for them a crucial loss.

Pindar, the great lyric poet of triumphs, wrote in the first Pythian Ode that the victory at Cuma redounded to the Siracusans' credit even more than their victory at Himera. To be sure, Pindar was living on grants from Hiero, for whom the victory at Cuma was the high point of his life. There was no denying, though, that winning at Cuma just six years after Himera endowed Siracusae with supreme glory.

Culture under Hiero

Closer to home, the city Megara Hyblea had produced a great dramatist. Epicharmus, born circa 525, satirized the gods in his mythological burlesques. Writing in the language spoken in southeast Sicily at the time, a Dorian Greek evolving into a Sicilian Greek, he produced over fifty plays. There's no indication that Epicharmus ever became part of Hiero's court, but then he might have had some reservations about doing so after Gelon destroyed his native city in 483. Gelon dragged Megara Hyblea's upper classes to Siracusae, which may explain why Epicharmus died in Siracusae, around 450.

While Epicharmus was working on his comedies, Hiero had theater pieces produced by Aeschylus. Already famous as a poet when he left Athens for Sicily, Aeschylus wrote choral lyrics, as did Pindar, and also dialogue; he was the first to have dialogues acted out by performers. He wrote with unique persuasiveness about human suffering — like many of his contemporaries, he was a war veteran. He sought to foster morality by always punishing the violence of his bad guys. Aeschylus' plays — he wrote ninety of them — were presented widely around Sicily as well as at festivals in the Greek homeland, and in due course he won thirteen first prizes at the Greater Dionysia in Athens.*

Another of Hiero's court poets (lyric and elegiac) was Simonides, funereally famous for his dirges and tombstone epigrams; for the Athenian soldiers killed at Marathon in the year 490 he wrote an epigraph that contemporaries regarded even more highly than the one of Aeschylus.

Achievements of Gelon and Hiero

To his aristocratic friends, Hiero was appreciated for his patronage of the arts. The temple that his brother Gelon had initiated in Ortygia Hiero completed, and dedicated it to the goddess of the arts, Athena.

Siracusae's population of at least two hundred thousand† made her the largest city of all Greece. The two tyrants added substantially to the territory dominated by Siracusae, making her the Greek

---

* Epicharmus is considered the father of Sicilian comedy. His exact contemporary, Aeschylus, is famous as the father of theatrical tragedy, for his introduction of actors, the scope of his poetry, and the profundity of his thinking. Of all his plays, seven, including *Prometheus Bound,* survive in full — the (Western) world's oldest extant tragedies.

† Estimates vary widely for the population of Siracusae during the third and fourth centuries B.C.; the minimum proposed exceeds two hundred thousand people.

world's greatest power. She had no authority as capital city, only the force of arms. When Hiero died in 467, Siracusae controlled half of Sicily, that is, the territory from Naxos in the northeast to Akragas in the southwest.

The eighteen years of Gelon and Hiero were a time of military victories and economic prosperity, from which many Greek Sicilians benefitted. But the tyrants left many others bitter. Hiero's brother Trasibulo acceded to the power but was destined not to wield it. The populace of Siracusae, and of the Chalcidian cities to the north, raised a hue and cry — they had had enough of that family, enough of despotism, probably at bottom enough of being forced to move from one city to another at the whim of the sovereign. Now the people forced the sovereign to move. Armed men from other Greek cities and from the Sicel community joined the Siracusans in 466 to dispatch Trasibulo into exile.

SIRACUSAE MEETS OPPOSITION

Siracusae, now administered democratically by representatives of the people, still pulled all Sicily's strings.

For example, in 461 the Siracusans protested Hiero's transfer, fifteen years before, of tens of thousands of people. From Katane-renamed-Etna they removed the Dorians, resettled them in a Sicel town called Inessa, and sent the original inhabitants of Katane back home. Katane would again be called Katane. It was Inessa, they decided, that would henceforth be called Etna. The Chalcidian cities in the northeast hated Siracusae for her military interference as well as for her wealth and power.

By now the greater part of Sicily's indigenous people had blended genetically or culturally into the Greeks, but evidently some Sicels were still distinct. In the southeast survived a marginalized group whose *killyrioi* grandfathers had seized power in Siracusae only to have the aristocrats oust them and install Gelon. Those forced to work the Greeks' land bided their time, seeking solace in their cult of Palici, "patron" of the oppressed, their shrine located twenty-five kilometers west-southwest of Catania.

Around 450 a Sicel of noble origins, Ducetius, roused his people to successful combat over some of the Greek colonies. The rebels first made their capital at Leontinoi, then they expanded. They held power for several years before being overthrown by armies of Siracusae and Akragas. Treating Ducetius as befit a deposed king, the Siracusans exiled him (to Corinth) to live at their expense. But somehow he returned to Sicily, to Kale Acte (on the north coast midway between Thermae Himerae and Mylae), where he established a community with old-country Greeks and some Sicels. The rebellion reminds us that Sicily's indigenous people hated the Greek colonization and fought for centuries against it.

Siracusae didn't always have the support of Akragas. Now ruled by aristocrats, Akragas continued to flourish. She had sided with Siracusae at Himera, but the location of Akragas within easy range of the tempestuous Carthaginians obliged her to maintain good relations with them. That policy proved so beneficial to Akragas that she acquired enough wealth and enough power to make her the only real rival of Siracusae in Sicily. Hardly interrupting her commercial activities, in 445 Akragas declared war on Siracusae. Siracusae won, but the two Dorian-speaking cities continued in conflict even after peace was arranged.

Peloponnesian War

This internecine warfare in Sicily occurred as the rivalry between Athens and Sparta intensified. The Greeks wouldn't let Sicily remain a bystander to this conflict of theirs, later known as the Peloponnesian War, because of Sicily's success in raising grains for the Greek metropoli. Although Athens had no need to import grain, Sicily had become by far the most important region of Greek expansion, and Athens particularly envied the power of Siracusae.

Athens vs. Siracusae

Leontinoi, Siracusae's bête noire, had allied herself formally to Athens in 432, and when Siracusae attacked Leontinoi in 427, Leontinoi sent to her ally for help. Athens, then four years into the war against

Sparta, had few resources to spare, but she was persuaded to send troops — if Athens sent a fleet in aid of Leontinoi and her allies, it would at least lower the risk of Sicily's grain going to Sparta or Sparta's allies. Fighting on the side of Athens and Leontinoi were the weakened but determined Sicels. Also allied with Athens and Leontinoi were the cities of Sicily's northeast; while some of the upper class there favored Siracusae, in this time of crisis these cities opposed her. Selinus had drifted into alliance with Siracusae; allied with them were Gela and Gela's dependency Camarina. (Gela had resurrected Camarina again in 461. The settlers might have done better to call her by the Greek word *phoenix*.) The hostilities between Siracusae and Athens convulsed the island.

The master of words who persuaded Athens to send troops to Sicily must be introduced. Gorgias, a native of Leontinoi, was in his fifties when chosen as delegation leader, already world famous for his ability to respond off the cuff to whatever question was put to him. His originality lay in striving to make oratory persuasive; that is, he wasn't so much trying to broadcast truth as to make people act. Gorgias' philosophy — which came to be called "sophism" — distinguished him from his younger contemporary Socrates not only intellectually but also in making him a lot of money. He used some of his wealth to erect a golden statue at Delphi. After securing help for his hometown, Gorgias remained in Greece. He survived for another half century, until 376 or 375, thereby making himself famous in the Greek world also for his longevity. Meanwhile at Athens, he argued (among other things) that the Greeks should unite against Persia and settle all the poor Greeks there, thereby facilitating peace in the Greek cities.

In 424 — that is, a few years after Gorgias moved the Greek war to Sicily — Gela and Camarina, both forced out of the war, took the lead in trying to end the hostilities. They arranged a peace conference, which was held in Gela. The negotiator for Siracusae, Hermocrates, made an impassioned plea: the cities of Sicily should act independently from Greece, and in the name of common sense they should unify. Now it was the Sicilians of Dorian origin fighting against Athens, but those of Chalcidian and therefore Ionian origin should not on that account consider themselves safe. If the Greek-Sicilians continued to brawl among themselves, he warned, they would all wind up controlled by Athens. The speech was highly praised; a truce was arranged in 422. It lasted two years.

The truce began after Spartan victories. Humbled Athens had lots of war matériel sitting idle, to say nothing of bored generals. The politician Alcibiades took it upon himself to persuade Athens to conquer Sicily with all its riches and thereby gain control of the Mediterranean. He argued that the Sicilians were a mixture of peoples, highly mobile, thus without attachment to their colony, so would not fight in its defense; each colony would sell out to the Athenians rather than cooperate with other colonies. Therefore, Athens would have no difficulty defeating Sicily; she need only conquer Siracusae. So persuaded, Athens sent troops, which besieged Siracusae for two long years. To no avail, for in autumn 413 the Siracusans roused themselves and in the famous Battle of Siracusae overcame Athens's fleet.

Siracusae, in victory, proved brutal. Executing Athenian generals was the least of it. A few other prisoners, the lucky ones, suffered the usual fate of being branded on the forehead and sold into slavery. But, unusually, the region to the west and southwest of Siracusae abounds in narrow canyons; with winter coming on, the victorious troops marched several thousand prisoners into these canyons and left them there, knowing that — escape precluded by the high rock walls — many would die of cold and starvation.

The Western Front

Sixty years before, the Carthaginians had gone to the aid of an ex-tyrant and suffered defeat and humiliation in the ensuing Battle of Himera. They even lost authority among the west's indigenous people. Their debility had perhaps a positive consequence: it's thought that around this time the people of Mozia substituted animal sacrifice for boy-child sacrifice, and if that is the case, it would have reflected the

Carthaginians' increased need for men. Until now the Carthaginians had never engaged (piracy apart) in hostilities against the towns of the Greeks.

Time heals all wounds, and seriously weakened as they were, the Carthaginians gradually reestablished good relations with the Greek cities. Enough so that around 427 they sent their own "colony" to Siracusae, for purposes of trade.

Meanwhile Selinus, fearing Carthaginian revival, tried to expand eastward, which led to disputes between Selinus and Akragas. More important to Selinus were her border conflicts with Egesta, continuing interminably. In the conflict of 416, for example, Selinus had the support of her ally Siracusae, so Egesta approached the Carthaginians, but they were not inclined to join this fray. Egesta then sought help from Athens, and eventually Athens sent a huge military force which, however, couldn't subdue Siracusae and Selinus. Eventually Athens sought aid from the Carthaginians. The Carthaginians still wouldn't help; they were busy with domestic and imperial problems in North Africa. Their conflicts in Greek Sicily had moderated and they wanted to keep it that way.

So the Carthaginians (and Akragas) remained unallied on the sidelines, in this war of Egesta and Athens against Selinus and Siracusae. Although Athens sent a great force against Siracusae, she was badly defeated, again. Again Selinus was on the winning side, and still rich: Thucydides notes that in 414,

> at the time of the Athenian invasion . . . there was no shortage of money among Selinuntans, neither to private persons nor to the shrines.

Egesta, on the periphery of the action, was not harmed. It was around this time, in the last decades of the fifth century, that she built her great temple, in Doric style. Despite the intermittent hostilities — or *because* she had to maintain an awareness of the protagonists' military activities — Egesta had acquired characteristics of a Greek-Sicilian city. Though the Elymi kept speaking their own language among themselves, they learned to write in Greek. They inscribed Greek letters to record texts in their own language. In due course they minted bilingual coins.

Selinus, from her position of strength, soon attacked Egesta. The Carthaginians had traditionally sided with the indigenous people against aggression by Selinus, and now when Egesta desperately called on the Carthaginians they were ready to help. The Carthaginians invaded Selinus in the spring of 409 and conquered in nine days. It all happened so fast that Selinus's allies didn't have time to come to her aid. As reported by Diodorus Siculus and the fourth-century Athenian historian Xenophon, the Carthaginians razed Selinus; they took five thousand slaves, and only twenty-five hundred Selinuntans managed to flee. The great majority of the men living in Selinus, some sixteen thousand, the Carthaginians massacred; henceforward the city was theirs.

Mazar in Sicily's southwest corner had developed as the shared possession of Selinus and the Carthaginians. A small and unaligned trading post, she had had no trouble. The Carthaginians weren't doing much farming, either around Mazar or around Carthage. At Mazar they bought the Greek-Sicilians' grain and bread, using them to make the twice-baked bread (*biscoctum*, ship's biscuit) so important for their sailors. The Carthaginians realized that Selinus was expanding as fast as she could into the interior so as to cultivate grains, which she then traded along with her pottery for the Carthaginians' luxury goods. A fine kettle of fish: Selinus's demand for goods pleased the Carthaginians while her expansion dismayed them. Once the Carthaginians vanquished Selinus, there was no longer any question to whom Mazar belonged.

Having conquered Selinus, the Carthaginians went looking for another target. After talking it over with Siracusae and Athens, the Carthaginians settled on Akragas, her longtime trading partner. (Later historians, Diodorus Siculus and Timaeus of Tauromenion, remarked particularly on the olives and wine going from Akragas to Carthage.) But the economic power of Akragas made her the rival of both Selinus and Siracusae: Siracusae would be delighted by a

Carthaginian conquest of Akragas. Akragas also looked *easy* to defeat: not having been at war for more than thirty years, Akragas would have gone soft from the lack of military exercise, from luxurious living, and because the previous oligarchs had been supplanted by democrats. In the event, Akragas held out seven months, then in December 406 surrendered. Her inhabitants were permitted to depart for Leontinoi, then the Carthaginians had an orgy of plunder, during which they caused serious damage to the temples. In the life of the splendid spirited city of Akragas it was the 175th year.

✺

Gela had been living anxiously under the threat of invasion from Carthaginians for twenty years. As soon as the Carthaginians attacked Akragas, the Gelans knew their days were numbered. Gela called for and received help from Siracusae. The Carthaginian attack on Gela came in the summer of 405, and the two sides battled under the fortifications. Gela was defeated, and the Gelans expelled.

Then there was the north coast. After winning the Battle of Himera, the Greek-Sicilians moved the surviving residents of the town to a nearby hot springs. Seventy years later, Thermae Himerae was a nice little city. In 409 Hamilcar's grandson Hannibal vengefully took his army of Carthaginians and Sicels into Thermae, destroyed the town, and massacred three thousand prisoners.

Sicilians Imitate Athenian Democracy
In the midst of all this warfare, Leontinoi's class war flared up again, causing the city great damage as the aristocrats sought to regain power. The poorer people sent to Athens for aid, but Athens at war was not inclined to cross the Ionian for Leontinoi a second time. In years of strife Leontinoi lost many of her aristocrats and common people. Tempted by her weakness, the Carthaginians attacked Leontinoi in 409 and razed her. Three years later the Siracusans marched into the debris of the once-prosperous Leontinoi, with the intention of remaining. Then the Carthaginians attacked Akragas, and in 406 the refugees from Akragas relocated in Leontinoi. A treaty between the Greek-Sicilians and the Carthaginians the fol-

lowing year stipulated (among many things) that Leontinoi should remain an autonomous city.

Clearly the Greek-Sicilians were having difficulty governing themselves. Certain problems were due to the recurrent transfer of populations from city to city and the residence in some cities of thousands of mercenaries. During the Peloponnesian War the different social classes of Siracusae united to suppress Athens, but as the war wound down they renewed their feuds, as did Leontinoi. War veterans conscious of their successes and sacrifices demanded governmental recognition; they wanted to participate in government.

While the Siracusans deprecated Athens as a military power, they nonetheless admired the Athenian way of governing. They watched with interest as Athens introduced a new system called "democracy." The Siracusan veterans in Siracusae succeeded in obtaining a written legislative code and an assembly based on the model of Athens, but the landowners circumscribed it: Athens chose her assembly by lot, whereas Siracusae would elect hers. Since members of the assembly served without pay, candidates for election came from the upper classes. The landowners (they no longer called themselves *gamoroi*) remained unwilling to share power with the populace. The veterans did succeed in strengthening the rule of law, even adopting the Athenian system of choosing judges by lot.

The Siracusans also adapted the Athenians' way of discouraging corruption. In Siracusae any assemblyman deemed to be exceeding his authority through influence peddling, nepotism, or financial irregularities would be banished from the city for five years. If we can believe the historian Diodorus, the new rule, aimed at keeping the representatives honest, resulted in many of the best politicians retiring from public life.

This Siracusan "democracy" hardly impinged on the power of the oligarchy and the perpetual conflict between rich and poor. The experiment lasted only a couple of years. When the Carthaginians started trampling the Greek colonies, the worried Siracusans clamored for a return to the old system with a new tyrant.

THE TYRANT DIONYSIUS

The god Dionysius had many attributes, including patron of the theater. In 406, a young man named after him dashed from the wings
onto the Siracusan stage, where he was to become one of Sicily's great
protagonists. Dionysius was only twenty-four when he took command
of the forces of an oligarch, Hermocrates, to become general, then
commander in chief, then, before the year was out, Siracusae's ruler.

He was a native Siracusan, without any particular pedigree;
nothing distinguished Dionysius from the rest of the Siracusan soldiers so much as his political savvy, his ability to seize an opportunity. He made a good political marriage, and he murdered some generals and civilian leaders who might have opposed him. He cleared
out all the residents from the Siracusan core, Ortygia, in order to
make the whole island his fortress, repopulating it with the entire
population of a town from the Italian peninsula he had vanquished,
with mercenaries (who were numerous in the area), and with a lot of
slaves whom he had freed to obtain their loyalty. He distributed
rewards carefully, so that leading citizens would support him in
order to maintain their position.

When Dionysius seized power, the revived Carthaginians were conquering Greek colonies right and left, and it looked like Siracusae
would be the next to fall. Dionysius made peace with them in a
treaty that recognized Carthaginian rights in the western part of the
island — although it had been evident to everyone for a long time
that the Carthaginians controlled that region, no Greek had ever
before acknowledged it officially. In return Dionysius wanted only
that the Carthaginians acknowledge him as ruler of Siracusae.

Meanwhile he had to tie up some loose ends from the last decades'
war between Siracusae and Athens. In 404 Dionysius went on a ram-
page, attacking everywhere in Sicily's northeast — all those cities that
had sided with Athens. He razed Naxos and sold her people into
slavery, ending the 330-year history of Sicily's first settlement. He likewise took revenge on Katane by deporting all her inhabitants into
slavery. The physical city he turned over to mercenaries who had served
him, and mercenaries are notoriously careless about their surroundings.

Dionysius transferred populations for military ends. He dealt with the Carthaginians just to buy time, while he sought to advance the art of warfare through handsome rewards for improvements in artillery. To discourage Athenians and Carthaginians and any other powers with designs on Siracusae, Dionysius had a wall built in an arc several kilometers out from Ortygia, in length some twenty-six kilometers, with moats and buttresses for catapults and the most modern defensive features. To deter enemy advance from the plain north of the city, he had the wall's strongest castle built on the Epipoles plateau, eight kilometers north of the city center, completing the fortifications around the year 400.

Once Dionysius had his territory secured, he could devote himself to domestic pursuits. He had been married only a few months when his wife died, before she could give him an heir. He was not inclined to let this happen a second time: on a single night during 399–398 Dionysius took to wife *two* women. By them he had enough sons and daughters for incestuous marriages and nepotism throughout his long reign. He acted as though no one would oppose him, and given his brutality, no one did.

Certainly not Damocles, one of his courtiers. Damocles was well aware of Dionysius's paranoia, a neurosis of dictators, perhaps, but in Dionysius particularly intense. One day, endeavoring to flatter Dionysius, Damocles itemized all of the sovereign's pleasures and properties. Dionysius, not so happy with his state, decided to show Damocles the fear that was his constant companion. He invited his subordinate to a sumptuous meal, arranged the most elegant table, and seated Damocles directly under the point of a sword that hung from the ceiling by a single horse hair.

❧

From the time he seized power, Dionysius exploited Siracusan fear of the Carthaginians. When, in 398, he felt ready to make war on them, he asked for support from the Siracusan assembly and received it unhesitatingly; the assembly had become just a rubber stamp. Disregarding Siracusae's accords with the Carthaginians, he purged the Carthaginians living in Siracusae, the envoys and the merchants. And one day, without notice, Dionysius had all the Carthaginian ships in the harbor destroyed.

He set out to ruin the Carthaginians' communities. First Egesta, because she had remained unscathed in the war a dozen years earlier that had destroyed Selinus. Next Eryx, the Carthaginians' city at Sicily's northwest tip, which yielded before a shot was hurled. Most important, Mozia.

Mozia was never a great city, like Athens or Siracusae, like Tyre or Carthage, but she was a major city of the Carthaginians and the biggest one in Sicily. For a long time after the Himera disaster, Mozia maintained her position as the Carthaginians' stronghold while staying out of the wars of Greek Sicily. Her people were devoted to crafts and public works. Of necessity they rebuilt the wall around the island with towers and main gates and postern gates. The wall was thick; along its length its outside surfaces were defined by two facing stone blocks, the space between them being filled by rubble. Like the Greek-Sicilians, the Carthaginians spared no effort to keep their defenses effective. But now with her two sister-cities defeated, Mozia realized that even unassailable fortifications wouldn't be enough to save her. Despairing of outside help, Mozia broke the causeway so that Greek forces could not attack from land. Dionysius's troops nonetheless blockaded the island and attacked it from their ships with a new kind of siege engine, and by late summer 397 Mozia could hold out no longer. The forces of Dionysius destroyed the island city, crucified the Greeks who had been living there, and deported the Carthaginians.

Dionysius allowed the core of the Carthaginian military to flee Sicily after paying him a large sum of money. Henceforward Dionysius controlled all of Sicily and was the most powerful leader in the Greek world. He spent the rest of his thirty-eight-year reign making intermittent war on the Italic peninsula and in Greece as well as on the Carthaginians. Mostly he sought military victories, but sometimes he gained control by negotiation and threat. On other occasions the Carthaginians won, as in 378 up near Panormus.

Most survivors of Mozia took up residence just across the lagoon from their ravaged island, on the westernmost point of mainland Sicily, a site inhabited by Sicani. The Greeks called the place Lilibaeum, meaning "opposite Libia."* Other Carthaginians came to join the refugees, and all determined to make this promontory like Mozia, only stronger. Their best engineers went to work immediately to construct a naval base truly unconquerable, and the military men brought their fleet there. Merchants soon built the headland into a commercial center for their Mediterranean operations. All around their new city's land borders the Carthaginians raised a mighty wall.

It had been a-building for almost thirty years, but finally, what a wall they had! The likes of it had never been seen before — more than six meters thick. Both external surfaces were of big cubic stones smoothed to a fare-thee-well for maximum stability. The channel between the cubed-stone faces was packed with smaller stones. The Carthaginians may not have built much, but when they did they proved themselves excellent engineers. Dionysius could hardly ignore the reports of Lilibaeum's military force and of her wealth so quickly acquired. He sent his soldiers in 368. Lilibaeum resisted effectively.

Being foiled may have killed him, for he died the following year. The payment he had obtained from the Carthaginians bolstered Siracusae's position as the Mediterranean's best fortified and most splendid city. But the city had no soul, her residents lacked roots there. While Dionysius greatly increased Siracusae's population, the motley migrants never blended into a nation, nor did they hold any political power whatever. Dionysius gave tyranny a bad name.

SOME TYRANTS OF THE FOURTH CENTURY
Dionysius the Younger, Dion, and the Philosopher Plato
Around 387, a score of years before the death of Dionysius, Plato visited Siracusae. He "didn't like the lifestyle *at all*":

---

* "Libia" then designated all the North African coast, not only today's country Libya.

> Where happiness derives from gorging oneself at table
> twice a day as the . . . Siracusans do . . . and never
> sleeping alone at night, such habits having been followed
> from youth, a man never has the chance to grow wise.

The son and heir of Dionysius, known as Dionysius the Younger, ascended when he was thirty; he had soft tastes and a weakness for liquor. And he had an uncle Dion (Dionysius the Elder's brother-in-law, also son-in-law), whose greater education and maturity led to quarrels between the two. Dion had been impressed by Plato on the latter's visit to Siracusae, to the extent that he declared himself opposed to tyranny in principle. Junior's unsuitability for rule led Dion to think of Plato and to summon him to inculcate some wisdom in the new tyrant. Plato, despite his sixty years, could hardly refuse, and he went willingly enough to instill in a tyrant the principles of the philosopher-king.

Once at the Siracusae court, he urged Dionysius the Younger to "live every day in a manner that will promote self-mastery, and to find yourself friends or supporters worthy of confidence, in order to avoid the fate of your father." He succeeded in annexing several important Sicilian cities laid waste by the Carthaginians, but in none of them was he able to establish a secure government run by his supporters. He made all Sicily revolve around a single city. "[What you should do, rather,] after establishing yourself in the weakened Sicilian cities, is to link them to each other through one legal code and one political regime, so that they will give you proper assistance against the foreign enemy."

This advice recalls that of Gorgias of Leontinoi sixty years before, when he was urging the Greeks to stop fighting among themselves and unite against the Persians. That hadn't happened, nor would Dionysius the Younger prove able and willing to unite the Sicilian cities against the Carthaginians. Uncle Dion now abjured his earlier philosophy and fought greedily to take power from Dionysius. Dionysius exiled him, and Dion withdrew to Athens. He frequented Plato's Academy and chatted with Plato at the Olympic Games. With clearer consequence he led the Siracusan aristocrats, self-exiled in Athens, who wished to overthrow Dionysius the Younger. Supported by Sparta, they sailed to Siracusae about 356 for a coup d'état, whereby Dion had two years at Siracusae's helm before being murdered by political rivals.

Dionysius the Younger returned to power. Plato in Athens persisted in broadcasting his ideas, warning the Sicilians against their continual bickering, about riches or form of government or whatever; they should concentrate their efforts on subduing the Carthaginians. He wrote to the tyrant:

> Your father's generation installed Dionysius [the Elder], because of his youth and his military skills. . . . Now, though, Sicily, Greek Sicily, runs a great risk that the Carthaginians will devastate the entire island and that it will fall into a state of complete savagery. . . . It won't take much for the Greek language to disappear from all Sicily and for the island to pass under the rule of the Carthaginians. What's essential now is saving the Greeks from the Carthaginian yoke, then later you can argue about your form of government.

Rather than cooperate with the Dionysian tyranny, Siracusae's aristocrats drifted away from the city. Without any Dion to lead them, this time they established themselves in Leontinoi and in due course sent to Corinth for help. Since founding her colony four hundred years before, Corinth had left Siracusae pretty much alone, free to exert her autonomy. But when Siracusae's erstwhile aristocrats called, Corinth's tyrant, Timoleon, led a mercenary force to Sicily and deposed Dionysius.

Timoleon

When Timoleon started ruling Siracusae around 344, he learned that Sicily included some new cities. Dionysius the Elder, shortly after expelling the residents of Katane and Naxos, established Tyndaris on a hill overlooking the sea twenty kilometers west of the Mylae penin-sula. Later, on the Ionian coast, some grandsons of the deportees from Naxos went to the old site and set about rebuilding the community, as their ancestors had done a century before. They found it disheart-ening. In 358, under the leadership of Andromacos, they moved to the top of Mount Tauro, building Tauromenion (Taormina), which was easier to defend than Naxos.

Timoleon, in his mid-sixties when he arrived in Siracusae, would stay in power only seven years, but they were busy years. He brought Sicily many thousands of immigrants from the Italian peninsula and from the Greek homeland, these last welcomed by the Greek-Sicilians, who after four centuries on Sicily still considered them-selves Greeks. Soon after arrival Timoleon set about improving Sicily's defenses. He refurbished Siracusan democratic government to the city's benefit. Purporting to rid some of Sicily's other cities of tyrants, he brought half the island under his control. Megara Hyblea, razed by Gelon around 483, and Agrigas, badly damaged by the Carthaginians in 406, developed into cities again through the efforts of Timoleon; he even helped Egesta get back on her feet.

This westward advance the Carthaginians watched apprehensively. They assumed that the Greek-Sicilians would soon invade Lilibaeum, now the Carthaginians' only city in Sicily. Her wall made Lilibaeum impregnable . . . they hoped. In the short run ships from North Africa brought soldiers to fight against Timoleon's troops near Egesta. There was a rainstorm, unusual in western Sicily in summer. The Greeks took advantage of it, and through superior tactics over-came the superior numbers of Carthage. The two sides arranged, around 340, to end the hostilities and, after long negotiations, Timoleon agreed to leave borders unchanged.

When Timoleon had first come to Siracusae, the Sicilians resented a sovereign who was not one of their own, but his performance won them over. From the start he had support from the Andromacos, who had led the founders of Tauromenion fourteen years previously. Andromacos's son Timaeus was only about twelve when Timoleon came to Siracusae; he would grow up to be a historian, writing about

Sicily's Greek cities and their relationship with the indigenous Sicels. He also, presciently, wrote of the up-and-coming Romans and their role in the fortune of the Greeks. As the first to argue the ancient origins of the Greeks in Sicily, Timaeus greatly influenced later historians. In the short run, Timaeus was exiled by the later tyrant Agathocles to Athens, where he dedicated himself to writing his *Sicelica* about the good old days under Timoleon.

Agathocles
Because of advanced age Timoleon retired, as few rulers ever did. He had been out of office for twenty years when Agathocles came to power as tyrant of Siracusae in 317.

Originating on the north coast of Sicily and experienced as a mercenary in Carthaginian wars, Agathocles gained control over most of Greek Sicily, including Lipari. Fearing Agathocles's power, the Carthaginians invaded Siracusae, and he struck back by attacking Carthage in 310 and the recently reconstructed Egesta in 307. The following year they established peace. Again. What's new is that Agathocles henceforward ruled as "king."

Another symbol: it was Agathocles who first decided to represent Sicily on his coins with the three-legged *triskelis* that became the island's emblem. The three legs are considered to point to the Italian peninsula (Europe), Greece (the east), and North Africa.

While cities came and went, Agathocles proved consequential for Gela. The Carthaginian attack on Gela in 405 was meant to empty the city, but a few people managed to hide themselves or quickly returned to devote themselves to the construction of what would be essentially a new city. The Carthaginians hadn't destroyed the seashore or the fertile soil, so the site attracted others. New houses went up, especially in the western part of the plateau, which previous Gelans had used for sanctuaries and cemeteries.

Timoleon had contributed to Gela's redevelopment around 342 by strengthening Sicily's fortifications. Timoleon preferred peace and prosperity to warfare; still, just in case, he had Gela rebuild her walls. When Agathocles, more bellicose, seized Gela in 311 to use as a base against the Carthaginians, he accelerated the pace of construction. In some stretches, the perfectly fitted sandstone blocks of previous walls were still serviceable for the lower layers of the new wall. As the nearest stone quarries lay several kilometers distant from Gela, the layers above the sandstone blocks were constructed of sun-dried clay bricks. The wall rose in some places to eight meters. Along the ramparts brick turrets were built to replace the stone ones. Inside the wall, the several large rooms of the barracks stood around a central court with wells and cisterns. Stairs led to the sentry posts, from where soldiers could watch the waves crashing onto a duned stretch of beach below. The Gelans knew they had the most imposing walls in Magna Graecia. (And the most durable. Parts of them survive as the best extant example of the ancient Greeks' military architecture.)

At the end of a shift of construction work, or at any hour during the hot summer, the Gelans would go off to the nearby public baths. Brick flooring and underground heating made a session here as pleasant as at any bath in Delphi or Olympia. A brick wall separated the two baths. Sitting here, or checking their clothing in the anteroom or retrieving it, patrons disbursed money and may have dropped some accidentally — coins have been found here from the Timoleon era, among them some coins from Siracusae. Also left in the baths were jars of Italic and of Punic origin, and salves.

Once again, in the later half of the fourth century and into the third, the Gelans lived comfortably. Always, even just after the disaster, they lived religiously, consulting their gods each day, about weighty matters and even about ordinary ones. They organized public rituals as prescribed, with all participants wearing white. Yet they could be lighthearted about their religion; they danced and sang and attended the plays of Epicharmus, whose lines made them laugh at the antics of their gods.

They honored their forebears with daily offerings similar to their own diet, based on grains and legumes. These were usually boiled separately or together into a porridge, which people seasoned with whatever herbs they had at hand and supplemented with wild fruits and meats, cheese, olive oil, and honey. The quantity and quality of the supplements depended as ever on the economic position of the diners. At least some among the rich cared about good meals, for Gela had her own cookery writer around the year 300, when Archestratus compiled some Greek recipes into a work called *Heduphagetica* (*Sweet Eating*).* Archestratus spread the gospel of good eating, but, like Plato a generation before, frowned upon overindulgence.

Indigestion existed then too, on occasion triggered by political worries. Sicily's century of tyrants, started 406 with Dionysius, was characterized by dynastic conflicts and civil wars, reflected in tyrants' invasions of other Sicilian cities. The tyrants of Siracusae evacuated other cities expressly to increase the population of Siracusae, bringing in peoples who would be loyal to them. Some of these received immediate citizenship, as did groups of mercenaries. Mercenaries cowed innocent farmers in the classical version of "the killing fields." When earlier residents sought redress for the distribution of lands to the newcomers, class wars erupted. Despite forced mobility, people identified themselves with their city of origin (or their fathers' origin); no one considered himself loyal to Sicily.

Between Siracusae and other cities of Greek Sicily, and between the Greek Sicilians and the Carthaginians, alliances shifted so often that keeping track of them would be difficult not only for the reader two thousand years later, but for people living at the time.

After Agathocles, Sicily's strong men continued to title themselves "king," as was common in other lands and as Plato had recommended, but that did nothing to decrease their brutality. The tyrants of Siracusae — including Dionysius and Timoleon and Agathocles — may be unfamiliar names now, but at the time they were among the wealthiest men in the world and were revered and greatly feared by millions of people.

---

* Already in the fifth century a certain Siracusan named Mithaecus had written on the art of cooking and apparently broke new Sicilian ground by doing so; after all, the first written records in Sicily date only from about 500 B.C. Although the work of Mithaecus is lost, a partial Latin translation of Archestratus survives. Anyone wondering about the quality of recipes in *Heduphagetica* may be reassured to know that Archestratus was a friend of Epicurus.

THE BEGINNING OF THE END

MAMERTINES

Even under Agathocles, Siracusae had been in the thrall of mercenaries holding citizenship yet supported discreetly by the Carthaginians. For a generation the mercenaries got into scrapes with the local population, as groups of inactive soldiers often did in ancient times. Especially, a large contingent of Mamertines was causing dire problems with the women. The Mamertines were mercenaries from the region around Naples; in their language the word for Mars, the god of war, was Mamerte, from whom these mercenaries took their name. Their custom for obtaining wives was simply to seize the women who attracted them. After the assassination of the Agathocles in 289, the Mamertines went so far as to seize the government of the city. Siracusae gave the soldiers money to go away, arranging for them to reside in the port area of Messena.

Around this time the Mamertine mercenaries went marauding

MAP 6. Towns of Greeks and Carthaginians, before 250 B.C.

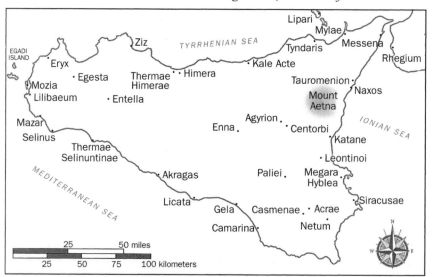

along Sicily's south shore. They razed the weakened Gela sometime in the mid-280s. (The tyrant Phintias of Akragas finished the job a few years later and took the survivors to Licata. So much for the strongest walls in the Greek world.)

In Messena the Mamertines' history repeated itself, and soon the good people there started complaining about them: they disparage our vendors, they brawl in the streets, they damage our property, and above all they molest our women. Here too the Mamertines went beyond rape and such military conviviality. They took over the city administration in 288, and then they extended themselves across the mountains until they controlled a vast expanse of northeast Sicily.

PYRRHUS

During the 280s, in a poor region of northwest Greece, the king Pyrrhus advanced a claim to sovereignty of Siracusae; he might profit by the city's troubles. Some years before, he had married Lanassa, daughter of Agathocles, so the dynastic claims were actually those of Pyrrhus's son Alexander. Nonetheless his pretension to Siracusae was taken seriously, because the king was Pyrrhus of Epirus, and he was a great general.

From his kingdom on the Ionians' eastern shore, Pyrrhus crossed over into Italy's heel and continued on foot, with an entourage including two sons (one of them the pretender), twenty-five thousand men, and twenty elephants. Lumbering toward Siracusae, Pyrrhus and his troops became embroiled with Roman forces. In a battle at Heraclea in 280, Pyrrhus defeated the Romans. Rather his elephants did, as the Romans were scared off by them. The following year the same opponents battled again, at Ausculum,* and Pyrrhus won again. This time his losses were so heavy that he declared, "Another such victory and Pyrrhus is destroyed."†

---

* Heraclea was on the sole of the Italian boot, around today's Metaponto. Ausculum, today's Ascoli Piceno, was in the center of the peninsula's east coast.
† Almost twenty-three hundred years later the phrase "Pyrrhic victory" remains alive in the major European languages.

Because of the significant reduction in his forces, he was persuaded to lower his sights — instead of taking on the Romans again, he could hasten to Sicily, build up his army, and take on the Carthaginians. Pyrrhus received a triumphal welcome in Siracusae, the keys to the city and all that. Indeed, the Siracusans conferred upon Pyrrhus the title "King of Sicily," making him the first named to rule the island as a single political entity.

In the absence of a strong Greek-Sicilian tyrant to restrain them, the Carthaginians had moved eastward as far as Camarina, conquering her in 279. The Carthaginians now controlled over two-thirds of the island, more than they had ever claimed before. Siracusae's acquisition of a king — of a great general and his forces — changed Sicily's balance of power. The Mamertines avowed their Carthaginian alliance. Sicily's new king set out to win the west of the island from the Carthaginians and for a while met with success.

After occupying the remains of Egesta in 277, he proceeded toward Lilibaeum, to the city that had thwarted Dionysius and fielded men who had withstood Timoleon. Pyrrhus had his troops begin their siege. But no efforts could get them through that wall. Unable to enter the city and engage the enemy, Pyrrhus's men chafed to the point that Pyrrhus feared for their loyalty. Lilibaeum stood fast behind her fortifications. After two months of frustration, Pyrrhus called quits to the siege and set sail. Lilibaeum proved the only city able to resist Pyrrhus, the supreme Greek general, king of Epirus and of Sicily.

On his way back from his failed siege of Lilibaeum, still in 277, the king conquered Panormus. It didn't help; the Siracusans no longer liked having a foreign potentate. Pyrrhus left the island after a couple of years.

THE ROMANS ARRIVE

The Romans saw two opponents in Sicily. Defeated in two battles by Pyrrhus, Rome was ready to retaliate against "his" kingdom of Siracusae. And the Romans had learned that the strait, where they had ambitions, was controlled by the new powerful alliance of Mamertines and Carthaginians. The new tyrant of Siracusae, Hiero II, likewise feared the Carthaginian alliance with the Mamertines. Correspondingly, the Mamertines in Messena grew increasingly fearful that Hiero would invade, so, in 264, went to ask help . . . of Carthage and of Rome. Just to be on the safe side. The Carthaginians arrived first and made peace with Hiero II on behalf of Messena. Then the Romans arrived and threw out the Carthaginians. War.

TRANSITION
The Romans Conquer Sicily (263–212 B.C.)

THE FIRST PUNIC WAR

Messena fell to the Romans in 263, the first of Sicily's cities to do so. "So the Carthaginian War had its beginning," wrote Diodorus. As the Romans called the Carthaginians "Poeni," and as the Romans proved victorious, the Greek-named "Phoenicians" came to be called "Punic" and the Carthaginian War the Punic War. Doubtless the Roman soldiers were called all kinds of names as they spent the next twenty years slashing their way across Sicily.

From Messena the Romans proceeded, logically enough, to the Aeolian Islands. For a couple of centuries the people of the little town of Lipari had been living prosperously and quietly, but as the Romans drew closer the Aeolians allied themselves to the Carthaginians. General Hannibal won a victory here over the Roman fleet. In vain, for in 252 the Romans occupied the obsidian islet.

༄

Lilibaeum's thwarting of Pyrrhus was a tiny hors d'oeuvre to the Carthaginians before the Romans swept down to devour them. For over two hundred years, ever since a treaty of 508 between Rome and Carthage, the two powers had observed an understanding with regard to the North African coast and nearby trade routes. Since then the military environment had changed in two relevant ways. First, in the Battle of Himera in 480 the Greeks had triumphed over the Carthaginians — true, that was two centuries before, but the Carthaginians had never regained their aura of invincibility. Second, the Romans had grown into a powerful nation; now they controlled virtually all the Italic peninsula. Their next logical move would be to cross the strait. Carthage, with a military presence on Sicily, was the most powerful city in the western Mediterranean, and Rome took that as a challenge.

From Messena the Roman legions spread relentlessly south and west. In 263 they made a puppet of Siracusae's ruler. The same year they conquered Katane, and then, moving westward into the interior, they won the alliance of Centuripe, and in 258 they sacked Enna. On the south coast, Akragas was now a town of the Carthaginians; the Romans besieged Akragas for six months in 262–61 and finally conquered the city. East of Akragas, the Romans in 258 stumbled on the largely destroyed Camarina, and with equipment supplied by Siracusae flattened what little was standing there.

The Romans, rapid and ruthless on land, recognized their inferiority to the Carthaginians on the sea. In 261 an opportunity came to the Romans and they seized it: they captured a Carthaginian ship (a quinquereme, with five levels of oarsmen) and had their carpenters duplicate it exactly, a hundred times . . . in just a couple of months. Now the Romans had a fleet worthy of them.

On land the Romans continued their advance. Compared to their progressions in the east and south, they encountered greater resistance as they moved westward along the north shore, that is, as they moved closer to the Carthaginians. Still, the Romans conquered: in 252 Thermae Himerae and the following year Panormus, heretofore central to the Carthaginian defenses. In 250 the Romans arrived in great force at Lilibaeum and surrounded her by land and sea. Then they discovered that they absolutely could not breach that famous wall.

The Romans established a naval blockade, which they maintained for a year until they lost ninety ships in a defeat up north and decided to leave Lilibaeum temporarily. Roman soldiers found it impossible to reach Lilibaeum by land because of the Carthaginian guerrillas in the interior; from 247 to 242 the Carthaginians were under the command of the skillful Hamilcar Barca from his nest in the hills northeast of Lilibaeum. The Romans renewed their blockade in 242, with two hundred ships, new or newly equipped.

The Carthaginians brought in reinforcements. The Romans may have had two hundred ships, but the Carthaginians had twice that number, which they deployed to the west and north of Lilibaeum.

✺

Over the waters, dense with ships out to the Egadi Islands, the cap-
tains communicated with each other by using smoke signals.
Although the Carthaginian ships were bigger and swifter than most
of the Roman, the Carthaginians needed more room to maneuver.
Bringing in their ships from the north, the Romans immobilized the
Carthaginians between the Roman ships and the land. Most of the
Carthaginian ships were sunk or captured in this Battle of the Egadi,
which the Romans won on March 10, 241 B.C.

Lilibaeum was now a Roman city. It was clear to all concerned,
Romans and Carthaginians alike, that the sea too was now Roman,
and therefore also the Sicilian shores where the Carthaginians had a
few remaining strongholds. From their redoubt at Eryx, their leader
Hamilcar Barca sued for peace. The ensuing treaty gave to Rome all
the Carthaginian territory in Sicily and its minor islands, and huge
reparations. The Romans had won all of Magna Graecia; here on the
west coast of Sicily the Romans grasped the Mediterranean world.

᧤

The Carthaginians, now effectively dead as a people, wrote no history. Nor were they kind to future archaeologists, as the Greeks
were. The Greeks in Sicily lived in cities; they constructed and
crafted things that we can see. Although most of what they constructed was destroyed by Greek-Sicilians themselves or else disintegrated with time, we still have tangible evidence of how they lived.
The Carthaginians in Sicily built only Mozia and Lilibaeum and a
couple of towns, and elsewhere crafted nothing of any size.

Even their greatest contribution to civilization came to us, ironically, through the Greeks. Phoenicians (shortly before becoming
Carthaginians) taught Greeks an efficient way to communicate and
conserve their thoughts, but when the Carthaginians wrote they
wrote mostly on papyrus, which disintegrates quickly on the sea-
coast. They left it to the Greeks, as it were, to transmit written
records. In consequence most of what is known about the
Carthaginians in Sicily comes from Greek sources and is biased, to a
greater or lesser extent, in favor of the Greeks.

SIRACUSAE

Greek Sicily was dying but not yet dead. There was still Siracusae with her native sovereign.

Hiero II came to power in 269 as a military man at the time when Rome was sailing cautiously into the Mediterranean. At first Hiero II sided with Carthage, but after a few months of evaluating the adversaries he cast his lot with Rome. Although much of Sicily became the battleground, and Sicilian cities were being devastated by the Romans, Siracusae supplied food and materials to Rome. Hiero II's policy paid off: Siracusae lived with a semblance of normality while the other Sicilian cities fell bleeding to the Romans.

Rome benefitted enormously by having Siracusae as her ally: she would have been hard put to conquer this great city, she did not have to worry about Siracusae while fighting elsewhere, and the Siracusaens contributed mightily to the Roman war effort. Hiero II was taxing Siracusae 10 percent of all her crops, and supplying at least that quantity to Rome.

At the same time — in a demonstration of her great wealth — Siracusae was exporting large amounts of grain to Egypt, as well as live pigs and horses and different kinds of fish preserved by drying, salting, and pickling. Trade with Egypt and Rhodes was important to Hiero II, and he maintained a large fleet for that purpose. While his ultimate aim must have been political, he was interested enough in agriculture to write a treatise on the subject. He kept large numbers of dairy cattle near Siracusae, and one had to be very wealthy to do that, because without special attention grass will not survive the region's dry summers.

Ambitious to equal the glory of Hiero I (who ruled two centuries before) yet prevented by the Roman war from territorial expansion, Hiero II indulged his grandiosity by building. On the site of a theater of Hiero I, Hiero II built the Greek world's largest theater, with seats for fifteen thousand spectators. He commissioned the carving, out of living rock, of the world's largest altar, large enough for the simultaneous sacrifice of 450 oxen. Some of the altarpieces rose to a height of fifteen meters. Commissioning a ship Hiero II outdid himself — perhaps because he had the technical help of the great Archimedes — the ship being so large that it could not dock at Siracusae. In fact the only harbor that could take it was Alexandria in Egypt, so Hiero II gave it to King Ptolemy there.

Hiero II managed to obtain sanction for his rule from Carthage as well as Rome, so he didn't face immediate invasion, but that could change at any moment. Dionysius the Elder had strengthened the fortifications around Siracusae a century and a half before; now the twenty-six-kilometer wall really had to be renovated. On the Epipolis plateau Archimedes worked as engineer to give Hiero II and Siracusae truly imposing fortifications bound to deter any invaders.

A younger relative of Hiero II, likewise a native of Siracusae, Archimedes was a whiz at things in the physical world. One day Hiero asked him how to determine the proportions of gold and silver in his crown, and the answer came to Archimedes in his bath as he realized that, as silver weighs less than gold, he could measure with displaced water. That's when, it's said, he shouted "Eureka!" ("I have found it!") and in his excitement rushed out into the street stark naked.

From the same experience he derived the principle of buoyancy. He invented the water screw so useful for irrigation, and he delighted in using levers to move great weights. His favorite achievement was the discovery of the relation between the surface and volume of a sphere and its circumscribing cylinder; in fact he ordered that a sphere and a cylinder be placed over his eventual grave. He wanted to work in mathematics and the pure sciences, but his kinsman and king feared war, so Archimedes busied himself with defenses and weapons and siege engines in case of invasion by Carthage.

Hiero II's diplomacy saved Siracusae from damage for over twenty years while Rome, in defeating Carthage, devastated the west of Sicily. Except for Siracusae and her nearby dependent towns, all Sicily fell to the Romans. After a respite of twenty-three years, in 218 another war started. Siracusae was still allied to Rome, as Hiero II and his upper-class supporters preferred. Those of the populace who disliked Hiero II's policy were restrained by the Romans and realized that the alliance would not change until Hiero II died. *If* Hiero II died. The tyrant lived to be ninety-two, expiring in 215 after a reign of fifty-four years. Over the next year Siracusae's anti-Roman faction gained strength and took Siracusae to war against Rome. Bad timing: as the rest of Sicily had already been vanquished, Rome could concentrate her forces on Siracusae.

Siracusae's wall held; the Romans entered thanks to a spy. A Roman soldier, neglecting orders, killed Archimedes in 212, shortly before Siracusae capitulated.

—⟳ 3 ⟲—

ROMANS

THE TAKEOVER

The Romans started their empire in Sicily. For more than a century prior to their attacks on Sicily, Rome expanded around the peninsula, without war, into territories of Italic peoples much like themselves in language and physical aspect. Now the Romans possessed an immense land of Greeks.

The Romans already knew about the Greeks, indeed they had modeled their own city-state on those of the Greeks. They saw Sicily — they called it Triquetra — as a conglomerate of Greek city-states that never learned to live together and continually fought against each other (which is why Rome could vanquish Sicily). The Romans were far superior to the Greeks in the techniques of administration, and they would administer Sicily as an entity. If the Greeks in Sicily weren't to continue wasting their resources in internecine wars, Rome would have to keep tight control.

The strongmen of Greek Sicily, as we have seen, often razed the island's cities only to restore them later. The foreign ruler would not so vacillate. Prior to taking Lilibaeum in 241, the Romans had demolished Katane (263), Akragas (262–61), Camarina (258), Enna (258), Thermae Himerae (252), Panormus (251), and many smaller places. Then toward the end of the century the Romans destroyed a slew of cities, for the first or second time, calling them "rebellious"; among them were Leontinoi (214), Megara Hyblea (213), and

Akragas (210). Sicily was a defeated land, a Roman property, to be exploited for the benefit of Rome.

The city of Rome was densely populated with a million inhabitants, and even if some residents kept chickens and pigs, Rome lacked space to grow cereals. Without importing grain, Rome could not survive. Sicily had roughly the same number of people as Rome — perhaps a few more — spread out over a huge island. That land and those people would be employed to produce grain for Rome. The Greek-Sicilians had lived like the Greeks of Greece; the Roman conquerors quickly made it clear that the Sicilians were not going to live like Romans.

If you don't like paying taxes and if farming isn't your thing, you wouldn't have enjoyed Roman Sicily.

ADMINISTRATION AND TAXATION

Greece, hundreds of years before, established its colonies so that Greek farmers might have grain to eat and to send to the mother country; Rome established her empire for much the same reason. The difference was less the end than the means.

Despite the importance of grain to the Romans, in conquering Sicily they damaged its agriculture. Not by devastating fields — the Romans never laid waste to wheat fields — but by interrupting the work. Most people in Sicily had been working the land in small, isolated groups, as their ancestors had done over five centuries; but when foreign armies came tramping and shooting and looting all around Greek Sicily, killing many, most owners and workers realized they were easy targets and left their fields.

In due course the Romans got those fields back into production, but with new owners. As befit the victorious, the Romans expropriated the lands of those whom they wished to punish, individuals or even entire communities.

This expropriated *ager publicus* (public land) ostensibly served two purposes: to increase the amount of land being cultivated, and to redistribute land among small farmers. It turned out though that much of this land went to favored individuals from Rome or from the south of the peninsula, either as a gift or for a nominal rent. Parcels of land were also put under the control of less privileged Roman homesteaders. Soon peasants in Sicily were dependent on the rich or on foreigners (usually on rich foreigners) for land to cultivate.

The smallest unit of Roman administration was the city, the Roman "city" (like that of the Greeks) including its rural surroundings. Roman Sicily consisted of sixty or seventy of them at different times. Rome's most important administrative change was the ranking of cities according to the degree of favor in which she held them; in the first years of Roman rule the degree of favor depended on how much cooperation the Romans had received from the city during the period of takeover. The more highly favored a city, the less she had to pay in taxes. Rome assessed taxes on cities rather than on individuals; then the city collected from its households. A family's wealth or poverty depended to a great extent on place of residence.

The basic tax was 10 percent of production. Exempt from that, and sometimes from other taxes, were the *civitates liberae*, the free cities, including Panormus, Egesta, and Alicie in the west and Centorbi in the east. The second category was *civitates foederatae*, cities that had allied themselves with Rome during the war, including Messena, Taormenion, and Netum. The third category, which included most of Sicily's cities, was *decumanae*, derived from the Latin word for "ten"; these were obliged to pay the annual *decima* tribute. The fourth and lowest category was *censoriae*, the cities that had most strongly resisted Rome, especially Lilibaeum; in these cities Rome confiscated extensive territories, which were given or rented to Romans.

Other factors might enter into the classification of a city, for example ancestry. The Romans liked to consider themselves descendants from the ancient Trojans. Egesta — which the Romans called Segesta* — they treated well because of her Elymi origins, in the

---

* The Romans altered the names of several Greek cities, e.g., Akragas/Agrigentum, Tauromenion/Tauromenium, Himera/Himerenses, Siracusae/Siracusa.

belief that the Elymi too were of Trojan descent. When the Romans were conquering the area, they either completed the theater that Segesta was building or they built the theater themselves. Another of the Romans' favorite cities was Centorbi, an old Sicel town in the southwest foothills of Mount Etna. A high natural fortress overlooking three river valleys, located at the northwest corner of the plain extending to the Ionian Sea, Centorbi had great strategic value. She also had rock salt to mine. Yet Cicero explained the Romans' affection for Centorbi by attributing to her people a descent from the ancient Trojans. If the Romans' beliefs were valid, then the peoples of Segesta and Centorbi and the new masters of Sicily were cousins, at a remove of eighty generations.

Lilibaeum, in contrast, came into the Roman family by force. The Carthaginians had built Lilibaeum into a strong port, where they had resisted the Romans long and hard. With the Roman conquest, the Carthaginians found themselves de-ported, in the original sense of the word. After the change of hands Lilibaeum looked much the same — she sent out grain, received (for example) wine from Rhodes, berthed and supplied the navy — but there wasn't a single Carthaginian in sight. The city was now the Romans' main Sicilian port, commercial and naval, whence ships sailed to invade North Africa. Scipio embarked here for his victory over Hannibal* and his conquest of Hannibal's Carthage in 202 B.C., which earned him fame and the distinguishing name Scipio Africanus Major.

When Siracusae yielded to the Romans in 213 B.C., as a token of her former glory she was allowed status as capital city of the Province of Sicily. In the days of Magna Graecia no one had ever thought of Sicily or even of Greek Sicily as a political unit, whereas now Siracusa housed a *praetor* (governor) for the whole island. As the Romans' only interest in Sicily was grain, their administration

---

* Hannibal was the son of Hamilcar Barca, the guerrilla commander who kept the Romans from attacking Lilibaeum from 247 to 242. This most famous Hannibal played no role in Sicilian history. He, even more than his father, had an illustrious military career, though at its end he was defeated and eventually exiled. At age seventy he killed himself to avoid being surrendered to the Romans.

focused first on maximizing grain output, and second on getting as much of the grain as possible to Rome. Apart from that, the Sicilians were free to do what they wished, and each city had the responsibility for local government. Siracusa, which in Greek times had dominated Sicily without formal jurisdiction, was now the official capital of all the island; but she no longer had any power.

∞

If the *ager publicus* program failed to turn peasants into small landholders, it did bring more of Sicily's land into cultivation, and into cultivation as Rome wanted it. Old and new farmers grew some olives, some vegetables (such as beans), some fruit (especially grapes), some barley, but overwhelmingly wheat. Wheat was the staple of the Mediterranean diet, and *triticum durum*, Sicily's hard wheat and the easiest food for Sicilians to produce, had the advantage of keeping better than other grains during the long periods of transport and storage.

Rome's taking 10 percent of Sicily's products came as no shock to the Greeks now part of Roman Sicily; some cities of Magna Graecia, one of them Hiero II's Siracusa, had had to pay a like amount as tax. The Romans, however, required that Sicily sell another 10 percent of her product to Rome, at a price determined unilaterally by Rome, whenever the Roman Senate deemed it necessary. This still does not seem harsh to us moderns who pay more than a third of our income in taxes, but ancient peoples couldn't produce much more than they needed to satisfy their own physical hunger. To the Sicilians of the time the taxes were heavy.

Besides, paying taxes to the foreign ruler was not like paying taxes in Magna Graecia, for now their produce was leaving Sicily for Rome. Previously when they had paid tax, even if a large part of the tax disappeared into the granaries of private persons, they saw benefit of the tax in their own city. Now for roads and bridges, building construction and maintenance, community and religious festivities, localities would have to levy additional taxes.

Then too it bothered many Sicilians that they were being taxed by an aggressor using food grown in Sicily to nourish soldiers embarked on conquests in other foreign parts. After Rome had won control of Sicily from the Greeks and Carthaginians, Roman legions had crossed the sea to continue the fight against the Carthaginians, and they won the Carthaginian province of Spain in the west. Then they went off to fight against the Greeks in the east. In 190 B.C. Rome demanded the forced sale of 10 percent of Sicily's grain, which was earmarked for the legions in Greece, and in 171 another forced sale for legions in Macedonia. That's a fifth of some annual harvests leaving Sicily to go to the aristocrats in Rome and their wars.

Legions of officials visited the fields to inspect the crops and then to observe the harvest. Given that the tax was 10 percent of a harvest that varied from year to year, around June of each year contracts were drawn up between the Roman publicans (tax collectors) and the individual cities. We have just seen that the tax burden was not distributed evenly between the cities. Publicans had a lot of leeway in the amount of tax they might demand, and could impose onerous contracts upon weaker cities. Then, when a city was unable to supply the grain stipulated in the contract, she was forced to borrow from the same publicans, at high rates of interest.

Besides the grain, which is harvested every year, Rome took Sicily's trees, which renew themselves only after thirty or forty years if at all. Except for narrow coastal strips and the precious plains at Katane and Gela, Sicily's terrain was heavily forested. The Romans saw a double benefit from cutting down trees: the cleared land would be used to grow grain or other foods, and the timber would be used to make ships. The Romans needed thousands of ships just to transport their legions around the Mediterranean, to say nothing of actual fighting.

Ships were needed to transport grain not only to the military men but also to the civilians in Rome. (Moving a bulky, low-value product over land was inconceivable.) One ship could carry a thousand tons in three days from Lilibaeum to Rome's port at Ostia. The costs of shipping Sicily's grain fell on the Sicilians, as the Romans imposed a duty of 5 percent *ad valorem* on all goods sent from or to any port in Sicily. The revenue from this tax went to Rome.

Piracy still infested all the waters around Sicily, ebbing and flowing like the tides but as continuous as the waves. The pirates would have damaged Sicily more than they did if Sicily had not fought against them. Sicilians paid for the war against piracy with a tax in kind: the governor requisitioned ships and troops as he felt they were needed. All of Sicily's cities had to provide these manned ships, on the grounds that every community lost from piracy. This tax weighed as heavily as the basic 10 percent tax on produce, even more so when governors took advantage of it to secure ships and men for their own personal activities.

SLAVES

Rome had not been a naval power before she took on the Carthaginians and won the battle of the Egadi in 241 B.C., but by 150 B.C. Rome ruled the Mediterranean. The Roman fleet went to Greece in 146 and conquered and sacked Corinth, the mother city of Siracusa. That same year, the Romans achieved an old military objective. Whipped into action by the words of their late statesman Cato, who had just died, the Romans sent their forces to destroy Carthage. They wracked the city until not a stone could be seen above the soil. But they spared the fields and incorporated the territory into Rome's possessions as the Province of Africa. Naturally Rome took many thousands of slaves, which was to have a particular effect upon Sicily.

All large landowners made use of slaves. Slaves had always been part of Greek agricultural life, and Greeks in Sicily had used slaves in cultivating grain. While grain production needs lots of land, it doesn't require much attention from the farm worker. Because grain required larger fields and less skill than were needed for the meat and fruit in which the Italian peninsula specialized, agriculture in Sicily always had larger landholdings and larger slaveholdings than the peninsula. Now, under the Romans, the expansion of wheat fields and the increase in slaves encouraged each other, raising the size of Sicily's landholdings and slaveholdings to a level well above that in the rest of the Roman Empire. Some slaves had inherited their position from ancesters who were slaves to the Greek-Sicilians, some slaves came into that position due to conquest of their land by the Romans.

As slaves bred more slaves, the trend accelerated. Landowners in Sicily, with a sure market for their grain, bought more and more slaves. Not only the large landowners but now the smaller landowners as well could buy slaves, increase their holdings, and live easier, richer lives. As the circumstances of the landowners improved, the circumstances of their slaves worsened. If the landowners could buy and replace slaves cheaply, they could treat them cruelly and even work them to death.

Being made to work long hours was the least of it. Their owners beat them and branded them like cattle. While slave owners had earlier gotten away with cruelty to their slaves, the groups enslaved from the conquest of Corinth and Carthage were different those enslaved during earlier conquests of the Romans. Most of the new ones were Greek, some of them cultured men who had grown up among slaveholders. They were not inclined to resign themselves to degradation for the rest of their lives. Among them were men capable of organization and leadership. They had one weapon, their numbers, and one key shared attribute, the use of a common tongue.

The Romans, whose skill in the organization of their legions had brought them victory after victory, made a mistake when organizing their captured Greeks into slave labor. Their mistake was not even due to ignorance; they had disregarded an oft-repeated warning to keep slave groups heterogeneous. Given that slaves vastly outnumbered their owners, the owners had to keep them subjugated, physically strong enough to work but psychologically weak and isolated. Individual slaves, brutally treated, would always try to escape, as exemplified by armed bands of escaped slaves who were by 141 demanding ransom in different parts of the island. But so long as slaves could not easily communicate with one another, they would be hard put to organize a mass escape. Now throughout grain-growing Sicily the Greek slaves could communicate; a revolt was waiting to happen.

SLAVE REVOLTS

It broke out in 135 at a large landholding near Enna in the island's center. Some slaves of a vicious landowner were plotting to kill him, and they asked counsel of their fellow slave Eunus, whom they respected for his magical powers. Eunus had been taken from Greek Syria by the conquering Romans. As things developed, Eunus ran off from his owner with a few hundred others to Enna and there joined other escaped slaves. Together they decided to kill the landlord and did so; they proclaimed Eunus their king. Within days of a few hundred men fleeing their bondage, several thousand escaped men considered themselves part of a nationlike entity, modeled on the Greek-Syrian kingdom and organized with courts and arms-producing workshops.

The exploits of Eunus and his followers gave courage to slaves-turned-bandits in the zone of Agrigentum. The leader there, Cleon, brought Eunus another few thousand men and became his commander in chief. Upward of fifty thousand men pushed eastward as

MAP 7. Towns, 250 B.C.– A.D. 900

legions, picking up food and fighters as they advanced. Eunus and Cleon ordered their subjects not to destroy fields and not to kill field-workers. The corps advanced toward the east, though hardly unimpeded; it kept meeting sequential fronts of the Sicilian militia and had to do battle numerous times.

Rome, on the other hand, reacted slowly. Even though many of the large landowners in Sicily came from Rome, to most people in Rome, Sicily was remote and rural; they knew little about Sicily and cared less. Sicily's landowners weren't about to report the events to Roman officialdom, who might blame the landowners for having brought it on themselves by their brutality and chastise them for this interruption in exporting grain. Roman administrators in Sicily likewise neglected to report, for as a group they benefitted by the landlords' cruelty and corruption. Eventually, of course, high-level officials in Rome became aware of the revolt, its size, and its progression. But as nothing like this had ever happened before, official Rome was uncertain how to respond. At first the Romans hoped that the problem would just go away, that the forces of Cleon and those of Eunus would begin fighting each other. When that didn't happen, but instead the rebels were gaining territory, the Roman officials hesitated to spend the money to crush them. As Rome dithered, the former enslaved fieldworkers managed to cut a swath from Enna to Tauromenium.

It took a few years, until 132, but Rome eventually dispatched to Tauromenium twenty thousand soldiers experienced in putting down rebellious slaves on the peninsula. After a series of sieges and treacheries, the Roman soldiers did what they were ordered to do: they captured and tortured the rebels before throwing them from the ramparts to their deaths or putting them in prison. Eunus met the second fate; he must have expected to die in chains one way or another.

Sicily could return to the grain business as usual in 131 — or almost as usual. Estates that had stopped functioning because of damage to the fields were gradually brought back into production. For the most part, Roman Sicily's landowners remained loyal to Rome because they knew that anyone deemed disloyal risked expulsion. Those few towns that had shown sympathy to the rebels found themselves run by men whose loyalty to Rome was clear. Of course there was talk of punishing the rebels, but they could hardly be killed or imprisoned as they were needed in the fields, and it was a bit late to threaten them with enslavement.

The Roman Senate did consider changing the system of landowner-ship, and went so far as to pass a law (the lex Rupilo of 131), but slavery in Sicily remained as horrible as ever. The legislators were not about to mitigate the cruelty inherent in the system, given that they and their class profited from it. In fact they paid little official attention to the slave revolt. They recognized other major events in Sicily and sometimes responded to them sympathetically — for example, after a major eruption of Etna in 122 Rome exempted Katane for ten years from the 10 percent tax. But although the slave revolt caused great loss to many Sicilian landowners, Rome gave them no financial aid.

✐

Rome was growing anxious about the northern part of the Italian peninsula, which was threatened with invasion by Germanic peoples. In 104 B.C. Rome asked military support from Nicomede III, king of Bithynia in Asia Minor and Rome's puppet. Nicomede said he couldn't comply because all the young men in his kingdom had been dragged off by slave traders to the Roman lands or had fled out of fear that they might be. Rome got the point and stopped abetting the slave traders; the Roman Senate decreed the manumission of persons belonging to Rome's "allies." Hardly had this news reached Sicily than Rome's governor in Siracusa found himself besieged by slaves seeking emancipation. Over the next few days he prepared the doc-ument to liberate some eight hundred slaves, then cried halt and ordered the slaves still waiting to return to their owners. Did he really believe they would? The slaves, denied and disgusted, ran off northwest toward the sanctuary of Palici and called for revolt.

They were joined by bands of other slaves who had liberated them-selves. Large groups came from far across the island — from western territory never hellenized, specifically from around the romanized port city of Lilibaeum, and from the nearby inland zone around

Alicie (modern Salemi) and Segesta. The revolt of the previous generation took place in the eastern half of Sicily; this was the moment
for slaves from the west. As in the first revolt, these rebels were
organized into a kingdom, under the rule of a certain Salvio, with its
capital in the mountaintop town of Triokala (modern Caltabellotta),
near the southern coast directly south of Panormus. This rebel operation was smaller but better organized than the preceding one. This
time however the Romans reacted immediately. Salvio and his troops
had to fight Roman soldiers from the start, especially when they
tried to reach the larger population centers. The Romans in fact kept
them from conquering any city, although the rebel forces gained control of the countryside throughout Sicily.*

The particulars aren't important; though the slaves carried on for
four years, their end was inevitable. For the last rebels there was a
final series of events, gratuitously tragic. The Romans promised several hundred holdouts that their lives would be spared if they surrendered. The slaves surrendered and were sent to Rome, to the circus
to be torn to shreds by lions.

TRAVELLING AND LANDSCAPE

The lions were shipped to Rome from the far shores of the empire,
just like the first generations of slaves. It's astounding how much
animal and vegetable matter the Romans transported around the
Mediterranean. About the time of the second slave revolt, the tiny
Greek island of Delos (where the Aegean meets the Mediterranean) became a huge slave market. The Greek region, long

---

* Footnote for feminists: There was something rare in this revolt, or at least in the
reports of it: women. In the first revolt the wife of the rich landowner was thrown
to her slaves to be tortured and killed, but the kindly young daughter was spared
and escorted to her relatives. (Diodorus Siculus, *Biblioteca historica*, xxxiv–xxxv, 2,
§§ 24b, 37) All other characters were men. Records of the second revolt indicate
that the Romans took prisoner many women; these women must have been slaves
in rebellion. Sad as it is to meet women in these circumstances, it's gratifying that
someone bothered to record their presence.

the Mediterranean's primary importer, lost that position to the Italian peninsula and Sicily, which were now the major purchasers of eastern slaves and goods.

Commerce predominated as the reason for travel, yet just as the Greeks had travelled often between the original Greek lands and Magna Graecia for cultural and family reasons, so did Romans travel around their empire. Besides, the Romans had a new main reason for travelling — the movement of their legions. For this they introduced another means of travelling, by road, though the lion's share of the traffic still went by water.

The Greeks' islands had dictated their becoming seafarers; to go inland the Greeks followed rivers. They never cared about roads, and they never built any serious roads in Sicily. The Romans, if less obviously, were also turned to the seas by geography: the peninsula has long coasts and a mountainous spine. And then, the conquest and rule of overseas provinces created a class of Romans familiar with the sea. Even so, from the first years of their expansion the Romans had army engineers constructing roads across the peninsula. In Sicily, the Romans built roads less durable and a road network less dense. Still, Sicily got its first roads from the Romans — some on the coasts, and two other principal roads that crossed the island in something like an X, from Panormus to Siracusa and from Katane to Agrigentum.

Although the Romans built them primarily for military purposes, soon the roads were used mostly for transporting grain to the rivers and seas. A few Greek-speaking traders, to be sure, loaded their mules with wine, honey, cloths, and (more often) oil. In the good old days the Greeks prided themselves on their temples and their pottery, and the Carthaginians on their purple-dyed cloth, but now in Sicily crafts were virtually unknown. They had given way to the imperative of wheat.

As had the trees, uprooted to open space for cultivation. Therefore a traveller noticed more soldiers, administrators, and traders crossing the fields (without any actual increase in their numbers), and escaped slaves had fewer places to conceal themselves.

The travellers would have seen, or heard of, the famous volcano dominating northeastern Sicily. From the southeast of the island to the west, the Sicilian landscape didn't vary greatly. Except for the narrow, flat coastal areas with the major towns, the island consisted of farmland and pastureland bordered by woods and hemmed in by hills. Large cultivated fields were planted entirely with wheat; smaller plots were given mostly to cereals and secondarily to vegetables and fruits. Interspersed among them were parcels set aside as pasture. Agriculture demanded livestock, at least oxen and mules, and sheep abounded. Cattle were essential for dairy products, and horses served for war — the cattle and horses raised on Sicily were world famous.

Where the hillsides were too steep for wheat, grapes were grown for the wine drunk by the local people and soldiers. Several hills had towns atop them, towns developed around military posts. This was the case in the west, near Palermo; in the southeast, between Gela and Siracusa; and west of Mount Etna. In the vast central area, on the other hand, there was hardly any Roman presence.

CICERO

The highest official in Sicily was the governor, with his office in Siracusa. Under him, for administrative purposes, Sicily was divided into two regions, each administered by an official (essentially a judge) flanked by two financial officers. The Romans made particular use of Sicily as a training ground for young functionaries whom they might later send on to higher-level jobs in places more distant or important.

One such functionary, Marcus Tullius Cicero, was born early in 106 B.C. in a town between Rome and Naples. Although Cicero did not have a distinguished family background, he received a good education. He tried to gain a foothold in the politics of Rome but failed — he belonged to the wrong political party — yet he embarked successfully on a lawyer's career. For further study in law and rhetoric he went to Athens, then to Rhodes. When Rome's political guard changed, the twenty-eight-year-old Cicero returned to Rome and found that people admired him for his knowledge of Greek culture.

After two years in Rome, he was sent to Lilibaeum. Sicily's slave revolts had ended a quarter century before, and the island had long since quieted down. In his administrative tasks Cicero made good use of his Greek, for most of the populace spoke Greek and official documents were issued in Greek as well as Latin. (The Romans naturally used Latin for government business, but they made no attempt to impose it.) The "Greeks" with whom Cicero dealt might be descendants of the colonists of Magna Graecia, or hellenized Sicels and Sicani, or even hellenized Carthaginians. He would have met them in their capacity of traders or landowners.

Cicero's duties, less than onerous, included visits to the governor in Siracusa. There on one occasion he made a personal pilgrimage to the tomb of Archimedes, only to feel grieved on finding it covered with brambles. During Cicero's year as quaestor, he acquired Sicilian experience and Sicilian friends, and he earned a reputation as a good and honest man.

GOVERNOR VERRES

Cicero went back to Rome, and when in 73 B.C. a slave revolt broke out in the south of the peninsula, he was not involved. He knew that Sicily had been the site of the two most serious slave revolts the Romans had ever experienced. But slaves rebelled from time to time, the upshot inevitably being suppression.

This revolt, led by Spartacus, came into Cicero's purview because its beginning coincided with the beginning of the term of Caius Verres as governor of Sicily. Wherever they served, governors generally appropriated local resources; Verres was to prove himself exceptional among them. In his preceding post in Asia he had made a name for himself in the fields of extortion and rapine. The term of office of governor lasting just one year, Verres would have to hurry to pick the plums from the trees (especially given Rome's policy of felling Sicily's trees). But an unexpected opportunity came to Verres toward the end of his first year in Siracusa, when the official who was to succeed him got enmeshed on the peninsula in the Spartacus affair. Verres's father, a senator in Rome, pulled strings so that Caius could remain in the post for a second year.

Verres's dedication to Sicily showed itself only in his plundering. He had the shipyards at Messena build a large freighter for his own use, suitable for shipping home his booty. From public buildings he carried off sculptures, jewelry, and mountains of coins. Even statues: from the temple of Hercules in Agrigentum he removed the bronze statue of the god, of which the chin and one knee had been smoothed by kisses of the faithful. He stole bronze statues from Thermae Himerenses and the likeness of Diana from Segesta; indeed it seemed that he left Sicily no well-crafted gods at all. What he could not hoist by himself he had carried by subordinates, whom he rewarded by letting them steal on their own behalf. Just a few years previously, when Cicero worked in Marsala, Sicily had many guides who showed visitors various exceptional artworks. Now the guides "explain everywhere what has been taken away."

The governor sold political offices, including that of senator. When he asked money of Rome for official purposes, he exaggerated and then embezzled all that arrived. He beggared the cities: cities legally exempt from the tithes, such as Alicie and Centorbi, were forced to deliver an amount of grain even greater than that levied on the tax-paying cities. Farmers around the island abandoned their fields, leaving the countryside desolate. Against wealthy residents Verres formulated false accusations to deprive them of their property. To add insult to tangible loss, he had his statue sculpted and placed in several cities, at the taxpayers' expense.

Sicily in this period was home to many wealthy officials and professional men who spent eagerly on goods from the east. One of them was Stenius of Thermae (Termini Imerese), a collector particularly of bronze from Delos and Corinth, and of wrought silver. Acting as a friend to Governor Verres, Stenius invited him to his house. Soon Stenius realized that the governor had removed most of his valuable pieces.

The Sicilian leaders, maltreated and menaced by the greedy governor, sent Stenius as their representative to Rome to complain. He found some support in government circles there and received a sympathetic hearing even at the Senate, but the Senate wasn't inclined to take any action — any interference with an aristocratic family was risky, any endeavor to curtail the activities of a senator's son would be very dangerous indeed.

Increasingly anxious about Verres, the Sicilians had a second preoccupation. Spartacus had returned from the north of the peninsula with his hundred thousand men because the crops up north proved inadequate to feed them all. Now they marauded at the southern tip of the boot, around Rhegium, just across the strait from Messena.* The threats to Sicily were clear even before they were voiced: Spartacus might invade, and even if he didn't the slaves in Sicily might themselves rebel.

Spartacus did in fact arrange to transport two thousand of his men to Sicily to agitate among the slaves there; he hired pirate boats, paying in advance. The pirates didn't show, perhaps owing to intervention by Governor Verres. For certain, Verres took steps to insure that the slave army could not travel through the ports, thus blocking Spartacus at Rhegium. Because of the menace on Sicily's doorstep, the senator's son remained in Siracusa as governor for a third term.

When Verres finally departed in 71, relieved Sicilians rushed to topple the Verres statues and smash them. Tauromenium threw down her statue but left the pedestal as a warning. The statue at Tyndaris depicted Verres on horseback; the local people destroyed Verres but left his horse. Centorbi — called by Cicero "the greatest and richest city in all Sicily" — had been honored by Verres not just with a statue of himself but also with statues of his father and his son. Rather than rushing to shatter the statues, the men of Centorbi requested the participation of high officials, and when

---

* In the day since Homer had written of Scylla and Charybdis, seafarers had crossed the strait regularly, and so had come to take its perils for granted. And by now it had been explained that the dangers were not due to monsters but to opposing tides, where the Ionian current meets the Tyrrhenian.

thirty senators arrived they all together toppled the statues, to point up that they were acting not in anger but in justice.

CICERO PROSECUTES VERRES

Verres was brought to trial in 70 B.C. in Rome, sued by Sicilians in a class action. They hired Cicero, who returned to Sicily for several weeks to collect evidence. Previously Cicero had pleaded cases as attorney for the defense; in justifying himself as the best attorney to prosecute Verres, he said that in doing so he would be "defending the entire province of Sicily."

In five long orations Cicero focused on two points: that Verres had damaged Sicilians criminally, and that Sicily of all places didn't deserve to be treated like that. Sicily was, after all, "the first place our ancestors learned how marvelous it is to rule a foreign country":

> No other nation has equaled her in loyal goodwill toward us: once the various cities on the island had embraced our friendship, they remained our friends. . . . Thus our ancestors made this province their first step toward empire, going from Sicily to invade Africa: for the great power of Carthage would never have been destroyed so readily had not Sicily helped us, supplying us with grain and a harbor for our ships.

Cicero revealed how under Verres every Sicilian lived in fear of financial loss and physical harm:

> In every town where the governor stayed overnight, some women of good family were taken to gratify his lust.
> Countless sums of money . . . were plucked from the farmers. . . . Roman citizens were tortured and killed like slaves. The most villainous man would be allowed to go free on payment of bribes, while innocent men of the greatest integrity would be tried in absentia, condemned, and banished. . . .

He would not let the judges forget Sicily's continuing military importance, which Verres disregarded:

> Strongly fortified harbors, mighty and well-defended cities, were left open to the pirates. Sicilian sailors and soldiers, our allies and our friends, were starved to death. . . . [The] governor despoiled and dismantled every one of the ancient monuments, some of them the gifts of wealthy kings who intended them as ornaments for the particular cities, others the gifts of our Roman generals who gave or restored them to the communities of Sicily which they conquered. . . .

Although we can read Cicero's strong and lengthy arguments,* there's no point in trying to imagine Cicero arguing them before judges, because he never did. He wrote out the briefs, but instead of presenting them to the court he jumped the gun and had them published. Even on parchment they proved so persuasive that Verres fled, to Marseilles.

Only thanks to the assignment and the skills of Cicero is Verres more than a footnote in the scrapheap of scholarly history. Though he showed great talent in stealing from the Sicilians, he was just one such official in a long line that extends to the present day.

CAESAR AND POMPEY

Politics in Rome rarely impinged on Sicily, but twenty years after Cicero prosecuted Verres the two top politicians of Rome found themselves in Sicilian rough waters. The aristocratic Julius Caesar was the general who had just conquered Gaul, the populist Gnaeus Pompey the consul at Rome. Pompey (later to be distinguished as

---

* Cicero, *The Verrine Orations,* for example in two volumes of the Loeb Classical Library. Harvard University Press, 1928; reprinted several times.

"the Great") was the first of Roman consuls to hold power alone, for Rome had always been republican, with the reins of power held simultaneously by two consuls.

Caesar, in 49 B.C. battling Pompey for political control, brought his fleet to Messena. Messena was still "the city of the Mamertines," as Cicero always called it, and given Caesar's drinking tastes it's likely Caesar thought of Messena as the city of the Mamertine wine. Pompey won the battle at Messena. But Caesar won the next round (in Greece), then proceeded to Lilibaeum, following Pompey to Egypt to prolong the attack.

Pompey and Caesar presumably enjoyed themselves sailing back and forth across the Mediterranean. It was Pompey's last travel, for he was murdered by the Egyptians, but Caesar lived to return to Rome (or he would not have become such a favorite of dramatists). In Rome he became dictator in the year 47, and in early 44 he declared himself *dictator perpetuus* (that is, for life). Just weeks later, on March 15, he too was murdered. The ensuing civil war, played out largely in Sicily, was brought about by the heirs of Caesar and Pompey in a classical example of feud between two political families.

Caesar's nineteen-year-old heir, Octavian, decided that republicanism wasn't for him, so he allied himself with Marc Antony and Marcus Lepidus in a triumvirate. Pompey's son Sextus favored a republic, in which he could expect to wield some power; the battle was joined. Sextus Pompey, with a huge fleet given him by the Roman Senate, decided to base himself off the Tyrrhenian coast and quickly seized Mylae and Tyndaris before sailing east to take Messena. A few cities, including Centorbi, supported Octavian's triumvirate, while most of eastern Sicily supported Sextus Pompey.

The young Pompey turned his ships to piracy, in the Tyrrhenian menacing all ships directed toward Rome and thereby cutting Rome's grain supply. Sicily's marginal classes loved Pompey; for them the Pompeys symbolized liberty. Slaves fled to Pompey in the thousands; so many of them left the fields that the vestal virgins accompanied their sacrificial rituals with prayers that the slaves would remain at their work. (To abandon fields was considered a sacrilege against Ceres, goddess of the earth.) Those fugitives who were galley slaves turned their ships to Pompey's use. The expanded blockade of Rome proved effective, forcing Octavian to accept Sextus Pompey as ruler of Sicily if only Pompey would lift the blockade. Rome needed that grain.

Soon, nonetheless, Octavian felt strong enough to quash Sextus Pompey. Hostilities reopened in the eastern Tyrrhenian. Battles involved hundreds of warships and more than a hundred thousand men. Lipari quickly fortified some embankments. For two years Octavian bloodied Sicilian waters. Though most of the battles took place at sea, Octavian also attacked hilltop Tauromenium (36 B.C.), but met defeat. In due course Octavian's proconsul, Lepidus, arrived in Sicily at the head of fourteen legions and obliged most of Pompey's forces to surrender. Pompey's hopes were finally dashed on September 3, 36, in the naval battle off Mylae (Milazzo). Pompey fled, and Sicily had to pay the price. For one thing, Octavian had all the inhabitants of Tauromenium deported. For another, though he had most of the captured slaves returned to their owners, he had thousands of slaves tortured and killed.

THE YEARS OF OCTAVIAN AUGUSTUS

This victory over Sextus Pompey in Sicily was a milestone on Octavian's road to imperial power. To be sure, Caesar had named him his heir, but he had to wait fifteen years, until 29 B.C., for the Senate to name him *imperator* (military commander). Now he held supreme power over Rome's conquered territories, from the coastal areas of the eastern Mediterranean to the Atlantic Ocean, from the North Sea to the Nile. The Romans' empire had started with their conquest of Sicily two centuries before; only when Octavian originated the post did the empire have an emperor.

Apparently Julius Caesar's to-do list included making Roman citizens of the Sicilians, or of some Sicilians, but his life ended before he could act; Octavian took up the idea, as spoils of war. Harking back to Siracusa's days of glory, Octavian decided to depopulate and repopulate cities.

Within a year of becoming emperor, Octavian ordered a census of people and lands. Sicily's inhabitants numbered seven hundred thousand. The biggest cities (that is, cities with their surrounding countryside) were Panormus, with perhaps thirty thousand inhabitants, having grown rapidly since becoming Rome's commercial port for Spain and France; Siracusa, with perhaps ten thousand, her population having dropped precipitously from the days of the tyrants; and Katane. Siracusa, Katane, Panormus, and the Tyrrhenian coast towns of Thermae and Tyndaris were named *coloniae*. So was the emptied, strategically situated town of Tauromenium, her name already changed from the Greek form.

Residents of *coloniae* were automatically Roman citizens, under the jurisdiction of Roman law (rather than the law for conquered territories), with rights to vote, to work for the Roman administration, and to hold high office. These honors would not go to the earlier residents of the cities but rather, as reward, to Rome's veterans of the last war. Most of the veterans were imported from the peninsula; the Romans were creating an Italic upper class.

Ever more Sicily had Romans in coastal cities, Greeks on farmlands. The clearing of Sicily's inland for grain-growing facilitated the transfer of people to the interior. There, the Greek language remained in common use, and the farmers arranged their lives not only around the natural calendar but also around the Greek religious calendar. The cities of the south coast that had been so important in Greek Sicily, namely Gela and Selinunte, didn't exist anymore. Even some smaller Greek communities, such as Leontinoi and Megara Hyblea, had become ghost towns. Only Akragas, with her fertile hinterland, survived as commercial center; the Romans called her Agrigentum and, considering that the Romans had twice invaded the city, now treated her well enough.

∽

Rome expanded around the Mediterranean primarily to obtain wheat. Some years before Octavian came to power, in fact prior to 41 B.C.,

Map 8. Sicily in the Mediterranean, 250 B.C.–A.D. 900

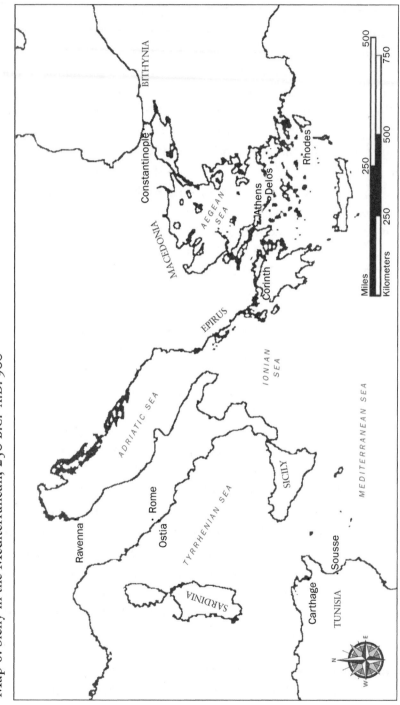

Rome's port Ostia had built a pavilion with mosaic decorations representing her four principal grain suppliers, of which Sicily was one. This
mosaic manifested Sicily's status as an important grain supplier . . . but
no longer an indispensable one.

In Octavian's first decades, the years leading up to our year 0,
Sicily was sending Rome something like two million bushels of grain
annually, yet Rome was no longer satisfied to receive Sicily's tax contributions in grain. Back when they conquered Sicily, the Romans
had levied an annual 10 percent tax on agricultural products to be
paid in kind; but with the decline of Rome's dependence on Sicily as
granary, Octavian replaced that with a fixed amount of property tax
to be paid in coin. For the individual Sicilian, the change in taxation
was the most notable event of Octavian's reign, more memorable
even than the visit Octavian paid to Sicily about 23 B.C. at the start
of a tour around his empire.*

Throughout Octavian's reign, and for some time thereafter, the
Roman market provided grain-related work for all Sicilians, not only
on the farmlands but also in the towns and cities. Grain from eastern
Sicily was shipped through Messena and Katane, and from central
Sicily through the smaller Tyrrhenian port of Thermae, all of it destined for Rome's port of Ostia. Rome traded with Spain mainly
through Sicily's port at Panormus. Sicily's largest port, Lilibaeum,
served the Romans especially as an entrepôt for the grain originating
in North Africa. Besides grain, Sicily sent Rome small amounts of
wool and wine, as well as horses.

The shipping required many workers, of course. Among them, at
every port government clerks had to weigh all arriving cargo carefully, if only for the assessment of taxes. Sicilian grain was usually
transported by privately owned ships under Rome's regulation.
Sellers who feared that their shipments might be tampered with en
route arranged for a kind of security: they took a sample from their
cargo and sent it by a different shipper to the addressee, who could
compare the sample with the big shipment when it arrived.

---

* By this time Octavian had received the title Augustus ("sacred," "revered"), and
historians usually refer to him simply as Augustus.

Sicily enjoyed a standard of living high enough to support a moderate amount of intra-Sicilian trade. In all urbanized communities the products and productive activities were but a step or two removed from the fields: the vendors in towns sold the simpler processed agricultural goods — honey, wine, cheese, and (especially) olive oil — and cottons, of which Siracusa was a major producer. Also some sea products (salt) and what we call manufactured goods, such as tools. The abundant pottery arriving at Messena and Katane was traded inland while grain and other farm products were being taken to the coasts. As the Roman population enjoyed prosperity in the larger cities, so did the Greeks on the farmlands.

Perhaps that was why Sicilians did not seize opportunities for work outside agriculture. To be sure, only citizens of Rome were automatically entitled to work in the Roman bureaucracy, and most of the Sicilians with Greek roots were not Roman citizens; still, the empire offered many kinds of work without discriminating on the basis of class, creed, or country of origin. Whatever the reason, Few Sicilians left their island to seek positions in the Roman capital or to join the military or the administrative services.

Octavian, or his courtiers, would have known about one Greek-Sicilian of the preceding generation who had been badly stung by the travel bug. Diodorus, born around 90 B.C., left his little hometown of Agirium (the name means "inscription"), on a hilltop twenty kilometers west of Centorbi, to see the world and write about it. He travelled extensively in Europe and in Asia Minor, then settled down in Rome for many years to create his voluminous *Historical Library*. The opus ends in 54 B.C., with *Caesar's Gallic War*. Although Diodorus wrote in Latin, like most small-town Sicilians he considered himself Greek to the end of his life.

We know of another writer who migrated from small-town Sicily to Rome. A younger contemporary of Diodorus, Caecilius didn't leave information about himself to posterity. It was mentioned elsewhere that he was a Jew,* the son of a slave, and from Kale Acte (the

---

* Yes, there were Jews in Sicily around the year 0 . . . which means that Sicily had Jews before it had Christians.

old north-coast town of Ducetius, the Sicel). In Rome, Caecilius became influential as a literary critic.

In a distant part of the Roman Empire, around this time, Jesus was born. The event went entirely unremarked in Roman Sicily, and it would be a long time before followers of Jesus entered Sicilian history. We should rejoice though if only because, by our calendar, years are now A.D. rather than B.C., meaning we can stop counting backward.

FIRST TO THIRD CENTURIES A.D.: AGRICULTURE AND SLAVES

As long as the Romans were expanding their empire, they considered Sicily valuable. Rome took all the Sicilian grain she could get in taxes, in forced sale, or, as a last resort, in normal purchase arrangements. With few exceptions, Sicilians were prohibited from selling their grain other than to Rome. Throughout his realm and throughout his reign, Octavian aimed to keep his subjects down on the farm.

But as Octavian's long reign wore on, it was increasingly apparent that the Roman expansion had stopped. Rome already possessed all the cultivable land around the Mediterranean, so there would be no further conquests to augment Rome's wealth in the forms of slaves and grain fields. Later in the first century A.D. the empire would add provinces in the east and the Rhineland and Britannia to the north, but these were not wheat-growing lands. While the Sicilians remained rooted, people from other provinces moved to Rome, and Rome needed additional grain to feed them. From the last years of Octavian, the Roman emperors concerned themselves anxiously with importing more grain.

∽

At this point many Roman senators and nobles cast their eyes on the grain fields of Sicily, especially the fertile lands in the north and east. Not since the Roman conquerors of Sicily distributed *ager publicus* lands to people from the peninsula had rural Sicily known any influx of foreigners. The patricians usually did not go to Sicily themselves but instead sent agents to buy and manage property.

Heretofore most of the grain had been raised by smallholders; the large landholdings, with their great number of slaves and their disproportionate political importance, had not been numerous.* With the migration to Sicily of many Romans ambitious to raise large quantities of grain, smallholdings began to be merged or incorporated into vast new latifundia. The slaves of the smallholdings went along with the land, while the latifundia had no place for the erstwhile small proprietors. The concentration took place gradually, during the first through fourth centuries. The individual smallholders weren't necessarily driven off, but their sons had to find other occupations and other places to live. Nor was the merging of smaller holdings into latifundia ever complete — there always remained some small and medium proprietors. But as a share of all Sicily's cultivated lands, the smallholdings declined significantly.

This transformation of Sicily's agriculture had a corollary. Latifundia by definition operate with legions of slaves. Sicily was like Rome's other provinces in supplying Rome with grain but different in having a plethora of slaves. Because Sicily lay so close to the peninsula and had optimal soil for the cultivation of grain, whenever Rome conquered additional lands she sent the captured men to work as slaves in her first "granary."

Those provinces that lost men to slavery had a reduced labor supply for producing the increased quantity of grain to satisfy Rome; they were consequently stimulated to use labor-saving devices, especially in their big landholdings. Imperial Gaul and Britannia, and the area that is today northern Italy, made modest technological advances in plows, harrows, mowers, threshers, and water mills. Granting that Sicily's different climate and topography could have led to different advances, the vast amount of archaeological and literary material yields no instance of any equivalent modifications on

---

*This is similar to the situation prevailing today in much of the Third World, where a relatively few big landowners control their areas and the export trade, while most of the people on the land are peasants or smallholders.

the island. Nor was there any upgrading in the few nonfarm activities such as forging tools and building roads. Extreme dependence on slave labor discouraged industry among the Sicilian landholders and encouraged indolence.

FIRST TO THIRD CENTURIES A.D.:
CITIES AND CULTURAL LIFE

Wealth depended on possessing land. In due course the managers of large estates merged with the circle of patricians come from Rome to govern Sicily. This aristocracy excluded smaller proprietors. Some smallholders persevered, growing grain and fruit, raising sheep, paying taxes, and complaining about the rich. Others, dispossessed, migrated to the coastal cities, or to Enna (Sicily's only inland city), where they augmented the ranks of artisans and small traders. Tombs of this period note weavers and dyers, carpenters and stone-cutters, dealers in spices and in foreign currency, sailors and doctors. Their presence meant city dwellers certainly didn't patronize the providers of crafts and services in the small inland towns. Nor did the big latifundia patronize the small-town traders; the latifundia were self-sufficient. Without groups of smallholders, the inland towns disintegrated. No longer did they attract new residents or erect impressive public works.

Just as Roman Sicily experienced no technological change, it made no new products. On the other hand, the Romans exploited one old product of the earth in a new way. On Sicily's east coast a bit north of Katane rose a lavic plateau with a town the Romans called Aquilea (modern Acireale). The Greeks (who called it Akis) had made it famous for its sulfur waters, of which the Romans too took advantage for pleasure and health — the Romans loved baths. Then in the second century A.D. they began also to mine the sulfur. They found more sulfur across Mount Etna, beyond Centorbi, in the area southeast of Enna, and put slaves and criminals to work extracting it. Called "brimstone" in the Bible, sulfur served the Romans as medicine, bleach, cleanser, and disinfectant for wine casks.

The quarrymen added to the occupational mix around Katane and doubtless patronized Katane's several public baths. The city built ships for Rome, turned wool into woolens, and prospered additionally by transshipping from her fertile hinterland. One indication of Katane's wealth and advanced development was that she received her drinking water over a three-tier aqueduct from twenty-five kilometers away, namely from Licodia. A second indication is that, although Katane already had a Greek theater, in the first century A.D. a new theater was built over it big enough for an audience of seven thousand. Katane during this period was paying more attention to public buildings than most cities, yet even this theater soon proved inadequate. Around the year 200 Katane built a new amphitheater on the edge of town with seating for some fifteen thousand.* Katane enjoyed a reputation as a cultural center, which this theater enhanced.

The Greeks, it will be recalled, had constructed theaters in many towns. In Roman times these theaters continued to produce Greek poetry readings and dramas. There's even specific reference to two plays by Aeschylus being performed in Siracusa's theater, namely *The Persians* in 472 and *The Women of Etna* in 476.

All the same, the Romans' favorite entertainment differed substantially from that of the Greeks, and Romans renovated theaters to fit their preferred spectacles. The Greeks, for their drama, had built theaters where all the spectators could hear the voices from the stage. They constructed their tiers of seats in an arc so that the performers' faces would be visible to the entire audience. The Romans, for their circuses and gladiatorial contests, needed more stage space and more storage space (those animals had to be housed). More patrons could be seated too — the Romans' tiers of seats completely circled the stage, which had no backdrop, for on the stage the men and animals

---

* The remains of the amphitheater can be seen in what is now Catania's center, in Piazza Stesicoro, named after the Sicilian poet Stesichorus of the sixth century B.C. The amphitheater was so large that any recitation of Stesichorus performed there would have been inaudible to most of the patrons.

moved erratically. The Roman patrons would not need to hear recitation, only roars and shrieks.

Roman circuses diverted Sicilians whose Magna Graecia ancestors had known a dynamic urban life. Sicily no longer had any intellectual life public enough so that we have heard of it. Nor creative activity. Rome's virtual prohibition on trade with other lands meant that Sicilians had little contact with foreigners, and Rome enforced that prohibition by using officials as watchdogs. Sicilians were hindered in developing not only commerce but also native leadership.

As though to underline Sicily's isolation, Rome exiled some of her prisoners there. Lipari's distance from the Sicilian mainland and from the Roman capital made her ideal as a prison. The soldiers who guarded those prisoners were Rome's only standing military force in Sicily.

One wonders why the Sicilians didn't rebel against their foreign masters. Other subject populations — in Palestine, in France, in Spain — took up arms against Roman rule. It seems that Sicilians did riot once or twice in a small way, not seriously enough to be recorded by the great historians. Sicilians may simply have lacked inclination for the organizing and struggling needed to rebel. And then the Roman rule wasn't such as to stir the Sicilians to revolt, in the way that (for instance) the big landowners' brutality had given rise to the slave revolts of centuries before. On the whole the Romans in Sicily weren't cruel, they were callous — they didn't whip the Sicilians, they squashed them.

There was something else, known to such leaders as the Sicilians had: Sicily as part of Magna Graecia was frequently at war, whereas Sicily as part of the Roman realm lived in peace.

ROME GOES INTO DECLINE

The imperial army, organized by Octavian, maintained peace within the empire for a couple of centuries and also built roads of great length. Peace and roads both facilitated movement; if Sicilians weren't inclined to emigrate, free men from the other provinces went eagerly to Rome. The imperial capital concentrated wealth and beauty and allowed citizens to live well without having to do much work. Leisure was in fact government policy: each year the citizens enjoyed some 150 public holidays, with a corresponding amount of entertainment. *La dolce vita* depended on slaves whom Rome had taken from the same provinces. The very urban capital of Rome suffered a malaise similar to rural Sicily's: slaves led to sloth.

With the end of expansion in the second century the Roman Empire stopped capturing slaves. Slaves bred, but their work lives were short. No longer did the increase in slaves match the Roman residents' increased desire for goods and services. Romans continued to demand luxurious imports, although Rome was producing nothing for which there was foreign demand. About efficiency and beauty the slaves couldn't have cared less; the Roman freemen weren't about to tighten their belts or dirty their hands. People in the provinces, provisioning Rome, reduced their effort.

To maintain the allegiance of the provinces, in 212 Rome extended citizenship to virtually all free men in the empire, including Sicily. To be sure, Roman citizenship was no longer the prize that it once was, for the reduction in Rome's resources led to internal tensions. People in turmoil listened receptively to offers of spiritual sustenance. It's not coincidence that a new religion grew up exactly when and where the Roman Empire was weakening.

THE COMING OF CHRISTIANITY

The new Roman citizens of Sicily included people from around the empire, among them many from the Mediterranean's eastern shores. Tomb inscriptions indicate that all were Greek-speaking and that they followed a variety of religions and of practices for dealing with the dead. The descendants of the Greeks, their dedication to their religion notwithstanding, had always been tolerant of others' beliefs. The Roman rulers never interfered with the Sicilians' practice of religion, if only because Rome's religion derived from that of Greece.

Rome embraced the Greek gods, giving them Latin names. The Greek goddess of agriculture, Demeter, the Romans called Ceres, and when they first learned of Sicily's great fertility they recognized the island as the goddess's home. As gods were working throughout the universe, Romans held, new gods might be discovered, and these too could be worshipped. When the Roman legions came back from the provinces with new gods, citizens in Rome thought it expedient to worship them. From this embrace of other gods it was only a short step to tolerance of other religions.

The Romans in Sicily, specifically, accepted elements of the religion of the majority into their own practices. For example, they made Latin-inscribed offerings at Greek temples. Another example: traditionally Romans cremated their dead, but in the second century some Romans in Sicily were buried, like Greeks. Even where gods were not shared, tolerance prevailed. Jews, identified as such, were buried in Sicily during the imperial era. And the Carthaginian religion was indicated on some funeral monuments at Lilibaeum, two or three hundred years after Rome had thrown the Carthaginians out.

Christianity was one of several cults that came to the Italian peninsula and to Sicily from the east. The emperors in Rome, trying to steady a shaky empire, saw a new faith as a political threat. They didn't scruple at adding Christ to the Roman pantheon, but they resisted the idea that the Christian god must be worshipped exclusively.

As early as the 60s, the emperor Nero persecuted Christians (but then, he was murderous generally); succeeding emperors fluctuated in their treatment of the new sect. Sicily was sheltered from the strongest politico-religious currents. During periods of severe persecution Christians, some known by name and by their hometowns in other imperial provinces, took refuge in Sicily in hopes of avoiding lions. There's no indication that the Christians suffered any hostility from the Sicilian populace. Nevertheless Christians in Sicily had to conceal their faith, so they buried their dead in secret underground chambers. That's less contradictory than it sounds, for the known world belonged entirely to the Romans, and within it Sicily offered relative safety.

The Christians dug catacombs in the west of Sicily at Lilibaeum, Panormus, and Agrigentum; and in some towns in the southeast, especially Siracusa. It seems that the Siracusa Christians extended their catacombs frequently, almost as the need arose with individual deaths, for their layout is anything but systematic; these catacombs are more complex and bigger than the ones in Rome. They were used throughout the third century and until the emperor Constantine decriminalized Christianity in 313. Then the religion spread quickly, especially among urban dwellers. Within a year Siracusa had a bishop, and here and in many other towns throughout the island Greek temples were recycled into Christian churches.

PATRICIAN IMMIGRANTS

Coinciding with the spread of Christianity, the Romans became aware of a reduction in the number of residents in their capital city.* The wealthy who now left Rome for Sicily often gave as their reasons leisure, hunting, and study. This noble group scarcely overlapped the proprietors of the latifundia, many of whom never visited Sicily at all.

The Roman aristocrats new in Sicily did, in time, buy land. The Romans as government built virtually nothing in their Sicilian province, but rich Romans did so as private individuals. Though the Roman Empire was in decline, its splendor continued, and the fortunate few could live luxuriously. On their Sicilian estates they built mansions suitable for lavish entertainment, where senators and generals and cultural idols could indulge their palates and other parts of their bodies away from the eyes of the public. Their houseguests included prestigious travellers appreciating a chance to get away from the ports, among them high-level officials and merchants from any of the Mediterranean shores, and maybe some closet Christians.

---

* As mentioned above, the emperors of the late first century concerned themselves about a sufficiency of grain for Rome's increasing population. Their worries proved needless, for the population soon decreased sharply: modern estimates indicate a drop from over a million at the time of Octavian (died A.D. 14) to less than half a million two centuries later.

At one of these houses, the Villa Casale (just west of today's Piazza Armerina), some North African business was carried on during the latter half of the fourth century; that's known because numerous Punic coins were found there. This villa was very remote — the closest ports, Katane and Siracusae, were eighty kilometers distant. A princely habitation with four dozen rooms, the villa might well have been built by workmen recently displaced as smallholders. Under the direction of a supervisor and a proprietor who were men of culture, they produced highly differentiated mosaics for the walls and floors of the mansion's every room. The subjects range from stories of the Greek gods to musical instruments to a gymnasium scene of girls in bikinis. Animals abound: oxen and hunting dogs and wild beasts from Africa. The latter, and a scene of a chariot race, seem to depict the circuses in Rome.

TIME TRAVELLER

The mosaics were destined to last through the centuries, and, unless you were extremely wealthy, you have a better chance of seeing them now that you ever would have fifteen hundred years ago.

If you did visit Roman Sicily then — despite my warning — chances are that someone would have invited you home for a meal. Perhaps not home-cooked: by now "the Sicilians" included many people of Roman origin, and Romans habitually purchased their cooked meals from a takeout for consumption at home.

After eating, if you were male, your host would probably have invited you to accompany him to a bath. Now *there's* an aspect of Roman Sicily that you would have liked: the baths were great stress relievers. As a traveller you would have heard about the impressive baths at Katane and at Tauromenium; on the south coast at Thermae Selinuntinae (Sciacca); and on the north coast at Thermae Himerenses, famous for her two springs of mineral waters that relieved arthritis and rheumatism. Virtually every community had its public bath, where, with Sicilians of our own gender, we could have talked for hours about the appeal of Christianity, the sexual orgies of an official, the excellence of ex-slave actors and poets now in favor, or, as ever, prices and taxes. Your businessman host, talking of Sicily's good economic fortune, would attribute it to the Romans' and Greeks' common worship of Demeter/Ceres.

My hostess *tsk-tsked* about the Romans' predilection for blood sports: "Throwing Christians and felons to the lions, applauding while the animals tear men apart — what is the world coming to?"

IMPACT OF ROMANS ON SICILY

Official visitors from Rome might have talked critically about Rome's balance of trade, poor and declining. Rome had already lost some of her power and a lot of her energy, which augured a dramatic change for Sicily.

Sicily was nearing the end of six hundred years in the Roman Empire. "The Roman Empire" has a magnificent ring. "The Roman Empire" makes today's traveller think not only of the triumphal monuments in Rome but also of the theater in Verona (northern Italy), of the theater and the aqueduct in Tarragona (Spain), of the Porta Nigra in Trier (Germany), and of Hadrian's Wall (across northern England). In Sicily, however, there is nothing that manifests Roman grandeur, and there never was. A visit to Roman Sicily would have given no more indication of the glory of the Roman Empire than a visit to today's Honduras would give of the American.

Rather, Roman impact on Sicily is epitomized in two details of language:

• The Latin word *fundus* applied to any landholding. The kind of landownership the Romans developed in Sicily was so different from their traditional practice that they needed a new word to distinguish it and preposed the word *latus* (wide), coining the word *latifundium*.

• When the Romans conquered Sicily in the late third century B.C., most of the inhabitants spoke Greek and a much smaller group in the west spoke Punic. The few Carthaginians who remained in Roman Sicily did not romanize, they hellenized. Through six centuries Rome sent Sicily legions of administrators, all Latin-speaking. Most of them spoke no Greek, and Latin was clearly the language of status. New Latin-speaking settlers came from the peninsula to integrate with the Sicilian population. The Romans did nothing to deter the Sicilians from speaking Latin. Yet after six hundred years the Sicilians are still speaking Greek.

TRANSITION
Germanic Peoples Move South (ca. 425–468)

The Vandals, in what is today northeast Germany, were disposed to migrate for better living conditions. During the fourth century they moved gradually southward, seeking richer lands for farms and pasture. Their leaders saw a Roman Empire grown flabby and thought they might be able to crop parts of it for themselves. Battling the Romans continually, the Vandals crossed the Pyrenees into Spain and at the same time developed their power on the seas. Under their king, Gaiseric, they sailed from Spain into North Africa in 429 and there defeated Roman forces. This affected the Sicilian economy immediately, even before the Vandals set foot in Sicily: when Rome lost North Africa as a supplier of grain, Sicily regained prime importance as Rome's granary.

—⌁ 4 ⌁—

VANDALS, GOTHS,
BYZANTINES

VANDALS

From the site of Carthage the Vandals could imagine themselves latter-day Carthaginians. They used their new naval strength to tyrannize the western Mediterranean, concentrating on the large islands that Rome considered her possessions but left devoid of a military presence. As Sicily lay closest to the North African coast, it was a principal target of Vandal raids.

King Gaiseric coveted the city of Rome. To defeat the Romans he needed only to cut off their food supply, that is, to stop the export of grain to Rome from Sicily. The Vandals invaded Sicily full-scale in 440, but the Sicilians ejected them. The Vandals continued their attacks, winning Sardinia and Corsica, but Sicily held out. Sicilian cities suffered horribly, among them Iato (south of Panormus), Segesta, and most of all Lilibaeum. (As compensation for damages suffered, Rome, perhaps amazed by the Sicilian resistance, amazingly sent Sicily a return of six-sevenths of its taxes.) Still, considering the Vandals' ravages further north in Europe, Sicily got off easy. And once the Vandals conquered Sicily in 468, King Gaiseric exercised his sovereignty with a light hand.

While they won over the Romans' forces just posted to Sicily, there's no indication that the Vandals made any effort to oust the Romans. In any case they wouldn't have succeeded, because generations of Romans had become part of the Sicilian people.

⌒

The Vandals had sacked Rome in 455, which led to the shift of the capital of the Roman Empire from Rome to Constantinople. (Constantinople was the new name for a city formerly called Byzantium.) Constantinople sent the general Odoacer to rule the Italian peninsula; Odoacer happened to be an Arian Christian.

Arians, in great numbers among the Germanic invaders, were scorned by the Greek Christians. In early Christian times the clerics were always on the lookout for beliefs and observances that deviated from the doctrine they had established. The difference of dogma may now seem minor — the Greeks held Christ to be identical in being with God the Father, whereas the Arians held Christ to be similar — but for a church defining its doctrines and establishing its power, the dogmatic difference was important not just religiously but also politically. The Greek church considered the Roman church an ally, while both Roman and Greek considered the Arians to be heretical. Rome and the Roman Christian church were now in the hands of a heretic.

Gaiseric, king of the Vandals, sovereign of Sicily, by now an old man, was also an Arian. He had spent his life fighting against the Roman-Christian Roman Empire, and in 476 that empire succumbed. Its pallbearers were Germanic — but he was not among them, for he no longer held power. Within months (for Gaiseric would die in 477) Gaiseric sold most of Sicily to Odoacer, in return for an annual tribute, sort of selling Sicily on the installment plan. For himself Gaiseric kept Lilibaeum and a small area around her, but with that exception Sicily was again united with the peninsula in the Roman Empire. However, the peninsula was now Germanic, the Roman Empire Byzantine; Sicily's Christians fell between the two stools.

∾

If confusion beset their church, the Sicilians could still rely on their grain. Wheat from the subdued Sicily kept the people of the central peninsula from starving after the Germanic invaders on the peninsula devastated the countryside and frightened the farmers into abandoning their fields.

When from Rome the emperor and the senators fled, the hierarchy of the church stood fast and gained immensely in power. The Germanic tribes knew nothing about governing conquered peoples. In the anarchic state it was the pope who reigned. As everywhere in Vandalized Europe, in Sicily the church provided stability and succor for a desperate populace. Individuals bequeathed land to the church gratefully, or, affected by the tumult, sold it cheaply. The Roman emperors who owned much of Sicily's land no longer had administrators to protect it. When the dust settled, the Sicilians saw two big changes from the time of their fathers: first, that a large part of the Sicilian grain fields had come into the possession of the church and religious organizations, and second, that literacy had virtually disappeared from the general population and was now a skill characteristic of churchmen.

Though evidence is meager, it appears that during the century of Germanic hegemony the church reduced slavery on its Sicilian holdings in favor of tenant farming. The change to a free peasantry may also have applied on lands not owned by the church. Any tenants or peasants were highly taxed by the officials, at the mercy of the large landowners, and probably not much better off than slaves.

We have no idea of how those engaged in agriculture — that is, the vast majority of Sicilians — viewed Christianity and church politics, but these were naturally the main interests of the clerics who kept the records. However distorted the vision of these scribes, the church's takeover of Sicily's lands and literacy would have repercussions that continue to be felt in our own time.

Most often a conqueror imposes his language upon those conquered. The Romans in Sicily were an exception, and the Vandals were another. The Vandals, adopting Christianity, began to use Latin, the language indissolubly linked with Christianity. Again Sicily had rulers who did their business in Latin; and again the Sicilians would not relinquish their Greek.

GOTHS

After the Vandals and the Arians, a third group of Germanic peoples, also Arian, allied itself with Byzantium. These were Ostrogoths, whose king was Theodoric. The Byzantine emperor, Zeno, was the patron of Odoacer on the peninsula and seemed to be his ally; nonetheless in 488 Zeno sent Theodoric to defeat Odoacer. Upon Odoacer's surrender, Theodoric killed him.

Sicily (still except for Lilibaeum) now belonged to Theodoric. Theodoric was not disposed to leave the Lilibaeum enclave in the hands of the Vandals, so in 491 he made his sister the wife of the Vandal king. Thereby Theodoric the Ostrogoth had effective control of all Sicily.

Theodoric freed himself from Zeno and assumed the crown of Italy (493), making Ravenna his capital. To Sicily he sent only a small military contingent, and he made no institutional changes. Although on the peninsula Theodoric redistributed a lot of land to members of his court and his army, in Sicily he did not interfere in the land ownership, probably because so much of the land belonged to the church. Nor did he interfere with the shipment of Sicilian grain to nourish Rome. There's no reason to doubt that he ruled Sicily, as he did Italy, with benevolence.

So the people of Gaiseric, and a few men of Theodoric, became ancestors of Sicilians. Other than their seed they left nothing of themselves in Sicily, not even personal names or place names. Men wrote of their slow, violent conquest of Sicily, but there's no evidence of any violence thereafter. Furthermore, during the fifth and early sixth centuries, while most Christian lands battled endlessly over heresies, Christian Sicily remained marginal to the conflicts. The Arian Germanic tribes, notorious throughout Europe for their depredations, gave Sicily a period of peace. Here too, as in their tenacity toward language, Sicilians went against the grain.

BYZANTINES

JUSTINIAN

Everyone noted the new star come to the political firmament in 527. The Byzantine Empire (the Greek or Eastern empire based in Constantinople) was in the ascendant when Justinian became its emperor. Already forty-five, he was religious, industrious, and wildly ambitious: he intended to reunite both the Roman Empire and the Christian churches.

However conciliatory that may sound, the means to those ends was war. In 533 Justinian sent his general Belisarius to take North Africa from the Vandals. When Justinian in Constantinople requested the Ostrogoths in Rome to let Belisarius refuel in Sicily — this without benefit of fax — the answer was cordially affirmative. So the Byzantine general had no problems when he stopped on the south coast of Sicily, near Camarina. Soon the North African coast was Byzantine. The Ostrogoths might have withheld permission to transit Sicily had they realized Justinian was invading North Africa to establish a base for seizing Sicily and Italy.

Shortly before Justinian came to power, Theodoric had died in Ravenna. His daughter and heiress, Amalasuntha — highly educated, with regal ambitions of her own — placed herself under the protection of Justinian. Soon, in 535, in her bath, she was strangled by an Ostrogoth, which gave Justinian a fine pretext for invading Italy. Within months Belisarius sailed from Tunisia to win his foothold in Sicily. The few Ostrogoth soldiers put up a show of fighting; civilians not being obliged to fight, Sicily scarcely resisted.

And why should the Sicilians have resisted the Byzantines? If the Germanic rule had been less oppressive than the Roman it was equally foreign. Belisarius and his men — glory be! — spoke Greek and followed the Greek religious rites.

Only Siracusa suffered from the change of sovereignty. Her centuries as world city were a distant memory, and she had been in decline since the Roman conquest, the Byzantine invaders dealt a fatal blow: Belisarius deported the population to Naples. The Byzantines affirmed Siracusa as capital, but they established their administrative center at Tauromenium.

They would administer Sicily much like the rest of their empire, in accordance with the old Roman model. Although the authority of the Roman church over Sicily was never annulled, Arian-ruled Sicily became part of the Eastern church.

Sicily came into Justinian's realm just after he published his great legal code. Though he called it a code of Roman law, Justinian's conception of law derived from Christianity and from his own omnipotence as ruler. The code would provide legal justification for the theocracy controlling every aspect of life in the Byzantine Empire.

Sicily and the south of the Italian peninsula formed the western part of the Byzantine (Eastern) Empire; to their north lay the Latin-Christian (Western) realm. Justinian had prepared his code to provide a stable legal framework for each province to exercise self-government within a restored Roman Empire. When, however, the code became the basis of the law throughout the Eastern Empire but not the Western, ironically it aggravated the split between East and West.

EDUCATION AND CULTURE

All along Sicily's east coast ships arrived from various ports in the Byzantine realm, carrying Greek-speaking soldiers and administrators at all levels. Monks came too, to illuminate books and, by establishing schools around the island, to illuminate boys. Their curriculum comprised grammar, rhetoric, and logic, as well as religion and church music. To those continuing school into adolescence, the monks taught about the physical world as well as more deeply about music and philosophy, even the ideas of Plato and Aristotle, pagans though they had been. While Byzantine law had its source in Rome, Byzantine culture came from ancient Greece and included a profound respect for learning.

Some of the monks were scholars who found cracks in the Byzantine-Christian monolith through which they might transmit the knowledge of the ancients, if not their questioning approach to the world. All monks, and the eventual homegrown men of letters, depended on the Byzantine church for sustenance. It followed that scholarship meant the producing and copying of material that the church wanted to disseminate.

The populace had no other channel to switch to. In any case, many Sicilians left the Roman church, which worshipped in Latin, to embrace the Byzantine kind of Christianity, which worshipped in a Greek approximating the Sicilians' language. Women, the strongest supporters of Christianity, particularly enjoyed Byzantine worship for its oriental music and rich color; doubtless they encouraged their men's piety.

ARCHITECTURE AND ART

In the first decades of the Byzantines, Sicily naturally worshipped in churches of Roman architecture, with a rectangular nave and semicircular apses, the form called "basilical." But in time new churches were needed, and these were built with Byzantine elements of construction and design, representing the Greek cross with its four arms of equal length. On occasion the Byzantines reconstructed old pre-Roman temples, such as the ones in Siracusa and Agrigentum. Outside the cities, the Byzantines built like the Greek Sicilians of a thousand years before: they dotted the landscape with shrines and small churches, especially on cliff tops. Typically these were roofed by domes, as the builders sought to have the church mirror the celestial sphere.

The magnificence of the Byzantine church was to be found, though, inside it: the church was conceived not only as a house of God but also as a showcase of frescoes and mosaics. The Byzantines developed their mosaics from Roman models — the early Christian churches in Rome used mosaics — but "developed" is the operative word. Whereas the Romans had used pebbles to achieve the effect of painting, the Byzantines manufactured and used bits of glass. Their highly skilled technicians selected glass cubes of appropriate sizes and colors and set them into plaster sufficiently damp to hold them in position; they had to work quickly before the plaster dried.

The characteristic Byzantine style developed from a few parts of the empire: the earthiness of the bodies created by the Greeks appeared spiritually enriched by the dignity of the bodies created by Palestinians and Syrians. But after blending these elements, the Byzantines made figures that seemed all alike; holy personages weren't supposed to be portrayed realistically. The Byzantine worshipper saw, wherever he might be, the same solemn stylized figures in the same pure, strong colors. What the artisans lacked in creativity of line, they compensated for in their lavish use of purple and blue, red and gold.

The Byzantines also wore bright colors, the complete palette. They said that the colorful garb displayed their joy in the knowledge that they would go to paradise; yet the colors were a novelty even for them, reflecting the recently increased accessibility of dyes and improved techniques of dyers. Sicily's ancient Greeks and Romans, then the Germanic administrators, had worn their tunics in natural white or neutral shades, so Sicilian cities suddenly looked more cheerful.

SICILIANS FEEL OPPRESSED

But the Sicilians, at first so happy with the change of rule, didn't remain happy very long. They disliked the Byzantines' garb, colorful as it was, for it draped in heavy folds completely hiding the figure. Of the live human body only the face showed, and not always that, for upper-class women were made to wear veils (the only women in Christian Europe to do so). In the hot weather it seemed that the Byzantines were punishing the body.

The new rulers likewise stifled the mind. The Byzantines gave their women little to do besides bearing and caring for children, and allowed them virtually no contact beyond their immediate families. Byzantine scholars, in sharp contrast to their Greek ancestors' open questioning, obliged the Sicilians to learn by rote. As the only patrons of art were the church and the church-imbued state, all art was religious art. Artists and craftsmen worked in groups with no chance for the individual to display initiative in what he would produce or how. Nor was the human propensity for fun to be indulged. The Greeks' popular god Dionysius, the patron of the theater and of merrymaking generally — known to the Romans as Bacchus — was transformed by the Byzantines into a demon. Bacchic feasting had characterized, particularly, the final days of the Sicilians' grape harvest; the Byzantines tried to suppress the festival. Byzantine priests interfered with carnivals, which they considered licentious, and refused to baptize actors so as to hinder theatrical productions. But the populace paid little heed, risking anathema to attend the amusements.

Their early Christian ancestors, not so far back, had felt elated about discovering the Word, but now priests were instructing them in detail about what to believe and threatening dire punishment for those who believed otherwise. After all, according to the Byzantines, a Christian could jeopardize his entry into the celestial kingdom by a theological error. As worship always took place indoors and as the worshippers always had to stand, they grew uncomfortable, and because the service and the music were always the same, they grew bored. But if they failed to attend a service on three consecutive Sundays, the Byzantine priest would excommunicate them. The Sicilian Christians soon lost their enthusiasm for the Byzantines' Christianity.

COMPARISON OF BYZANTINES AND ANCIENT GREEKS

In general, the Greek-descended Sicilians found their Byzantine rulers stodgy and severe. Actually, apart from their language, the Byzantines had little in common with the ancient Greeks.

Greece let her Sicilian colonies manage their own affairs; Byzantium ran an intrusive bureaucracy of church and state. While both peoples practiced their religion devotedly, the Greeks endowed their gods with human personalities of great strength and variety, whereas the Byzantines allowed their sacred figures hardly any individuality at all. The Greek colonists in Sicily respected and adopted the gods of others; the Byzantines were intolerant and judgmental.

As for fine arts, the Greeks specialized in large forms, constructing temples and theaters; the Byzantines specialized in small forms, organizing bits of glass into pictures and decorating letters on book pages. The Greeks thought three-dimensionally, of temples and sculptures, while the Byzantines concentrated on two-dimensional forms such as triptychs and frescoes. As a corollary, perhaps, the Greeks tried tirelessly for perfect perspective, whereas the Byzantines showed no interest in it.

We can hardly fault the writers of the time for writing about a subject of primary interest to their public and their patrons. Still, what a great contrast there was between them and the Greek-Sicilian writers — Epicharmus, Empedocles, Archimedes, Diodorus — who told us at length about their lives, their politics, and their physical world.

POST-JUSTINIAN STAGNANCY

During the thirty years (535–65) that Justinian ruled Sicily, he doubled the size of his realm. Although Sicily wasn't involved militarily in his expeditions, it was taxed ruinously to pay for them. The Greek-speaking ruler benefitted Sicily no more than had his Gothic predecessors.

Three years after Justinian's death, Sicily felt the serious threat of war. The north of the Italian peninsula had been invaded, again, by Germanic tribes — this time mostly Lombards, joined by Heruli (the people of Odoacer, who had purchased Sicily from the Vandal king Gaiseric a century before). Justinian had drained his empire's treasury, so the invaders could advance down the peninsula without having to battle defending soldiers. Sicilians lived in constant fear that the Germans would soon reach them. This accounts, in part, for the post-Justinian period's absolute stagnancy.

Of domestic importance was the Byzantine control of all productive activity. The Byzantines held trade and industry to be a matter of national concern, just like foreign relations. In this the Byzantines were similar to the Romans, and just as Rome had destined Sicily for a granary, so did Byzantium, though not as explicitly. The Byzantines made government monopolies of the two most profitable commercial items of the era: silk, the former pride of the Carthaginians, and grain, far and away Sicily's most valuable export.

To meet its needs other than food, Sicily depended on trade. Given the Byzantine monopolies, Sicily had little of its own to sell. Whatever luxury items Sicilians might produce, they were stopped from exporting them by the vigilant government inspectors. Any Sicilian attempts at trading other goods were discouraged through heavy taxes on sales and duties on imports and exports. Consequently, Byzantine Sicily experienced hardly any social or economic change, just political events and conflicts.

RELIGION AND THE SOCIAL ORDER

Byzantines of the upper class in Constantinople lived lives of consummate luxury, while all their subjects worked to produce for them. Religion provided a rationale for this, for in an empire obsessed with Christianity the only value was religious. If the Sicilians were forced into living with the bare essentials, well, Byzantine morality gave high value to asceticism. Justinian had written Christian dogma into law, and he and his code would dominate Sicily as long as the island remained Byzantine. The civil and religious machinery collaborated to regulate every aspect of life, more so as the years passed.

In this epoch prior to the development of nation-states, every person's primary allegiance was to his religion. Like other subjects of Byzantium, Sicilians were caught up in the drive to defend orthodox Christianity. When building its own empire, the Christian church feared everyone outside it and sought to impose homogeneity of behavior and belief. Only people of passion bother to announce themselves as heretics, so heretical groups posed to the church not just a philosophical but a political threat. Persecute the heretics or tolerate them? It was a hot issue.

Another was celibacy, because married priests would divert economic resources from the church. Some Sicilian priests with wives and children were doing just that, and Pope Gregory was concerned about them. The bishop of Tyndaris, for one, complained to Pope Gregory about priests who were leaving the priesthood, but Pope Gregory insisted on priestly celibacy. Actually the church in Sicily lacked direct corporate experience with poverty — the church through its various agencies was Sicily's largest landowner, with about a third of Sicily's land. Some of that land was indeed inherited by Pope Gregory himself, on the death of his father, which may account for his particular interest in the island.

Then there was the role of the church in regulating private behavior unconnected with belief or ritual. Early in his reign Pope Gregory told his bishops not to interfere in Sicily's secular affairs except in regard to the poor. But Byzantines, innate autocrats, resisted the idea of secularity. Travel permits were rigidly controlled, as were workers' hours and wages. People were enjoined from dressing in certain cloths and colors. And the Sicilians had to pay for the army of government employees who ordained and enforced all these restrictions.

FOREIGN ENTANGLEMENTS

To control their subjects and their enemies, imperial powers generally threatened physical force; in contrast the Byzantines depended largely on threats of perdition, which were effective only for Christians. Throughout the Mediterranean but especially around Sicily, Byzantine commerce was suffering from the piracy of North Africans zealous in their new Islam. Rather than reacting militarily, the Byzantines lessened the risks by sending their ships in great convoys. But when a ship became disabled near the shore, it was menaced not only by Muslims — the impoverished Christians living nearby would swarm to the ship for plunder.

While the Sicilians still feared the Lombards, the Muslims were closer. A small force of Muslims made forays into Sicily in 652, but that was only twenty years after Mohammed's death, and the holy warriors weren't yet well enough organized to do Sicily any damage. To drive them away came Byzantine soldiers from Ravenna, led by the governor.

Before the Byzantine governor could return to Ravenna he died, leaving Italy without a Byzantine representative. The emperor in Constantinople, Constans II, was giving his attention to more urgent matters, like branding dead popes as heretics . . . and then, the living one, Pope Martin, whom Constans deposed from the papacy and banished to the Crimea. The reaction against Constans was so strong that he decided to transfer himself to the West, from where he could also better govern Italy. His first thought was naturally Rome, but a visit there proved unpleasant, so he settled at Siracusa. When the Byzantines first occupied Sicily, they said that Siracusa would remain Sicily's official capital; now, eight emperors later, in 663, Constans II honored that promise.

Upon hearing of the emperor's move, Siracusans entertained hopes that his presence would benefit them, but once settled with his fashionable court, Constans comported himself like one of the extravagant rulers of Siracusa who had long ago tyrannized Magna Graecia. The Sicilians found themselves footing the horrendous bill for his expenses. Their release from this financial burden came through some Byzantine nobles in Sicily who conspired to murder the emperor. Perhaps thinking of the first days of Byzantine rule and the daughter of King Theodoric, the chamberlain charged with the deed killed Constans II while he was bathing, clubbing him with a soap dish. The dead Emperor's son, Constantine IV, arrived in Siracusa at the head of an army to transfer the court back to Constantinople. So ended Siracusa's five-year spell as capital of the Byzantine Empire.

After the adventure of Constans II, Sicily seemed ever more remote to a Constantinople beset by troubles in the East. Still, Sicily being under threat from both Lombards and Arabs, the Byzantines had to devote some attention to its defenses. Around 687 they declared the island a *theme* (military province) and installed a military governor at Messena. They strengthened the defenses of some inland towns —

for example, fifty kilometers west of Siracusa at the small town of Ibla (Regusa); in the island's center, at Enna; and in the west, next to Segesta, at Catalafimi. Panormus, otherwise unimportant to the Byzantines, was to be defended for her strategic position. But these defensive efforts were to prove too little and too late.

The problems of the Christian church in Sicily would soon become moot.

TRANSITION
The Coming of the Muslims (827–902)

When Muslims set out from North Africa to challenge the Byzantines' control of the Mediterranean, Sicily heard echoes of ancient conflicts between Greeks and Carthaginians.

Actually, the interlopers weren't descended from the Carthaginians; rather they had swept in from farther south in Africa and from the east in Asia. Brandishing the Islamic message around what we now call Tunisia, they developed Kairouan as capital and religious center, then continued a hundred kilometers north and in 698 occupied the spectral Carthage. Basing themselves on that headland, they traded and raided around the Mediterranean, and, starting around 820, they set up a few trading stations in Sicily.

They must have pinched themselves in disbelief when they received an invitation to invade Sicily. A Byzantine general in Sicily named Eufemius, aware of the Muslims' designs for the island and wanting to extend his own power, incited a rebellion in Sicily and went to the Aghlabites in Kairouan for support. If he had known his history, he would have recalled that the Mamertines had sought help from North Africa a thousand years before, and that the upshot was the Roman conquest of Sicily . . . and the political end of the Mamertines.

Probably not even thinking of that, the parliament in Kairouan proposed to invade Marsala, then feared that that port would be heavily fortified and decided to land farther south at Mazar. On June 13, 827, from the town of Sousse 120 kilometers south of Carthage, ten thousand foot soldiers and seven hundred cavalrymen, each with his swift horse, embarked in a hundred ships. Although the invaders originated in many parts of the Muslim empire (including Spain), most of the men were Berbers (from the North African coast) and Arabs (from farther east). After three days' voyage they found awaiting them at Mazar an armed force led by Eufemius, yet these men together were outnumbered by the

Byzantine defenders. It took the Muslim forces a month to conquer Mazar, which they called Mazara. Leaving a garrison there, the victors moved off toward Siracusa and further conquest.

Their first siege of Siracusa failed, partly because many of the Muslims contracted the malaria endemic to southeast Sicily. In the northwest they fared better, taking Drepanum (Trapani) in 830 and Panormus the following year. From this corner of Sicily they could ply the waters to the mercantile cities of the northern Italian peninsula as well as to their lands in the western Mediterranean.

To save Christian Sicily from infidel incursions and eventual conquest you'd think that other Christian peoples would fight ardently. In fact they offered little help. The Byzantines were straining their resources as it was — in the eastern part of their empire trying to ward off Muslims and Bulgars and Slavs — whereas Sicily lay far, far to the west. The Romans, for their part, didn't much care what happened to a province of Byzantium; still, one wonders that they accepted the risk of Muslims using Sicily as a stepping-stone to Rome. The Muslims, sending forces from North Africa, began their Tyrrhenian campaign in 839 at Lipari, killing many of her residents and enslaving the survivors, thus emptying the island. Four years later, when the Muslims went to attack Messena, the duchy of Naples sought to benefit commercially by sending help . . . to the Muslims. Once the Muslims won Messena, they of course controlled traffic between the Mediterranean and the Tyrrhenian.

The Muslims weren't opposed by the Sicilian populace, which feared Muslim fanaticism but had had enough of Byzantine fanaticism. Sicily's Byzantines, on the other hand, fought many a hard battle, usually ending in their defeat; one can hear them screaming to Constantinople for reinforcements, which never came.

Enna, at the heart of the vast grain lands, had been a hub of the Roman road system. The Byzantines had fortified the city heavily and, after Panormus fell to the Muslims in 831, concentrated their forces here. The Muslims besieged Enna for a long time, until they finally took her by storm in 859. In 878 the Muslims again targeted Siracusa, Sicily's principal city. This time they used underground mines and succeeded in cracking her walls. The ensuing massacre and flight removed all life from this city whence hordes of soldiers had marched forth to ravage Magna Graecia with impunity. Almost all the residents of Tauromenium too lost their lives, when the Muslims reduced the city to ashes. The Byzantines' hilltop capital was the last Sicilian city to fall to the Muslims, on the first day of August in 902, seventy-five years after their first invasion.

During that long period the Arabs brought about many changes in the land they were conquering. Like the ancient Greeks, the Muslims came to Sicily to stay.

—◦ 5 ◦—
MUSLIMS

This chapter of Sicilian history is generally labeled "Arab," but we have just noted that the Muslim conquerors of Sicily included several peoples. More important for the Sicilians, though, was that their new rulers had languages and a religion quite unlike those of the island. The Muslim practice of putting nonbelievers to the sword terrorized Sicilians, with good reason; the conquest proved brutal.

Once the Muslims secured themselves, the surviving Sicilians found to their relief that the new rulers had no intention of killing them. At the start of Islam its adherents had broadcast Mohammed's words in countries largely pagan, generally offering the conquered a choice between Islam and death. By now, though, Muslims had two centuries of experience in ruling subject peoples, basing their rule on the Koran. Their new subjects in Sicily were not pagans, nor converts, but Christians and (perhaps 7 percent) Jews, groups the Koran discussed explicitly. Islam acknowledged its debt to Judaism and Christianity as the faiths from which Islam arose. It categorized the adherents of those faiths as *dhimmis*, ranked between Muslims and pagans. Because *dhimmis* believed in Allah even if they didn't accept Mohammed as prophet, Islam directed Muslims to treat them with dignity and allow them freedom in following their older religions.

The ruling Muslims would nonetheless burden nonbelievers with higher taxes than believers paid. The Muslims justified the tax differential as a protection tax, for they exempted nonbelievers from military service. Sicily knew differential taxation from the ancient Romans, who had imposed taxes according to one's residence; now the Muslims imposed taxes according to one's religion.

RELIGION

At this stage of Western history, religion dominated life. Muslims, Christians, and Jews would all have agreed that no person could live without belonging to a religious community. Not only where a man worshipped, but also when he could do business, whether or not he would join the military, whom he married, what he ate, his name itself, all depended on his religion. It was fundamental to a man's identity; without religious affiliation he would be cut off from society.

Every aspect of conduct being regulated by religious law, Jews and Christians were left free as communities to live according to their own laws, so long as they did not interfere with Muslims. The Jewish community and the Christian community had autonomy regarding their internal affairs: commerce, schools, criminal justice, religious buildings and rituals, and so on. On the other hand, *dhimmis* were forbidden any religious activity that might be perceived as courting attention of Muslims: ringing church bells, drinking wine in public, or reading scriptures where a Muslim might hear. The construction of new churches and synagogues was prohibited, although existing ones might be repaired. (When Muslim officials received petitions for "repairs" that were in fact renovations, they tended to be lenient).

A law obliged all *dhimmis* to indicate their community on a badge on their clothing and a plaque on their houses. And the Muslims promulgated some laws of which the sole purpose was to remind everyone of Muslim superiority — for instance, laws prohibiting *dhimmis* from building houses higher than those of the local Muslims, from carrying weapons, or from riding horses. Certainly this body of *dhimmi* laws irked the Sicilians, but it seems not to have hurt them materially. The Sicilians paid lower taxes under the

Muslims than they had under the Byzantines, and, the change in official religion notwithstanding, the Sicilians felt more at ease under the
Muslims.

Direct benefit from the change of rulers went however to only half
the Sicilians, the male half. The Muslims continued and extended the
Byzantine restrictions on women. Under the old regime women of
the upper class went around veiled, but now all women had to do so.
The Byzantines had given their women little to do besides bearing
and caring for children, and had allowed them virtually no contact
beyond their immediate families. This segregation of women doubtless facilitated the Sicilian acceptance of polygamy when that practice arrived with the Muslims.

The Muslims were as theocratic as the Byzantines, but they were
less narrow-minded and officious. Islam was a young and dynamic
religion; the Muslims were eager to win friends. Byzantium in Sicily
was always stagnant, its adherents unimaginative and defensive; now
most Byzantines fled rather than live under Muslims. Although the
conquerors transformed some churches into mosques, generally they
did this not to limit the practice of Christianity but rather because
the Byzantines had departed and a great number of arriving Muslims
needed houses of worship.

AGRICULTURE, FOOD, AND TRADE

In the first period of Islam the Muslims went abroad for the purpose
of spreading their religion, but by the late ninth century they had
other motives for occupying Sicily. Like earlier invaders, the Muslims
hungered for the island's grain and for its central location for
Mediterranean trade. They had an additional reason, peculiar to
North Africans: they thirsted for Sicily's water.

Children of the desert, their experience in administering Muslim
colonies in the Tigris and Euphrates valleys whetted their appetite
for water-fed crops. The Persian melons and vegetables would grow
well near Sicily's many rivers and rivulets. (Sicily had more rivers and

streams then than now.) The Romans had cleared the land; now to distribute water throughout that land the Muslims built canals and installed irrigation systems of waterwheels and siphons.

The Muslims were always fighting among themselves just as Christians were, and Muslim refugees crossed the rough waters from North Africa to Sicily by the thousands. Fortunately for them, Sicily's population had decreased since Roman times, and a large amount of land lay unused despite its suitability for farming. Many of the refugees settled on farmland near the towns, and when that ran out they found themselves heretofore-unused bits of land in rural areas. To create still more farms, Muslims built canals to drain the flatlands ridden with malaria.

Like their predecessors, the Muslims cultivated primarily Sicily's common durum wheat. One way they used it was to make the *rishta* noodles they had eaten in Persia; this seems to be the first pasta in Europe. For making couscous the Muslims tried durum wheat and then some new varieties; they topped the dish with the seafood abounding off the Sicilian coasts. They experimented with new strains of cereals, and delighted in those places with sufficient water for growing rice.

The land took on a new look, with variegated fields of melons, eggplant, and saffron. Muslims planted Sicily's first date palms and trees for bananas and for citrus fruits (though not the common orange, which didn't arrive until much later). On hillsides they grew almonds and pistachios. Besides the new fruits and vegetables they brought in cotton, mulberry trees for the silkworms, sumac for tanning and dyeing, and hemp for caulking ships. Although the ancients' attempt to cultivate papyrus in Sicily had proved unsuccessful, the Muslims did grow papyrus and prepare it as a writing surface.

Sugar too arrived in Europe with these Muslims, who cultivated sugarcane to satisfy their cravings for sweets first tasted in Asia. Even in summer on the coasts, they indulged in cool sweets and cold drinks, made with ice carried down from the mountains in spring and conserved by a method the ancient Romans had used but the Europeans had meanwhile forgotten.

Long before the Romans, people on Sicily fished for tuna to eat and to export. Each spring this fish, two to two-and-a-half meters long, comes in great schools from the west. That it arrives in Sicily just off Mazara was convenient for the Muslims, who increased the efficiency of tuna-fishing. In an operation called the *mattanza*, they rowed out into the teeming currents and arranged their boats in circles. Beating the water while making each circle smaller, they drove the tuna inside the circles. Once a circle was small enough to allow the fishermen, leaning over the sides of their boats, to reach the tuna, they whacked them to death. Like their predecessors, the Muslims preserved their fish with salt (extracted on Sicily's west coast).

To round out their diets, the new rulers intensified Sicily's raising of livestock: sheep, goats, and cattle. They also raised horses, for war. No pigs, which their religion forbade them to eat; for the same reason they did not much turn their grapes into wine. A strange omission from the Muslims' produce was olives — they imported olive oil into Sicily from North Africa.

Maritime traffic had dwindled under the Vandals and further under the Byzantines. Now the ports were alive with the colors of crops and the sounds of shipping. Sicily's forests, regrown after the Romans had cleared the land, were cut down again by the Muslims, likewise to build ships to maintain trade and empire. They sent off some hardwood to North Africa, which had none of its own. They exported the tuna they fished in the western waters and the sulfur they mined in the eastern mountains. They processed their sugar for use in medicines and sold it in the north, in small quantities as it was very expensive. Under Muslim tutelage Sicily expanded from being a granary to being a supplier of a wide range of products. This was real economic development.

LANDHOLDING PATTERNS

Agricultural diversification came about in response to social necessity. For grain to be profitable, it must be grown on extensive holdings, whereas a living could be made from smallholdings planted with fruits and other luxury crops. On the death of a Muslim all his sons were entitled to a share of his lands; the greater numbers in the succeeding generations could live from a given amount of land only if the land was used more intensively. The sharp drop in the average size of holdings meant a corresponding decrease in slavery. Economic reasons reinforced religious to improve the conditions of the remaining slaves.

These circumstances prevailed more on the west of the island than the east. The incidence of Muslims was higher in the west, because virtually all the Muslims arrived in Sicily from the Tunisian headland, and they settled in the west because it was so convenient for them to go back and forth and participate in the life of the wider Muslim world. Their staying in the west was facilitated by the trade pattern: Muslim Sicily traded primarily south and west of the island, for to the east was the Byzantine empire; the Muslims used Balerm (Palermo) and the ports of the west coast more than they used

MAP 9. Sicily as divided administratively by the Muslims

Messena and Siracusa. In eastern Sicily the Greek and Latin elements still prevailed.

Western Sicily blended into eastern somewhat to the east of Balerm and Girgenti (Agrigento). The Muslims divided the island administratively into three provinces or "vals," roughly equal in size. The western Val di Mazara extended almost as far east as today's city of Enna. A line from slightly north of Enna to the Ionian coast just north of Catania divided the eastern portion of the island into a southern Val di Noto and a northern Val Demone.

When Berbers immigrated throughout the tenth century, they were given small plots carved out from western latifundia. Eastern Sicily retained its latifundia, which accounts for far-ranging differences between western and eastern Sicily even today.

POPULATION NUMBERS

The impact of the Muslims was greater, logically enough, where there were more Muslims in the population; but determining the numbers and the proportion of Muslims in Sicily is not easy. For one thing, the continual movement between Sicily and North Africa would have complicated any efforts to assign residence. For another, over the two centuries of Muslim rule the proportion of Muslims in the total Sicilian population increased significantly — in the first years the Byzantines departed, and then many conquered Sicilians converted to Islam. Apart from the general expedience in sharing the faith of the rulers, a couple of considerations led to conversions: the Muslims were more capable economically (which may have been seen as characteristic of the religion), and Muslims paid lower taxes than non-Muslims (though the difference in Sicily seems not to have been great). A further, though smaller, complication was the Jews. Some Jews were already living in Sicily under the Byzantines; some came from North Africa with the Muslims. Some Jews converted to Islam, and even those who remained Jewish considered themselves part of the Islamic (rather than Christian) world. And then there

MAP 10. Sicily, 900–1100

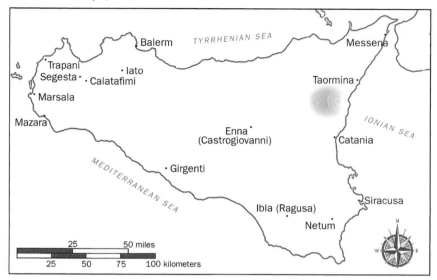

were the many slaves who accompanied their Muslim lords — are they to be considered in the calculations?

Still, some rough estimates have been made for the end of the Muslim period. Sicily's total population was then about 1.6 million, substantially higher than when the Muslims arrived. During the period of Muslim rule, some half-million Muslims immigrated. That is, toward the end of Muslim rule roughly a third of Sicily's inhabitants had their roots in the Islamic world.

CITIES

As the Muslims advanced agriculture and commerce, urban life flourished once more. If towns grew in size and number throughout the island, they benefitted particularly in the Muslim-dominated west.

Mazara, important for the North Africans as the port closest to the Tunisian headland, was fortuitously a good port, in that the natural harbor lay at the wide mouth of a navigable river where many ships could be berthed at a time. Ideal for tuna fishing, Mazara had a fertile hinterland as well. The spot had served since time immemorial as a landing place for traders and pirates. The local residents who took care of them were, at the start of the ninth century, Latins and Greeks in roughly equal numbers, and a few Jews lived outside the city walls where the big markets were located. When Muslims settled in the area and began to farm, their officials established a major military post. What for a thousand years had been at most a village became a flourishing city enclosed in a high thick wall.

As her population swelled with immigrating Berbers, Mazara expanded in the Muslim way. Houses were built attached in groups circling a courtyard, which contained a well and a cooking place for the use of those who lived around that courtyard — often members of a single family. From the courtyard an alleyway intersected with other alleyways leading usually into similar courtyards, less often into secondary streets with their mosques and public baths and eventually into the major streets. Thus the residential areas consisted of private little neighborhoods, each closed off from the noise and traffic of the major streets. The narrowness of the streets and the contiguity of the buildings assuaged the heat of the sun, while the sharp curves of the streets maximized breezes.

Resembling a branching tree, this street configuration looked and felt quite different from the Romans' grid pattern. The Arabs had not invented it — in fact the ancient Greeks had laid out Siracusa this way — but it was characteristic of Muslim cities, in Sicily and elsewhere.

Marsala (*Mars-al-Allah*, "port of Allah") became the name of the old Carthaginian and Roman Lilibaeum. A depressed town under the Byzantines, Marsala became under the conquering Muslims a base from which to subdue the interior as well as an important city.

Trapani, slumbering as Drepanum since the Battle of the Egadi in 241 B.C., was developed by the Muslims as a port and as a commercial and handicraft center. Like the rest of western Sicily, Trapani fished for tuna and extracted salt, although she specialized in the working of coral and of gold. Figuratively as well as literally, Trapani enjoyed a golden age.

The port the Muslims called Balerm had been, under the name Panormus, the Byzantines' second city in Sicily, although the Byzantines had done nothing to develop it. The Muslims were not going to let the port remain unproductive, given its location on a bay sheltered by mountains, with nearby rivers north and south, with fertile coastal strips, and with a location between North Africa and the commercial cities of the Italian peninsula. The conquerors chose to make Balerm their capital, and, on a slight rise about two kilometers inland from the gulf, the emir had his castle built.

As Sicily's commerce grew, Balerm expanded quickly into Muslim Sicily's greatest city. Larger than any city on the Italian peninsula, Balerm offered a profitable market for merchants from the peninsula and beyond. During the two centuries of Muslim control, the city's population trebled to one hundred thousand or more. Residents included Arabs from Arabia, Berbers and black-skinned peoples from North Africa, Greeks, Jews, Persians, and soldiers from as far away as Russia. The Byzantines' bright colors, coupled with the Muslims' elegant clothing and jewelry, made Balerm a gay meeting place.

Balerm catered also to the mind, an aspect of the human spirit neglected in Sicily since the ancient Greeks. Scholars flocked to the capital. Muslims opened education to all — for instance, in the towns they provided public lectures once or twice a week on a wide range of topics, while in Balerm one could hear lectures all week throughout day and evening. As to Balerm's schooling for boys we have a suggestion of its high quality: Ibn Hawkal, a merchant from Baghdad visiting around 970, commented that "although schoolteachers are notorious for their mental deficiency and light brains," Balerm's three hundred teachers were accorded great respect by the residents.

It doesn't surprise us to learn — from Ibn Hawkal — that Balerm's public schools were mostly in a walled central district (namely, Cassaro) inhabited by the rulers, high officials, and the other wealthy. Along with the castle there were the numerous civic buildings that one would expect in a capital city. And of course mosques, in the city considered the Medina of the west; those who counted minarets reported several hundred. These public buildings were located on thoroughfares from which branched off narrower dead-end streets with traverses into courtyards, like Mazara's layout. The much larger Balerm, though, was zoned into districts according to use. The unwalled district containing many warehouses of foreign merchants was called Schiavoni, from the eponymous pirates with quarters there — it was probably the scariest area of the city.

Travellers considered Balerm splendid like Cordova and Cairo, yet dirty and smelly. Overall it was exciting — few other cities were as dynamic and cosmopolitan. Many particulars about Balerm have come down to us, and one kind of report strikes by its omission: notwithstanding the hodge-podge of ambitious people, there are no mentions of hostilities between ethnic groups. That's not only remarkable for the period, it's remarkable, period.

MUSLIM DIVISIONS AND DECLINE

On the other hand, the Muslim world experienced continual conflict. Just as the Christian church was split contentiously between Eastern and Latin branches, Islam was split between Sunnis and Shiites. The Muslims who conquered Sicily were Aghlabite caliphs, Sunnis with their capital in Kairouan. A different family of caliphs, the Fatimids of the Shiite branch, overthrew the Aghlabites in 909, thereby acquiring Tunisia and Sicily. It was the Fatimid governors who fostered culture and economic growth. When the Fatimids established their capital in Cairo, they greatly increased the geographic distance between the rulers' seat of power and their territory of Sicily.

In consequence the Fatimids made Sicily a semiautonomous emirate. The increased autonomy intensified rivalries within Sicily's ruling group. Ministers grew quarrelsome and shortsighted, then hedonistic and lazy. The Muslims working in administration and the military in Balerm were still mostly Arabs (Sunnis), inevitably with different priorities than those of the Muslims working small farms in southwest Sicily who were Berbers (Shiites). The Berbers feared Arabization. When great numbers of Berbers immigrated to Sicily during the tenth century, they were doing it, at least in part, to strengthen the Berbers in Sicily against the Arabs. Throughout the century the two groups viciously contested the dominance within Sicily. The Arabs winning, the Berbers retreated into North Africa (1015). Southwest Sicily's population dropped sharply, eventually weakening the ports and naval capacity.

This hardly went unnoticed by the merchants of Pisa and Genoa and Venice, nor by the Byzantines. They each saw themselves the protagonists in the next act of Sicily's drama. It seemed only a matter of time before the Muslims would lose the island to them.

SUMMARY OF MUSLIMS

The Muslims enjoyed secure rule of Sicily for only about a century before their internecine conflicts and the menace of foreign invaders diverted their attention from governing the island. They had invaded a culture hugely different from their own yet were well on their way to absorbing it. During their short stay they transformed Sicilian agriculture, improving the diet and the export trade. In many cities they introduced an urban design noteworthy for fostering calm living. They left good memories of a prosperous period, so that most people in Sicily were sorry to see them go. Their greatest legacy was of harmony among the different peoples.

Though they built no great public works as the Greeks had, a thousand years later one can't drive around Sicily without being reminded of the Muslims. Innumerable directional signs point us to Muslim localities. From Palermo fifteen kilometers southeast lies Misilmeri (manzil al amir, "resting place of the emir"). Going southwest from Palermo on the road to Mazara — the most used route at the time — is one of the first Muslim settlements, Alcamo (manzil alqama), named after a man called Alqama. On the coast just north of Alcamo is Castellammare (Arabic al-Madarig). Southwest, just south of the Elymi (S)egesta, is Calatafimi, the Byzantine Castrum Phimes, which the Arabs deformed into Kalat-al-Fimi, *castrum* being the Latin and *kalat* the Arabic for the English "castle" or "fortress."

Farther south, halfway between north and south coasts, lay the ancient Egesta ally Alicie, which the Muslims developed substantially and renamed Salàm ("health" or "safety") and which we know as Salemi. Fifteen kilometers to the east stood old Gibellina *(gibel* is the Arabic word for mountain). South to the coast and a few kilometers eastward lies Sciacca, the old Thermae Selinuntinae of the Romans, which the Muslims renamed as-Saqqah ("fissure"). A detour twenty kilometers northeast of Sciacca and a long drive up a high, steep rock brings us to the ancient Caltabellotta (*Kalat-al-ballut*, castle of the rock).

Now we're departing from the area of the Muslims' heaviest settlement, so we'll see fewer Arabic names. Still, from Agrigento (Arab Girgenti) we can go northeast seventy-five kilometers through Caltanissetta (*Kalat an-nisa*, castle of women) to Enna. A bit to the east of Enna stands the mountain topped by the town Calascibetta (*kalat* plus Scibet, the name of the mountain). The Arabs changed the name of Enna to Kasr Iani (*kasr* being another word for "castle"), from which the city would long be called Castrogiovanni. There are many more place names from the Arabs, but I'll finish forty-five kilometers southeast of Enna with my favorite in the east, Caltagirone — the Arabs called her Qal'at-al ganom, "castle of the genies," for the spirits who dwelt in the nearby caves.

TRANSITION
The Coming of the Normans (1061–1091)

All during the tenth century the western Mediterranean belonged to the Muslims, but starting around 1015 they gradually withdrew into their huge, trade-rich land mass. Sicily was at the edge of their empire and therefore vulnerable. The Byzantines ached to recapture eastern Sicily, since they could reach the peninsular trading cities only through the Strait of Messina. The Byzantine general George Manikes (Italian: Maniace) put together an international force of fighting men: a contingent of the emperor's guard from Constantinople,* Lombards and other groups from the north of the peninsula, and some three hundred Normans from northwest France. The troops of Manikes took Messena easily in late summer 1038 and set out for Siracusa, which finally yielded in 1040. But the Christians were able to hold their gains for only a few months, and soon Sicily, except for Messena, returned to Muslim rule.

Although Manikes was called back to Constantinople at the end of the hostilities, his soldiers remained in eastern Sicily. In Messena around this time one began to hear the shout "Matagriffone!" — literally "kill the monsters," but Messena's way of saying "kill the Greeks." Greeks for them signifying the mixed Greek-Byzantine people.

The conflicts among Christians and among Muslims encouraged the dreams of mercenaries on the Byzantine ships. Although in theory the mercenaries were fighting for the Byzantines, many had their own agendas and changed their loyalties more frequently than their clothes. Norman knights had ventured to the Mediterranean for mercenaries' pay and booty, but before long, at propitious moments, they grabbed land for themselves.

---

* This was the Varangian Guard of Scandinavians. With them was the renowned Norwegian king Harald Hardrada (the Pitiless), returning from Jerusalem, who in 1066 would lead an unsuccessful invasion of England.

THE HAUTEVILLES

In the continued battling around the south of the peninsula and the island of Sicily, members of the prolific Hauteville family began to win the prizes.

The Hautevilles were of Viking stock. Their forefathers had left Scandinavia and, after a few generations of plundering northern Europe, in the early tenth century settled down as small landowners in Normandy and became Christians. The establishment of the feudal system in Normandy, with the consequent redistribution of lands, encouraged younger sons of the region's large families to venture out, as had the Vikings, in search of fertile lands sufficient for all. Thwacking around the central Mediterranean, they won impressive amounts of loot and land.

Among them Robert de Hauteville stood out for his strength and determination, which is what we would expect of a man achieving command. He acquired the nickname "Guiscard," meaning crafty, foxy. That was a compliment, for craftiness was regarded a positive quality around the Mediterranean in the eleventh century, just as it is among Sicilians today.

Despite his being "of insignificant origin" (Byzantine historian Anna Comnena's phrase), Robert Guiscard got himself recognized by the pope. Once upon a time, in the days of the Vandals, the papacy had held lots of land in Sicily, which now it would happily recoup. So Pope Nicholas II supported the Hautevilles' fight for Sicily as though it were a holy war, whatever misgivings he might have had about the warriors. The swashbuckling Normans were at least Christians of the Latin church — far better to have *them* ruling in the south than the Muslims and Byzantines currently there. In 1059 Robert Guiscard bound himself as vassal to the pope, promising loyalty and tribute; and the pope invested Robert "Duke of Apulia and Calabria, by the grace of God and Saint Peter, and, by their help, of Sicilia." The last phrase meant that Robert was entitled to rule Sicily as soon as he could conquer it.

That was hardly a foregone conclusion. The Mediterranean waters were rough, scene of the three-way struggle between Latin Christians, Byzantines, and Muslims, and simultaneously of savage piracy. Here Robert Guiscard had to be fierce just to survive. Once he conquered, he behaved mildly. Rather than killing or deporting the vanquished, he asked only that they recognize his sovereignty with an annual tribute. Rather than forcing the Muslims to convert to Christianity, he allowed them to maintain the practice of their religion. He couldn't afford to antagonize the Muslims, as the land he was striving to rule contained so many of them, and they were the ones who knew how to administer it. The pope-anointed pirate had to trim his sail to demographic winds.

THE CONQUEST

Having established a beachhead on Sicily, Robert left most of the fighting to his brother Roger — younger than Robert by fourteen years and no slouch either. Roger's first conquest was of Messena, in 1061; he soon learned though that conquering Sicily wouldn't be easy. Come summer he marched his troops 150 kilometers in ten days, across the mountains to a steep ridge with a magnificent view of Mount Etna and the area's highest settlement, Troina. There he posted soldiers and deposited his new wife, Judith, while he went west to besiege Nicosia. But the Greeks of Troina, hating the Norman invaders even more than they hated their Muslim rulers, tried to kidnap Judith, which occasioned fighting in the streets and the quick return of the worried husband. Greeks and Muslims having joined forces against him, Roger, with wife and troops, retreated into his fortress. They spent four months there, under siege, gradually coming to appreciate how frosty this Mediterranean island could be. They lacked fuel, and Roger and Judith had a single cloak between them, which by night they used as a blanket and by day they wore (or, if Roger was chivalrous, she wore). This continued, chillingly, until one evening they could hear Arabs warming themselves with local wine. A few hours later the Normans crept over the snow to the besiegers' lines and slaughtered them.*

Robert Guiscard led the successful invasion of Balerm in the first week of 1072, but increasingly he concerned himself with his duchies on the peninsula and with Byzantine lands farther east. Roger took command, but his offensives were slow because he generally lacked the manpower to deal effectively with the resistance of the Greek-speaking Sicilians in the countryside and the attacks by sea of men from Byzantium and North Africa. When Robert died in 1085, Roger finished the conquest as "Grand Count of Sicily."

These two Hautevilles spent half their lives embroiled in armed struggle around the Mediterranean; of Sicily, in the Mediterranean's center, they apparently never doubted the value. The evident riches of the island, the diversified agriculture and the optimal location for worldwide commerce — their Northmen ancestors would not have dreamed for more.

୬୬

The Muslims had needed seventy-five years to occupy the entire island, and they weren't going to give it up without a struggle. For instance, after the Normans won Catania in 1071 Muslim rebels drove them out, obliging the Normans to conquer a second time in 1081. To take control of all Sicily, the Normans needed the thirty years, from 1060 to 1091, which is when they captured the Muslims' last major stronghold at Noto, inland, south of Siracusa.

As warfare goes, this conquest was relatively unbloody. Many Muslims fled, of course, among them a certain young poet who was

---

* The activities of Robert and Roger were major news in their homeland of Normandy, followed most attentively by the Norman duke William "the Bastard." He was irritated that these Hauteville brothers, mere knights, had conquered rich territories in the Mediterranean and had won honors and support from the pope. The Hautevilles' successes fed his ambition for a realm of his own, while providing him with military and diplomatic models. Without the spur of the Hautevilles' invasions of Sicily in the early 1060s, it's questionable whether William would have become, in 1066, "the Conqueror."

born in Siracusa in 1055 or '56, was transferred as a boy to the redoubt Noto, and abandoned Sicily for Tunisia in 1078–79 because of the conquering Normans. All his long life Abu Mohammed Ibn Hamdis felt himself an exile . . . :

> Recalling Sicily provokes pain,
> it fills my heart with regret.
> The land which turned silly youths into noble men of
> talent — that land is now gone.
> A paradise! And I was expelled from it.
> I grieve for that land with tears which I would call a
>   river,
> if they were not bitter.

Ibn Hamdis would live on in Sicily as the greatest poet of the epoch.

_꙰ 6 ꙰_

NORMANS

To the foreigner seeking animation and uniqueness, the history of Sicily suggests a barbell, the "bells" being the classical period and the modern period and the "bar" the intervening centuries. What invalidates this image is the bump toward the middle of the bar, the century of the Normans. Count Roger transformed himself from consummate plunderer to consummate politician, elevating government to gratify ethnically diverse subjects.

COUNT ROGER (I)

Palermo, in the Mediterranean area second only to Constantinople in size and in grandeur, excited visitors both as cultural center and as vast emporium. Count Roger would climb the mountain, from where he would look out over the city's domes and minarets to the bay with its myriad boats. Descending, he would refresh himself at the fountains, stroll through the markets, and greet the craftsmen. And marvel that this great capital was *his*.

KEEPING MUSLIM BUREAUCRACY
In Roger's long military career he had battled fiercely against Muslims, devastating their fields and demolishing their towns, sometimes proudly. But now he was sixty years old, ruler of a large, rich,

and mild land — he wasn't looking for trouble. While he kicked out the emirs, he appreciated that under Muslim rule the Sicilians had lived contentedly and prosperously. Count Roger, dwelling in the emirs' palace, would treat his Muslim subjects with respect.

Moreover, he would maintain the Muslims' administrative system. The Muslims' laws and regulations generally remained in effect, and, along with Latin and Greek as languages of official business, Arabic would still be used. Although he expected his highest officials to become Christian, Roger had his Norman councillors keep the competent Muslim functionaries in their posts and offer Sicily's Muslims new positions in the civil bureaucracy, in the military, and at court. Community life as represented in commerce and justice was to proceed as it had before the conquest.

Count Roger's motive for this policy wasn't religious tolerance, certainly not as the phrase is used in our time. Rather, as his Muslim subjects were many and his Christian soldiers few and unruly, Roger had to win the support of Sicily's Muslims, or they would embark on seafaring adventures of their own and leave Roger a half-empty realm.

GREEKS

As for the non-Muslim half, the Greeks were resentful. Not because the Normans sometimes warred against the Byzantines — the descendants of Byzantines in Sicily were few and were generally disliked by the descendants of the original Greeks. Rather, the Greek-speakers resented the Normans on a practical ground. Though both Greeks and Muslims lived all around the island, the Greeks lived especially in the countryside of the eastern part. As the Norman invaders had first approached Sicily from the east, the Greek farmers had suffered more damage than other groups. They cried that the Normans were brutal, that although the Normans called themselves Christians they were a plague much worse than the Muslims. Certainly the Normans invading did more damage than the Muslim rulers grown lackadaisical. Afterward, the Normans' continuance of a Muslim administration added fuel to the fire.

Under Muslim rule, to be sure, Greek-speakers had played little part in the administration. A small number of Greek Sicilians earned their living, as Greeks have ever done, in maritime activities. In Count Roger's Sicily, although most of the military and commercial seamen were these "Greeks," they were commanded by the powerful *admiratus admirateorum,* a Latinization of *emir of emirs* (and the short bridge to our word *admiral*). Regarding the majority, well, the ancient Greeks had colonized Sicily to till its fertile soil, and their descendants seventeen centuries later continued to till it.

In recent times the line between Sicily's Greeks and Muslims had blurred. Under Muslim rule, some of the Greek-speakers converted to Islam, and as time went on many who didn't convert nevertheless adopted the customs and the language of the Arabs. Muslims were cultivators too, but the Muslims had been instrumental in advancing agricultural methods in Sicily, and consequently they dominated the agriculture that was conducted on a large scale. Ergo, in a world where almost everyone worked the land, Muslims tended to be wealthier than Greeks. Now that Sicily was ruled by Christians, the Greeks hoped for succor.

Count Roger intended that the three religious communities be treated equally. The Muslim rulers had avoided interethnic conflict by assuring autonomy to each religious community, and the Norman rulers saw no reason to modify that practice. Just as the Muslims had taxed their co-religionists less heavily than nonbelievers, the Normans would do the same, only now it was the Jews and the Muslims who had to pay the head tax. (In recompense, both groups were excused from military service.) The Latin-speaking Normans, not numerous, could be expected to establish themselves within the Christian religious community without much trouble. The difficulties that arose were due to the Normans' introduction of feudalism, a system encompassing economic, political, and social life.

REDISTRIBUTING LAND

It was part of conquest — almost a definition of it — that the conqueror took over the castles with the rest of the defensive structures and that he dispossessed those landowners who had actively resisted his forces. In Sicily, Robert Guiscard and later Count Roger seized lands, keeping some of the best for their own use, giving some to relatives, and distributing some to Normans and to men from the mainland who had allied themselves with the Normans in the conquest.

The conqueror needed to know what his realm possessed. After the Normans had subdued England, in 1085–86 they took a census of men and lands (recorded in the *Domesday Book*), and the Arabs had maintained such a record through their *diwans*. Count Roger ordered an enumeration, showing for each landlord the number of his peasants and artisans as well as the size of his lands. In 1097 he assembled his knights at Mazara and gave them the results. This seems to be the first time that a European sovereign gathered his leading subjects to discuss state business, and it's the basis for Sicilians' claim to having the oldest parliament in Europe.

FEUDALISM

Although it was the evolution of feudalism in Normandy earlier in the century that had pushed the Hautevilles off their lands and into their Mediterranean adventures, Count Roger and the Normans considered feudalism the normal way to order their lands and their community lives, and so distributed their lands in the feudal pattern. The change to feudalism was not meant to be, and in fact was not, cataclysmic; the Normans weren't ideologues. When, for example, in 1094 Count Roger granted lands to the bishop of Messina, they were to be allotted "according to the earlier divisions of the Saracens"; this was bureaucratically convenient. But Roger did move Sicily toward feudalism. Indeed feudalism seemed for Sicily a natural, as Sicily was an agricultural land and feudal organization was based on landholding.

The feudal system considered all the lands of the realm as belonging to the king (or in Sicily's case, the count). Among an upper class called "lords" or "barons" the sovereign distributed lands called *"feudi"* or "fiefs," then each lord could (and usually did) divide his *feudo* among a lower strata called "vassals" who directly managed the estates. The actual agricultural work was done by serfs, in this book (for the sake of consistency over time) subsumed under peasants. In return for the perpetual use of land, a man bound himself to the grantor by a pledge of loyalty and by obligations that impinged on every area of life, from marriage to military service. The oath by which he bound himself being Christian, Muslims and Jews were kept outside the feudal system. Moreover, Count Roger decided to grant fiefs only as rewards to his fighting companions or as incentives to Normans to migrate to Sicily, so he limited fiefs to Latins. The Greeks were unhappy about being outside the Muslim administration and outside the Latin land-grant system.

Wouldn't the vesting of all the country's land in the ruler bring Greek and Muslim landowners to ruin? Not necessarily. Other feudal countries had resolved this difficulty by allowing for land to be held in *alod* — that is, held without any obligation to an overlord. In Sicily, in general, those who had held land before the Norman conquest could keep it, in *alod*. That produced two distinct groups of landholders: those feudally obligated to the sovereign and those owning property independently of him. Count Roger found himself sitting astride two horses.

COUNT ROGER'S ADMINISTRATION

Sicilian society had always been stratified less by class than by ethnicity. The count ruled a Sicily divided sharply into religious communities, ruling from the top of a Muslim-created pyramid. He was also the feudal overlord of the Normans living in Sicily. Each system demanded its own bureaucracy, which became very complicated. Taxation, for example, was managed from two offices. The Duana de Secretis, dealing with ordinary royal revenue, oversaw the tax collections carried on by the three religious communities. The Duana Baronum dealt with feudal revenue. (The words themselves reflect the ethnicity: *secretis* is Greek, *baronum* is Latin, and *duana* — whence the modern French *douane*, Italian *dogana* — is a Latinization of the Arabic *divan,* meaning writing place or office).

Count Roger made use of the confusions and jealousies to

strengthen himself as ruler. Keeping the final say for himself fostered centralized government. He wanted Muslims as civil servants because, no longer part of the ruling class, they would feel dependant on him personally. Virtually all the other men Roger appointed came from outside Sicily, for much the same reason. Not only the Greeks but also the Norman barons demurred; in most feudal hierarchies the barons would have been able to influence their lord and enhance their own positions, but Count Roger derived heightened authority from having conquered the land.

Just in case, the count discouraged baronial resistance through his regulations for their fiefs. He generally granted lands for life only, so that the heir would have to ask to keep them. He demanded that the barons' close female relatives not marry unless and until he, Roger, consented; by delaying marriages he could limit the birth of heirs, and in the absence of heirs a fief would revert to the lord. By prohibiting the construction of castles without his consent he reduced the barons' control over the lands they held and accordingly over their vassals. He also insisted on his right as sovereign to give justice to a vassal at the expense of his lord. If these measures didn't suffice to keep a baron quiet, Roger would simply take back the land.

CHRISTIAN POLITICS

From their first days in Sicily the Hauteville brothers distributed lands to the church. As the Normans advanced, in their wake came Latin priests and monks, whom the Normans helped to establish. Needless to say, Palermo's cathedral, used by the Muslims as a mosque, had been duly reconsecrated, to be the episcopal church of all Christians — in fact during the first years of Roger's rule the bishop was a Greek. The Normans made no attempt to impose the Latin rite on Greek Christians, who remained free to worship in their own churches according to the Greek rite. As an expression of his support of all the religions of his subjects, Count Roger intervened personally to aid the reconstruction of those Greek church buildings damaged in the warfare. And as the church hierarchy became predominantly Latin, the count made it a point to see that the Greeks were treated fairly in church matters, on occasion exempting a Greek community from the jurisdiction of the Latin bishop. On the other hand, as the Church of Rome became the official religion, and as hostilities continued between the Normans and the Byzantines, Sicily's Greeks were requested to sever their ties to Byzantium; but they resisted.

As a successful Norman approaching the end of his life, Count Roger fostered the Roman church in his realm. Yet he made equivalent donations to the Greek monasteries in Sicily, just as he sent donations to churches in Normandy. As the Greeks saw it, it was one thing when the Normans gave to the Latin church some lands that Muslims had been using for public purposes. It was quite another thing for the Normans to assign to the Latin church other large parcels, especially further inland and in the south, traditional areas of Greek farmers. So the Greeks kept petitioning Count Roger.

At the same time the count was receiving forceful messages from the pope, Urban II. The pope was claiming a right to control secular sovereigns, not least Roger, and it goes without saying that as No. 1 defender of the faith the pope would insist on favoring Christians over infidels. If the Normans were conceding residence to Muslims in Sicily, Count Roger should at least make strong efforts to convert them to Christianity. But not *any* Christianity, not the rite of the majority of Sicily's Christians. Muslims and even those Christians following the Eastern rite should be encouraged into the Latin church.

Pope Urban's interests in this regard extended far beyond Sicily, as shown by his call in 1096 for a Crusade to win back Jerusalem from the Muslims. Sicily was barely affected by this Crusade. A few of Count Roger's vassals did run off to join it, and he grumbled that he had thus lost half his army. On balance he sympathized with the ambition to Christianize Jerusalem; he himself would have preferred a realm with fewer Muslims and more Christians. But he intended to accomplish that without killing Muslims, and without going to the ends of the earth to do so.

Pope Urban wasn't getting very far in his efforts to persuade Roger into active cooperation, so he tried to bribe him. In 1098 the pope met the count and made him his deputy. Specifically he conferred upon Roger the power in Sicily to appoint the bishops, to act as judge in ecclesiastical matters, and to act as treasurer for church revenues. That's a lot of power. The Vatican had already begun its fight, elsewhere in Christian lands, to *deny* kings the right to name bishops, fearing that kings might choose them for temporal (that is, political) reasons. More broadly, the Vatican wanted to *restrict* the power of kings in all matters even tangentially ecclesiastical. Against that background, the appointment of Roger as apostolic legate was extraordinary. But then, other sovereigns didn't have a realm full of Muslims and non-Latin Christians to be brought into the fold. In granting the ruler of Sicily this authority as apostolic legate, the pope opened a Pandora's box.

LOMBARDS

All along, Roger worked to bring Roman-rite Christians into Sicily. He brought in, especially to the Lipari Islands, religious and lay people from Tuscany, France, and England. And most of all, he brought in Lombards.

Among the eastern Germanic peoples who since Roman times had been drifting south in search of better fields, the Lombards in the sixth century occupied the Byzantine-ruled northeast of the peninsula. By then they had been dubbed *Langobards* ("long beards"). Originally pagans and Arians, like the Viking-Normans the Lombards eventually settled down into the Christianity of the surrounding population. They expanded and dominated — in the seventh and eighth centuries they occupied a full two-thirds of the peninsula. In their capital south of Milan at Pavia, they elected their king, lived under codified laws, and enjoyed freedom of worship, three practices unusual for the times. Their independence was, however, washed away in Charlemagne's tide. Intermarriage with the Franks was diminishing them as a people. Some Lombards joined the Normans in the Mediterranean fighting against Byzantines and Muslims. A few Lombards drifted down into Sicily, and during the Norman conquest they provided infantrymen to Count Roger in his campaigns around Troina and Nicosia.

Map 11. Sicily, 1100–1300

Thirty years had passed since Roger huddled with his Judith in the Troina fortress. In the interim Judith died, as had Roger's second wife. With children still to marry off, he sought another wife. Since the unforgettable siege at Troina Roger had won all Sicily — in fact following his brother's death Count Roger was the most powerful man in the Mediterranean region, a very desirable "catch." He married Adelaide, forty years his junior, a Lombard of noble family, whose clan was keen to acquire a new home. Count Roger founded for them, in 1090, the town of San Fratello, a few kilometers inland from the Tyrrhenian coast, north of Troina.

COUNT ROGER'S LEGACY

Count Roger died at age seventy in June 1101, having run Sicily for some twenty years. He left Sicily a wonderful place to live, full of all the things that money could buy and with a high degree of human decency. The people of his realm spoke different languages

MAP 12. Sicily and Italy, 1100–1300

and worshipped in different ways, yet Count Roger treated all the communities with respect amounting to equivalence.

Though a strong and absolute sovereign, Count Roger ruled through law rather than arbitrarily. This made for domestic order. Additionally, the count organized his military well enough to deter foreign challenges. His sovereignty was solid enough and his diplomacy skillful enough to withstand the church, even to have the church augment his power.

Count Roger had in fact developed something of great historical importance: the pattern for a modern state. Elsewhere in Europe at the time such effective rule over a large territory was unknown. While long princely minorities usually lead to chaos, Sicily continued to live peacefully after the count's death, reflecting his achievement of a competent and loyal administration.

KING ROGER (II)

From Count Roger's marriage with Adelaide came Roger Jr., born in Palermo three days before Christmas 1095. The only son to survive the count, young Roger was to become Sicily's remarkable royal.

The self-made Count Roger created in Palermo a court where his son could grow up a sybarite. The count had risen to power by fighting Muslims, yet here was his son with Muslim nurses, tutors, and councillors. Only in Sicily did Muslims share a land with Christians and owe allegiance to the same sovereign.

The young prince typified a new breed of Sicilian, combining as he did the blood of Normans and Lombards. But there was little Norman in his upbringing; raised by Muslims, he was influenced secondarily by Lombards.

Adelaide was regent for her son, the office lasting until his eighteenth birthday. As Roger approached majority, she naturally still wanted the best for him, and that was among her reasons for marrying Baldwin, king of Jerusalem: the prenuptial agreement made it likely that young Roger would accede to Jerusalem's throne someday. But the venture turned sour. As soon as Adelaide entered into Jerusalem she saw how primitive the city was compared to Palermo. Her disillusion turned to anger when she learned that Baldwin already had a wife. Adelaide's marriage was annulled by the pope, but she returned to Sicily in 1117 feeling humiliated, and she died shortly afterward. For the rest of his life, Roger II could hardly think of Jerusalem without antipathy.

EXPANDING THE REALM

Intelligent, clever, and adventurous like his father, Roger II also inherited an ambition to make Sicily the center of a powerful Mediterranean state. As a first effort toward that goal, in July 1123 he led his army and navy in an invasion of Mahdia, the old Fatimid capital on the coast two hundred kilometers south of Carthage; but he was repulsed.

Before he could try again, he was called to the peninsula to deal with a crisis in family politics, the perennial problem of feudal rights. By diplomacy and arms, Roger II won for himself the two duchies at issue, Calabria and Apulia, the toe and heel, respectively, of the peninsular boot. The instep between them, the duchy of Lucania, was uninvolved in the dispute and so didn't pass to Roger II, but he and his army soon took care of that. Roger's realm increased thereby not only in size but also in diversity, for the three duchies had known no rule by Muslims; rather their experience was Byzantine. Consequently the issue of religious tolerance would not be significant in Roger's realm outside Sicily.

He wanted to keep the governance of his big new realm, of the southern peninsula as well as Sicily, in his own hands, although traditionally barons held effective sovereignty over their duchies and fiefs. In 1129 Roger II summoned his many barons to a *parliamentum*, at Melfi in the north of Lucania, where he spoke of his rights and duties. He cited the Roman law, codified by Justinian, that placed the king above the law. He demanded the end of hostilities between his vassals. He would continue his father's tight control over feudal inheritance in Sicily and extend the policy to the southern peninsula. (It was an important way of controlling his vassals' behavior.) He insisted on safety for merchants and the roads they travelled. He would provide justice throughout his territory. These weren't new ideas, although more than earlier sovereigns he intended to control these functions from his own court. It was novel in Europe that where the king could not appear personally to dispense justice a circuit judge would do so in his name. King Roger's centralization as outlined at Melfi was one of a long series of steps toward the nation-state.

He had prevailed and he had proclaimed, but he still wasn't quite yet ruler of the southern peninsula. In feudalism all land belonged ultimately to emperor or pope,* so Roger II's land wouldn't be officially his until the pope "invested" him with it (that is, granted it to him). Once land was conquered, investiture was usually a formality, but in this case the emperors argued that the south of the peninsula was German land. Moreover, Pope Honorius II himself didn't want the Normans to rule such a vast territory. Emperor and pope roused cities and duchies to rebel against Roger. When Honorius died in 1130, a big issue in the ensuing papal elections was what to do about Roger. In the event, two men were named pope: Innocent II, who would adhere to the policy of Honorius, and Anacletus II, who had family ties with Roger but no following among the monarchs on the continent. Anacletus immediately accepted Roger's fealty, along with his pledge (common at such times) of a sizeable annual contribution to the Holy See, and he duly named Roger king.

The three months of ceremonies terminated in splendor at the cathedral of Palermo on Christmas night, 1130. Against an oriental backdrop of silks, Roger received the sacred unction from the cardinal representing Anacletus. Robert, prince of Capua and the strongest of Roger's vassals, placed the crown on his head. Roger II was now King of Sicily, Calabria, and Apulia. As such, his financial and military resources were as great and his lands were as vast as those in any Christian kingdom except for England and France. He styled himself "King of Sicily and of Italy." From the end of 1130,

---

* That "or" was going to create big problems.

Roger II de Hauteville was the first sovereign of what today is (approximately) Italy's Mezzogiorno.

Earlier in the year, while Roger was intriguing to be invested as king, duty had called him out of Sicily to North Africa. Political weaknesses there as well as among the Byzantines made it seem a felicitous moment to invade. But the new king had to wait five years for the Normans' major success, in 1135: the conquest of Djerba, four hundred kilometers south of Carthage, where the Normans might base themselves in future campaigns. Perhaps for Roger the greatest benefit of these military expeditions was as diversion from the tumult at home. Ever since he had acquired the peninsular duchies, the rebellions against him, whipped up by Pope Innocent, had been constant, and his Anacletus-invested lands had grown anarchic. For nine years he raced around his duchies trying to extinguish fires.

KING ROGER'S ADMINISTRATION

During periods of peace, Roger lived with his court alternately in Sicily and in Calabria. In either place the king, at the summit of power in the Latin feudal world, speaking Norman French, appeared a Mediterranean Arab potentate. Stocky, bearded, his Viking-blond hair falling down to his shoulders in the fashion of the day, Roger II was often seen in Arab robes and surrounded by Muslim advisers and entertainers. Count Roger had felt constrained to employ many Muslim administrators because of their great numbers and experience in his realm; his son continued the practice for pleasure.

King Roger faced the same administrative duality as his father. In regard to his Norman community, he stood at the pinnacle of a pyramid of nobles, all hierarchical rights and duties already established, even codified in a *catalogus baronum*. In contrast, the Muslims, alien to feudalism, were under Roger II's direct jurisdiction; they owed him a personal loyalty. The king deflected resentments against the Muslims in his employ by putting them in posts unconnected with landownership and farming. Most of the artisans were Muslims, and Muslims manned the offices dealing with finance. They were preeminent among the soldiers, although Latins too provided armed service, as part of their feudal obligations. (Those Muslims who fought did so as professional soldiers, while Latins were obligated for short terms.) For personal bodyguard and militia, both Rogers had a corps of Muslims.

It helped King Roger in his direct rule that he understood Arabic as well as a little Greek. He fashioned a strong central government and decided the policies in the economic sphere. Yet he chose good men as advisers and knew how to delegate. Even those European sovereigns who opposed his papal politics envied him his corps of administrators and his personal gift for administration.

∽

While he preferred Muslims for his court, Roger II pursued a policy of Latinization. In the mountainous land in eastern Sicily where his father had settled Lombards, Christians now predominated from San Fratello near the north coast down two-thirds of the way to the south coast. In this broad strip the Normans developed — fortified, refortified, expanded — several towns: Troina, Nicosia, Centuripe (the old Centorbi), Agira, Castrogiovanni (Enna), Caltanissetta, Piazza Armerina. Continuing migration brought into the area many non-Lombards (especially from France and the northwest of the peninsula, that is, Pisa and Genoa), but "Lombard" came to be used comprehensively. They were all Latin, their organization feudal. Among the vassals a baronial class duly developed, and the barons came to be responsible for local peacekeeping.

Even with these Latins imported, most of the people in "Norman Sicily" weren't Norman. The populace was Greek-Sicilian, and the administrators were Muslim.

ARCHITECTURE
It was during the 1130s, when King Roger was burdened by hostilities inside and outside his realm, that he initiated churches

> . . so splendid that travellers extol their architectural beauty, their structural refinement, and their vivid originality.

The new style blended Byzantine and Muslim elements. Curiously, the Byzantine and Muslim regimes left Sicily no great art or architecture; it's as though the peoples of those centuries put their artistic talents on hold until they heard King Roger's call for great expressions of faith. Just as soon as he received his crown, he had work started on the church where he planned to be buried. He chose a location seventy kilometers to the east of Palermo, at Cefalù, the old Greek coastal town whose name derives from *kefalé*, the rock that dominates the town and into which Roger built his church.

Scarcely had work begun at Cefalù before King Roger put other teams of architects and construction men to work on his chapel in Palermo. At thirty-six, not feeling death imminent, he could give the royal tombs lower priority than royal splendor he would see every day. In his palace, one flight up from the ground, rose a three-naved basilica, covered, in due course, by a wooden stalactite ceiling most unexpected in a Latin church. The floor was (and still is) of mosaic arabesques. In fact every bit of surface in the chapel — ceiling, floor, walls, columns — is covered with complicated design in an orgy of colored stones, carved wood, and swirling marble. Yet the affect is integral and appealing. In the cupola it's noted that the chapel was consecrated in 1143 — in all the intervening centuries it's unlikely that anyone ever went into this chapel and concentrated on prayer!

Of course this Palatine Chapel was for King Roger's intimates, not a place open to the general public. But about the time that the chapel was completed, work started on the Church of St. John of the Hermits, outside the palace but only a couple of minutes' walk away. This church was used for funerals of court dignitaries. Still, anyone walking by on the street would have noticed an oriental aspect to this austere Latin church: above the square construction rise four big domes, plus a little dome atop a bell tower — and the domes are brick red.

The same period saw the construction of a church where worship would follow the Greek ritual. Since the 1120s King Roger, in his battles around the Mediterranean, had depended on the skill of his admiral, George of Antioch, and it was in his honor that this church was built and called "Santa Maria of the Admiral."* The church was built in the form of the Latin cross, with a domed roof. Its walls hold a splendid cycle of Byzantine mosaics. On one side wall are two mosaic portraits: *Admiral George at the Virgin's Feet* and *Roger II Crowned by Jesus*. It's the only likeness of King Roger known to have been produced by men who had seen him.

So the Christian king who liked to dress as an Arab had his churches adorned in the styles of Muslims and Byzantines. Maybe during the building of these churches the ancient Greeks were in the wings as well, giving pep talks on speedy industriousness. For in Palermo this series of architectural splendors rose within a span of twenty years.

KINGSHIP CONFIRMED

The death of Pope Anacletus in 1138 forced a showdown between Roger and Pope Innocent. It came to arms, and in July 1139 up near Naples the soldiers of Roger won over those of the pope. Three days later Innocent recognized Roger as king and agreed to invest him. Naples and the nearby Capua recognized Roger's sovereignty too, so that Roger was now doubly confirmed as ruler of all the southern half of the peninsula as well as Sicily. He made one concession: he dropped the title "King of Sicily and Italy" and agreed to call himself "King of Sicily, of the duchy of Apulia and the principality of Capua." But how can one be king of a duchy or a principality?

After decades of bitter bargaining and wearying wars, after being invested as king by two different and opposing popes, Roger II was indisputably king. He was, as it happened, a thinking man who reflected on the meaning of kingship; and he was a strong man, naturally dominant, severe in his official relationships, who knew himself as the source of power and broadcast his ideas. "A baptized sultan," King Roger also had a streak of the Byzantine: while in theory feudalism is a system of reciprocal obligations, the Byzantine king gets his sovereignty from God. It cannot be happenstance that

---

* This church has been called the Martorana since around 1700.

his mosaic portrait shows him in Byzantine regalia being crowned by Jesus directly, although in real life he received his crown from a vicar of the pope whom he had defeated. He was born to be the Christian king of a Latin kingdom, and by God he wasn't going to let anyone, not even the pope, tell him how his kingdom should be run.

Not that the popes didn't try. They argued that the sovereign of Sicily was a vassal of the pope, from the days when Roger II's uncle, Robert Guiscard, fighting for Sicily, won the pope's support.* Later on, Count Roger had been commissioned explicitly as apostolic legate. As such, uniquely in Europe, the Hautevilles held final authority over all the prelates in their realms. As though to taunt the pope, Roger II turned that authority to his own advantage in maintaining the multi-religious character of the island.

CULTURE AND LEARNING

Even the Christian religious, who gained in numbers and power, were heterogeneous. The Byzantine monks had left Sicily during the ninth century as the Arabs poured in; now that Sicily was again secure Christian country, Byzantines returned. Roger II, to mollify the pope, made a point of inviting Latin churchmen; some came from England, more from France, to set up schools and abbeys. While in Christendom generally around this time the monasteries played the principal role in advancing culture, in Sicily the monks were more the recipients and transmitters of old knowledge.

King Roger's court was famous not only for its oriental luxury but also, among scholars, as a center for intellectual discourse. Sicily's long and close connection with the Muslim world primarily, and with the Greek and Byzantine world secondarily, distinguished it from the northern peninsula and the countries north of the Alps, which had for centuries been cut off from learning. When the northerners revived their interest in the broader world, they found that culture had become a virtual monopoly of the Orientals.

---

* Robert Guiscard had not deferred to the pope. In fact he was excommunicated three times, apparently without its having done him any harm.

Likewise the practical application of learning in technology. For example, from North Africa the Arabs in Sicily had imported a new kind of material on which to write, made of flax and old linen. Unlike the usual papyrus, it didn't crack when folded. Palermo was the first city in Europe to use paper for documents. In the first years of the century, before Roger II came to his majority, the chancery was issuing documents on this new material and the Countess Adelaide was signing them. From his accession, young King Roger affixed his seal to documents on paper, some in Greek and Arabic, some in Latin.*

Not for many years did this "new papyrus" come to be called "paper." The new papyrus lacked the resistance of the old; it was more than a century before the product could be improved sufficiently for common use. Later, in the first half of the 1200s, the emperor Frederick II would decree that all documents on paper should be copied on parchment for safekeeping.

In Sicily as in Spain, men familiar with the ancient sources and capable of translating them into Latin could be found among the Arabs and the Jews. The Byzantines in their monasteries had scrupulously kept alive the wisdom of the ancient Greeks, and the Byzantines were after all Christians in their fashion; but their nation's political reversals had lessened their accessibility, and among Greek-speakers now available many were living in Sicily. So Sicily channeled the culture of ancient Greece into Latin Christendom.

THE GEOGRAPHER IDRISI

King Roger invited to his court mathematicians and astronomers, poets and philosophers, intellectuals from all spheres and nations; thus Palermo abounded in polyglot scientists and men of letters. One of the immigrant scholars, a man of both science and letters, called himself a geographer. Ash-Sharif al-Idrisi (or Edrisi) was born into a noble family in Ceuta, the small island in the Straits of Gibraltar. He grew up wanting to see the bigger world, studied in Cordoba, and in

---

* The oldest still conserved, found in the Palermo archives (Archivio di Stato), was written in Greek and Arabic and signed by Countess Adelaide in 1109; it dealt with the monks in the monastery San Filippo at Enna.

due course visited most of the Mediterranean littoral, Asia Minor, and much of Europe up to the far north. When in his mid-thirties he decided to settle down, he did so in Palermo.

Four years younger than Roger II, he became devoted to the king. It's known that Idrisi gave Roger two objects reflecting their main common interest — a map of the earth engraved on a silver tray, and a silver globe of the heavens. King Roger would commission travellers to bring back information, which Idrisi would then write up. Integrating these reports with what he had learned in his own travels, he compiled a *Diversion for those eager to travel in the world*, titling it also *The Book of Roger* (1154). In it Idrisi described the earth, dividing it into seven horizontal climatic zones. As it presented new material, *The Book of Roger* was a major work of geography for its time.

More pertinent, he described Sicily. We have Idrisi to thank for most of what is known today about Muslim Sicily. Years after coming to live in Sicily he writes as though he were still overwhelmed by the island:

> Sicily is the gem of the century . . . its beauties of nature, its collectivity of buildings, the remoteness of its past, make it a country really unique.

He sounds as though he were writing for a tourist office — to be sure, attracting new people was an aim of his patron. One of my own problems in writing about Sicily also bothered Idrisi:

> Sicily . . . is an island of momentous events, with vast regions, numerous towns, infinite beauties and attractions, so that if we were to try to calculate its merits separately and to talk about its conditions town by town, we would find ourselves facing a task not only complicated but unmanageable. . . .
>
> At the moment when we are finishing our text, the sovereign of this island (the exalted King Roger) possesses a

hundred towns and an additional thirty localities of a size between cities and citadels, without counting the small-holdings, the bigger farms, and the villages.

ETHNIC MIX

The larger towns and cities consisted of distinct quarters or neighborhoods, as the population was still organized administratively into religious communities and residential areas generally weren't mixed. Any village likely had residents from a single religious community. King Roger arranged some autonomy for the Muslim enclave at Monreale (just southwest of Palermo) and for the Greeks around their monasteries. The ethnic separation facilitated order, since the leaders of each community dictated different beliefs and behavior, values and loyalties, and could make their people behave. But more and more in Sicily's towns the peoples lived similar lives, associated with one another, and intermarried.

The ethnic mix was naturally most evident in the port cities. Palermo's streets in mid-century boasted mosques, synagogues, and Latin and Greek churches, along with palatial houses and luxuriant parks. A bird's view of the town centers would show monks' cowls, Arabs' turbans, and soldiers' helmets. And what a babel of sounds! They were overwhelmingly dialects of Arabic and Latin, occasionally Greek and the diverse languages of the scholars and sailors and merchants passing through from all the nations of the world. The calls of the muezzins sounded five times a day, sometimes in cacophonous concert with the ring of (reinstated) church bells. The daytime din included vendors shouting their wares, Arabs chiseling and clanging, students disputing, soldiers brawling, Latin monks muttering their offices, Greeks telling their beads, pigs oinking and donkeys braying, and, last but not least, coins jingling.

Jews on the street did not distinguish themselves by language, as they used Hebrew only for prayer and in their secular lives spoke Arabic or Greek. The Jewish community was simply one of the communities; it seems that the others paid it no particular attention. Few among the locals would even have noticed when a new group of Jews arrived in Palermo in 1147. They came from Thebes (Greece), silk weavers at the top of their profession in a city renowned for its silk. From one of his victorious campaigns against Byzantium, King Roger brought the silk workers back, probably as captives, to develop Sicily's silk industry begun by the Muslims. Roger had the silk workshops located right in the palace, as the industry would be important for profit and status.

The foreign trade of Arab times had made Mazara a principal port, but the Normans destroyed her when conquering Sicily. They rebuilt the town's defenses and port so that she again exported grain and was again significant in the North Africa trade, but by that time the Latins had conquered Jerusalem and shifted commercial interests eastward.

Messina, because of her exceptional geography always a major commercial city, flourished under the Normans as she had not since the days of the Mamertines. Maybe even under Mamertine hegemony Messina had Jewish residents; now, in any case, descendants of the Mamertines and of the ancient Greeks worked with Jews producing silk for export. Back in Homer's epoch Messina had been a center of Greek trading; ships still called regularly from Greece and occasionally from Armenia, while the largest fleets came from Genoa, Pisa, and Amalfi. Much of the traffic sailing between northern France and the Latin Kingdom of Jerusalem — both of them Norman lands — passed through Messina, so that in the course of a season Messina provided for the personal needs of a hundred thousand men or more, and for their ships.

FOREIGN POLICY

The Second Crusade embarked in 1146, led by King Louis VII of France. Invited to go with it, King Roger declined. For one thing, his resentment still smoldered over the way his mother had been treated by the king of Jerusalem, so he didn't want to fight for that kingdom. Yet in May 1147 he offered his fleet to King Louis, only to have his offer rejected. He was turned down because the others realized that he wanted his fleet used not against Muslims but against Byzantines.

Map 13. Sicily in the Mediterranean, 1100–1700

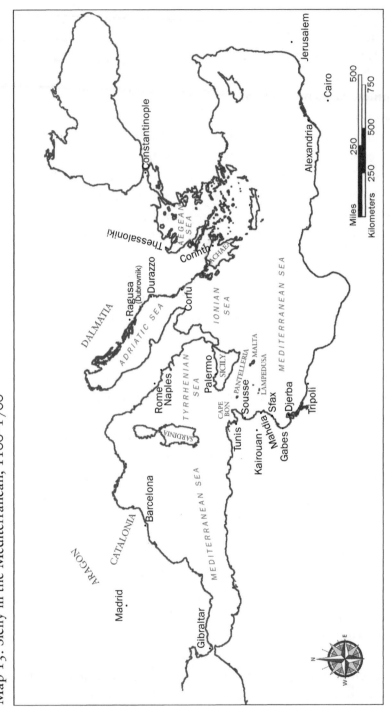

By usual military means, King Roger had gained possession of small islands lying between Sicily and Africa, namely Malta and Pantelleria. On the Mediterranean coast of Africa, twenty years before, he had failed in his attempt to conquer Mahdia, two hundred kilometers south of Carthage; now he succeeded, and for good measure he took Sousse (to Mahdia's north) and Sfax and Gabes (to her south). The Normans tried to take Tripoli in 1142 and failed, but the city fell to them four years later. By 1148 the Normans held all of the coast from Cape Bon (that is, the Carthage headland) to Tripoli, and the important inland city of Kairouan. During the same years he made war against the Byzantines, conquering Corfu in 1147, entering the Bay of Corinth, and threatening Constantinople. While the Crusaders at the eastern end of the Mediterranean kept trying to win Byzantine and Muslim lands for the Roman church, King Roger was trying to conquer Byzantine and Muslim lands for himself.

DOMESTIC STRIFE

At the same time he was facing opposition from some of his subjects at home. The flourishing Messina and the Lombard feudatories were each claiming many rights that the king was not prepared to grant. Roger II had always feared cities and merchants, the groups that were acting with too much independence in the north of the Italian. For that reason he promoted ruralization, but now even landowners challenged him.

Lacking a reasonable alternative, King Roger, as a Latin Christian and a Norman, continued to bring in other people like himself. He still expected, or he hoped despite evidence to the contrary, that the grant of a fief would secure the newcomer's loyalty to him. But by now feudal lords were working the system, increasing their lands and their power, to the point where they achieved a quasi-military strength. Both ethnic and feudal bonds caused the Latins to support one another.

Gradually the Arabs moved away from the fertile lands. That hurt Sicilian agriculture, because the Arabs had traditional knowledge of Mediterranean soils and had used it to develop this land to great profit, whereas the Normans had less familiarity with Mediterranean conditions and less incentive to do farm work themselves. Many who had left the north as mere knights were now barons with vast lands, thanks only to King Roger; still they lusted for more power.

When the king made attempts to restrict the barons, he found himself frustrated by family ties with the Lombards and ethnic ties with the Normans, by the fact that the northerners had won important positions in his army, and by the very fact that immigrant barons now controlled his countryside. By his immigration policy he had managed to keep at bay his merchants and artisans, but his efforts to keep Sicily profitable were being hindered by bunches of greedy, squabbling barons. He had always trod warily vis-à-vis the lower orders, but they had got the best of him.

Though maybe not yet. He could turn to the northern merchants who were — another threat — gaining control of his Mediterranean. Their presence was really nothing new; over a hundred years earlier, even before the Byzantine Manikes invaded eastern Sicily, Genoa had taken Caltagirone, and the Genovesi still had a colony there. But now many more ships than before were coursing around the Mediterranean from the northern peninsula's mercantile cities: Genoa, Pisa and, the strongest, Venice. They were standing by in 1150 as King Roger's grasp loosened. He granted all three cities special trade concessions, in order to contain his barons commercially. The barons howled that Roger was favoring northern interests at the expense of Sicilian.

THE DEATH OF KING ROGER

Idrisi had written that King Roger "does more in his sleep than common mortals do when awake." But by 1150 Roger II de Hauteville was feeling old and tired. Of his five sons, four had died; their mother had died earlier. Roger married again in 1153, and started a child. He was never to see his daughter Constance; before her birth in 1154 he died, aged fifty-eight. We will see Constance briefly, at a crossroads of Sicilian politics. Meanwhile, King Roger was survived by his son William.

Count Roger and King Roger had given Sicily its most centralized government since the Roman Empire, and its most efficient government ever. During the eighty-two years since the Hautevilles had taken Balerm, they ruled over a peaceful and prosperous Sicily. Moreover, they added the south of the peninsula and Tunisia to their realm.

These achievements would prove less significant for Sicily's future than three other occurrences brought about by the Rogers: the arrival of merchants from peninsular maritime cities, the establishment of a special relationship with the Church, and the immutable division of lands between sovereign and barons.

KING WILLIAM I
Considered bright but lazy, William served as his father's associate for three years before he succeeded at the age of thirty-four. Once king, he devoted himself entirely to pleasure in his oriental court, showing little interest in his realm and seldom rousing himself even to sign documents.

The new king was observed closely by the North African coastal towns King Roger had conquered several years before. In the town of Sfax, on New Year's Eve 1156, the Christian community was celebrating with wine, women, fireworks, and a parade of richly decorated cows. Some Muslims joined in the festivities, then suddenly and in concert drew out their weapons and retook the town. Within five years, Sicily lost the rest of her territories in Africa.

Sicily's agricultural sector was functioning better than its military. It was fortunate that Sicily's main crop was durum wheat, requiring no particular intelligence or industry to grow, because after the Muslim cultivators left even the Christian landowners could produce it with success. The high grain yields in the west of the island and on the Gela plain were legendary. Along with wheat, a little macaroni was now being exported too: Idrisi mentions a pasta factory just west of Termini Imerese. Sicily continued to export animals skins and cotton and her highly prized silk, and, in smaller amounts, flax (especially from Milazzo) and henna (from Partinico).

Though Sicily prospered, the feudal lords weren't happy. Up north the lords, residing in towns, controlled the food chain from field to port; in Sicily (apart from Messina, which handled her own food trade) commerce was essentially managed by Palermo, which meant by the Muslim bureaucrats. From the time of the trade accords of 1150, most of the income from Sicily's produce finished in the coffers of other trading cities — Pisa and Genoa and Venice.

As long as the strong and popular King Roger ruled Sicily, the barons bided their time, but when the new King William proved unpopular, their grouching turned bellicose. Some of them were Hauteville relatives or at least of Norman origin, and the Lombards too seemed cut from the same cloth as the Hautevilles in their ambitions and eagerness for battle. They wanted power, and King William's favoritism of the Muslims galled them.

The open rebellion started in 1160, triggered by a fiscal matter and aimed at getting Lombards into the administration. It spread rapidly. When King William learned of rebels in the fortress at Caccamo, fifty kilometers east of Palermo, he reacted by dispatching his soldiers eastward to the Lombard fiefs. On the morning of March 9, 1161, some barons stormed the royal palace and massacred the unarmed Muslim employees while holding King William prisoner. Inside the palace they pillaged, raided the treasury, carried off the harem girls, and burned the records of landholdings. Rioting in Palermo's streets, the Christians broke into Muslim-owned businesses, killing the proprietors or driving them out of Palermo. In the countryside they usurped the Muslims' farmlands. The Lombard barons were behaving toward Sicilian Muslims like the Crusaders were behaving toward Muslims on the road to Jerusalem.

William's supporters — Muslims and others — retaliated by ravaging the barons' lands. Piazza Armerina and Butera were among the Lombard towns devastated in late summer 1161; their refugees ran east to Caltagirone. Back in Palermo, King William replaced his lost Muslim administrators with other Muslims and allowed them, as bureaucrats, to take their revenge. But on the farmlands there was no replacing the Muslims, who had fled — as had Idrisi and other high-level advisers. Sicily is estimated to have lost 10 to 15 percent of its total population when the Muslims left.

Eventually the hostilities died down, and some rebellious heads rolled. Carrying weapons was henceforth forbidden to Muslims. The shambles embodied a sorry and certain end to the religiously open policy that had been the pride of the two Rogers.

❧

King William, aged forty, effectively retired, to devote himself entirely to the luxuries of kingship. He embarked on one big project, a massive new palace on Palermo's outskirts. He called it by the Arab name "Zisa" ("splendid"), which suited the oriental style he had in mind, with several fountains, pools, and fishponds. It cost a large fortune, of course, but that hardly mattered, as King William was rich even by the standards of sovereigns. The construction proceeded apace, especially once King William's health declined.

While King William suffers from a long illness, we might note that his inner circle included two bishops from England, Bartholomew and his blood brother Walter of the Mill. The Hautevilles had heartily invited foreign men of the cloth, and (like the Hautevilles) most priests in England had their origins in Normandy. Not only the several who served at William's court, but virtually all these ecclesiastics spent their time politicking in Palermo to the utter neglect of their nominal flock. It seems that some of them, to further their political ambitions, encouraged the anti-Muslim violence.

King William did not live to see the sumptuous Zisa completed. He died in May 1166, mourned (they say) only by his Arab women and destined to go down in history, exaggeratedly, as William the Bad.

KING WILLIAM II

William left a thirteen-year-old son and heir of the same name. He also left that passel of English churchmen salivating.

The widow, Margaret of Navarre, now regent, caught between Muslim administrators and Latin barons, immediately summoned help from her homeland. Spain and France both sent large armed forces, and for a while it looked like Sicily was to be ruled by a bunch of corrupt Spanish and French barons. Perhaps in answer to the prayers of Englishmen, an act of God intervened. A major earthquake hit the east coast in 1169, destroying Catania and shaking Messina. (When word reached sixteen-year-old King William, he evinced his multicultural upbringing by asking those in his palace to pray, "to whatever god they wished.") In the earthquake's aftermath, people in Messina heard that the prime minister, the regent's cousin from France, was on his way to France with a lot of Sicilian money. Messina rioted against rule by Spaniards and Frenchmen. The bishop Walter of the Mill stepped in, obtained the people's acclaim, got himself named archbishop of Palermo, and filled the political vacuum.*

The conflict in Sicily about whether the authority over the clergy belonged to Hautevilles or popes had an equivalent in England, where the English king Henry II had a longstanding quarrel with his friend the archbishop of Canterbury, Thomas Becket. In January 1171 the Sicilian churchmen learned to their horror that, at the request of King Henry, the archbishop had been murdered. As some of the bishops had known Becket personally, they were bereaved as individuals. The shock touched the entire Christian world, and the church canonized Becket in less than three years. At this time Marsala's town center was being graced with its first major church, which was duly dedicated to the new saint.

Sicily was soon to strengthen relations with England in a royal fashion. After long negotiations, fostered by Walter of the Mill, young William II married the ten-year-old Joan, daughter of England's King Henry II, on February 13, 1177, whereupon Palermo's English archbishop anointed and crowned her queen of Sicily.

William reached majority in 1172 but was unwilling or unable to

---

* Probably the first and last cleric ever to do so, Walter of the Mill signed himself "Emir and Archbishop." This is one quick illustration of the inter-ethnic complexity.

take the reins himself. By then the English archbishop Walter was sharing rule with his brother Bartholomew and the bishop of Siracusa, Richard Palmer: power in the three-cornered island was held by a triumvirate of English bishops. The chancellor was a Frenchman, and gradually Norman-French supplanted Arabic as the language of the administration. This somewhat mollified the Lombard barons.

∽

Although Sicily's tide had turned against the Muslims, the king himself would have liked to maintain the easy relations with them that the earlier Hauteville sovereigns had enjoyed. But to keep them around him William II was obliged to give the Muslims protection. He enjoyed living among Muslims, dressing like them, reputedly taking pleasure in their men of culture and in their women. He seldom left his palace.

Outside his court, the realm took on a more Christian appearance. In the cities mosques still stood, but churches were going up everywhere. More brown and black habits on the streets reflected the swelling ranks of the religious. The church-building Cluniacs and the Cistercians augmented their landholdings and their treasuries. In the countryside too ecclesiastics were gobbling up lands. This surging wave of Latinization almost drowned the Greeks. Visitors to Palermo and other cities still remarked on the Christian women veiling themselves and on the "oriental flavor," but from month to month Sicily grew more European.

Some churches were built through the patronage of King William, and the year after the canonization of Becket he started one as his own royal project. It was to include concepts from the newest iconography on the Italian peninsula. William II's grandfather, King Roger, having realized two or three of the most beautiful churches in Christendom — everybody said so — King William may well have wanted to continue the tradition . . . or to outshine his ancestor. Doubtless he received encouragement from the archbishop Walter.

He chose to build eight kilometers southwest of Palermo, where his grandfather and great-grandfather had especially liked to hunt, on a hill that had come to be called Mons Regalis ("royal hill"). In earlier times, though, an Arab hamlet lay here; and now William II worked with Arab architects designing a Fatimid building to incorporate the best Christian ornament. Between 1174 and 1176 the great Monreale church came into being, with a twin-towered facade. Over the next decade King William rode to Monreale many times, flanked by his black African bodyguards, to watch the Arab craftsmen apply geometric patterns amid the arches. Meanwhile, inside, Byzantine designers planned the mosaics illustrating both Old and New Testaments, with reference to the newest iconography from the Italian peninsula; and in due course Byzantine craftsmen erected these in the nave and a huge *Christ Pantocrator* in the apse. To the right of the church, as part of a Benedictine abbey, cloisters took shape like a Muslim courtyard with porticos. It's not too much to imagine that Roger II would have been proud of his grandson's effort, though he might have considered the mosaics a bit crude.

∞

Walter of the Mill directed William II's domestic policy throughout the reign, leaving the king free to devote his efforts to church-building and (concurrently) to warfare. Like his forebears, William II interested himself in Jerusalem and the eastern Mediterranean. As early as 1174, he sent a great naval force against Alexandria, then he began to reach seriously for the Byzantine crown. He spent the winter of 1184–85 in Messina, assembling a fleet of twenty-five hundred ships and eighty thousand men. In June 1185 he sailed up the Strait of Otranto for Durazzo, which surrendered quickly. Equally smoothly King William's forces marched east to Thessaloniki, the second city of the Byzantine Empire. Thessaloniki resembled Palermo in her diversity and her prosperity. She fell, unprepared for the Sicilians' invasion and savagery. William II's conquests, however, proved short-lived.

History calls him William the Good, to distinguish him from his father, William the Bad. The behavior of William II merits rather the sobriquet William the Worse.

SUMMARY OF NORMANS

The Sicily that had attracted the Hautevilles in the 1060s was an Arab land politically and culturally. As the Hautevilles took over land and power, they brought in Latin Christians, gradually moving Sicily from the oriental to the feudal world and into European politics.

Just as the ancient Romans pushed the Greeks into the interior, the Normans pushed the Muslims into the interior. The Muslims had earlier transformed Sicily's countryside; the Normans transformed the cities.

During the scant century of their rule, the Hautevilles tried to create an empire. King Roger succeeded in joining the south of the Italian peninsula with Sicily in one realm. He seized coastal Tunisia, but within twenty years his son lost it all. Now Sicily's overseas possessions were barely a territorial footnote, a couple of little islands to its south. Though Sicily was never militarily invaded, during the last Norman decades Sicilians fought with arms among themselves.

Using income from their immense landholdings, the Hautevilles left a prime artistic legacy. How ironic that rulers leading lives so antipathetic to the church would be instrumental in creating paragons of churches.

TRANSITION
From Hauteville to Hohenstaufen (1189–1194)

In the early part of his reign, William II fought against the emperor Frederick I (Barbarossa) when the latter was trying to limit the autonomy of his cities in northern Italy. In this battle William II joined with the pope. But when new politics allied Barbarossa with the pope, William withdrew from that fray.

Though married for many years to Joan, William II had no children with her. Nor had he any surviving siblings. Remember that Roger II had a posthumous daughter, Constance? She was about the same age as William II. Early in 1186 King William took his Aunt Constance from her convent at the ripe old age of thirty-two and married her off to Henry, eleven years her junior. Henry was Barbarossa's second son, a prince of the Hohenstaufen family of Swabia (southwest Germany). Then William II made Constance his heir. Whatever short-term benefits he may have desired from alliance with Barbarossa, William must have known he was gambling with Sicily's independence.

In 1189, three years after Constance's wedding to Henry, William II died at thirty-six. Although Constance was heiress, many in Sicily did not want her German husband ruling them. Besides, some held (with Salic law) that sovereignty should not pass through a woman. So there was a lot of family fighting, reaching far into Europe, about who would be the next king of Sicily. The crown went to Tancred, a Hauteville cousin.

Most Sicilians, though, were touched more directly by the continued fighting between Christians and Muslims. There were Muslim communities even in Sicily's eastern cities, and as the Latins' numbers and power increased, their tolerance of the Muslims decreased. According to the Muslim voyager Ibn Jubair, writing in the late 1180s, all that remained to the followers of Islam in Sicily were "a religious judge to whom to direct their legal questions and a principal mosque in which during Ramadan they were permitted to meet under the lamps." The Muslims struggled to maintain their religious and economic life, for they no longer had protectors in high places. The hostilities flared into civil war, with razed villages and with the peaceable fleeing to the mountains.

RICHARD LION-HEART

Into this woeful situation sailed a strong king with a hundred ships and thousands of men, mostly Normans. He was the new king of England, Richard Lion-Heart, with no claim at all to the Sicilian throne. He did have business to attend to in Sicily, in that his sister Joan, widow of King William II, was being held prisoner by King Tancred. There were money questions too.

But what brought Richard Lion-Heart to Sicily at this time was the Third Crusade. His men were mostly Normans because few Englishmen went on Crusades. Richard had agreed to lead the Crusade only if the French king Philip Augustus would go along — a condition based not on affection, but rather on Richard's fear that if he went without him Philip would steal his French possessions. The two young kings agreed to meet in Messina, in September 1190, and from there proceed eastward together.

Philip arrived first and put up at the royal palace. Richard made trouble even before landing in Sicily: he detoured slightly to invade the coast of Calabria and then, touching Messina, seized her small peninsula of San Salvatore with its great Greek monastery. The populace of Messina took to the streets in anger. King Tancred wasn't going to risk an armed battle, given the Norman legions waiting in the outskirts of the city; rather, Tancred sent negotiators to Richard to resolve the conflict. The release of Joan was soon arranged. But the locals knew that one of Richard's party was receiving hospitality from Tancred, and they had little patience for negotiations anyway. Shouting obscenities against King Richard and against the English, they rioted so clamorously as to derail the negotiations.

King Richard stormed out of the meeting room. He called his troops and had them disperse the rioters, killing whomever they wished, then had them lay waste to the city. He gave orders to leave unharmed the royal palace with Philip inside, but to set many other palaces afire, making a special point of destroying the buildings of Tancred's negotiators. Meanwhile Richard had sent men to the port to burn the Sicilian ships docked there, so that the people of Messina couldn't flee. Tancred was, to be sure, king of Sicily, but Richard Lion-Heart ruled Messina.

To ensure that Messina's populace wouldn't riot again, Richard took hostages from the city's upper class. On a hill in the outskirts, just opposite the Greek monastery he had seized, he tauntingly constructed a quickie fortress, of wood, which he called "Matagriffone" ("kill the Greeks," see p. 141). November 11, 1190, was Armistice Day: Tancred agreed to give one of his daughters in marriage to a nephew of Richard's. (There's no record of the young lady's having taken part in the discussions.)

Tancred also agreed to pay Richard twenty thousand ounces of gold, more than enough for him to travel in style to the Holy Land. But he had just spent two glorious months in Messina; he decided to winter in Sicily. Philip Augustus could no longer even stand the sight of Richard, nonetheless the two kings spent the next months quarrelling and carousing around the island. They finally left for their Crusade on April 10, 1191, assured that Sicilians would remember them for a while.

Within a month the German king Henry VI was to arrive, but he was no longer the king first in Sicilians' thoughts.

—⟡ 7 ⟡—
HOHENSTAUFENS

When Constance, heiress to Sicily, was wed in 1186 to Henry, the second son of Holy Roman Emperor Frederick Barbarossa, the concern of Sicily's barons that their land might fall to the Germans seemed exaggerated. A spate of deaths, though, changed things: not only did Sicily's king die young in 1189, but Barbarossa died in 1190, and his eldest son, the new German king, died a year later. That made a whole new ball game, for now Constance's husband ruled as the German king Henry VI and as Holy Roman Emperor. The earlier disquiet in Sicilian quarters about being ruled by a German prince intensified to dread of being ruled by a German king and emperor. Nor did the popes want Sicily and the empire ruled by the same man. But Henry VI coveted Sicily as gateway to a Mediterranean realm.

By promising Messina tax breaks as a free port, Henry VI incited the city to rebel again in 1194 against Tancred. In the conflict Tancred died, his heir just a boy. Henry profited from this new Hauteville weakness by conquering Constance's homeland.

As Sicilians had feared, the advent of Henry changed Sicily from an independent country to a subordinate part of the Holy Roman Empire.

Some of the Sicilian nobles favored Henry VI for their king because he was sovereign of a distant land and would leave them alone. They proved correct in their belief that he had no interest in governing the Sicilians, but he would not leave them alone. He saw Sicily less as a granary than as a treasury. Like the Roman governor Verges, Henry VI took from Sicily everything he could get his hands on. Sicilians considered him rapacious and cruel, having done only one thing acceptable, and that nine months before his coronation: he made Constance pregnant.

FREDERICK

FREDERICK'S EARLY YEARS

Constance was on her way to Palermo for the coronation, to take place on Christmas Day 1194, when she realized that maternity was imminent. On the Adriatic coast near Ancona she had to stop. Forty years old, nine years into a childless marriage, she feared that people might question her being the mother and thus her child being royal, so she decided to give birth publicly. In the main square of Iesi she had her servitors erect a tent into which, at the appropriate hour, some twenty prelates crammed themselves. The baby was born on December 26, the day after his father, Henry, received the crown. The newborn was named Frederick Roger after his grandfathers.

Less than three years later King Henry, at thirty-two, got sick and died. German barons of his entourage leapt to take control of Frederick. Constance, ruling as regent for her infant son, knew she was no longer physically strong and feared for the future of her son and his realm if her husband's barons should take over. Consequently she paid Pope Innocent III to be the boy's guardian in matters political. The German barons did arrogate power in Palermo, triggering race riots. Dispossessed Muslims and the survivors of others, seeking revenge for 1189–90, wreaked havoc around Sicily and even conquered Girgenti (Agrigento) to use as a port for communications with North Africa. Escalating into civil war, the disturbances would continue for many years.

Frederick, three and a half years old, was crowned king in May 1198. Constance succumbed six months later, leaving the boy king quite unprotected. The racial turmoil may have worked to protect and strengthen Frederick, because no one had much time for him. More people had witnessed his birth than saw to his needs as a young child. Sometimes neighbors had to feed him, and he was left to run in the streets like ordinary boys. Although Palermo was a very big city, a boy there had the sea at his doorstep, a nearby mountain to climb, and countryside just a short dash distant; he grew to love nature and animals. Physically strong and short of stature, he learned to fight; and in cosmopolitan Palermo he learned the ways of different peoples and their major languages.

∽

The pope's guardianship lasted until Frederick reached age fourteen. Frederick was bright enough to realize that the pope hadn't been guarding much. During the short reign of his father, Henry VI, the king was the largest landholder in Sicily. But with the papacy claiming feudal lordship over all Sicily, religious and lay associates of the church had taken advantage of Frederick's minority to appropriate vast estates for themselves all around the island. They had carved up virtually all the royal demesne. This might well have contributed to Frederick's lifelong lack of reverence toward the church.

Nor had the papal representative serving as regent done anything toward ending the island-wide disorders; Frederick's minority had been a period of continual racial strife. Action was desperately needed, especially inland. Fear of violence kept people at home, severely reducing town business and agricultural production. The Muslims were rebelling even now — how could he restore the calm that his grandfather Roger had fostered? Frederick grasped the situation with the quick decisiveness, or impatience, that was to continue throughout his life. With troops ordered from his barons, he organized squads to burn all crops in targeted areas so as to starve the rebels into submission.

Another problem was the Ligurians, who had appropriated his ancestral lands not usurped by the church. The Ligurians had been around for a long time, merchant-sailors from Genoa who had settled themselves over the years in the Rogers' fiefs in southeast Sicily. Now though they considered themselves the rulers of Caltagirone and of Siracusa, as well as of Sicily's small island of Malta. Caltagirone, located favorably at the junction of the great plains of Catania and Gela, was important as a road hub and commercial center, and in the minds of many people she was a Ligurian town! On the other hand, the Ligurians hadn't taken as much land as the church, and they should be easier to displace than the ecclesiastic usurpers.

The loss of royal land to church agencies and to Ligurians reduced Frederick's revenues, of course, and when Frederick reclaimed the lands the evicted barons caused disorders that were expensive to pacify. Nor did Innocent III scruple at draining away Frederick's money directly. Disregarding the fact that Frederick's mother, Constance, had paid him well to guard the heir and his realm, the pope now billed Frederick a large sum for maintaining law and order, even though what the pope and his associates had encouraged was disorder. Some cities came to the young king's rescue with donations; otherwise he would have lacked money to start his rule.

The pope's interest in Frederick extended to picking his wife. Frederick was only fourteen when he was wed to Constance of Aragon, several years his senior. If the name Constance was an appealing coincidence to the motherless king, Constance's origin in Aragon was what appealed to Pope Innocent: she had no German connection. Germany ruled the lands north of the Papal States, and the "Sicily" of the time reached to their southern border. Innocent III didn't want Sicily and Germany ever to have the same ruler — he didn't want the Papal States pressed by one ruler from both sides. Frederick, to be sure, was half-German with a German legacy, which could well become a threat. But at least, married to the Aragonese, Frederick couldn't compound the threat by taking a wife with German loyalties. Constance did come to Sicily with five hundred Aragonese knights, and the pope was hardly surprised that Frederick employed those knights in his struggle to gain control of Sicily.

Ruling Sicily was already a challenge. His subjects' heterogeneity was like a coin, double-sided. The Muslims as a community were troublesome, but as individuals he liked them, and he had Muslims among his courtiers. He enjoyed being among men of different faiths and ideas; that ran in the family. In recent decades Sicily's Muslims had lost most of their power, and its Greeks much of their Greekness; still the island remained a mosaic of peoples. Some spice was added to the Sicilian pot when soldiers and troubadours from western France, come with Richard Lion-Heart, took up residence in Messina. Although the five hundred Aragonese knights brought by Constance were decimated by disease and many of them returned home, we can assume that the soldiers, like the troubadours, left Sicilian progeny.

The problems immediate to the young king — the place of the Muslims, the shortage of funds for administration, and division of power with the papacy — were to dominate his reign and his life. Sicily's special relationship with the papacy, so frustrating for King Frederick, would impinge on Sicily's development for centuries after him.

FREDERICK GETS HIS CROWNS

To celebrate his coming of age, Frederick went to Germany. He left his homeland during a terrible famine, an event fortunately rare in Sicily. He named his foreign wife as regent, and the Sicilians resented that too. After being enthroned as king of Germany at Frankfurt in December 1212, he stayed in the north to fight for the crown of the Holy Roman Empire. He won papal support by promising that he would keep Sicily administratively independent of the empire and that he would not directly rule Germany; still it was a long battle. When he was finally crowned emperor at St. Peter's in Rome on November 22, 1220, that same day he proclaimed the Kingdom of Sicily to be legally separate from his empire. Yet Frederick chose Palermo as his imperial capital, and immediately after his consecration he returned there, at long last to build his kingdom.

Vis-à-vis Frederick, the Sicilians were of two minds. He was, after all, the son of the universally hated grasping German, and he himself was wearing German crowns. But he was also the son of Constance: in his veins coursed the blood of King Roger, from birth to death a true Sicilian.

FREDERICK IN SICILY: ADMINISTRATION

Frederick's heart was in Sicily. Even though he travelled extensively throughout his life, he always spoke of Palermo as home and of her gardens, which he loved. His empire was divided into three parts: the Germanic realms; the north of the Italian peninsula; and his Sicilian kingdom, called the Regnum, consisting of the island of Sicily and the southern half of the peninsula. In the first two (where the weather did not permit Mediterranean gardens) he delegated the rule to princes, and he allowed increasing power to the upper ranks of the feudal landowners. In contrast, he considered his Sicilian kingdom, his Regnum, to be his personal fief. He gave top priority to recovering his lands around the island, enforcing his decrees with arms when necessary.

✑

To assure his actual control of Sicily, he hastened to centralize power. Roger II had employed his barons as rural judges, but Frederick would do the major judging himself. When arranging his absences from Sicily he would have to delegate governance, and he concerned himself greatly about getting the best men possible to act for him. Along with improving his corps of officials, he desired to transmit the original culture of his courtiers. With this dual objective, he proceeded in 1224 to found a university in Naples.

For this university Frederick cast the mould. He would have no religious patronage — thus he established Europe's first state university. For teaching law he had a model in the university at Bologna, but Frederick wished to go beyond law to provide explicit training for public officials. For the same reason that King Roger had preferred to employ men from outside Sicily as his functionaries, Frederick wanted civil servants working throughout the realm whose sights would be set higher than local or familial graft. His graduates would serve alongside nobles in administering the kingdom. He would subsidize the study of bright but needy young men, thus fostering their dedication to him personally. So that his functionaries would regulate everything as he wished, he employed teachers who shared his conservatism and appreciated the prestige of the job. To prevent the importation of radical ideas, he forbade his subjects in the Regnum to study at other universities.

Frederick saw some problems as peculiar to the island of Sicily. It was unnecessarily complex to have as subjects so many different peoples, each in an autonomous community, following different calendars, eating different foods, even paying different taxes. His officials never really knew who was supposed to be doing what. The feudalized Latin Christians knew what hierarchy was, but the others would obey only their own religious leaders, never having been called on directly to obey the state officials.

So Frederick abolished the religious communities that had legislated and judged for their members for three hundred years. He did not interfere with the freedom of Muslims, Jews, or Greek Catholics to worship in their own ways, but he watched them carefully, for they were alien to the feudal system. He couldn't abide collective behavior conflicting with Christian morality — for example he forced prostitutes to live outside the city walls. In the same way, non-Christians posed a threat to a well-ordered society, so he banned them from high-level work in the administration. The Muslim rulers of long ago had mandated that nonbelievers wear badges; Frederick went further and decreed that henceforth all non-Christians wear distinctive dress.

Against the background of the riots he took Muslims and Jews under his protection (without, however, making any change in the discriminatory tax rates). This was analogous to his legislation regarding Jews in his German lands, where he made them his own private vassals ("serfs of the royal chamber"). Later he was to foster money-lending by Jews, though with restrictions. Toward Muslims he seems harsher. Even if their dominance in western Sicily had ceased, in parts of western Sicily they still felt at home. Frederick moved large groups of them away to the other end of his Regnum, to the peninsular heel (Apulia). He told them that in the small town of Lucera, near Foggia, they would be able to practice their religion openly; and there he trained them as soldiers.

Muslims had been among Sicily's skilled silk workers; those

remaining were Jews, and he soon sent them to Foggia too. Gradually Frederick came to spend most of his time in Foggia, and by 1225 he had transferred most of his administrators there. Soon Palermo was his capital in name only.

FREDERICK'S COURT AND CULTURE
Early in Frederick's reign, Palermo had an active court life. A bright young man with a passion for learning, the king interested himself in the arts, of which he was patron. He gave high priority to introducing Greek and Arabic science into Europe, and like his Norman predecessors he employed Arabic-speaking and Greek-speaking scientists at court to do the translations. Frederick's personal bent was scientific, however the main development in the seventy years since King Roger's death was the educated courtiers' change of emphasis from the study of the natural world to the humanities. The Jewish and Muslim peoples had a long tradition of writing poetry, and men in these groups joined other men of Frederick's Regnum in the court poetry circles.

Participating in these circles were also the French troubadours from Messina, who introduced into Sicily the elegant new poetry of southern French aristocrats. Their lyrics, relating to court life and courtly love, had nothing to do with Sicilian traditions or with the populace. The upper classes, especially in eastern Sicily, were replacing Latin in their everyday speech with a proto-Italian, so the troubadours sang in this contemporary language. The troubadours lasted in Sicily only a short time, because when Frederick left the island the courtly entertainment wafted away. But their language and literary style, taken over and adapted by the Tuscans, were an important phase in the development of modern Italian.

On balance, court life under Frederick probably sparkled less than it had under King Roger and the Kings William. In the intervening decades the great multicultural intellectual ferment shifted to the Iberian peninsula. Frederick's Norman ancestors enjoyed culture for its own sake, while the more complex Frederick mixed his sincere cultural interests with ulterior motives of politics and propaganda.

Besides, Frederick was always on the move. King Roger and the Williams had been kings not only *of* Sicily but also *in* Sicily. It was far more common in these centuries for a king to move with his entourage frequently from one part of the realm to another, and that was what Frederick did. His peripatetic retinue included men of letters and of music, while some of these types remained to work in one or another of Frederick's palaces even when Frederick was absent. But planets need a stable sun around which to revolve.

Frederick and the Papacy

Frederick had delegated the rule of his German lands in order to devote his attention to Sicily, but the popes wouldn't let him.

Though the conflict between temporal sovereigns and the papacy engulfed all Europe, it had a particular immediacy for Sicily. The contest over Sicily, as seen in previous chapters, began with Robert Guiscard and heightened with Count Roger and King Roger. With Frederick it erupted, because he ruled the territory on the far side of the Papal States.

Besides, he was a type that aroused the popes' dander. Even as a boy, Frederick was independent and stubborn, unwilling to yield to the religious groups living on his lands. He treated Muslims with respect and cordiality. He violated sexual morality by maintaining a harem (which he maintained poorly, according to the righteous or the jealous). He blasphemed constantly and showed no deference to God's representatives in the church. Whether or not irreligious, Frederick was irreverent in a world where papal politics were as scheming as secular politics.

Frederick showed no gratitude to the pope who had facilitated his crowning as emperor. Indeed, as the popes considered Sicily to be a papal fief, Frederick wouldn't even have been able to reign over Sicily without papal acquiescence. For his coronations in 1212 and 1220, he met the request of the popes to take vows of crusade. Then he didn't go. In 1239, Pope Gregory IX lost patience with Frederick and excommunicated him.

FREDERICK'S CRUSADE

Excommunication of royalty in medieval times being fairly common and seldom permanent; the freethinking Frederick might well have disregarded it. Now, though, he was seriously planning to go to Jerusalem, not for any religious reason, but because his second wife, Isabelle (Yolande) of Brienne, was heiress to the Latin Kingdom there. Defending the rights of his wife, he might acquire for himself an additional crown and the income that went with it. That scarcely warmed the pope's heart; in fact pope and emperor quarreled so much about it that Frederick wound up going to Jerusalem in defiance of the pope. Shortly before the scheduled departure in 1228, Isabelle died giving birth to Conrad. Immediately Conrad was lawful king of Jerusalem, so Frederick made the imperial venture to protect the rights of his son. To placate the pope he called it his Crusade, but there was something fishy about that: Crusades were meant to protect the Latin Kingdom from the Muslims, and this so-called Sixth Crusade included in its forces Frederick's loyal legion of Sicilian Muslims, those whom he had trained as soldiers in Lucera.

Frederick went on Crusade as a German, for virtually all Crusaders came from Germany and France. People in the southern zones of Europe had pretty much ignored the whole business. Sicily, central to Mediterranean politics, hadn't even been considered part of Europe before the time of Frederick's father, Henry VI. Then too, during the period of the first five Crusades so many Sicilians were Muslims that the idea of an anti-Muslim venture would have been unthinkable.

With hindsight it's clear that however vicious and silly the Crusades were, the Sicilians lost out by not participating. They never saw the technological wonders of the East, which Crusaders adopted or imitated on return to their home countries. The Crusaders carried back into Europe new desires for creature comforts and new ideas about culture. They left in Jerusalem their belief in the supremacy of the church. Sicily missed those stimuli to development. By the time Frederick went to Jerusalem, the moment had passed. And even then he had no large force of impressionable Christians.

Frederick's activities in Jerusalem need not concern us here, except that his every step riled the pope. The facts that the king of Sicily placed the crown of Jerusalem on his own head, and that in Jerusalem he consorted with Muslim leaders, are relevant to Sicily only because they turned papal enmity into vendetta.

POLITICAL PHILOSOPHY

After Frederick returned in 1229 from Jerusalem, he devoted himself to the governance of Sicily. From the start he had governed his Regnum much as King Roger had done, with the difference that Frederick was more successful at extending his rule in the peninsular part of his realm. Feudal holdings were not to extend into eternity; on the death of a noble the heir had to apply to have his titles and fiefs reconfirmed. When the king did allow the inheritance of lands, the beneficiary had to pay a corresponding tax. Nor was the use of feudal lands unrestricted: mineral and forest rights belonged to the crown. Frederick commanded the barons to dismantle any castles built since the disruptions of 1189, and if they wanted to make substantial repairs to an earlier castle they would have to get his approval. *That* would discourage landowners from fighting private wars, giving force to his decree that all military activity in the Regnum be the exclusive province of the king.

Feudalism defined the classes rigidly and regulated the relations between them, but additionally Frederick wanted a legal framework to justify his position as sovereign. With the aid of lawyers, he drew up the first comprehensive code of law since Justinian's seven centuries before. Frederick's special homage, however, he paid to his grandfather King Roger, by revealing his new code to his vassals at Melfi, where Roger had held his momentous *parliamentum* a hundred years before. That Frederick harked even further back, to the Roman empire and its venerable emperors, he made clear by titling his work *Liber Augustalis*. Also known as the Constitutions of Melfi (1231), it published a new theory of absolutist monarchy for Sicily, a notion of which Roger could only have dreamed.

A king rules by divine right, Frederick declared, and is subject only to divine authority. God ordained princes to settle the conflicts inevitable among mankind, the king being the prince with absolute and final authority over his realm. It followed that, as this authority comes directly from God, the pope is here irrelevant. Frederick wrote his law code without reference to the pope.

Frederick stood on slippery ground. According to the church, the island of Sicily was its fief, and its king a vassal of the pope. Being a papal fief, Sicily could not be part of the Holy Roman Empire. But when the pope's vassal king of Sicily and the emperor of the Holy Roman Empire are the same man, does the pope or the emperor hold the final authority over Sicily? Frederick chose not to address what would be the defining question for him and his descendants.

Frederick had no doubt that only strong central power could prevent anarchy. His contemporaries believed this valid, as had the ancients who deified their rulers. What was novel in Frederick's political philosophy was his separation of strong central power from religious practice.

To be sure, he introduced his specific laws by genuflecting to the king's accepted duty to defend the church. The usual formula related the defense of the church to the defense of the peace in the realm, but Frederick chose to identify peace in the realm with social order. He made heresy criminal not because it offended against God but because it disturbed the peace. Denouncing the Albigensians who were then running riot in southern France and in Frederick's lands in the north of the peninsula, he encouraged priests to question his subjects about their beliefs, and for those found to be heretical he decreed death. In his ardor for law to serve the social order, Frederick started an Inquisition.

On the other hand, so long as his subjects worshipped in conventional quiet, he didn't care which religion they followed. The *Liber Augustalis* declared all individuals equal before the law; indeed, his code mentions specifically that Jews and Muslims have the right to initiate lawsuits just like Christians. Frederick had abolished the religious communities because that system bound Sicilians of different religions to different codes of law. Frederick wanted everyone in his realm to be subject to the same laws, as that would facilitate the autocracy he desired.

The strife between Muslims and Christians continuing, Frederick tried to discourage the persecution of non-Christians by the Christian populace. Not only did he call the persecution "excessive," he decreed that, in cases where culprits could not be found, officials would impose a fine on the whole locality.

FINANCE

Legal codes and colleges, crownings and Crusades, these don't come cheap. The Norman kings, as feudal lords, had assessed property taxes on lower lords for the defense of the realm in times of crisis. Frederick, being in continual crisis, levied the tax every year, its rate depending on immediate needs; he used this *subventio generalis* as his largest finance tool. When his subjects complained about taxes, this was the tax on which they focused. Of course Sicilians paid dozens of other taxes, including import duties, harbor dues, warehousing fees, and fees for the right to graze animals. The taxes were very heavy, and the more Frederick absented himself from the island, the more his island subjects resented his taxation. Not only did the taxpayers suffer directly; on balance the taxes hindered production, even though some of the revenue was spent for agricultural development.

Frederick applied himself to the island's economy with a sincere desire to improve the lives of his subjects. Even when absent from Sicily, he would write letters of inquiry and admonition about small matters. He built bridges, improved the irrigation system, and protected debtors from the confiscation of their tools and animals. To stimulate the sale of goods he abolished the locally imposed tariffs and insisted that towns hold annual fairs. He had less success in imposing two measures that would have proved useful for development: he tried to replace the differing local systems of weights and measures with an island-wide system, and he tried to reduce the damage from locusts in bad years by assigning every individual a quota of the bugs to catch.

On the island a small amount of iron was mined, so Frederick made trade in iron and steel a royal monopoly, along with hemp, dyes, pitch, tallow, and Sicily's famous products, salt and silk. The export of grain (as ever, the most remunerative crop) increased as North Africa suffered reverses and had to import more of this fundamental food; for a while Tunisia was Sicily's biggest wheat buyer. When Frederick regained his place as Sicily's largest landowner, he became a major grain exporter, and he had the advantage of being able to export in his own boats. Others had necessarily to deliver their export grain to agents of the northern maritime cities or of Ragusa (the later Dubrovnik) on the Adriatic coast. The foreigners spent in Sicily little for consumption and less for development. Although Sicily had an adequate navy, it apparently lacked a merchant marine — it certainly had none of any strength — and the amount of money lost to foreign shippers is incalculable but great.

Mercantile Cities

Commerce was simply not a Sicilian priority. At a time when northern Europe and northern Italy were fostering cities, Sicily lagged behind. Nonetheless, cities are generally at the cutting edge of economic development and social advance, so the importance of Sicily's cities is disproportionate to their size.

Messina

The fortunes of Messina, more than of most cities, ebbed and flowed. We saw Messina at the catastrophe of Richard Lion-Heart. Shortly afterward, the city abetted the invasion of the German Henry VI. As king, Henry rewarded Messina by making her a free port, granting tax concessions to any ships that might dock there. Like Trapani (the major port of northwest Sicily), Messina was assessed lower taxes than other cities. Foreign maritime cities naturally rushed to open offices and warehouses in Messina. They received economic advantages, such as highly preferential treatment in buying wood for ships. Politically the merchants living in Messina enjoyed aspects of the autonomy once known by the Normans' religious communities; for example they could select and be judged by their own magistrates.

It was a further boon for Messina when Frederick's transfer to Apulia turned Palermo into a sleepy town. Messina became the major producer of silk. The city teemed with Crusaders and with sailors from Pisa and Genoa and Venice, all of whom spread news about the happenings up north. Merchants arrived also from Greece and Dalmatia, and pirates from all the shores of the Mediterranean who needed places to meet and commit commerce.

Growing rich, and ever seeking new opportunities for growing richer, Messina's merchants negotiated as a group to expand their activities. They claimed rights, for instance, to fish anywhere in the Tyrrhenian or Ionian and to dig iron from the mines south of Messina far beyond the city walls. A proud city, Messina now boasted a mercantile class almost as strong as that of the Lombard cities scattered across the north of the Italian peninsula.

Almost as strong. Some time back, during the reign of Sicily's William II, Frederick's German grandfather (Frederick Barbarossa) found that the mercantile cities of the north were stronger than he was. Now our emperor, Frederick II, liked Messina — at least he had graced her with the only church he ever built* — but he didn't like Messina's recent claims; they were a potential threat to his personal and complete rule of the Regnum. He abrogated the tax benefits granted Messina by his parents, reduced her trading privileges, and seized some of the merchants' property. Even more galling for the merchants, he had them watched so closely that it hindered their cheating.

Angered by the imperial strictures, in 1232 Messina rebelled. Frederick reacted by sending soldiers from Calabria and stringing up the rebellion's leaders. Then he detached Messina administratively from Sicily and joined her to Calabria.† To destroy Messina as a port would hardly be to Frederick's advantage. Rather, he imposed a tax of

---

* Frederick built the church in Gothic style around 1220 and called it Santa Maria Alemanna (that is, in Messina's German quarter). It has been badly damaged by natural forces, and now its ruins are being excavated.
† Strange as that sounds now, it has a geographical rationale: until modern times Messina was cut off from the rest of Sicily by the mountains behind her, while the Straits provided easy passage from Messina to Calabria.

3 percent, a rate that would allow Messina to compete with the other maritime cities but would limit merchants' possibilities of putting aside profits. That would keep the mercantile class within bounds.

Suppressing the Merchants

Desiring their own autonomy and believing that Frederick had over-reacted in Messina, other cities in the east grew restive, but they yielded to him. Exceptionally, the year after Messina's rebellion the hill town of Centuripe (the Romans' rich Centorbi) started to rebel. Frederick demolished the town.

Frederick's policy of suppressing Sicily's cities can be traced to King Roger, who feared barons and artisans and any group with aspirations. The threat that King Roger could sense only vaguely had become quite concrete by Frederick's time, when ambition was embodied in the mer-cantile class of his German lands and his Lombard lands. When Frederick delegated the governance of these he gave them license to strengthen themselves. For one thing, they were able to reduce their tax burden (with the result that the Sicilians had to pay a disproportionate share of the empire's taxes). Frederick's direct authoritarian rule of Sicily, in contrast, squelched anyone there who might challenge him.

Frederick moved Centuripe's survivors to the coast north of Siracusa, specifically to the new city he named Augusta. The city name was a manifestation of Frederick's desire to be not just an emperor, but an emperor in the classical mold. Another was his issuance of a new gold coin, which he called the *augustale* and which showed him not in the usual kingly profile but sitting in the manner of a Roman emperor. If he fancied himself as a Roman, in resettling the Muslims, and then destroying Centuripe and transferring her survivors he acted like a tyrant of ancient Greece. He treated cities harshly, just as he had snubbed the church, because he brooked no challenge to his authority.

Parliament

Frederick had his modern side — indeed he is credited with making Sicily a modern state. Assemblies similar to his *parliamentum* at

Melfi had been held for a long time. A feudal sovereign generally summoned his nobles and prelates to inform them about changes he wished to make in law or in public behavior and to ask them for support or ratification. Less commonly the king would treat his nobles as a council, asking them to discuss the proposal with him before he issued a decree. The feudal lords didn't attend at the king's request but at his command. The king also charged them with staying abreast of public matters in their districts, so that they could keep him informed of what was going on. As the years passed during Frederick's reign, such assemblies — in Frederick's Regnum and elsewhere in Europe — increased in frequency and regularity.

Around the time of the Messina rebellion, Frederick began to summon some representatives of the cities to join the feudal lords at assemblies. That was an advance, though a limited one. Not the cities themselves but the king's officials decided which urban worthies would participate in each assembly. If Sicily's cities ever tried to have assemblies of their own to deal with local affairs, they didn't succeed.

The War Between Frederick and the Papacy Turns Hot

Frederick's interest in parliamentary problems often had to give way to the urgency of papal problems. For many years he battled the papal forces about heresy and about the rule of the Lombard lands and the Papal States. One Sicilian phase of the strife centered on the maritime cities of the peninsula, with which Frederick was constantly negotiating about trading concessions. In the late 1230s the pope (Gregory IX) began to entice Genoa and Venice into making war on Sicily. Genoa had dominated Siracusa at the beginning of the century, until young Frederick reclaimed her; now the pope promised Genoa she could have Siracusa back.

To motivate its animus against Frederick, the papacy never stopped citing the Muslims, so no one was surprised when a new pope (Innocent IV) lambasted Frederick as a Muslim-lover. Then on July 12, 1245, Innocent declared his war against Frederick to be a holy war. To fight Frederick would be to defend the faith, and participants in this Christian action would be treated as Crusaders with all corresponding benefits. The war of words escalated into armed battles, and Frederick found himself with prelates as hostages. He sought to make peace, but the pope proved intransigent. On the grounds that Frederick had long been excommunicate, the pope freed all his subjects from allegiance to him. And since Frederick no longer had subjects, he was thereby deposed as king and emperor.

∾

According to the church, if a pope had the authority to put the crown on Frederick's head, then a pope has the authority to take it off. The church hoped that Frederick would be driven out by the Sicilians, long suffering from the taxes that Frederick levied for his wars. Now that the action of deposition had ended negotiations with Frederick, there would be more wars and higher taxes.

Actually the island of Sicily was fighting again already. Frederick transferred most of western Sicily's Muslims to Lucera in the 1220s, and the few who remained were quiet workers on the land. Yet the Christians kept persecuting them. When the Muslims finally reacted in 1243, inland Sicily was torn by hostilities, which ended only when Frederick evicted the Muslim peasants and shipped them to Foggia.

The Christians in Sicily were even unhappier than before. Their bishops harangued them about Frederick's irreverence and despotism and assured them that he was no longer their king. Frederick was on the defensive; there wasn't much he could do beyond denying papal representatives entrance into his Regnum and banning the reading there of papal communications. Still he kept busy trying to suppress opposition, especially after he learned of a plot to murder him.

Into the countryside depopulated of Muslims Frederick brought settlers from the north of the peninsula who were unprepared for farming in Mediterranean conditions. So he turned to North Africa, not for other Muslims but for Jews. Unlike Muslims confident in their vast Arab territories, Jews were a small people with no political muscle, so Frederick had nothing to fear from them. The newcomers were directed to introduce into Sicily the cultivation of Tunisian products, especially dates and indigo. Half of their product they could keep, half went to the state.

Frederick returned north to fight against his deposition, leaving Sicilians further embittered about being taxed for foreign adventures. Their anger was to smolder for another generation, even though, toward the end of 1250 when Frederick was suffering from dysentery, he revoked forever the *subventio generalis*.

∽

Frederick died in Apulia on December 13, 1250, two weeks short of his fifty-sixth birthday. His life had been very full though not very satisfying. At his request, his body was put to rest in the Palermo cathedral near that of his grandfather Roger, whom he never saw but whom he often emulated.

SUMMARY OF FREDERICK

Like King Roger, Frederick was an intelligent man with a strong personality — it was unfortunate for Sicily that Frederick's realm was so much larger than his grandfather's. Frederick faced peculiar disadvantages: his German father sufficed to make Sicilians suspicious of him, and his inheritance of Sicily's throne through his mother, contrary to Salic law, assured that many Sicilians would have done him out of that throne. To make matters worse, Frederick was an intellectual. The breadth of his interests, the energy of his mind, elevated him to the company of certain Muslim princes, but he stood alone among European sovereigns. Moreover, it's said that as kings have no peers, they tend to feel isolated; an emperor stands apart even from kings.

Frederick was rare among humankind not just in being royal. He was rare in having grown up as an orphan without brothers or sisters — indeed, at least in Sicily, without any relatives at all. That Frederick was not born on the island of Sicily is a technicality; he was to all effects a homegrown prince, and he considered the island his home. In his youth he knew the reality of his subjects' lives as well as anyone of any epoch born to the purple.

Although he spent in Sicily very little of his adult life, he worked assiduously to modernize it. He thought that a centralized state might advance the welfare of the people, and to this end he instituted changes in commerce and in the administrative system. He improved agricultural infrastructure, built many fortresses, and fostered a short-lived musical entertainment for the rich. He expelled Muslims from their home on the island and similarly transferred some Jews, yet he also brought to Sicily some other Jews from North Africa and some Christians from the north. Sicilians applauded his ideas, though they hated the taxes he collected to make his projects operational.

With an empire including realms on both northern and southern borders of the Papal States, Frederick was pushed into warfare that demanded huge amounts of time and Sicilian money. His papal problems marred his reign. He might well have proved an outstanding king of Sicily had he not been Holy Roman Emperor.

Frederick was the most complicated of Sicily's kings. His natural intelligence and energy led him to pursue multiple ventures. Let's observe one of his pastimes, reflecting different aspects of his personality. A love of animals, developed as a boy in Palermo, was to continue throughout his life, perhaps as a substitute for human friends. The grown man infused that love with scholarly concern. He bred poultry and pigeons and hunting dogs and (in Malta) camels. His passion was falconry, in which he became expert — he wrote a long and excellent book on the subject, and he introduced some fine points of Islamic falconry into Europe. He may have been the first to cultivate game systematically, by watching and noting when animals mated and gave birth. When he decreed limited seasons for hunting particular animals, the animals of Apulia (it's said) wrote to thank him. Pertinent here is that Frederick pursued his husbandry entirely outside the island of Sicily.

In his lighter moments he behaved in such a way that court circles knew him as a womanizer. Yet he must have taken seriously traditional marriage, as he would have four wives. He grieved deeply on the death in 1221 of his first wife, Constance, the mother of his first child, Henry (who was to become Germany's Henry VII). As noted above, his second wife, from Brienne, died in 1228, leaving him a son Conrad. In 1235 he took Isabella of England as his third wife, but she too predeceased him. On his deathbed he married for the fourth time, to Bianca Lancia, the mother of his son Manfred. (Soon Conrad and Manfred would each rule Sicily, briefly.)

Because of the variety and intensity of Frederick's activities, people throughout Europe spoke of him as "Stupor Mundi," the wonder of the world. From the thirty-eight-year rule of a strong, knowledge-able, and industrious king, one wonders if the Sicilians might have expected more.

∽

To protect his position up north, Frederick impoverished Sicily. Just in recent times, Sicily's wealth had already been depleted by three Hauteville in-laws: Baldwin of Jerusalem embezzled Adelaide's dowry (before sending her back, crying, to Palermo), Richard Lion-Heart had made off with a substantial sum (before he left for Jerusalem), and Henry VI had grabbed what he could during his brief reign. The projects of the Hauteville grandson were more hon-orable but similarly ruinous. Like the destroyed Greek cities that rose again, Sicily's wealth renewed itself.

The burden of taxation lay heavily on Sicilians, who had always produced enough to tempt greedy foreigners. Yet before long princes would shy away from Sicily.

FREDERICK'S HEIRS

Frederick would prove to be, in Sicily, the only Hohenstaufen who ever counted. Faced with a church antagonistic to him from his birth, Frederick had put up a good fight until his dying days, but the papacy lived on to fight his successors.

CONRAD

From 1245, when Innocent "deposed" Frederick from the Sicilian throne, the pope had sought to fill the position. In 1247 he anointed as his own "king of Sicily," William of Holland, incompetent but innocuous. When Frederick died at the end of 1250, his crowns passed to his twenty-two-year-old son, Conrad. The new king of Sicily had his father's qualities and greater financial savvy; his subjects

regarded him optimistically. The pope, on the other hand, was ener-
gized by the succession to find a better man for the role of anti-king.
Never again, the pope reiterated, would the crowns of Sicily and of
the empire be worn by the same man. Primary job specifications for
the new "king": to have no lands in Germany and to have ample
money for the wars inevitable before he could actually rule Sicily.
After all, King Conrad was young and strong.

Innocent duly proposed to his council two men: Alfonso of Castile
(soon to be King Alfonso X), and Richard, Earl of Cornwall, brother
of England's King Henry III. Both Alfonso and Richard had
Hohenstaufen blood — even though the pope was out to destroy the
rightful Hohenstaufen heirs, he preferred to keep the throne in the clan.

England's Richard was chosen. When informed of his selection to
(in effect) fight for the kingship of Sicily, he responded that that was
like offering him the moon, provided he could take it from the sky.
So Alfonso of Castile was invited to fill the anti-throne, but he
refused too. Alfonso had the support of King Louis of France, and
when Alfonso said he didn't want the job, it was offered to King
Louis's younger brother, Charles, count of Anjou. But Charles didn't
want to get involved either.

Before long it occurred to England's King Henry that he had a
younger son, Edmund. Early in 1254, on behalf of the nine-year-old
Edmund, King Henry applied for the pope-called kingship of Sicily. In
the negotiations Henry agreed to pay the costs of making his son
Sicily's ruler in fact as well as in name. Pope Innocent was delighted:
on May 14 he was already sending out letters referring to young
Edmund as "king of Sicily."

That's when the news arrived of the death of Conrad, King of
Sicily, on May 11, of a fever. In his deathbed weakness he com-
mended to the pope the protection of his toddler son, born of a
Bavarian mother and called Conradin; now Conradin was the king
of Sicily, the hope of the Hohenstaufens. As the boy had been
entrusted to Pope Innocent, the pope didn't know what to do. He
didn't want to act rashly, and was spared the need to decide by dying
in December.

MANFRED

King Conrad's half-brother Manfred, aged twenty-two, was already experienced as Frederick's regent in Sicily. On Conrad's death, Manfred (though he was not in line for the throne) applied his great energy to the everlasting diplomatic and military battles because he had little alternative. Wresting Sicily from the Hohenstaufens had become the popes' obsession.

Of all the nobles throughout Europe whom Innocent had tried to interest in taking over rule of Sicily, England's king Henry was the first to nibble. England had, in fact, long had commercial and ecclesiastical interests in Sicily. Henry had been taxing his subjects heavily so that he might go on Crusade (although he didn't really want to go so far), and Innocent had been trying to get him to change his Crusade project into a crusade closer to home against the godless Hohenstaufens. A new pope, Alexander IV, continued Innocent's endeavor. But while the English populace was resigned to paying taxes to send their sovereign to Jerusalem, it refused to finance a holy war in Sicily. The idea absolutely shocked English prelates. The pope, hoping he could loosen Henry's pursestrings through a fait accompli, in October 1255 had one of his legates anoint young Edmund king of Sicily. Henry III received a horrendous bill, with the threat of excommunication if he didn't pay it.

The pope needed the money. He was running a military campaign against Manfred in the southern peninsula. The papacy had no devoted troops, just mercenaries who seldom got paid. Manfred, knowing that the papacy was out to destroy him, waged effective battle using his dedicated Muslim soldiers from Lucera. By 1257 the island of Sicily, in fact the whole Regnum, was in Manfred's hands.

Manfred had accepted his role as regent for his young nephew Conradin. The Sicilians, for their part, had little enthusiasm for a child king; regencies always created problems, and the boy was living in Bavaria anyhow — they had never even seen him. On the other hand, they saw, admired, and applauded the handsome blond Manfred, who was charming, bright, and victorious.* Manfred

---

* Dante in *The Divine Comedy* described Manfred as blond and handsome.

embodied the ideals in the myth of the emperor Frederick, which the Sicilians loved. After some politicking by Manfred among Sicily's barons, in August 1258, in Palermo, the archbishop of Girgenti crowned Manfred king of Sicily.

By Christmas, Edmund's shadow kingship had been revoked. Sicily had had real English queens (Joan, wife of William II, and Isabella, wife of Frederick), but it was not to have even a fake English king.

Manfred soon had something else to celebrate. As king of Sicily, he arranged a marriage for his daughter Constance with Peter, the heir to Aragon-Catalonia.

❧

Re-enter Charles, Count of Anjou.* King Conrad's death had raised the prize value of a papally ordained sovereignty over Sicily. Like his brother, King Louis (later Saint Louis), Charles was a pious supporter of the church. Both brothers had looked with antipathy on the emperor Frederick, and they condemned Manfred as usurper of the throne. When the pope, from 1261 the Frenchman Urban IV, went to the French court dangling the Sicilian crown, King Louis hesitated, thinking about the rights of young Conradin — to disregard royal heredity would be to open a can of worms. But when Charles expressed interest in the crown, King Louis told him to go for it. Louis warned Charles, though, that his support of Charles's endeavor would not extend to the financial.

Perhaps to a French count coveting Sicily a French pope might offer a discount? Think again. Urban's terms would have deterred any prince of merely extraordinary ambition. To assume the role of Sicily's anti-king that England's Edmund had vacated, Charles would have to take over England's debt to the papacy. Additionally, he would have to pay the papacy a huge annual tribute, some thirty times what the popes had demanded of the Normans. Whenever a pope demanded military aid, Charles would be bound to furnish three hundred ships or knights. If Charles was going to have to spend all

---

* Anjou was a territory in northwestern France, around the river Loire. The adjective is "Angevin."

this to obtain sovereignty of Sicily, guess where the money would come from.

Pope Urban also specified what he wanted in church-Sicilian relations. No longer would Sicily's king be an apostolic legate — he would have no control over the appointment or scope of bishops. Sicily's clergy was henceforward to be tax-exempt. To assure that the king of Sicily would not develop too much power vis-à-vis the Papal States, Charles would have to agree not to seek lands or positions in the empire north of Rome nor in the Papal States themselves. He would have to promise to provide a good administration. Charles was not to tax Sicily excessively; to offset any loss, the pope would allow Charles a tenth of the ecclesiastical revenues in France for the next three years.

Charles was still game — he wasn't yet forty, and once he was in power he'd have time to change the terms.

So the papacy had a working partner, a sworn angel, in its drive to rid Sicily of Hohenstaufens. As often in partnerships, Charles of Anjou and Pope Urban did not always see eye to eye, especially when Charles, within months of his agreement with the pope, violated it by getting himself appointed senator in Rome. But Urban never wavered in his support of Charles in the battle against King Manfred.

The military conflict centered on the borderlands of the northern Regnum and the southern part of the Papal States; Manfred generally had the advantage. Cardinals began sharp questioning about the purpose of the war and the sincerity of Charles, but Pope Urban insisted that Manfred posed a real threat and that they needed Charles to defeat him. When Urban died in October 1264, the fighting continued with Pope Clement IV, another Frenchman, directing the papal side. Then, at Benevento, in a battle against Charles at the end of February 1266, Manfred was killed.

CONRADIN

Naturally Manfred's death had great impact throughout the entire Regnum and the empire, but on no one as much as on the Hohenstaufen heir Conradin. Besides being the rightful king of Sicily, the boy was now fourteen and ripe for adventure. Although he had been raised in the Germanic realm, the Sicilians didn't hold Germanness against Conradin the way they had against Frederick, because the political climate had changed so disastrously. Manfred's routed army included many Sicilians who now fled to Bavaria, joining the delegations of politicians determined that Conradin be enthroned. The adolescent was in his glory.

The leaders in Rome had scarcely thought of Conradin during all the years of fighting against Manfred; now, in September 1266, apprised of all the activity in Bavaria, the pope promptly threatened excommunication for anyone supporting the young prince in his royal designs. Regardless, Sicilians rallied in Conradin's favor.

Charles of Anjou, heeding warnings from Rome about the volatile Sicilians, remained in the north of Italy although he commanded military forces in Sicily. Pope Clement augmented his decrees against Conradin's supporters, with little effect. To assist the Sicilian partisans, Tunisian soldiers arrived on the island. As of November 1267 Charles's forces held Messina and Palermo, while Conradin's partisans held all the rest of Sicily. Muslim forces from Lucera, naturally favoring the Hohenstaufens, extended the battle to the peninsula.

By then Conradin, disregarding his mother's fears, had left Bavaria with a small army. For three months of the winter, from October 21, 1267, to January 17, 1268, he camped at Verona with his soldiers — soldiers from Germany, from the north of the peninsula, and especially from Sicily. Probably he and they hoped that other fighters would join them. Conradin's strategists hoped also that Charles and his Angevin forces would move south to respond to the Sicilian revolt. Neither happened; in fact some of Conradin's German men abandoned him and returned north. Conradin couldn't wait any longer — he set off for Milan, then stayed a bit south of Milan with his supporters at Pavia for three weeks, crossed the mountains to the coast, and sailed to Pisa. He met with no opposition from the Angevin forces.

Arriving at Pisa on April 7, Conradin was welcomed with all the ceremony due a king. He knew how to respond. Pisans had long held lands and trade privileges in Sicily, especially eastern Sicily; Conradin would confirm all those privileges and give Pisa the west-coast cities of Marsala and Trapani, as well as the island of Malta. Three weeks in Pisa, then Conradin travelled south through Siena and Viterbo, where Pope Clement from behind a window witnessed the enthusiastic reception. Conradin continued euphoric to Rome, arriving there on July 24.

Likewise Rome gave the sixteen-year-old a reception not seen there since the time of the ancient Romans. Such a welcome in the capital of the Papal States was all the more remarkable in that the papacy considered Conradin its prime foe. Pope Clement, to be sure, was out of town. Rome's buildings were hung with banners, her streets strewn with flowers as he passed. The city resounded with songs, games, parades; the exultant crowds couldn't be quieted. Such glee for Sicily's young king.

It was matched, however, by the bitterness of the pope. A month after arriving in Rome, Conradin's troops moved eastward to Avezzano, to be met in battle by the much larger forces of Charles. Decisively defeated, the young king was captured at the end of August. Pope Clement may or may not have urged the boy's death; in any case he didn't oppose it. Charles had Conradin tried in a kangaroo court, and on October 29, 1268, in the piazza of the Naples market, the king of Sicily was beheaded. He had never seen the island of Sicily.

Charles of Anjou

With Conradin died all Hohenstaufen hopes. The battle of the papacy against Holy Roman Emperor Frederick and his line had ended in conclusive victory for the former. Frederick's son Manfred and Frederick's grandson Conradin had lost their lives to the popes' *idée fixe*. The way was now clear for the French count, Charles of Anjou, to reign over Sicily — except that the execution of young Conradin had propelled the Sicilians into revolt.

The execution had incensed not only the Sicilians but virtually everyone else in Europe as well, for it was against the rules of war for a victor to kill a captured enemy prince. Pope Clement was apparently very upset by it, and he died a month afterward; Charles of Anjou, on the other hand, seemed undisturbed.

Subduing the Sicilian rebels was naturally Charles's first priority. Before long his army captured their headquarters at Sciacca. In keeping with his lack of remorse about putting Conradin to death, Charles treated the rebels harshly. Their leaders he beheaded. Those from the peninsula who had borne arms against him he deported. Sicilians who had joined the rebellion saw their property confiscated. A greater number of Sicilians were damaged by another of Charles's punishments, one more legalistic. He decreed that from the time Pope Innocent deposed Frederick, Sicily had no legitimate sovereign; therefore the Angevin rulers would not recognize any title to land unless it had been registered prior to 1245. Any lands granted in the last years of Frederick's reign, or during the reigns of Conrad and Manfred, would revert to King Charles, as would any lands that had never been officially registered, of which there were many. Lands of Sicily's oldest families, their ownership known to everyone but never officially registered, fell to the new king.

Through these laws, Charles took possession of a lot of land. Much of it he distributed, as fiefs, to the hundreds of Frenchmen and Provençals who had come to Sicily with him. To minimize the risk of barons weakening his power, he granted no fiefs of great size. To intimidate landholders who might think about plotting with foreigners, he ruled that anyone who absented himself from the Regnum for a year would forfeit his land. The resurgence of feudalism went hand in hand with the replacement of local landowners by foreigners, and both developments were hated by the Sicilians.

To the established barons of Sicily, it seemed that Charles of Anjou did not respect the conditions that traditionally had warranted duty toward the sovereign. The feudal system, like Charles an import from northern France, had spread slowly in Sicily as the different religious communities became absorbed into the Christian. Feudalism was working in Sicily insofar as its fealty and reciprocal obligations were based on honor among families down through generations. But feudalism in France had evolved — the lands once granted as fiefs were by now virtually the vassals' private property, and the powers of the barons had shifted in favor of the king. The French officials expected the king to hold absolute power in this new realm, whereas the Sicilian landholders (putting aside their resentments peculiar to Charles of Anjou) expected the king to deal with them according to a code of mutual obligations.

Sicilians seethed as Frenchmen and Provençals came in to replace local landholders. When people in Sicily saw the newcomer landholders as "them," it became easier for the Greeks and Latins to think of themselves together as "us." This was the final stage in blending the Sicilians into a single Christian community, a community to whom the Norman kings had become a sacred symbol, a community of hate toward the Angevins for destroying the Norman line.

∽

Charles further alienated many people on the island of Sicily by choosing to live on the peninsula, in the continental part of his Regnum. He first stopped on the island in 1270, during the fourth year of his reign, on his way to Tunis for a crusade with his brother King Louis. Actually the crusade was Charles's idea. Tunis had been paying annual tribute to the king of Sicily for over a century, from the time of King Roger; but when Manfred died, the Tunisian king, Mustansir, decided to stop paying. Mustansir went further: he sent troops to Sicily to fight with Conradin's supporters against the Angevins, and when the rebels were defeated, Tunis offered them refuge. Charles, for revenge and for money, wanted to make Tunis his own puppet state, and he convinced King Louis that the Christian world would gain by the conquest of Tunis. King Louis put together an army and arranged to transport it in ships from Genoa, against the advice of his counselors.

King Louis sailed from the south of France. Charles of Anjou left Naples on July 8 for Palermo and anchored there five days later. For five hot summer weeks he waited at Palermo until the ships arrived. Finally in command of a fleet, Charles proceeded to Trapani, whence he set sail the evening of August 24. When he arrived in Tunis the next day, he learned that King Louis had just died.

However much grief he may have felt at the loss of his older brother, Charles rallied the French forces and supplemented them with his southern troops accustomed to the hot weather. They easily overcame Mustansir's soldiers. Charles imposed a crushing treaty. Tunis would have to pay all the expenses of the war, and would have to pay the Sicilian king an even larger tribute than she had been paying previously. (A third the tribute would go to Charles personally.) Mustansir would have to release all Christians held in his realm and to allow Christians trade concessions in Tunis. Tunis was now Sicily's dominion. Not quite as much under Sicily's rule as Sicily had once been under Arab rule, but still Charles of Anjou had acquitted himself well.

∽

The Sicilians really had no interest in Charles's exploit, inasmuch as they experienced their sovereign primarily through his taxes. The more their king adventured abroad, the less he would be concerned about Sicilians and the higher the taxes he would impose on them. Just like the warring Frederick. Frederick's *subventio generalis* — the property tax that his subjects had hated above all others and that he had finally cancelled — Charles imposed again. It appears, however, that the taxes imposed by Charles never reached the heights of those imposed by Frederick.

Other complaints concerned the administration. The Angevins left in place their predecessors' Norman-Hohenstaufen administrative system, but they changed all the administrators. Now all the functionaries on the island were from France and Provence. Charles sought to discourage corruption by employing in each part of his domains officials from elsewhere, much like the Normans and Frederick had done. But compared with Normans and Hohenstaufens, Charles's Frenchmen were suspicious, joyless bigots. The Sicilians hated them. Speaking their foreign language, treating the Sicilians with disdain, collecting tax money from them to send abroad, they encouraged no respect for their king.

Of course Charles of Anjou — having executed Conradin, usurped the throne, and confiscated lands of pacific Sicilians — would have been hard put to do anything right in his subjects' eyes. To Charles's credit, he instituted an honest judiciary and undertook public works (though he did much more in the peninsular part of the Regnum than on the island). Charles considered himself a good administrator and labored to earn a reputation as such. Had Sicilians used trains, he would have made them run on time.

While micromanaging his realm, Charles of Anjou had risen to great power. He became count of Anjou only because his brother King Louis created the title for him; now he was "Count of Anjou, Maine, Provence, and Forcalquier," which meant his domains were huge. By defeating the Hohenstaufens he became king of Sicily and king of Jerusalem. Between his Regnum and Jerusalem he conquered the mountainous land of Albania, and he won over the Greek district Achaea. He had defeated Tunis. His international interests were thus considerable.

And soon he would be master of the Mediterranean. During all of 1281 and early 1282 he worked in Naples preparing a military expedition to the East. By mid-March his forces from Naples and Provence were on their ships at Messina, waiting for his orders to depart. Charles had been frustrated in this project three times, first at Tunis by the death of his brother, King Louis, and twice more for reasons of weather and papal politics. Finally he was on his way.

Vespers

On Palermo's periphery and of simple appearance, the Church of the Holy Spirit caused no foreboding. To be sure, the English bishop Walter of the Mill had laid its cornerstone in 1177 on a day when the sun went into eclipse, and some observers considered that an omen, but through the following century the church maintained a churchly calm. For the people of Palermo and thereabouts, the church distinguished itself by its festival on Easter Mondays.*

The city experienced some rebellious agitation during the early part of 1282, but there was nothing new in that. Things calmed down for Easter week. Now, on March 30, as the festive period drew to a close,

---

* The day after Easter continues the holiday in most of Christian Europe.

the faithful were ambling toward the Church of the Holy Spirit for its Monday vesper service. People from miles around greeted each other and sang while they waited for the service to begin. They were joined by some French soldiers, likewise in joyful mood, but they had been drinking. Oblivious to dirty looks from the crowd, the soldiers flirted with local women. When a sergeant named Drouet pulled a young bride over to him, her husband reacted and attacked the sergeant with a knife. The startled crowd looked on as the sergeant succumbed to multiple stab wounds.

The other French soldiers jumped to do battle. The Sicilian men, all armed, greatly outnumbered them. When the church bell tolled Vespers, not one soldier was alive to hear it.

The bells of Palermo's other churches were pealing to announce their vesper services, coincidentally attracting attention throughout the city. Self-appointed messengers ran from the Church of the Holy Spirit into the city along different routes, crying out the massacre and screaming "Death to the French!" They gave weight to their words by attacking every Frenchman in their path. The men of Palermo left their vesper services and raced through the streets looking for Frenchmen, invading the taverns of soldiers and the monasteries of the French orders. At least two thousand of the French — soldiers and civilians — were slain in Palermo that night.

All Monday night Palermitani dashed forth to rouse towns and villages. A quick response came from Corleone, the old Arab fortress thirty kilometers south of Palermo. Once all the French there lay dead, Corleone dispatched emissaries to Palermo to suggest joint action. Runners were sent east to Messina, southeast to Caltanissetta, and west to Trapani. Soon the entire island was up in arms. Messina, the only city on the island to have received decent treatment from the Angevins, allowed some of her Frenchmen to escape before allying herself with Palermo. Similarly, the small town of Calatafimi, near Segesta, spared the life of her benevolent administrator and facilitated his return to Provence. But exceptions to the general slaughter were few.

TRANSITION
From Angevin to Aragonese (1282–1285)

Their fury triggered by chance, the rebels went on to organize themselves well for their immediate affairs. Palermo and Corleone led the towns in establishing communes. The Sicilians knew that winning their freedom from the Angevins wouldn't be easy. King Charles, soon after learning of events in Palermo, sent ships there from those awaiting him in Messina. But when Charles's admiral, approaching Palermo, found the city protected by a fleet supporting the rebels, he simply sailed away. Charles had no reason to hurry to restore order in Sicily; he rather sought allies in foreign courts so that he would have a large and strong army for striking later on.

The Sicilians meanwhile sent a delegation to Pope Martin, asking his support for their communes on the island. He shattered their hopes absolutely, saying that God had appointed King Charles as Sicily's sovereign. The delegates reflected that, after all, Count Charles of Anjou had been raised to king of Sicily by the papacy. How, then, could a pope collaborate in his dethronement? The disappointed Sicilians saw that if they wanted help, they would have to seek it elsewhere.

We recall Manfred, Emperor Frederick's son who gained the throne of his young nephew Conradin and ruled over Sicily for several years. Manfred's daughter Constance was the wife of Peter, by now the beloved king of Aragon. With the end of the males in the Hohenstaufen line, the position of Constance as heiress assumed an importance she would not have imagined at the time of her wedding.

From Peter's accession in 1276 Aragon traded importantly at Messina. King Peter knew all about the rebellious Sicilians and was not surprised to receive their envoys. Begging the king's sympathy for their exploited island, they implored him to let his lady queen accede to the throne that was hers by hereditary right. Peter acquiesced. On August 30, 1282, five months after the Vespers slaughter,

King Peter of Aragon sailed into Trapani at the head of a huge military force.

Palermo had no archbishop handy, so on September 4 the commune invested Peter as king of Sicily. Again Palermo was the capital! The Sicilians of the island had so hated government based in Naples, under the emperor Frederick II and under Manfred, and for the last twenty years under Charles of Anjou — finally Palermo was their capital again. King Peter promised to give them good government and proclaimed his resolve to honor the Sicilians' rights.

✑

To secure Sicily within his Aragonese realm, King Peter would need to overcome the Angevins. He had the disadvantage of fighting far from home, so he called upon Sicilians to join his army. Peter was also financially weaker than his adversary, but he was able to raise money from the Byzantines, who considered any enemy of Charles of Anjou to be their friend.

Charles too was having financial problems. Earlier he had gone into debt for his foreign ventures, which had brought him glory but no money. While his property in Greece could support itself, barely, Jerusalem and Albania needed aid from him in order to feed and defend themselves. Of course he taxed all his vast lands, but if he raised his taxes further he would risk other rebellions like Sicily's. If he lost Sicily he would receive neither the feudal dues from his Sicilian vassals nor his tribute from Tunis. At fifty-six, he feared for his comfort.

Charles's anxiety about holding Sicily surfaced in a pledge, early in 1283, by the sovereign's son and temporary regent, Charles of Salerno. He promised the Sicilians that certain taxes would be abolished or reduced. He promised the lords that their position would be more greatly respected. Henceforth they could marry when and whom they wished; if accused of misconduct, they would be tried by their peers; and they would be safeguarded from expropriation of their goods by overzealous bureaucrats. He promised the populace that they would benefit from better control of the markets and better administration of the forests. It was a nice package full of goodies, but it came too late.

In mid-April, Messina celebrated the arrival of the royal family from Aragon. King Peter made an overland tour of Sicily's north coast before returning home, while Queen Constance remained in Messina as his regent. The lords were told about the line of succession: on King Peter's death, his second son, James, would become king of Sicily.

Although still vital at forty-one, King Peter had to consider his imminent death: a few months earlier Charles of Anjou had challenged him to a duel, to be held in Bordeaux. Apparently Charles, though determined to hold Sicily, was not so determined to wage war. He was not alone in seeking alternative ways to prove superiority; many of his contemporaries argued that modern warfare cost too much. Wars may have made some sense in past centuries, when a lord could draft his vassals with their horses, but now soldiers had to be equipped with horses and shields, with lances, swords, and bows, and with arrows reaching to infinity. The soldiers even expected a stipend. So, while waiting for their dueling date, Peter of Aragon and Charles of Anjou engaged in some desultory battles and lots of diplomacy. Then, on June 1, 1283, they came to the chosen field at different times, so that each could claim the other hadn't come. Both, it figures, announced victory, and thus sovereignty over Sicily.

∞

Whenever Charles of Anjou left his son Charles of Salerno as regent, he gave him orders to stay put. One day in late May 1284, while King Charles was in Provence, the Naples dockyards finished some new galleys and Prince Charles was eager to try them out. He armed them lightly and on June 5 sailed away. Near the harbor rested a big fleet with Peter of Aragon's admiral, ready to attack King Charles on his return. Instead it was Prince Charles who sailed, unwittingly, to meet the Aragon ships. Utterly unprepared for battle, Prince Charles lost two of the new galleys and was himself taken prisoner. News of his capture sparked riots in Naples, where the locals celebrated by slaughtering Frenchmen.

The entire affair delighted Queen Constance in Messina. Her half-sister Beatrice, one of Manfred's children, had been in an Angevin prison since Manfred's death eighteen years before. The queen knew that hostile subjects of Charles of Anjou would rip his son to shreds if they got the chance. Immediately she wrote to the son's wife, the princess of Salerno, to say that the prince's life would be at high risk unless he was delivered to her at Messina. Soon the Angevins freed Beatrice; Charles of Salerno was in an Aragon prison but alive. Alive for the nonce, as many Sicilians itched to kill him to avenge Charles of Anjou's killing of Conradin.

The prisoner was Charles of Anjou's only surviving son, and it pained the king that his heir should be held by his enemy. The king was by now an old man of fifty-seven, who had once had a marvelous career but had seen most of his gains disintegrate over the last twenty years — that is, since he had started ruling Sicily. He was still proud, pious, and moral. Just recently he had learned that some of his administrators sought to lower their tax bill by assigning their property to the church; scorning such conduct, on January 2, 1285, he issued a decree to forbid it. Five days later he died.

∽

Since that unforgettable Easter Monday almost three years had passed, by which time the Sicilians might have expected to see results. But no notable changes had occurred in their lives, nor had the hostilities stopped. Their chosen king, Peter, was in Aragon trying to prevent the invasion of his land by the Angevins. Their pope-imposed king's heir, Charles of Salerno, was imprisoned in royal comfort in Aragon; we too should keep an eye on him. Pope Martin, denying the legitimacy of both of them, declared an interregnum, which gave the pope the authority to rule the island as its feudal overlord. As the consequence of their great uprising, the Sicilians now had three rulers, none of whom cared much about the Sicilians.

~ 8 ~

SPANISH

ARAGON RULES THE KINGDOM OF SICILY

THE NINETY YEARS WAR, 1282–1372

Back in late Norman times, when Sicily was threatened by civil war between Muslim administrators and Latin barons, the regent Margaret of Navarre brought in forces from Spain and France. Now the Spanish and French were contending Sicily's rule, in warfare that would drag on and on and on.

Peter of Aragon, as soon as he was crowned Sicily's king, returned to Aragon and royal business more important to him than Sicily. His wife, Queen Constance, remained in Messina with little money to meet the expenses of the ministers and the mercenaries who were supposed to be protecting the Aragons' position; for two years she sent nagging letters to King Peter about Sicily's needs. Before he could do much he died, prematurely, in November 1285, leaving Sicily and its problems to his son, James II.

The son and heir of the hated Charles of Anjou, Charles of Salerno, tried to get out of jail in Aragon by renouncing his rights to Sicily and Malta, and had he done so, his Aragonese captors were quite ready to release him. But the pope, now Honorius IV, ruled that out; previous popes had not exerted themselves to win the throne for Charles of Anjou only to have the younger Angevin yield now. The pope didn't want the Aragons ruling Sicily and demanded that Charles of Salerno fight for the kingdom. Charles was still incarcerated when papal forces invaded Sicily through May and

June 1287, besieging the new city Augusta before having to retreat. Negotiations involving England and France led to the release of Charles of Salerno from prison in October 1288, and six months later the next pope, Nicholas IV, crowned Charles king of Sicily.

Rather than feeling honored by having two rival rulers, the Sicilians swore that they would never again accept an Angevin as king, whatever improvements he might promise and whatever guarantees the pope might give.

The situation troubled Charles of Salerno himself. A pious and honorable man, he had been coerced into this kingship by the pope. Now he had papal funds thrust upon him for reconquering Sicily (and for pursuing the pope's larger war against the Aragonese). Charles of Salerno undertook instead to travel around the Papal States and through France trying to arrange truces, even offering to return to prison if it would help. But the antagonists paid little attention to his cries for "peace now."

Politics went no smoother for Sicily's King James II, who drew apart from his family in Aragon. Barcelona supported King James, but Pope Nicholas IV excommunicated him (not for the first time) and excommunicated the Sicilians for good measure. Papal politics and royal politics interplayed inimically, for the most part north of Sicily. Alliances kept shifting, and eventually the Aragonese James II, the Angevin Charles of Salerno, and the pope found themselves on the same side.

After James II moved back to Barcelona in 1295 as king of Aragon, the pope (now Boniface VIII) agreed to invest James's brother Frederick as the Sicilian King Frederick II.* According to the treaty finally arranged in 1302, Frederick wouldn't be *called* king of Sicily, but rather "king of Trinacria" (the island's old Greek name) so that the name Sicily could go with the peninsular part of the Regnum to the Angevins. This Treaty of Caltabellotta stipulated that on the death of Frederick II the island of Sicily would revert to the Angevins, who would then again rule the "greater Sicily," the

---

* This Aragonese who ruled Sicily from 1296 as King Frederick II is not to be confused with King Roger's grandson Frederick, king of Sicily 1197–1250, called Frederick II as Holy Roman Emperor.

Regnum. As compensation for their withdrawal from Sicily, the Aragonese were to receive from the Angevins the island of Sardinia or the island of Cyprus, neither of which, as a matter of fact, was the Angevins to give. The pope annulled the excommunication of the Sicilians and their royalty.

This treaty, also called the Peace of Caltabellotta, seemed to end the Angevin-Aragon conflict and in fact ushered in some years of peace and good feeling. But the treaty included plenty of clauses to fight over, and after the death of Charles of Salerno in 1309 the Aragonese and the Angevins stoked their fires. As they extended their hostilities around Europe and the Mediterranean, their interest in Sicily dwindled. Sicily remained an independent kingdom, its capital at Catania, its Aragonese sovereign Frederick II styling himself "king of Sicily."

∽

While the Angevins received support from France and from the papacy, the Aragonese stood alone and (as royalty goes) they were poor. Yet in Sicily they dared not cut corners on defense, not with Angevins menacing the eastern shore and with pirates everywhere. Bringing armies from the distant Iberia was impractical. Employing mercenaries was too expensive. To protect their Sicilian realm the Aragonese had little choice but to use Sicily's feudal soldiers, although that was easier said than done.

Certainly the landholding barons had military obligations toward their lord and king; toward the new ruling house, though, they just didn't feel obligated. The Aragonese weren't inclined to obtain the Sicilians' compliance by force. For one thing, the Sicilians had approached the House of Aragon to rule them because (oversimplifying) their Angevin rulers had overtaxed them and treated them with contempt — the Aragonese dared not make such mistakes. Aggravating that risk, those Angevins stood ready to exploit any Sicilian displeasure with the Aragonese. So the Aragonese had to ingratiate themselves with Sicily's barons, who had stables of horses and men.*

---

* We noted in the chapter on the Greek-Sicilians that the island gained renown for its horses. The military use of these horses continued throughout Sicily's history, like the production of wheat.

Holding a monopoly on essential resources, the barons enriched themselves. As the king's military officials mixed socially with the barons, some of the royal domains became barons' lands. In the other direction, by transferring land to Aragonese officials the barons could buy themselves certain privileges, along with exemption from military obligation. Some barons not gratified by the Aragonese allied themselves to the Angevins.

Messina was in a different position, having been administratively linked to Calabria, which remained under Angevin rule. The Angevins had treated Messina decently, so the Messinesi tended to support the Angevins. Moreover, many of the merchants in Messina were immigrants, from the north of Italy and from England and France. No such rationale explains the other Sicilians' lack of loyalty to their fellow islanders — the feeling of common identity seems to have flared up during the week following Vespers and then sputtered out. The guerrilla warfare around the island was bad enough, but Sicilian barons worsened the ravage by using guerrilla warfare as cover for sacking neighboring towns.

Feudalism's wheel had turned since Norman times. Like the Normans, the Aragonese had few of their own people in Sicily, so they depended on locals to govern the island. However, Count Roger and King Roger had kept the existing Muslim bureaucracy, whereas the Angevin administrators were eliminated before the Aragonese arrived. Count Roger and King Roger bolstered their sovereignty by granting fiefs to immigrants, whereas the Aragonese had very little to give to Sicily's established landholders. The power of the baronial class over Sicily would grow enormous.

AGRICULTURE DETERMINES POLITICAL DEVELOPMENT

The Aragonese were addressing immediate needs. To understand why Sicily reinforced its feudalism while other feudal regions of western Europe were evolving new systems, we must also look at something more fundamental: geography.

As the ancient Greeks found to their delight, the island of Sicily has extensive plains suitable for grain, and by Roman times everybody knew that the cultivation of wheat was practical only on large tracts of land. And there it grew, requiring from the cultivators little labor and less thought. The growers of grain didn't even have to think about exporting it, since export was handled by royal functionaries.

Let's contrast with northern Italy, where political evolution moved the towns and the merchants to center stage. The climate and topography of northern Italy favored a variety of crops rather than a single staple. The greater diversity of crops cultivable in northern Italy meant that the local landholders had to think about what they would grow, an effort spared the Sicilians. Then too, the Sicilians produced far more than they needed for sustenance, whereas the northern Italians needed more food than they could grow and looked to their seacoasts for trade. In short, Sicilians got their food from local fields whereas northern Italians got their food mostly from merchants and towns.

As northern Italians bought food abroad and as they considered with great seriousness which sector would best reward their farming efforts, they changed their thinking from that of subsistence producers to that of traders. With their commercial strengths the urban people could easily control the simpler people who remained on the land and sold their products in the towns. Just as logically, the more able among the Sicilians strove to increase their feudal holdings because the island had no other remunerative activity and no great need to develop one. Sicily's big, strong landholders could control the weaker townsmen.

Again it's useful to distinguish Messina: while Sicily in general was a granary, Messina was not. She traded like a northern town, and for the same reasons. Sicily's grain fields bordered on one or another of the ports: Palermo in the north; Trapani, Marsala, and Mazara in the west; Girgenti and Gela in the south; Siracusa and Catania in the east. The only Sicilian port without agricultural hinterland was Messina, and this situation Messina had in common with Amalfi, Pisa, Genoa, and Venice. Messina's location on the strait guaranteed her maritime importance. Reinforcing her commercial bent were the Peloritani Mountains separating the city from Sicily's grain lands. Messina had to look to the sea for sustenance. And not only for trade: because the city occasionally suffered a real shortage of grain, special laws allowed Messina to block grain-carrying boats along her coast and confiscate the cargo. The city's prominence as port facilitated her claiming a certain independence from landholders and royal officials, much as cities up north were doing.

THE BLACK DEATH AND ITS CONSEQUENCES FOR SICILY

For a short time even the barons and the merchants forgot about political power. A pestilence struck in 1347, mostly likely attributed to rats on a ship arriving in Sicily from the eastern Mediterranean. Far worse than preceding epidemics, the Black Death spread northward and killed more than a third of the people of Europe over the next twenty years. No one knows how many Sicilians died of the disease, for recordkeeping ceased.

Survivors scrambled for lands deprived of owners. The spectacle resembled the seizure of lands vacated by the Angevins by Sicilian barons at the turn of the century; in the aftermath of the Black Death, the Aragonese aristocracy competed with Sicilian barons to the point of employing soldiers from abroad. The young King Frederick III, called the Simple for the weakness of his character, fell prisoner to different belligerents in turn, as some barons aligned themselves with the Angevins in Naples and others with the Aragonese.

THE NINETY YEARS WAR CONCLUDES

The Black Death accelerated the population decline, which in turn aggravated the general disorder that characterized Sicily from the start of the fourteenth century. Angevin partisans fought Aragon partisans. The papal support of the Angevins ensured fighting between religious and lay Christians. Landed barons fought townsmen; at least one of Messina's attempts to organize a commune was foiled in a massacre. Fieldworkers, afraid to go to work, moved elsewhere. Many villages were abandoned and eventually disappeared. Into this chaos sailed armies of the Angevins, who sporadically attempted reconquest. Pisa and Genoa participated, sometimes with representatives on both sides. Marriages were arranged to serve dynastic policy, one reason for the constant shifts in alliances. Treaties were drafted and refused, or signed and broken. An occasional surcease allowed hope to bud before it was trampled. From the Vespers it took ninety years before peace was restored.

The pope, Gregory XI, worked to regularize the political status of Sicily, now impoverished. The treaty of 1372, signed at Avignon, proved definitive. The pope restored relations with the Aragonese, conditioned on Aragonese recognition of Sicily as a papal fief. Aragonese rule of Sicily was recognized by the Angevins, who renounced their right to rule it even later. The island of Sicily was thereby assured its place as an independent kingdom, linked in a special way to the church but separate from Naples.

THE BARONS COME TO THE FORE

During the reign of Frederick the Simple, the grandest barons carved the island into four spheres of influence, those of the Ventimiglia (whose lands included most of the north coast), the Chiaramonte (based in Palermo and the southeastern town of Modica), the Peralta (the south, based in Sciacca), and the Alagona, representing the Aragonese (the east coast, based at Catania, which was still the capital). These names would echo down the Sicilian centuries. The baronial families each tried to win royal support and naturally fought against each other. Effectively they ran the island, ineffectively.

When Frederick the Simple died in 1377, his baby daughter, Maria, succeeded; in due course she married Martin, the nephew of Aragon's king. The young couple went to Palermo in 1392, where Martin ruled jointly with his father, also named Martin. Barons struggling against each other unsurprisingly competed to win royal support, and in the clashes the co-kings ordered the execution of the leading Chiaramonte, which added to the discord. Martin the Younger flexed his political muscles by declaring himself, as ruler of Sicily, to be apostolic legate, thereby regaining stature for the Sicilians vis-à-vis the pope. On balance, though, the relative poverty of the House of Aragon limited its control of Sicily.

The Aragonese rulers did make efforts to clear up the shambles caused by a century of war. To quiet the turmoil, they brought in troops from Aragon (at the Sicilians' expense, naturally). Officials gave high priority to compiling new records of feudal land grants, as some of the old records were missing and their lack encouraged people to usurp land.

Each baron claimed sovereignty over his *feudo,* making laws and enforcing them. When Martin the Elder returned to Aragon as its king in 1395, Martin the Younger, having difficulty exerting his authority upon the barons, tried to circumscribe their power. While he did not go so far as to forbid barons to act as judges on their fiefs, he granted vassals the automatic right of appeal to the king, and he limited the judgment of serious criminal cases to the royal court.

Parliament was another venue of the struggle between barons and king. Sicily's parliament, initiated by the Norman King Roger and Holy Roman Emperor Frederick II, developed as three arms: the church, the barons, and the *demaniale* (representing the cities belonging to the king). It was at parliament that the first two groups might concertedly oppose the king, although even in the best of times they showed little initiative. In the fifty years after the Black Death the parliament was moribund: the Aragonese rulers left the Sicilians to their own devices, and the barons did as they wished without presenting formal requests. When Martin the Younger called a parliament in 1397 at Catania and another the following year at Siracusa, the barons used these opportunities to ask for basic changes. They wanted the king to rule according to Sicilian laws, not those of Aragon. And they wanted fewer Aragonese officials and more Sicilian. Although in Aragon itself the sovereign often considered parliamentarians' proposals with respect, King Martin told the Sicilian parliamentarians in no uncertain terms that he would promulgate laws as he wished. The barons, disappointed as they must have been, made no great fuss. The episode augured the end of Sicily's political autonomy.

Upon Maria's death in 1402, her widower continued as Sicily's King Martin I. When he died in 1409 the Sicilian crown went to his father, who was ruling in Barcelona as King Martin I of Aragon and now became additionally King Martin II of Sicily. Martin Sr. died the following year, leaving no direct heir. Aragon's nobles held family conclaves to select the next king, and the crown went to Martin the Elder's nephew Ferdinand. His titles included "King of Sicily."

Prosaic as this assignment of titles seemed, it would prove momentous for Sicily. This transition contrasted sharply with the drama of Vespers and the invitation to the Aragonese a century before. Then, most Sicilians favored the Aragonese to rule an independent Sicily rather than be ruled by the Angevins from Naples as half of the Regnum. The resultant wars so fatigued the Sicilians that they hardly noticed Sicily's quiet absorption into the Aragonese kingdom, to be ruled from Barcelona.

SICILY AS PART OF THE KINGDOM OF ARAGON

As long as it was an independent kingdom, Sicily had its capital at Catania, where its Aragonese kings held court. When Sicily became a part of the Kingdom of Aragon, the government shifted Sicily's capital to Palermo. That symbolized the larger practical change: Sicily's new capital was to function as an Aragonese administrative center.

From 1415 Aragon ruled Sicily through a series of viceroys. These deputies of the king acted almost exclusively to further their personal ambitions and cared not a whit for Sicily. Sicilian barons, resentful, petitioned Barcelona for some autonomy for Sicily, in vain. Still they were not about to yield the political power that they had acquired during Sicily's first century with an Aragonese king. If Sicily's absorption into Aragon's empire deprived its barons of any say in making laws, well then, they would ignore Barcelona's laws.

THE BARONIAL ECONOMY
The Land and Agriculture
Politics being no more consistent then than now, barons courted Aragonese officials because baronial wealth and status depended on

the pleasure of their Aragonese sovereigns. The sovereign — we recall feudal theory — owned all the land in his realm and could, as an extreme measure, seize the estate granted to a baron. To be sure, the risk of seizure was not great in the time of the weak Aragonese kings, yet a baron always had that risk in the back of his mind because the lands a baron held were the basis of his wealth and status.

The land was valued by its size rather than by its product. As a class the barons cared about land only as their basis of power; they showed little interest in land as the basis of agriculture. Since the expulsion of the last Muslims, no one experimented and no one encouraged diversity. To be sure, Sicily's dry summers limited the crops that could be grown. In any case, Sicily's huge fields produced a crop much in demand.

The Sicilian climate — winters mild with some rain, summers hot and dry — favored hard wheat, durum wheat. This is a winter wheat, which ancient peoples learned to plant in the autumn and harvest in the late spring or early summer. Hard wheat was so easy to grow that little was needed of the fieldworkers beyond submission. Just as the ancient Romans had taken advantage of that, a millennium later the barons kept the workers tied to the land, virtual slaves. From time to time legal documents denominated fieldworkers by new names, but that didn't change their condition. They worked from dawn to dusk, for a food ration sufficient to keep them toiling and breeding throughout short lives. Those who slacked in their work or supplicated more food were severely punished. Intrinsic to feudalism was the lord's control of food supplies. For one thing, peasants were forbidden to hunt, trap, or fish on the feudal lands; for another, the peasants were obliged to grind their wheat and press their olives in the lord's facilities, for a fee. Those who grumbled risked denunciation by a coworker wanting a small coin.

ᗡ

In the aftermath of the Black Death, up north the decimated land workers used their scarcity value to raise their living standards, but the Sicilian peasants never exercised concerted strength. It's most unlikely that the peasants knew of Eunus and his slave rebellion under the Romans, but they realized intuitively that no good would come of such an effort.

Likewise, up north the shortage of workers had led to mechanical and organizational improvements in cultivation, but these were not introduced into Sicily. For example, while northern fields were objects of sophisticated experiments in crop rotation, the Sicilian barons let their fields lay fallow half the time.* They did this even though the Aragonese, and through them several other countries, would buy all the crops that Sicily produced.

While up north feudalism was disintegrating, Sicily's feudalism remained rigid. That suited the Aragonese, who maintained a feudal system in Iberia too. Actually, so long as the Sicilians could provide Aragon with wheat and with profits from trade, Aragon didn't much care what Sicily did. Aragon certainly didn't favor modernization in Sicily, as modernization cost money. And Aragon saved the cost of maintaining soldiers in Sicily when Sicily's own barons kept their peasants under control. It turned out that Sicily's lack of a king of its own facilitated the barons' rule of the island.

Justice

To protect his wealth and his class, a baron had to control his inferiors absolutely. Should his manager prove an inadequate barrier between him and the workers, the baron needed legal authority. The barons fought long and hard for the right to purchase and maintain tribunals.

The baronial courts served to resolve minor conflicts between ordinary persons of similar rank, but they eliminated any hope of a hearing in regard to a wrong perpetrated by the masters. A dispossessed tenant could scream for a year that the hut in question had always been his, but it was no challenge to his lord to tear up his document or shut up his witnesses. The royal court was supposed to serve as a counterweight, and occasionally it recognized rights of

---

* It's just possible that there was more involved here than inertia, as crop rotation benefits humid lands more than dry lands, however, so far as we know, the Sicilians made no relevant experiments.

commoners over barons, as when the barons wanted to enclose the village commons that had always been used for grazing. However, a peasant with a grievance was unlikely to know that the royal court might hear his argument, and, even if he knew it, reaching that tribunal took a lot of money and persistence.

The trial of capital crimes, even those committed within a *feudo*, had been decreed by the first King Martin to be a royal prerogative. But the next generation of barons began to regain the power and in the 1430s they set up gibbets all around the island. Justice administered by the barons meant that ordinary people had no recourse to justice, no way short of arms to express their dissatisfactions.

The costs of baronial justice were borne by the vassals and the villagers, for the funds from whatever a defendant lost and from the court costs went to the judging body. The baron thus received direct and immediate revenue that was more than sufficient to pay for the administration of his tribunal. This was a new way for barons to extract money from their inferiors.

The viceroys occasionally pronounced against baronial "courts of injustice," just as they did against the baronial control of all peasant food supplies. But the income from the courts, like the fees from the baron's "company store" and olive press and grain mill, supplemented the barons' income, so such royal interdicts went unheeded.

As subjects of the weak kings of Aragon, Sicily's barons were making good money. Running Sicily, they left the running of their feudal estates to poor kin or vassals. Soon no self-respecting feudal lord dwelt on his lands.

Urban Development

City land manifested a baron's power to his peers much better than did an isolated *feudo*. The barons wanted their own palaces as a perquisite of the ruling class and began to invest in them. They were encouraged by laws from early in the 1400s that permitted private persons to expropriate in order to build private *palazzi*. Individuals of means now found it easy to acquire large city tracts for private parks around their dwellings; further to accommodate them street plans were modified. Their city property brought aesthetic and social enjoyment to the individual owners while it could also be expected to hold its economic value for them.

Some of this construction added to the city substance, as when the Chiaramonte family built Palermo a wall edging the inlet of her port. In due course Palermo charmed visitors with her rectilinear streets, luxurious villas, and magnificent public buildings. Construction in Trapani and the other maritime cities elicited much the same reaction. Siracusa, in decay for a thousand years, recovered some glory under Aragon. But most building projects contributed little to the commonweal. Even a big philanthropic gesture, however welcome, was not an unalloyed service to the city, inasmuch as it showcased the wealth of the barons to the detriment of the civic entity.

While the barons indulged in conspicuous consumption, the king had his own motives for beautifying Sicily's growing cities. King Alfonso, who ruled Sicily from 1416 to 1458, sought to keep the Sicilian barons happy while they supported him in his wars on the Italian peninsula. (One of his outstanding captains was Giovanni Ventimiglia.) The king developed a scheme to add to baronial assets while obtaining immediate revenue for himself: he sold Sicilian towns. That is, in return for a baron's cash payment into the royal coffers, the baron came into possession of a city's lands and inhabitants and all her revenues from sales and taxes and official business. The more attractive the town, the more money it would fetch.

If the citizens of a town wanted to buy their freedom from the baron and their resources enabled them to do so, the king would just sell the town again. Among the towns delivered into fiefdom by Alfonso were Lentini, Siracusa, Sciacca, Corleone, Erice, and (four times) Mazara. The city and port of Marsala were similarly sold, so that the city, deprived of her revenue, was always in debt.*

The Sicilian wealth so ingeniously redistributed among the upper classes was taken, in one way or another, from the peasants. As

---

* The Marsalesi were to endure this for a century. Then in 1574 they made the port inoperable by filling it in with rocks rather than having to pay for its fortification.

barons allotted the tax burden, they made sure that most of the taxes fell on the poor. Then when landlords changed their domicile from rural areas to cities, their rents from the land were no longer spent even partially in villages but entirely in the cities.

Demographic shifts resulting from changes in taxation had occurred even in Roman Sicily. A recent example was a heavy export tax levied from 1423 on grain and other agricultural products that had undergone processing, primarily meat, cheese, wine, and silk. Production of these consequently fell. This in turn occasioned peasant migration to the cities, especially to Palermo, which offered jobs in construction. The city had not taken measures to make a corresponding increase in grain reserves. A bad harvest in 1450 led to a riot by the hungry populace. Convinced that barons were hoarding essential foodstuffs, the rioters invaded the barons' cellars, emptied them of wine and olive oil, and threw the liquids into the sea.

Alfonso spent in Sicily to enrich the lives of barons. In Aragon his subjects called Alfonso "the Magnanimous" for his generosity and for his patronage of the arts. In Sicily too he promoted humanistic studies, endowing Messina with a school of Greek and Catania with Sicily's first university (1434–44), dedicated to law and medicine. But in his reign of forty-two years he might have contributed more, such as roads or hospitals. Or even the fostering of a court of cultural importance, given that at this time in northern Italy the Renaissance flowered. But Sicily was in another world, a world controlled by feudal barons.

King Alfonso Expands His Realm

Sicily's taxes helped to pay for King Alfonso's wars. He conquered Naples in 1442 and shifted his royal residence there, taking the title "King of the Two Sicilies." For a dozen years this time, the island of Sicily would be united with Naples. As Alfonso had planned, he used Naples as his base for expansion into the north of Italy. He regularly sent his soldiers swarming over the Two Sicilies to seize peasants from their fields and carry them off to fight Aragon's wars far from home.

The war most damaging to the Sicilian economy didn't involve Sicily or even Aragon directly. When Constantinople fell to the Turks in 1453, Sicily's trade with the eastern Mediterranean and with North Africa dropped sharply. It wasn't much use being in the middle of the Mediterranean if one couldn't trade around its periphery.

As a consolation prize the Turkish expansion brought Sicily a group of Christian immigrants. Some Albanian soldiers of the Greek rite, having fled Muslims invading the Balkan peninsula, landed in 1453 at Sicily's southwest corner. They spent a couple of years in a hamlet near Mazara before fetching more of their countrymen and moving inland to establish a village of their own. In the subsequent decades the government offered other groups of immigrants from the Balkans a kind of homesteading arrangement: newcomers received uncultivated land if they would promise to cultivate it and to submit themselves to the jurisdiction of the local lord. Albanians and Greeks eventually settled a wide strip southward from Monreale extending two-thirds of the way to the southern shore.* Two centuries had elapsed since the descendants of the Greek colonists and of the Byzantines blended indistinguishably into the Sicilian people, and now again Sicily had a significant number of Greek-speakers.

KING JOHN AND PARLIAMENT

When King Alfonso died in 1458, he bequeathed Naples to an illegitimate son and left Sicily and the rest of his kingdom to his brother John. Sicily was thereby separated, again, from Naples, and the new king emphasized this by declaring Sicily forever part of Aragon. In politics "forever" seldom lasts long; in this case, as we shall see, King John himself deliberately put an end to the Aragonese dynasty.

Meanwhile, at the start of his reign, King John convoked a rare Sicilian parliament. Barons in earlier parliaments had generally

---

* The largest of their settlements was Piana dei Greci, for which the archbishop of Monreale gave them the land in 1488; naming it "of the Greeks" was an error, rectified only in 1941 when the town was renamed Piana degli Albanesi. Other Greek-Albanian settlements were Contessa Entellina (1448), Biancavilla (1480), Mezzojuso (1487), and San Michele di Ganzaria (1534). Even in the first years after 1860, that is, after Sicily became part of the Kingdom of Italy, these "Greeks" maintained their distinct identity, as reflected in their clothing, dialect, and customs. Now though these have died out, leaving only particular church rituals.

functioned as a rubber stamp for the king, but this time they presented several petitions. The king agreed to reduce the period of military obligation and to refrain from imposing certain taxes without the consent of the parliament. He also went along with the barons' request to ban non-Sicilians (in effect, merchants from Genoa and Pisa) from acquiring lands and castles. On the other hand, the king refused to deal directly with what was frightening his barons: that in the continuing Turkish wars the Sicilian merchants faced danger in the eastern Mediterranean, while the Turks could sail in Sicilian waters without risk. His predecessor, King Alfonso, had taken away some of Sicily's galleys, and now the Sicilians couldn't even defend themselves.

Wars were a fact of life, like pirates and earthquakes, from which Sicilians suffered, both directly and through high taxes. Notwithstanding the riot in 1450, King John increased the amount of the export tax (in part to finance battles against the Turks), raising the tax eventually to a level one-third of what the grain sold for. Sicily had always submitted without argument to Aragon's taxation, but the burden was becoming unbearable. When a rebellion broke out in Sardinia, King John tried to raise still more funds. Some Sicilian cities reached deeper into their coffers, but others said *basta*, it's enough. In 1478 the king took the unusual step of going from city to city to solicit the funds. His viceroy convoked a parliament in Messina, and when the funds still weren't forthcoming he convoked another in Catania that he thought would be more favorable. The parliamentarians couldn't even be swayed by bribes. The king never did extract this money. It was a rare example of Sicilian barons actively resisting their king, and they won.

FOREIGN COMMERCE

Barons and king found a fundamental common interest in commerce. Sicily had been trading with Barcelona at least as far back as the 1260 marriage of King Manfred's daughter to Peter of Aragon-Catalonia. Around the time of the Vespers in 1282 the Aragonese were eager to rule Sicily because they saw commercial advantage in doing so —

Sicily had always produced a large agricultural surplus. During the century that Sicily was an independent kingdom ruled by a prince of the House of Aragon and then when it had been integrated into the Kingdom of Aragon, the Aragonese profited through Sicilian trade. Sicily's wheat went increasingly to Iberia and as ever to North Africa, to the Italian peninsula (where Sicily maintained commercial relations), and to the eastern Mediterranean (until the Turkish expansion). Minor products from the land included barley, rice, cotton, and silk, as well as wood and its products. Sicily's exported sugar and sugary confections delighted generations of European nobles. From the animal kingdom Sicily's largest money-earner was still tuna; Sicily also exported a few horses and some cheese. Last and least in weight were ostrich feathers, used to adorn hats and helmets.

All around the Mediterranean Sicily's exports were carried in Catalan ships, since the great maritime power Catalonia was united with Aragon. To further their commercial advantage in ruling Sicily, the Aragonese sent Sicily's raw silk to Catalonia to be woven into silk cloth, while obliging sheep-raising Sicily to import wool clothing from Aragon's domains.

Sicilians, apart from a few dominant barons, were not meant to gain from the island's economy. The Aragonese kings used their lands in Sicily for growing grain that they sold for personal profit. Sicily's barons, privilege-oriented, liked to see a coincidence of their own interests with those of their sovereign. To be sure, after a century and a half of Aragonese rule, many of Sicily's barons had Spanish origins — and those barons without them emulated those with. The barons cared more for economic gain than for political independence; as long as the economy was good, why should they seek change?

Sicily's traders were running into contrary winds: the direct harm to commerce from the Turkish hostilities, and the indirect harm to commerce from the Aragonese-Spanish policies of taxing exports and seizing peasants for warfare. Yet the serious long-term damage to Sicily's economy resulted from a change in the physical climate. Over the fifteenth century rainfall declined, thus irrigation dwindled and the diminishing rivers became inadequate as waterways for those crops that were harvested. The cultivation of sugarcane and rice, requiring large amounts of water, came to a standstill. By the 1480s Sicily's exports of animals and their products, and of wood and silk, had dropped significantly.

THE NEW KINGDOM OF SPAIN: FERDINAND AND ISABELLA

In the 1480s Sicily also suffered from a dynastic shift. King John's heir, Ferdinand, married the princess Isabella of Castile in 1469. Upon the death of the elderly king in 1479, the young couple joined their realms. The new sovereigns focused on the mainland; Sicily was just one bulge of little interest among their vast domains. Once the sure center of the Mediterranean sphere, Sicily would now be buffeted by Spanish waves.

THE INQUISITION

Ferdinand and Isabella, endeavoring to mold a nation from diverse realms, ardent about their new nationhood and their religion, wanted all their subjects to share the same faith. As soon as they acceded they intensified efforts to drive the Muslims from Granada (their last stronghold in southern Spain) and established courts to try heretics. Their appointment of the first inquisitors in September 1480 in Seville had no immediate affect on Sicily: few Sicilians could have imagined that this official delving into beliefs would prove incomparably more cruel than the Inquisition sponsored by Frederick II some 250 years before.

Sicily's Jews, though, were leery. From the time the Turks approached Constantinople in mid-century and wrote *finis* to the Byzantine empire in 1453, Sicilian Christians had become infected with Spanish hostility toward non-Christians. It culminated in Sicily's southeast, when members of the Christian community massacred the Jews of Modica in 1474 and of Noto a short time later. So Sicilian Jews had reason to be anxious about their sovereigns' religious policy.

Jews had been living in Sicily from time immemorial, their incidence in the Sicilian population being among the highest in Europe. In some towns in the west of the island, one Sicilian of every ten was

Jewish. Jews lived in most urban areas of the island, working at urban occupations. In the smaller towns they were often the only agents of commerce. Jews lived with political handicaps, but they could practice their religion without serious interference and, in Palermo and several other towns, maintain their synagogues.

Palermo's main synagogue stood a ten-minute walk east of the Norman palace, about halfway between the palace and the sea. A Jewish visitor to Palermo, Obadiah Bertinoro from the north of the peninsula, wrote of this synagogue's beauty. He spent several months in the city in 1487, the year Palermo received the first inquisitors from Tomás de Torquemada, the Inquisitor General appointed by Isabella and Ferdinand. We have reason to believe that both Obadiah and the inquisitors were warmly welcomed, to be sure by different groups.

Given Sicily's foreign merchants and its nearness to Muslim North Africa, Isabella and Ferdinand were determined to assure the Sicilians' religious orthodoxy. By this time about half of Sicily's barons were of Spanish origin, and these usually supported Spain because of loyalty or similar ways of thinking: they obliged Sicily to go along with Spain's wars against the Muslims in Iberia and with the establishment of the Inquisition in Sicily. (On the Italian peninsula, where Spanish hegemony was more recent, many men argued against inquisitorial "justice," and Naples refused to accommodate an inquisitorial tribunal.)

On the announcement in Sicily of the edict expelling all its Jews, many Sicilian Christians raised their voices in protest. They argued that their Jews were a peaceable people and that the Christians would be harmed by the loss of Jewish business. It's conceivable that protests made earlier might have mitigated the expulsion decree; in the event, many of Sicily's Jews were taken to Messina in 1493 and sent across the strait. Other Sicilian Jews, unwilling to give up their homes and all their possessions, accepted baptism. They spent the rest of their lives in fear of being denounced as apostates.

∽

The Inquisition was a child of Madrid (not of Rome), and in Sicily its main officials were virtually all Spanish. The viceroy too was

Spanish, but the Inquisition was controlled directly from Madrid, independent of the viceroy, and as a result much of the viceroys' energy went into jurisdictional squabbles with the inquisitors. After all, the ruler of Sicily was supposed to have the final say over the religious on the island.

Sicily's barons fared better than the viceroy. For privilege-loving Sicilians, the Inquisition created places as lay assistants, called *familiari*, also known as informers. These positions entitled holders to tax exemptions, to extensive legal immunities, and to weapons permits. Thus outfitted, the Inquisition's lay assistants might set up small armies to use in their private battles. The baronial families concerned themselves overwhelmingly with protecting what they had; they saw some of the changes occurring up north, and they didn't want any part of them. It suited Sicilian barons that the Inquisition demanded orthodoxy: although the inquisitors demanded only religious orthodoxy, in Inquisitional Sicily religious values were paramount and pervasive, so unorthodoxy of a political nature could also be challenged.

Baronial families allied themselves with the church because baronial families had members *in* the church. The system of primogeniture encouraged many younger sons and (given the shortage of eligible men) daughters to follow the religious life. When the Inquisition dispossessed the unorthodox, the spoils might well finish in the hands of barons' relatives. As a class, Sicily's barons loved the Inquisition.

∾

Once Sicily's ethnic cleansing succeeded vis-à-vis Muslims and Jews, the Inquisition targeted Christians of the Greek rite and merchants flirting with Protestantism. They all quickly learned to not even hint at criticism of the Inquisition, for which crime a gentleman might spend years in prison, whereas an ordinary man could be sentenced to an hour bound to a stake.

In previous dark times Sicilians turned to the church for solace, that is, for security and moral direction. Now the church was central to the confusion. It seized property in the name of religious purity. Many peasants knew themselves to be working on lands obtained by the fraud of their religious or baronial lords. The richest prelates were often foreigners, most frequently Spanish, whose positions were sinecures and who had no more concern for the ordinary Sicilian than did the barons. For the Sicilian laity this muddied the distinction between the Spanish Inquisition and the Roman Catholic Church.

What particularly galled the peasants were the tax exemptions granted to the church and the clergy; while these were not new, they gained significance with the increase in religious officials. Furthermore, the lands confiscated by the Inquisition were lost to the tax rolls. Notwithstanding their lack of education, peasants understood that the reduction of tax income from these sources would be compensated by an increase in the levies upon the peasants themselves.

The peasants could not appreciate, and only a few barons did appreciate, another of the Inquisition's damages: the loss of Sicily's young publishing industry. Foreign typographers had set up shops in Palermo and in Messina during the period from 1473 to 1476, their output a significant adjunct to the island's cultural life during the following two decades. Then the Inquisition discouraged all broadcasting of ideas, and Sicily's cultural stagnation followed.

Spain's Maritime Expansion

In Spain toward the end of the fifteenth century, a second great drama started playing. Atlantic discoveries quickly made Spain rich, although Sicilians participated neither in the explorations nor in the prosperity. Sicily was of course known to Columbus — we have evidence from his journal entry for October 28, 1492, when he first saw the island of Cuba and wrote: "all the country is high like Sicily." But when the Spanish heard of his landfall in "the Indies," Sicily was swept completely from their thoughts.

In Spain merchants and intellectuals could escape the Inquisitional pall by interesting themselves in Atlantic explorations, but Sicily was too far away. Sicilian cosmopolites were few and resided mostly in the eastern cities, the part of the Spanish empire closest to the Turkish shores. On that coast of Sicily everyone suffered when the Turks blocked Christian trade, and even those tolerant of the Muslim religion lived in fear of Turkish invasion.

SPANISH RULE, 1516–1700

CHARLES V: HIS TAXES AND HIS WARS

Ferdinand's crown passed in 1516 to his grandson Charles, the heir also of the Hapsburgs. Holy Roman Emperor Charles V (Carlo II of Sicily) ruled an empire larger than any in Europe since the Romans. His empire included the island of Sicily and the southern half of the Italian peninsula, as well as most of the Iberian peninsula. His Spanish domain included parts of South America, a land exuding silver. All thinking people thirsted for news of the New World, while Sicily was encapsulated in the Old.

Despite the Turkish problems in the east, during the first half of the 1500s the Mediterranean was still a major trading zone. But over the next decades Sicily was stung from the west as commercial activity shifted to the Atlantic. Associated with that was an improvement in ships. Sicily had had steady customers for its hard wheat because of its keeping quality; as the velocity of ships increased, keeping quality lost some of its importance, so Sicilian wheat lost some of its advantage. Competition developed from the soft wheat of western Asia and northern Europe. Still, one can just hear men on Messina's streets grumbling that Sicily's business reversals were America's fault.

Throughout Charles's reign over Spain (1516–56), the Spanish court exulted as ship after ship arrived with gold and silver from America, making Spain the world's richest country. Of this wealth Sicily saw nothing. During this period Sicily, like the rest of Europe, suffered serious price inflation, due primarily to demographic expansion and secondarily to the increase in money minted from the New World's gold and silver. Price inflation meant reduced purchasing power.

The emperor was fighting against the religious reformers in his own realm and against the French. Sicily's eternal role as granary for foreign rulers continued, as Sicilian grains were taken to feed Hapsburg troops up north. Charles sent his forces far afield — to the east against the Turks and to the west against the natives of the New World — and as his foreign operations became more extensive, his administrators commandeered more men and wheat from Sicily.

The Spanish had a whole arsenal of taxes, the collection of which they often delegated to "tax farmers." These bought from the government the right to collect taxes, and the tax farmers — greedy by definition — forced peasants to pay higher sums than the king's officers would have demanded. Partly attributable to the tax farmers was the fact, as indicated in a 1540 letter from the viceroy to Emperor Charles, that most of Sicily was starving.

King Charles's son took over in 1556, ruling "the double kingdom of Naples and Sicily" as Philip II (until 1598) without mitigating the taxes or the wars. Barons had no problem inciting hungry peasants to rebel; between 1512 and 1560 there were five riots just in Palermo. The rebellion of 1560, unusually, spread from Palermo to other cities, expanding its objectives as it went. Spain responded in 1564 by supplementing the export taxes with a new kind of tax, the *macinato*, on the milling of grain. Until now the barons charged the peasants for milling and pocketed the revenue; but the Spanish officials saw a milling tax as ideal for themselves, because, where everyone's diet was based on grain, a milling tax would fall on everyone who ate.

Spain needed more wood than ever to build warships, so under Philip II the deforestation of Sicily accelerated. From the conflicts between the Spanish Inquisition and the ecclesiastics in Rome grew a fight between Philip II and Pope Paul IV. The pope called the king a heretic and, inevitably, excommunicated him. Reiterating the papal claim to hold Sicily as its fief, the pope took Sicily from Philip's domains and turned it over to the Venetians. During the following years the papal navy sank Sicily's commercial vessels, while Turks and North Africans made continual raids along Sicily's coasts.

THE BARBARY PIRATES

The offensive of Charles's grandparents Ferdinand and Isabella culminated in Spain's expulsion of its large Muslim population. Muslims had lived in Spain for seven centuries, and the evicted generations found themselves at sea literally and psychologically. Joining the pirates who had always terrorized the Mediterranean shores, the new Barbary pirates (from "Berber") were angrier and hungrier than their habituated colleagues. They seized Sicilian ships, raided Sicilian coastal towns, and devastated fields with greater sanguinity.

Of course Sicilians were not passive victims of Muslim raids. Any ship might be manned by Muslims and Christians together, and Sicilian sailors were useful on the ships of North Africans raiding Sicily. Furthermore, Sicilians participated actively in the North African slave trade.

Still, Sicily suffered more than elsewhere from piracy, because of its size, location, and lack of warships. Sicily's coasts had always been vulnerable, given that the island's riches were along the coast and that the coastline was too long to be defended in its entirety. New in Spanish times was that the Muslims now marauding had the blessing of their North African rulers, which made them technically not pirates but corsairs. Their raids on Spanish property were therefore legally warfare.

Spain defended Sicily as best it could, turning eastern Sicily into a giant fortress. Notably, to protect from Turkish raids the residents of Lentini, in 1551 the Spanish built Carlentini on higher ground nearby. In contrast to earlier periods when potentates in North Africa wanted Sicily as a stepping stone to the continent, the Spanish used Sicily as a base for fighting North Africans.

When, almost three hundred years previously, it had come under the rule of Iberian princes, Sicily included the island of Malta, 120 kilometers south of Gela. Even further back, since the Norman king Roger, Sicily had held Malta as a dependency, supplying cheap grain and other economic aid. The Spanish saw the tiny island as strategically important, and they long maintained a military base there. But the battles against the Turks had dragged on for decades without result, and King Charles decided that maintaining Malta cost too much. In 1530, for the annual tribute of a falcon, he granted Malta with Tripoli as a Sicilian fief to a military order, the Knights of St. John. The knights preyed upon Muslim ships and succeeded in reducing the damages of Muslims against Sicilians.

Nonetheless, Tripoli fell to the Muslims in 1551. Fourteen years later the Turks tried to take Malta, but, after vicious fighting that cost the lives of almost half the knights, the Maltese defense proved successful. The Muslims suffered a second humiliating defeat in 1571 at Lepanto (in Greece, between Patras and Corinth), where Sicilians were among the Spanish empire's fighters.

The Muslims' losses curbed their plundering, at least on most Mediterranean shores. But after the English defeated the Spanish Armada in 1588, Spain could no longer spare ships for the central Mediterranean, with the result that North Africans could act with impunity. They not only blocked Sicily from sailing to markets around the Mediterranean but also inhibited grain buyers from sailing to Sicily. Even the merchants of Naples, like Sicily part of the Spanish empire, often made the long trip to the Balkans to buy grain rather than risk having their cargo seized in the Sicilian waters.

BITS OF NEW CULTURE

England's commercial interest in the area went back to the Middle Ages. English merchants had been residing in Messina for the past two or three centuries. As part of the Spanish empire, Sicily was stage for some of the Spanish-English rivalry. The name of the city was well enough known in England so that Shakespeare, after setting plays in Verona and Venice, used Messina as locale for his comedy *Much Ado about Nothing* (1598/1600).*

Messina by now had a university, having begged for one ever since 1434, when a university charter had been granted to Catania. Though Sicilian cultural life had been stagnant during the first half of the 1500s, it advanced during the second half. Time had assuaged the obsession of the inquisitors, and such great wealth had accumulated in Spain's coffers that the sovereigns could spare a little for Sicily. The two developments worked together to provide Sicily with some new academies.

On the other hand, it's important to note that while most of Western Europe derived philosophical and scientific stimulus from the discoveries of Columbus, Sicily remained outside that current.

---

* Shakespeare was the second literary genius — the first being Homer — to set drama in Messina. Moreover, a dozen years after *Much Ado*, Shakespeare wrote *A Winter's Tale*, which has Sicilian characters.

BARONS, PEASANTS, AND THEIR CHURCH

The cheerful silliness of *Much Ado* was far from reflecting contemporary Sicilian conditions, which were grave. In Sicily at this time, as in England's "enclosure movement," the lords were appropriating common lands, depriving the peasants of pasture. In both countries, as in Europe generally, peasants were severely punished when caught hunting, trapping, or fishing on the lords' lands.

In Sicily the Inquisition played some role in the redistribution and consolidation of estates. On a parallel track, religious orders competed for status, using their tax exemptions to build up fortunes. Meanwhile hungry peasants were taxed into destitution — taxes levied on Sicily remained fairly constant over the Spanish rule, but the tax burden was redistributed to the disadvantage of the peasants. They struggled to survive until the next religious holiday, when their lord condescended to set out tables with food for his villagers. Many peasants, wishing to feast more often, turned to poaching and banditry.

Some barons did conscientiously offer great quantities of food to their dependants on religious holidays and days of family celebration, although we don't know how many — such ordinary activities are mentioned only peripherally in archives and court proceedings, which then as now focused on the deplorable. We can nonetheless be sure that reciprocal responsibility, the hallmark of feudalism, had not disappeared. Some baronial families dowered peasant daughters and cared for ill fieldworkers as a matter of course, if only to save their souls and impress their friends. Frequently they channeled these charities, like their large-scale philanthropy, through the local church (itself maintained by the baron).

As the feudal hierarchy ignored younger sons, the church absorbed many of them, assuring them lifelong sustenance and training them to imbue the next generation with the values of the nobility. The brightest and most ambitious of these men became Sicily's prelates and scholars.

GOVERNMENT AND PARLIAMENT

And lawyers. Although the barons generally scoffed at learning, they were amenable to a son becoming a lawyer. As most barons were illiterate and incapable of the simplest bookkeeping, they needed someone in the family able to protect their estates. The University of Catania taught the young men to read better and to read law. The typical law graduate spent his life redistributing lands among the barons. A few of them went sometimes to Parlamento, where most of the men were lawyers; it was there that a man could do most to protect his family's property.

As in Europe generally in this period, Sicily's parliamentary institution was a creature of the crown. (The development of parliaments into representative lawmaking bodies needed centuries.) Parlamento had no legislative function; parliamentary business was mainly the announcement of royal decrees for ratification. An important exception, though: the sovereign was bound to ask the parliament's approval for *donativi*, that is, for levies of taxes beyond the regular. The barons might discuss with each other the merits of an item, but in the end, almost always, they cooperated in giving their Spanish rulers loyalty and financial support. Parlamento gratified the barons by bringing them together where their association with the rulers could be *seen*. It served the barons mainly for status, as a kind of club for select gentlemen. In return, the Spanish officials met some of the requests presented by the barons in parliament (for example, to strengthen fortifications) and generally favored the barons at the expense of the other Sicilians.

Parlamento, as noted earlier in this chapter, had three arms. The baronial arm though overwhelmed the other two, if only because some baron's blessing was always needed by anyone seeking advancement or favor. Proud as the barons were of their Parlamento going back centuries and of their own participation in it, it held little power. Just as lesser mortals had to kowtow to barons, the parliamentarians manifested loyalty to the Spanish crown, because all privilege was subject to the king's approval.

The "vice-roy," as the word indicates, represented the king. But the Spanish sovereigns appointed their viceroys in Sicily with little concern for their qualifications to govern and then limited their powers. During most reigns the military was completely independent of the viceroys. The Inquisition maintained such independence always. Though by 1600 the Inquisition had pretty much burned itself out, in Sicily it still wielded political power because the sovereigns were not enough interested in Sicily to establish there an effective administration. Lacking authority over the institution ultimately responsible for maintaining order and over the strongest religious institution, the viceroy was very weak. This facilitated the corruption of his subordinates, to the degree that by 1600 the situation bordered on anarchy.

In Parlamento, at least, the viceroy could manipulate the barons. It was he who convened the infrequent parliamentary sessions and who selected the parliamentarians for each one. There was no secret voting. Any parliamentarian wishing to be named to a future parliament dared not oppose the viceroy.

In all this the barons acquiesced, since they shared the conservative views of the Spanish. The Inquisition, as long as it lasted, served to stifle any criticism of Spanish activities and made thinking inadvisable even for the rich, who feared that any change at all might lead to loss in their own landholding position.

The paucity of educated men constrained the viceroy to appoint mostly lawyers for all three parliamentary arms, and lawyers, being employed by the wealthy, tend to be conventional. The University of Catania surely didn't direct its law students toward social challenges.

And it hardly had to teach them to argue. Whatever the barons thought about, they fought about: their lands and their relative position in the hierarchy and their family's accomplishments (real and spurious). They vaunted the supremacy of Palermo's land barons over Messina's rich merchants, and they jostled for favor in the Inquisition's bureaucracy. They seemed to quarrel about everything except the glory of association with the Spanish court.

The barons liked to consider themselves Spanish first and then, maybe, Sicilian. However, even in Spain's brightest hour — the mid-sixteenth to mid-seventeenth centuries —the sovereigns treated Sicily negligently. The viceroy made an annual visit to Madrid to report on conditions in Sicily and to receive relevant orders, but indications are that Spain generally left Sicily to its own devices. Not that Sicily's barons made claims on Spain's riches to improve conditions on their island: they were too busy feuding with each other to cooperate in any common activity, and they remained hostile to innovation.

If not by philosophy, the barons were restrained by their finances. Many of them had purchased their titles at great cost, and had to pay further to maintain them. They had to pay to build and maintain their *palazzi* in condition better than their neighbors', and the expenses for the *palazzi* and *giardini* never stopped. As feudal lords they held their lands in perpetuity, but they did not own them outright and so could not sell them. They had to have some sort of dwelling on their fief, which they were obliged to maintain as well as their *palazzo* in the city — or if not as well as, in addition to. They felt obliged to keep the property secure for their sons.

Only members of the baronial class or of religious orders had a political voice. The commercial classes, weak both in capital and in social esteem, depended on cities, and a city belonged either to a baron (who was sometimes a bishop) or to the king. Without franchise, Sicily's urban residents had no say in their governance and no locus for collective proceedings. In other regions of Europe, including northern Italy, autonomous cities were common and members of the upper classes, with visions beyond cities, were leading their people into national consciousness. This, no longer a new development, seemed likely to affect all peoples sooner or later.

Sicily's barons opted for later; generation after generation, they contented themselves with the status quo, and they were able to get away with it. This, more than anything else, distinguished Sicily from most of Western Europe. If, as was sometimes brought to the barons' attention, they used their lands inefficiently and they strangled the towns, why should they bother about it? They expressed no concern that the world was moving on and they no longer fit well in it.

THE BARONS' OCCUPATIONS

The feudal grant, which was the ultimate source of the baron's wealth, obligated him to serve with his horse in the king's wars.

Should the Spanish realm suffer an invasion or a major rebellion, the barons of Sicily had specifically to provide troops to a maximum of sixteen hundred knights, to serve without pay for the first three months and then to receive a stipend. But as feudalism declined generally and as gunpowder came into use, the conditions of the military changed, giving rise to Sicilian-Spanish conflicts on such matters as the necessity of a particular callup, whether an experienced soldier might be considered equivalent to a man and his horse, and the number of fighting men (even drum majors) required.

For local needs Sicily had a militia, more theoretical than active. Sicilians didn't relish military service, and the Spanish were inclined to reject them anyhow as too undisciplined. On the same grounds the Spanish didn't want Sicilians in the administration, objecting that they were too lazy or that they spent all their time seeking favors for their relatives. The barons might have disproved those charges by becoming successful in other fields, but they hardly ever tried.

Trade, for instance, provided ample opportunity that the barons didn't seize. Just as Sicily's Christians had never replaced the Muslims in agriculture, they never entered the commercial sector in which the Jews had predominated. What remained of Sicilian commerce was largely in the hands of northern Italians and English. Few Sicilians went to sea as international traders or as sailors. Nor, when Spain and Portugal were discovering new worlds and northern Italians were exploring the seas for different nations, did Sicilians take part. Descendants of Greeks, Phoenicians, Catalans — some of the finest seamen and traders the world has ever known — the barons would not have stooped to a maritime career.

GABELLOTI
They didn't even work on their lands; some barons lived long lives without ever visiting their feudi. To be sure, most barons would have been useless, as they knew neither agriculture nor accounting. Starting around 1600 and increasingly through the seventeenth cen-

tury, the feudal barons hired managers for their lands. Called a *gabelloto* — the word derives from *gabello* ("tax collector") — the manager was a member of rural Sicily's small middle class who might have risen from the peasantry, or descended from the nobility, or be a foreigner. Yet as *gabelloto* he enjoyed supreme power over the estate he managed.

No more than the barons did the *gabelloti* concern themselves with future or even present productivity. Such profits as were seen on the fiefs went into *gabelloti* pockets, not into investments for the land. *Gabelloti* didn't bother with irrigation. They cut down young trees for firewood, and they neglected olives, citrus fruits, and even grapes. Grain grew virtually by itself, so they let it grow wherever possible, and they had the peasants harvest it.

The *gabelloti* exerted their power essentially by controlling the peasants' access to land. The feudal system of minimal security for the loyal peasant gave way to a ruthless serfdom. The *gabelloti* attracted the peasants by offering contracts of four or five years, then gradually they decreased the term of contract to a single year. They continually threatened the peasants with nonrenewal, and by carrying out those threats they gave rise to a class of landless peasants forced to toil in the fields as day labor. The shorter the contract, the less anyone cared about what was good for the land.

Gabelloti were characterized by ambition to join the aristocracy, to which end they needed to amass fortunes far more quickly than anyone could accomplish through agriculture. They administered the barons' tribunals, and when the law seemed inadequate for their purposes they resorted to violence. They victimized their employers, demanding a third to a half of the estate's profits as their fee for managing it, and even then they delayed payment of the rest. Not infrequently the *gabelloti* allied themselves with bandit gangs, providing them with refuge or employing the gangs as their own security force. Gangster tactics often won the *gabelloti* great fortunes and brought them to positions of power over the feudal lords. In the anarchic Sicilian interior, the *gabelloti* could act with impunity.

CITIES

The warlike conditions of the interior gave the barons an additional reason, if one was needed, not to go there. It was enough reason that, for centuries now, the interior had been primitive. Improvements in Sicilian rural life had been few and far between, as the products of rural areas were taken to the cities to be sold, and the income from them was spent entirely in the cities.

Catania, which the Aragonese had made their Sicilian capital and an important city, lost her significance once Aragon merged into Spain. As soon as Spain absorbed Sicily into its empire and transferred the capital to Palermo, the only cities vying for Sicilian primacy were Palermo and Messina.

Palermo was the barons' city par excellence. Here they disported themselves, flaunting their titles and estates. Ever since the Normans, each ruling house coming to Sicily from abroad had granted lands and titles to its favorites. When that royal house was ousted its officials departed, but many of its land barons remained. Not all landholders were nobles, but those who weren't were striving to become so. As in much of Europe, buying a title wasn't difficult if one had the money. Nobility required a large, elegant dwelling, so the aspirants also needed one, in Palermo *comme il faut*. Spain's capital in Sicily grew during the 1500s into one of the largest and most attractive cities of the vast empire.

The viceroy Maqueda commissioned a new street that was to culminate in a small square embellished with strikingly Spanish architectural detail; via Maqueda became the main street of Sicily's barons.* The church too exhibited its Sicilian wealth in Palermo, where religious orders outdid themselves in constructing sumptuous churches and monasteries around the city. In the first half of the 1600s the bishops and the barons carried on a lively competition to produce the most costly, elegant structures.

The Spanish called Palermo a beautiful city, but that adjective

---

* Maqueda was viceroy only from 1598 to 1601; the street was named Maqueda after his untimely death, they say from a disease caught while he was engaged in the slave trade.

could be applied only to the baronial and monastic quarters. Most of Palermo's inhabitants lived in miserable hovels, in filthy, smelly alleyways. Although the barons refused to risk the dangers around their feudal estates, they made their homes in a city where armed robberies and murderous feuds were commonplace. In this capital of a country famed for its agriculture, a key city of an immensely wealthy empire, criminals abounded because the populace frequently went hungry. Corruption led to the lack of grain reserves. In the mid-1640s Palermo (and other coastal cities) reduced the quality of bread and fixed the price of it, and prohibited ships carrying food from leaving ports.

In 1647 the barons were up in arms particularly about Sicily's militia, though they were also unhappy about the flourishing *gabelloti* and the degenerating Spanish. (Spain, fast dissipating its riches from America, reduced its spending in Sicily.) A hungry populace quickly joined barons in rebellion. The marshalling of men to riot occurred particularly in Palermo because that's where the barons were. Riots depended on a mass of wrathful men but also needed barons with cooler heads to lead them. This was a period of rebellion in Europe generally, a situation that would have been known in Sicily only to the upper classes.

Consequent to the 1647 riot, in the 1651 Parlamento the barons complained about having to do military service without pay, noting particularly the high costs involved in preparing a horse for battle. They asked that their obligation to supply knights with horses be reduced by a sixth. They also wanted to reduce the obligation for men for the infantry; they objected that fighting men were being employed as sailors and suggested ways of limiting the practice.

∞

The Spanish had quashed the 1647 Palermo riot with the help of Messina. One would expect rivalry between Sicily's two major cities, the political capital and the commercial capital.

Owing to her unique geographic situation, Messina was almost an independent city-state. Used to special privileges from the time of Henry VI and more entrepreneurial than other Sicilian cities, Messina argued from a position of economic strength: her port at times earned half the income of all Sicily's ports, and her silk was also a major source of revenue for Sicily. Messina clung tenaciously to her monopoly of Sicily's raw and manufactured silk. Supplementary businesses such as shipping agents and banks established their Sicilian branches in Messina. Foreigners predominated in the city's commerce. If the wealthy in most of Sicily scorned work, the mercantile aristocracy of Messina relished it. The other Sicilian cities hated Messina.

Nor did the viceroys like the city. Messina kept petitioning to house the viceroy's court at least part of the year, in vain. Largely over this issue of administration — and corresponding revenue — Messina rebelled against the Spanish in 1674. The city refused to admit Spanish soldiers and executed some of their local supporters. Prepared to go to war, Messina sought help from France, rather desperately, as at this time France was Messina's main rival in the silk trade. Messina made contact too with the English nobility, presumptuously offering to the king's bastard son the crown of Sicily. On this issue though the English and the French were allies and unwilling to help Messina; the rebellion was put down by French troops. Messina suffered severe war damage, then was punished by military occupation, tax discrimination, and the loss of her silk monopoly and of her university.

Palermo, twenty years after the riot, was still suffering. At the worst moments, as in 1671, Palermo rationed bread and limited it to city residents. A dozen years later, in an attempt to rationalize the grain market on a more permanent basis, the city established an agency with complete control over the buying and selling of grain and the selling of bread. Even the baking of bread at home for family consumption was prohibited; such was the threat of starvation in Palermo that the populace hardly objected to the severe controls.

Sicily's general situation was so bad that even the barons suffered. Their occupation of redistributing lands made no contribution to the cities' assets nor, collectively, to their own. Revenues from their lands, like the lands themselves, were drying up. Although they paid very little tax, they were often in debt, to the point that some of them borrowed from their *gabelloti*. Getting a job was seldom an option:

in a country like Sicily under foreign rule, most respectable jobs went to compatriots of the ruler.

Barons who could still afford it left Sicily's despair and violence to live in Naples or Spain. Although in Sicily's cities, thanks to the Jesuits, even nonwealthy boys might get some schooling, Sicilians of talent and energy who wanted to make a career were still obliged to go abroad. Among the emigrants, lovers of baroque music will recognize Alessandro Scarlatti, born in Palermo in 1660, who at age nineteen departed to join musical circles in Rome.

Outside the big cities, food shortages were naturally less common. Some smaller cities were prospering. Trapani, the port closest to Iberia, flourished from the advent of the Aragonese and was now unquestionably a major shipping hub. English goods were sold to such an extent in Trapani that the English had a consul there as well as at Messina. A particular alliance existed between Trapani and Messina, aimed at countering the power of Palermo.

Across the island from Palermo, some barons were experimenting in city management. Caltagirone was thriving under the Genovesi who had dominated this area for centuries. Here the nobles — they called themselves "gentlemen" — assured themselves the control of the city by getting the king to sell them the exclusive right to administer her. Further southeast, the barons of Siracusa limited city administration to those families whose title went back at least two centuries.

EARTHQUAKE OF 1693

Lineage was no help against the catastrophe that brought southeast Sicily to world attention. On the afternoon of Sunday, January 11, 1693, a major earthquake struck. As the area experienced seismic activity occasionally, a quake two days earlier had sent only a few people running from their homes into the cold countryside to avoid the collapse of buildings; but those who did flee were more likely to survive what followed. In the corner of Sicily extending to Catania and Gela, some sixty thousand people died. Shocks were felt as far north as Lipari and as far south as Malta.

The broken earth swallowed people, animals, and rivers. Etna erupted violently, and immense waves swept coastal localities into the sea. Some twenty-five towns turned into piles of rubble, and at least as many suffered lesser but serious damage. About a third of Sicily, approximating the Val di Noto, would need massive reconstruction.

Barons throughout the afflicted area commissioned an orgy of building. Forty kilometers north of the earthquake's epicenter at Modica, the town of Occhiolà lost half her people; three months after the quake, the first cornerstone was laid in a replacement town two kilometers to the south, to be called Grammichele. The prince offered survivors from Occhiolà and nearby communities free building lots on the condition that they build in accord with the new town's hexagonal street plan. Thirty kilometers east of Modica, the survivors at Noto decided not to clear up their debris but to resettle at a new site an hour's walk southeast. Grammichele and Noto would become famous for their urban layouts, among the designs of architects who swarmed to the area from Italy and beyond. In most towns a shortage of money aggravated the usual inertia to delay the implementation of plans.

✐

The earthquake came as a crashing coda to one of Sicily's worst centuries. The European expansion across the Atlantic changed the Mediterranean into a backwater. Sicily's crops lost to new competition; for example, in Latin America's warmer climate the sugarcane grew higher than in Sicily. Other traditional money-earners suffered because Sicily failed to modernize: exports as different as sulfur and silk saw reduced markets because other countries could produce and transport at lower cost. Sicily wasn't even making its own basic wearing apparel, because England manufactured vast quantities of cloth and clothing and insisted on having Sicily as a sellers' market for them.

Summary of Spanish Rule
Sicilians were not the only European people to experience natural catastrophes and foreign rule and competition from larger countries,

MAP 14. Modern Sicily, from 1300

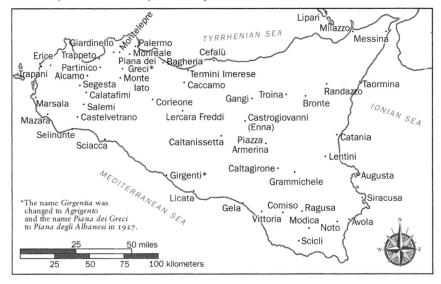

nor even the Inquisition and religious wars. Sicily suffered particularly from being mired in a feudalism facilitated by its economic base and accepted by its sovereigns. In Sicily's every sector, advances were obstructed by infighting, either by the barons who wanted no economic development at all or by the cities who favored it for themselves but not for other cities.

The three-cornered island with its three major cities was milked dry by the three dominant groups of barons, clergy, and Spanish. Relations between them varied over time, but they all benefitted by a passive populace. Once in every generation, roughly, barons roused peasants from their resignation to fight for the barons' particular objectives. In other countries members of the upper classes sometimes offered themselves as leaders for political change, but none did so in Sicily; they were too intent on maintaining their status. Elsewhere the military helped to develop discipline, leadership, and a sense of patriotism, but Sicily lacked a cohesive military body. A Sicilian identity might have grown had the Spanish kings been wicked despots, but, regarding Sicily, they were just indifferent. The Spanish crown was too distant, too abstract, to arouse Sicilians' enmity; insurgents directed their ire not against the king but against the viceroy and his policies.

It had been like that ever since 1282, the moment when resentment in Palermo against the French officers erupted into an island-wide revolt against the king. Nothing similar to the Vespers took place again. Under the Spanish, the Sicilians' resentment did occasionally boil and explode into violence in some city or town, but these riots hardly ever ignited the fury in smaller localities or inland, because of the limited roads and learning. So long as the rebellion didn't spread, the Spanish could put it down. The brutal repression of any militant protest was meant to discourage other rebellion, and it succeeded in that aim.

THE SPANISH LOSE SICILY

In 1700 Charles II, king of Spain, Naples, and Sicily, died childless. The French, waiting for such a moment to gain control of the Spanish empire, had persuaded him to name as his heir the grandson of the French king Louis XIV, young Philip, duke of Anjou. The Sicilians' proudest moment had been their Vespers uprising against Charles of Anjou, start of a struggle to end Angevin rule of Sicily forever. After a four-century hiatus, a duke of Anjou came to the Spanish throne as the first of the Bourbon dynasty.

The Sicilians were spared by the English and Dutch, who went to war (the War of the Spanish Succession) to prevent a union of France with Spain. In Sicily the Bourbons had not yet installed any military force, and the few soldiers on the island were presumably loyal to the Spanish Hapsburgs, so when Hapsburg Austria threatened to invade the now–French Bourbon Sicily, there was a scramble about who was to defend the island. Internecine battles erupted over who had the right to fight from Palermo's bastions, over the use of defense funds for private purposes, over who would protect the honor of Sicilian women in houses where foreign soldiers might be billeted. Accusations flew about locals spying on behalf of the English or the French. The guilds fought among themselves and against the nobles. Some of the nobles escaped the fray by retiring to their country estates. Officials joined them, leaving Palermo ungoverned.

For the Palermitan populace and the bands of peasants attracted from the countryside, the high point of the war was their rioting of May–June 1708. Houses were looted and food shops closed; beyond that, some of Palermo's foreign residents were murdered and their heads impaled. When Philip sent in Irish troops to crush the rebellion, he inspired further hatred. Meanwhile ships of a few countries lay in Sicilian waters — the French decided not to intervene, the English off Sicily's southwest coast once bombarded Mazara. But everything considered, the island suffered little physical damage and eventually settled down.

The European powers continued their war a while longer, the major participants France and Spain on one side and virtually the rest of Europe on the other. Savoy, a dukedom where today's Italy borders on France, was first allied with France and Spain, for the duke of Savoy had relatives in both, indeed his daughter Marie-Louise was married to the Angevin-Bourbon Philip who was Spain's king. But then the duke of Savoy changed to the English side and fought usefully until they won the war. England and its allies could now deprive Spain of its Mediterranean possessions. The Austrians, having obtained Naples, wanted to join Sicily to that realm. But England insisted that Sicily be ruled by a house too small to threaten England's commerce (which really meant the English wanted Sicily under its control). The victors agreed to reward the House of Savoy for its wartime shift of alliance. Having taken Sicily from Spain's Philip, in June 1713 they gave it to the duke of Savoy, his father-in-law.

TRANSITION
A Break from the Spanish (1713–1734)

SAVOY (1713–20)

Victor Amadeus II, Savoy's autocratic ruler, never expected to be a king. He made it clear when awarded Sicily that he didn't really want such a distant land, and especially not one reputed to be difficult to govern. But he was already forty-seven years old, and offers of king-ship don't come every day. Intelligent and industrious by nature, he rushed to prove himself a king worthy of the title.

Arranging for his trip, he learned that his new kingdom had no modern ships. Two centuries after the Genovese Columbus had crossed the Atlantic Ocean, the best of Sicily's ships could barely reach Genoa. He ordered a large sailing ship to be constructed in England so that Sicilians might use it as a model for building more. Meanwhile in October 1713 Victor Amadeus sailed to Sicily in an English ship with his household and with cash to buttress Sicily's treasury, escorted by other English ships with thousands of soldiers.

The king, subsidized by the British, applied himself to his new job as though he were an American efficiency expert. His patrons told him that their first priority would be the establishment of law and order, for pervasive criminality was ruining his kingdom and English commerce with it. The king already knew this and acted on it by punishing corrupt nobles. To diagnose and strengthen the Sicilian economy, he brought from the north a small army of technical specialists, financial experts, and skilled workers. He had them compile lists of infrastructure so that every street and bridge might be maintained. He undertook to modernize the arsenal at Palermo, funded new professors for the University of Catania, and restored some of the old privileges to Messina. He considered how best to reduce the size of a bureaucracy so swollen as to be ineffective.

Realizing that change arouses ire, he endeavored to placate the aristocracy by giving administrative jobs to vetted nobles and by not moving against baronial privilege. Although aware that the whole system of taxation needed overhaul, for starters he confined his measures to reducing outright fraud.

It was reported to him that too few men worked in the fields, a consequence of the miserable conditions the *gabelloti* imposed on their peasants; as the king learned about the situation, he decided that in due course he would require the Sicilian landowners to use with their peasants the contract used in his Savoy duchy. Nor could he do much in the short run about the barons' huge landholdings left partly uncultivated, but he decreed new measures to inhibit further consolidation of lands. Meanwhile he encouraged the use of local products to manufacture wool cloth and paper. He interested himself in irrigation, in fruit trees, and in animal husbandry. In September 1714, he ordered a census of the people (the count came to 1,135,000) and their income and animals.

Victor Amadeus II, the first king of Sicily to visit his realm in 180 years, made the rounds of the coastal cities. His subjects saw him not in royal silks but in working clothes of dull wool and serious boots. His choice of attire symbolized his first year as king in Sicily.

There was no second year. To deal with changes in European politics, the king went back to Savoy in September 1714 and delegated rule of Sicily to a council in Turin. The council in turn sent northerners to Sicily to improve the administration and the military, and they in fact implemented his policies.

The people who counted in Sicily resented the foreign functionaries who told them what to do. During the centuries under Spain, the Sicilian barons had in effect ruled Sicily, and they wanted to continue doing so without interference. They decried the king as insufficiently regal, and, principally, they feared that his projects would saddle them with higher prices and higher taxes. The nobles really wanted royalty just to provide pomp and parties, but Savoy was much too small to do that in the manner to which they had become accustomed under the Spanish. In short, the Sicilian barons did not appreciate their hardworking Savoy prince.

Sicilian aristocrats had long taken vicarious pleasure in the role of the Sicilian king as papal legate; they felt it connected them in a special way to the Vatican. When Lipari officially became part of Sicily in 1609, nothing was said about whether the apostolic rights would extend to the little archipelago, and the matter was forgotten for a century. Then some bureaucrat imposed a duty on beans being delivered to Lipari's bishop. As the bishop was tax-exempt, he did not have to pay, and he received an immediate official apology. Out of this trifle the bishop chose to make a case, supported by the pope.

These events occurred a couple of years before Victor Amadeus came to power, but once in Sicily he found himself involved. The pope declared that no king would be papal legate without asking the pope to install him according to feudal tradition, but Victor Amadeus preferred feud to feudality. Too modern for such rigmarole and already fighting the pope on other fronts, he countered that papal decrees, such as excommunications, would be null in Sicily unless royally confirmed. In this bloodless battle those priests who supported the king were excommunicated, and those priests who supported the pope were imprisoned or exiled. King and pope proclaimed that Sicilians need not obey the other. Religious life came to a standstill, which angered the mass of Sicilians.

The disenchantment was mutual. Trying to exchange his Sicilian kingdom for a more congenial one, Victor Amadeus embroiled Sicily in a conflict between Spain and Austria. He could not have foreseen its developing into Sicily's worst war since ancient times. Throughout 1719 the armies of Spain and Austria fought brutally all over the island. They razed suburbs around Palermo and refrained from fighting in the city only when paid huge sums. They ravaged the fields behind Marsala and Messina. Austria emerged victorious thanks to the naval support of Britain. The retreating Spanish forces followed a "scorched earth" policy, burning trees and carrying off animals. The Austrian ruler, Hapsburg emperor Charles VI, was now king over a million Sicilians and their devastated land.

HAPSBURG AUSTRIA (1720–34)

Nature would in due course return the land to productivity, and then the Austrians would have their turn to take Sicily's excess wheat and its olives turned into oil. Determined to increase yields on the island, the new rulers planned economic reforms similar to those of Victor Amadeus. More than he, though, they appreciated that the whole island was controlled by, and bled by, a few dozen baronial families whose support they would need if they were to effect changes.

That support would not be won easily. The Sicilians who cared who ruled them didn't want Sicily rejoined to Naples, didn't want still another foreign king, and didn't want officials who spoke no Sicilian. They showed their distress by rejecting the first Austrian viceroy, ostensibly because he flouted religion — he lived apart from his wife and employed some non-Catholic functionaries.

Yet the Sicilians acquiesced when the Austrians defied Catholic tradition by opening negotiations with Muslims, about the corsairs. This engagement helped reassure Sicilians who thought the Austrians too removed from problems in the Mediterranean. To provide reassurance vis-à-vis religion, the Austrians manifested their Christianity by reviving the Inquisition and by seeking reconciliation with the Vatican; relations were reestablished in 1728.

In the cultural sphere the Austrians satisfied one of the barons' perennial requests by opening and financing a school for the young nobility. In another attempt to improve the aristocracy, namely by bringing new blood into it, and at the same time to gratify barons on a personal level, the Austrians handed out titles lavishly; in consequence fewer men were prepared to buy titles, which meant a significant reduction in government revenues. The new rulers courted the barons while struggling to apply fiscal measures adequate and fair.

The Austrians set out to augment revenue from grain by increasing the price of the export licenses and requiring Sicilian merchants to buy the licenses at the new price. But the higher costs of export drove merchants to abandon Sicilian ports for foreign, and after good harvests grain piled up in Sicilian storage. Sicily's grain consumed domestically was still a major source of royal revenue through the *macinato*, the tax on milling. Hardest to evade, this tax was the most regressive. When the Austrians tried to shift the tax burden away from the poorest Sicilians, they met with the barons' intransigence.

As they had under Spanish rule, Sicily's barons rebuffed economic development generally. The Muslims had long ago taught Sicilians to raise sugarcane, and since then the Sicilians shipped sugar intermittently to northern Europe. Aware of the new suppliers in the western hemisphere, the Austrians realized that Sicily's sugarcane fields needed modern equipment and techniques if they were to compete. Officials were ready to impose a duty on imported sugar, with the dual aim of protecting the industry and of raising the funds to modernize the refineries. But on hearing of the sugar tax Sicilian aristocrats, grown accustomed to drinks and sherbets made with sugar, raised Cain. By winning the battle, they killed off Sicily's sugar industry.

Sicily's soil was known to contain significant amounts of sulfur and some alum (used for tanning and dyeing). Recent rulers had dreamed of ways to get the mines going again. Now the Austrians established a Sicilian bureau with authority to mine on private property. They brought in engineers and skilled labor from their lands in Hungary and eastern Germany. But the Sicilian feudal lords discouraged the operation by arousing the local populace against the foreigners.

Likewise the Austrians projected workshops for silk in Palermo and Messina, in response to Messina's demand to reestablish the silk industry there. Messina had lost her silk industry fifty years before, in the wake of her rebellion, and with the change of sovereignty she hoped for a return to her ancient economic position. The Austrians heeded, because Sicily's silk industry was moribund: it exported only some raw silk, not yet spun into thread, while Sicilians were spending money abroad for silk cloth and silk garments because those produced in Sicily were of poor quality and priced too high. The skilled silk workers had died off; to restore the industry the Austrians agreed to import replacements. As Jews were famous for weaving silk of high quality, the Austrians consented when Messina wanted to facilitate Jews' living there; but the idea came to naught due to objections of the resurrected Inquisition. Messina further implored the Austrians to reinstate her monopoly on the export of silk. Palermo would have none of that, and Catania voiced objections. As a result, time and effort that could have been spent in developing a silk industry for Sicily were wasted in fighting out Sicilian intercity rivalries in the Austrian court.

∽

As they opposed Austria's projects, the barons strengthened their political voice. When the Austrian rule started in 1720, the Sicilian barons who had known the good and lazy life under the Spanish were past their prime. Their sons, coming to maturity, showed a greater interest in politics and economics, as did those recently ennobled by the Austrians. Lines blurred between the old nobility and newcomers whose fathers had risen through their own efforts. In a parallel movement toward modern times, Austrian rule took more account of parliament than had Spanish, and around 1730 half the barons were taking part in parliamentary discussions. It all heralded baronial leadership.

Early in 1733 the Polish king Frederick Augustus died. That sounds quite irrelevant to Sicily, but the consequent War of the Polish Succession returned Sicily to Spain, now Bourbon Spain. The political growth of Sicily's barons was nipped in the bud.

~9~

BOURBONS

It was as though, after four centuries of living with Spanish rule, the Sicilians had taken a vacation with Savoy and Austria and then gone back home. Even during the intervening thirty-three years, Spanish influence on Sicily remained strong.

Europe had entered the period the historians call "modern," but the term seemed hardly applicable to Sicily. Every aspect of Sicilian life, from sovereignty to scholarship to sulfur mining, appeared primitive to the foreigners who came, saw, and compared.

The Bourbon Spanish taking up official positions in southeast Sicily saw the aftermath of the 1693 earthquake. Modica, the epicenter, Scicli halfway to the south coast, and parts of Catania now boasted magnificent religious and public buildings in the contemporary baroque style. Obliged by the earthquake damage to renovate her old Greek temple of Athena for the nth time, Siracusa gave it a baroque facade. On the other hand, Ragusa, twenty kilometers north of Modica, had come close to war between her old class of land barons who wanted to restore their old urban center and the newer aristocrats who wanted a new urban center built on a neighboring hill. In 1733, forty years after the earthquake, the building of the new center had barely begun.

THE NOBILITY

Concurrently, for different reasons, Palermo and its environs also experienced a building boom. Still the capital city, Palermo as Sicily's administrative and amusement center was where the wealthy wanted to live. The city kept expanding because there were lots of barons, at this time around two thousand of them, the highest incidence in Europe. The Sicilian capital was reputed to have more private palaces than any other city in Europe — and to have the greatest number of palaces whose owners suffered chronic debt.

The *nouveaux nobles* were an embarrassment to those of hereditary wealth. The inherited possession of luxurious furnishings and legions of slaves and servants no longer served to distinguish old money from riffraff. As a showcase for their superiority, families of great wealth and ancient pedigree built themselves fancy second homes outside of Palermo. Bagheria, on the coast fifteen kilometers east of Palermo, developed as a town of second homes for Palermo's nobility. Some houses here with beautiful baroque facades long remained empty because their owners couldn't afford to furnish them.

Contemporary writers (themselves of the upper class) said that Sicily's barons lacked skills and lacked guts, that they dedicated their lives to partying, gambling, and sucking up to their rulers. This generalizes too much, of course. The doctors, lawyers, and scholars all came from the baronial class. Urban beauty was conceived and commissioned entirely by the barons. To acquire the money necessary to purchase titles and houses, in a world only partially monetized, required perseverance and political skill.

Especially, through a variety of machinations, the barons kept their tax bills very low. In Parlamento they acquiesced in the king's levies, then assessed higher per capita taxes on royal towns than on feudal towns. The barons arranged that those who resided in Palermo would not be subject to tax in other cities, even on property they held in those other cities: reason enough for all barons to maintain a residence in Palermo.

This economic benefit accrued to the entire baronial class, and within that class the few barons selected for a parliament enjoyed high social status. They vaunted their participation in the ancient body and liked to imagine themselves sharing in government with the king, though Parlamento still had little money under its control and no legislative power. Even petitioning the king on serious matters such as defense or transport was something the parliamentarians rarely did. It behooved them to confine their requests to matters of protocol and to treat the parliamentary sessions as social occasions. Earlier in the century King Victor Amadeus complained that the parliamentarians gave most of their attention during the short sessions to eating sweets: he dubbed them his "ice cream parliament."

KINGS CARLO AND FERDINAND III

The new king of Naples and Sicily, heir to the Spanish throne, sailed in March 1735 into Messina. He was met by the locals' objections to his choosing Palermo for his coronation, even though tradition obliged him to receive his crown there. Soon the Palermitani were attending the banquets and balls of the new king, who was known variously as Charles or Carlos or Carlo, reflecting his French-Spanish-Italian connections. If the cosmopolitanism had no meaning for the ordinary Palermitani, the royal celebrations did bring them coins and free meals. Under Savoy and Austria the previous generation had missed out on Spanish pomp and parties, and now they reveled in them and looked forward to more. How disappointed they were when the new king left Palermo shortly after his crowning ceremony.

From his capital at Naples, King Carlo established a bureau, a *giunta*, for the governing of Sicily even in day-to-day affairs. To head the *giunta* he named one of the island's wealthiest barons, the prince of Palagonia. Lesser Sicilian barons, happily back in the Spanish fold, anticipated a return to their pre-Savoy world where no one tried to impose progress.

The barons soon learned (in a phrase not yet a cliché) you can't go home again. They recollected earlier Spanish rule as beneficent, following from Spain's immense wealth and power. More accurately, at a time when Spanish interests lay overwhelmingly in America, the viceroys were not pressured to make Sicily remunerative for the crown, so viceroys and barons were left free to fill their own purses. By the time Sicily returned to Spanish rule in 1735, Spain had squandered its gold and now required each part of its empire to contribute to the Spanish coffers.

King Carlo wanted to mitigate Sicily's poverty. Like his predecessors of Savoy and Austria, he aimed to increase grain production by employing lands and workers more efficiently than did the contemporary feudalism. A more modern agriculture would increase Sicily's income, with the dual benefit of adding to the royal revenues and improving the lot of the ordinary Sicilian.

The barons, for their part, cared only about the extent of their lands; they cared nothing about productivity. They were feudal lords and intended to remain so; their revenues depended on a submissive populace. By now the barons possessed about three-fourths of the villages in Sicily and a higher proportion of the peasants. The bigger barons who lived in the cities dominated the smaller ones, often their kin, who lived in the villages on the feudal estates and shared local power. The baronial class was a network of power that pressed the Bourbon *giunta* into its service.

FEUDALISM

Though Sicily's feudalism was now anachronistic, it wouldn't have lasted seven hundred years without providing some advantages for someone. For one thing, its hierarchy was well defined, and able men knew how to climb the ladder into the aristocracy. The upper rungs could expand without any churning of the social order. Those successful within this system naturally saw no reason for change. When change threatened, they tightened their hold on their property (including peasants) and they used lawyers to protect their interests.

In Naples, King Carlo succeeded in reducing the amount of land held feudally. The Sicilian lawyers' job was to defend the feudalistic status quo; during the 1740s, they argued successfully that any land once granted as *feudo* was to remain so forever, and that the king, barring exceptional cases, had no right to confiscate it. The land was a private possession of the lord, and even if the dwellers on that land wanted to buy their way out of feudalism, they could not legally do so. Yet barons had the right to take back land from peasants; this was confirmed in a law of 1752.

Although barred from selling their feudal lands, the barons could otherwise act with impunity. For example, a peasant needing cash would have nowhere to go except to his lord, who would lend it at high interest. Toward the end of the 1600s the Spanish had tried to temper this particular exploitation by providing peasants with a source of cheaper agricultural credit, but since then the barons commonly refused to rent land to a peasant unless he foreswore to borrow from anyone other than the lord. The Bourbon functionaries, for the most part, viewed the world as the barons did. In cases where an official entertained ideas about greater productivity or humanity, he wasn't able to do much. When a baron entertained such ideas — and some did — he didn't broadcast them. Class loyalty prevailed, or else fear of being silenced.

During the twenty-five years that Carlo ruled Sicily, the barons controlled every aspect of Sicilian life. It happened to be a prosperous period in Sicily, but improvement in a region's general economic situation often does nothing to improve the standard of living of its poor. The barons still held most of the land, and if a peasant wanted to keep eating he would have to do as his lord wished. The lord wanted the peasants in his fields, uncomplaining, too fatigued and ignorant even to dream of a better life. When King Carlo left Naples to rule Spain, he made such improvements in the economy and in administration there that he is considered the greatest of the Bourbons. But during his rule of Sicily he couldn't overcome the feudal lords' resistance. Naples has good memories of Carlo; to Sicily he was impotent.

GRAIN PRODUCTION AND DISTRIBUTION

In the first years of Bourbon rule, Sicily produced much more grain than needed for domestic consumption. The surplus was sold to traders, almost all of them Genovesi (there were a few Englishmen), who exported it through Termini Imerese and Sciacca.

The dietary staple of most of Europe and the Mediterranean region, wheat is *importantissimo*. As the amount of wheat harvested from a given amount of seed can vary widely from year to year, governments have always made it their business to set aside some of the wheat from the good years to distribute in the bad years, and Sicily did so. Administrators need to insure that reserves of grain are sufficient for local needs before selling any excess grain abroad. For this reason Sicily, like many other countries, required producers of grain to obtain a permit before exporting any of their product.

Wheat's importance in the diets of Sicily's trading partners made the control of wheat a lucrative matter. Wheat was unusual among food products in that in its harvested state it can keep without spoiling for a few years or longer, and this gave its producers options about whether and when to sell it. Speculation ran rife.

Sicily's rules required every wheat producer to deposit two-thirds of his crop in government storage; then after the administrators had calculated the total amount of wheat in storage and the amount of it needed for reserves and for next year's seed, they would determine the amount available for export, if any. In case of availability, anyone willing to pay the fee could apply for a license to export a certain quantity of this wheat. The fee varied each year in accord with quantities and market conditions. That gave those few dealers with large reserves of money the chance to buy licenses corresponding to the entire amount of grain for export and then resell them to smaller exporters for what the traffic would bear. In effect, the law required wheat producers to yield two-thirds of their crop to urban moneymen.

Some northern countries, for whom export trade was as important as it was in Sicily, crafted policies (called mercantilism) that encouraged the export of products so they would bring in revenue from abroad;

Sicily taxed and thus discouraged export. Its system of export tariffs actually meant monetary loss for Sicily, due to grain not exported at all or not officially exported. It was absurdly inefficient. But efficiency wasn't the Sicilian way.

The system stimulated corruption, such as wheat producers smuggling their grain out of Sicily and administrators demanding bribes of anyone applying for a permit. It transpired that in some years illegal exports of grain exceeded legal. In this environment officials were paid to disregard the need for reserves.

So government grain policy was dirty, even in good times. Then, as the century advanced and King Carlo aged, the excess wheat production diminished and less grain reached the cities. This was the barons' fault. To them could be traced the sheer lack of interest on the part of whoever was running the farming operations. Directly the barons were responsible in that during their good times they purchased more and more land rather than making improvements on the parcels cultivated by their ancestors. That brought land into cultivation which was less suitable for cultivation and was more distant from the coasts, raising costs of providing food for the cities and for export.

NEED FOR REFORM

Grain production was declining in a period when Sicily's population was rapidly increasing; Sicily's residents numbered about 1.1 million in 1700, 1.3 million at mid-century, and 1.7 million by 1800. The poor management of the fields and the brutality with which peasants were treated led to the abandonment of villages, in turn causing massive internal migration and vagrancy, and then higher food prices, starvation, and disease in the cities. When peasants, egged on by the barons for political reasons, invaded the cities in 1763, officials felt obliged to close city gates to refugees. And though the cities disbursed a lot of money to import food, it was too little or too late for the estimated thirty thousand people who died in the famine.

The problems were obvious to everyone familiar with Sicily, and foreigners, at least, freely suggested improvements: land should be redistributed in smaller parcels, landholders should treat their vassals better, and the government should change its tax structure. As it was, the tax system required the poor to pay for the rich; still the Bourbons kept the regressive *macinato* because, the barons favoring it, it was the easiest tax to collect.

Any worthwhile changes would have to restrict the barons, a tricky matter. As the rules forbid the selling of feudal lands, even getting the barons to pay their debts would be politically impossible — it would bankrupt many of them, thereby weakening the feudal system and the whole social structure that was in turn the foundation of the monarchy. Sicily offered the barons no way to maintain themselves other than their feudal lands and their export manipulations. Few of them had saleable skills.

The occasional schooling, usually by Jesuits, ignored all practicalities, transmitted orthodoxy, and discouraged initiative. King Carlo deplored these values and therefore those who inculcated them. In Sicily virtually every family settled a child or children in the church, much of the barons' debt was incurred to help relatives live a worldly religious life, and church bodies owned a third of all the land. Behind all this, even if not alone, stood the Jesuits, in Sicily and in the rest of the Bourbon empire. Like the barons, the religious contributed too little to the realm, and there were too many of them. Up north some Christian countries had recently evicted their Jesuits, deeming them too powerful, and in 1767 the Bourbons did likewise, expelling the order and expropriating its properties throughout their empire.

The estates of Sicily's Jesuits were earmarked for redistribution as small parcels. But how many peasants could afford to purchase? A few smallholders might have raised some money, but the church threatened to excommunicate anyone who bought the expropriated land. Barons, not easily intimidated, bought up the land in the confiscated large parcels.

∽

The order to expel the Jesuits from all Bourbon lands came from Carlo after he moved to the throne of Spain in 1759. In Naples he left his young son, Ferdinand, to reign over Sicily.* During Ferdinand's minority the regent, Bernardo Tanucci, advanced many of Carlo's modernizing policies, and in due course Ferdinand himself did as well.

For one thing, as the expulsion of the Jesuits had sharply reduced the number of schools in Sicily, the young king ordered the remaining religious to offer boys elementary instruction, and he detailed his edict so as to assure that poor boys could attend without paying — a program never implemented inland and of limited effectiveness in the cities. Having lost her Jesuit scholars, Palermo petitioned King Ferdinand for a university, and he was willing to establish one, but Catania fought successfully against a second university on the island.

Although obliged to employ the religious as elementary teachers, Ferdinand sought to limit the influence of the religious and also their landholdings — for example, by taking from them the remunerative maintenance of cemeteries. In accord with modern principles of sanitation, Ferdinand proposed to establish cemeteries on the outskirts of towns. But the faithful would have none of it, for they believed that the salvation of their souls depended on being buried in a churchyard.

Like his father, Carlo, and the preceding kings, Ferdinand found that his proposals led to continuing battles between government officials and Sicilian barons. As conservatism throttled the reforms, Ferdinand became discouraged, and his liberalism gradually succumbed to the strong reactionary influence of his wife, Marie Caroline, daughter of Holy Roman Emperor Francis I and Maria Theresa, and sister of Queen Marie Antoinette of France.

---

* This is the third of the four King Ferdinands who ruled Sicily. Their numeration is confusing because their realms were not identical and they belonged to different dynasties. This Ferdinand had a reign of exceptional length (b. 1751, reigned 1759–1825).

THE ENLIGHTENMENT REACHES SICILY

CARACCIOLO

While still hopeful of dragging Sicilians into modern Europe, King Ferdinand appointed Domenico Caracciolo as viceroy. Caracciolo had held posts in Turin, Paris, and London; to Palermo in 1781 he went grudgingly. But accepting the professional challenge, he dealt with fundamentals. Bread-making in Sicily had long been restricted to particular bakers (one result being, said Caracciolo, the worst bread he had ever tasted); he threw out the congeries of laws regarding grain and bread, thus permitting anyone to produce and sell them. As catalyst for his employment policy, he brought in German and English merchants and settled them in Messina. Under his direction, attention was finally given to developing the port at Catania, and a botanical garden was inaugurated near the shore at Palermo; banking and postal services were restructured to be more accessible and secure for the public.

In keeping with his king's priorities, Caracciolo first undertook to suppress the Inquisition. For fifty years there had been no burning at the stake, and in recent decades the Inquisition had done little more than harass old witches and homosexuals and the few writers and publishers of books on secular subjects, so the viceroy expected no objection from the laity about terminating it. But some barons screamed bloody murder, for they would lose the revenues and perks that came to them as the Inquisition's lay assistants. In bitter battles, Caracciolo confirmed himself as enemy of the large landowners by terminating their control over local courts, restricting their rights over their peasants, and rationalizing the tax system so that they would finally have to pay their fair share. The small middle class loved him.

In Palermo the small middle class, like the powerful rich and the numerous poor, also loved Santa Rosalia and celebrated her feast in July with a five-day holiday full of processions, music, fireworks, and horse racing. When Viceroy Caracciolo dared to cut the 1785 festival to three days, all classes in Palermo rioted against him, and he was obliged to resign. Like the well-intentioned King Victor Amadeus seventy years earlier, Caracciolo was defeated by the Sicilians' devotion to the trappings of their church. He stands out among the four centuries of Spanish viceroys as one who tried to do some good for Sicily.

MASONS

Some shafts of Enlightenment did pierce the baronial murk. The old European association of Masons, for one thing, actively spread ideas about the new toleration in religion and in politics. Some intellectually adventurous upper-class Sicilians listened to them, evidently, for by Caracciolo's time, the mid-1780s, the Masons had lodges in Palermo, Messina, Catania, and Caltagirone. To attend a Masonic meeting was not a casual matter, given church opposition; a man had to have a bent for independent thinking and a dash of courage. In the Sicilian climate one waxed warm about liberal ideas only among friends. Friends and friends of friends supported each other and in time would affect Sicilian politics.

THE START OF TOURISM

Once the Bourbons began to rule from Naples, the influence of Italy on Sicily grew. Naples was, after all, the largest city on the Italian peninsula, the third largest city in Europe, a capital city in every sense. She transmitted to Sicilian cities Italian conceptions of architecture and literature; also by the 1770s or 1780s Sicily's upper classes had adopted the Italian language. Academies and libraries became a normal part of Sicily's urban scene.

Around this time too Sicily's barons were meeting northern travellers in Naples and in Palermo. Sicily's first tourism can be traced to a resident of Rome who never even set foot in Sicily. Johann Joachim Winckelmann, the son of a German cobbler, became the father of classical archaeology. Between 1754 and 1768 he worked in the Vatican Library, explored the Roman ruins near Naples, and fell in love with ancient Greece. His systematic style of writing about Herculaneum and Pompeii — the first treatises on them — gained him recognition in scholarly circles throughout Europe. The authority and enthusiasm in his *Geschichte der Kunst des Alterthums (History of the Art of Antiquity,* 1764) stirred travellers to visit the remains of earlier civilizations.

While there was nothing new about well-heeled northern Europeans sending their offspring on a Grand Tour of Italy, very few journeyed down into Sicily to marvel at volcanic Etna and to experience that sunny land where oranges and lemons actually grew.

One of these few adventurers, Patrick Brydone, visited Sicily in 1770 and wrote reverently about Mount Etna and the Greek ruins. He delighted too in the ice cream served in several fruit forms and flavors. Attentive, enlightened, and a Mason, Brydone met with local Masons, and also with liberal priests. He sent his journal home as letters, which were soon published.

Sicily's bandits being notorious abroad, Brydone may have wished to reassure his compatriots; he cited an "intelligent long-term resident" who had a different perspective.

> . . . criminal they may be with regard to society in general. . . . The magistrates have often been obliged to protect them, and pay them court, as they are known to be perfectly determined, and desperate, and . . . extremely vindictive; . . . yet, with respect to one another, and to every person to whom they have once professed it, they have ever maintained the most unshaken fidelity. . . . [I]t was never known that any person who had put himself under their protection, and showed that he had confidence in them, had cause to repent of it, or was injured by any of them . . . on the contrary, they will protect him from impositions of every kind, and scorn to go halves with the landlord, like most other conductors and travelling servants; and will defend him with their lives, if there is occasion. . . . [I]n some circumstances, these bandits are the most respectable people of the island.

The books by Winckelmann and Brydone provided an educational motive to venture below Naples. During the rest of the century thousands came from England and France, from Germany and Denmark, to look around Sicily. The ruins at Taormina, Agrigento, and Segesta had always been visible, while at the Roman villa near Piazza Armerina important discoveries were made in 1761. Several other men of influence in their own lands had their journals published, further stimulating travel. Collectively the tourists made a substantial contribution to the Sicilian economy, for which innkeepers and coachmen especially thanked them.

Sicilian aristocrats were thrilled to welcome the foreigners, if only as a new source of diversion and status. Unlettered and intent upon their own constructions, the barons generally knew nothing of their forebears' public works that had survived through two thousand years. Their interest was kindled by the travellers' excitement, so that whenever the language barrier could be crossed the talk turned to Sicily's Greek past. Many barons reached modern Europe by way of Magna Graecia.

GOETHE

Complementarily, the splendid reception they would get in Palermo was well known to travelling classes up north. Among them was that personification of the Enlightenment, Johann Wolfgang von Goethe, thirty-seven years old, a Mason, famous as a writer. Responding to the call of the ancient Greeks, he arrived at the port of Palermo on April 2, 1787, a Monday morning, at eight o'clock . . . and after bureaucratic procedures was allowed to disembark at three in the afternoon. Goethe took it in stride, quite prepared to see Sicilian life as it was really lived. Not that he refrained from constructive criticism.

Goethe could speak enough Italian to make conversation with local storekeepers. In Palermo one day while he was purchasing small items, a sudden wind blew clouds of dust into all the shops.

"My god," Goethe cried, "how can your city have so much dirt? Can't you people find a place to put it?" On this elegant street the shopkeepers kept sweeping the refuse on the sidewalks into piles, and every new breeze carried the refuse onto the horse dung in the middle of the street. Goethe told the shopkeeper about garbage collection in Naples, where all day long donkeys were put to carrying the city's garbage into the fields; then he demanded, "Why can't you people here do something like that?"

"Here that's the way things are," replied the Palermo man. "Whatever we throw out of our houses rots before the door. Just look at that stinking straw, the fruit peels, the leftovers! We do our best to keep things clean — we sweep, but our besoms wear out and finally just become part of the filth in front of our houses."

With his Germanic urge toward efficiency, Goethe kept asking why some collection procedure couldn't be instituted. The shopkeeper shrugged and responded that the men responsible for street-cleaning were powerful, that they received money for cleaning, but no one holds them to using the money for that purpose. "And then there's a rumor," he went on, "just a rumor, mind. Some people say it's the barons who want to keep it like this, so that in the evening when they take their carriage rides the street will be soft and springy." Having gotten started, the Palermitano went on about police corruption.

∾

Goethe had received his *von* of nobility five years before, yet he was hardly an aristocrat like Sicilians thought of aristocrats — Goethe interested himself in the countryside. Within two days of his arrival he remarked on land being left fallow every third year. He went around asking questions about forage and the practicalities of husbandry in an area lacking meadows and therefore hay. Then he realized that there were few horses in the fields, the locals all plowing with oxen; northern Europe had replaced oxen with horses hundreds of years before.

Riding across the plains from Agrigento to Catania so as to see the extensive grain fields, he passed through a "mass of uninterrupted fertility," sown entirely to wheat and barley, without a single tree to be seen; the next day he was "wishing for a winged horse to escape from this monotony." Economists studying the situation would have added something about the scarcity of cattle, for as more land was sown to grain, less land was available for pasture.

To Goethe's party peasants offered food, some familiar to Goethe — which he found succulent — and some not. He was amazed to see some "serious people," with apparent pleasure, eating thistles. Agrigento, once the haughty city of the Greeks, lacked any kind of inn, so Goethe's party rented space with a local family. The girls of the house, cutting and forming pasta, bragged that the pasta from Agrigento was the best, "without equal for whiteness and softness."

Among upper-class people, Sicilian or tourist, Goethe was rare in venturing inland and, it followed, in making contact with peasants. (Goethe was, to be sure, exceptional even at home.) Nonetheless, Sicilians sometimes heard other northerners explaining that they had come to Sicily (all the way to Sicily!) to explore and to learn, an explanation that injected an active element into an environment of indifference. Asked about their homelands, the visitors spoke of the new liberalism sweeping the north, of progress and of governmental responsibility, concepts alien to Sicily. If only for the sake of polite conversation, the Sicilians tried to clarify and defend their own practices. Often Sicilian barons envied the foreigners' wealth and freedom while disapproving of their modern ways.

THE PEASANTS AND LAWLESSNESS

Up north feudalism was dying,* but in Sicily in the late 1700s it was still very much alive. Northerners' reference to better techniques and Bourbons' grant of new facilities were simply irrelevant to the island's interior. The vast majority of Sicilians were living out their short lives in primitive conditions that had not improved (in fact, had probably regressed) since the era of the Normans.

Typically, and perennially vexing, the peasants dwelt far from the

---

* By 1774 only 6 percent of the French population still labored under serfdom (Harry Elmer Barnes, *An Economic History of the Western World* [New York. Harcourt, Brace, 1942] p. 253).

lands they worked. Reasons were three. First, the banditry in the countryside discouraged isolated farmhouses. Second, the lack of rain in summer meant that during the growing season springs were few and far between. Third, most peasants worked the fields of a large landholder, who shifted his peasants around in accord with seasonal or weekly tasks.

The peasants' dwelling in distant villages led to multiple inefficiencies. It precluded the raising of cattle. The women couldn't do fieldwork part-time. The men of some villages slept at home every night, but then they had to spend several hours each day travelling by mule or on foot to the fields and home again. This meant a great loss of time and energy, for one thing. For another, not daring to leave their tools in the empty fields at night, they had to transport them each day, so they were limited to small, primitive tools for use by one individual. The peasant men of other villages lived at the fields during the busy seasons, in huts or barracks if they were lucky, returning to their women only Saturday and Sunday. Goethe mentioned hillside villages near Caltanissetta, in the center of the island, seemingly inhabited only by women. Goethe noted also — as had others — that the horses in the city, employed to draw the carriages of the rich, had their sleeping quarters in brick stalls lined with straw, whereas the field hands sometimes slept outside with no cover whatsoever, targets for disease-carrying insects.

Some mule tracks were such that horses could ply between the coast and the interior; Goethe managed to ride through a long swath of wheat land, but how many Sicilians had Goethe's good health, self-assurance, and purpose? Or a horse? In Goethe's Europe and in North America, horses and wagons wended continually over roads or established paths, and every hamlet could be reached by horse. Not so in Sicily. Coastal areas of course were served by boats, but Sicily's rivers are few and short. Those who lived inland had to walk.

Country folk were cut off from the life of the cities and even of the towns; many a peasant was born on his lord's lands and died there without ever having left them. The rare peasant who farmed his own little plot was obliged to sell his produce to the agent of a baron, for he had no access to any other buyer. The peasant did his fieldwork as he was told, or as his ancestors had been told. He had no way to learn to do anything else. Chances are he had never heard of schools.

He had heard of laws, those of the baron and of the king, those of the church and of the Inquisition. Should anyone have determined to remain law-abiding he would have had to learn these four complicated codes punishing different transgressions. The peasant knew laws and courts as instruments of the barons, meant to work against his class. The violence in his world could be put down, if at all, only by other violence.

The poverty and the legal position of the peasants was not much worse than elsewhere in rural Europe, but the banditry was. Occasionally a viceroy sent soldiers to fight against bandits, of whom some were killed; but the banditry continued as ever. Horse thievery, protection rackets, crimes of honor, kidnaps for ransom — eyed askance by all, and perpetrated by almost all.

In the local scale of values, most admirable was any action against the lords and their system. Most heinous was disloyalty — that is, telling an outsider about the actions of a local person. Called to testify in court, no Sicilian ever admitted to having seen or heard anything at all. He feared the bandits much more than he feared the officers of the king.

Controlling the bandits would have required a strong and engaged central government; such a government had been lacking in Sicily for a donkey's age. Officials in the cities knew little about what was happening inland, and if the topic should come up, the barons made clear that pursuing the internal matters of a *feudo* was not in the officials' best interest. Meanwhile the barons themselves didn't visit their estates, fearing to venture into a roadless backwater teeming with armed bands.

By now the *gabelloti* had made themselves absolute masters of inland Sicily. Even as royal officers attempted to reduce baronial exploitation of peasants, the *gabelloti* pocketed the fees the peasants were forced to pay to grind grain and press olives. The barons' courts were run by *gabelloti* to their own advantage, and among other things used their power to settle old scores. Another kind of justice was rendered by secret societies, with whom the *gabelloti* connived. The government reacted inconsistently, sometimes penalizing *gabelloti* for cooperating with armed gangs, sometimes ignoring the violence and the cooperation, sometimes using the *gabelloti* forces for official purposes. Although in inland Sicily violence was more pervasive than elsewhere in Europe, the Sicilian bandits were doing what bandits have done in every time and place — what was extraordinary was the weakness of the law.

NOBLES AND THE LAW

The many changes of sovereignty had left Sicily with a legal strata as muddled as her archaeological. The complications naturally worked to the benefit of the lawyers. For example, to bring suit it was first necessary to find the court that had jurisdiction — different courts dealt exclusively with nobles or clergy or landowners or businessmen or artisans or foreigners or customs or admiralty. This task by itself was enough to discourage a would-be lay litigant. Once a case reached court, it was sure to drag on for years or decades. Complexities and delays in the legal system led the wealthy too to prefer the efficacy of violence.

For a price one could call on associations in the violence business. Stories grew up around the group called the Beati Paoli, followers of the apostle Paul, if in name only. Supposed to have been in the first half of the eighteenth century as active as the Mafia would be in the twentieth, the Beati Paoli remain a mystery — hardly surprising, for such associations don't like to record their activities, and they operated among a people almost entirely illiterate. Hence the Beati Paoli became the stuff of romance and legend. Certainly they (or colleagues of unknown name) sprouted in soil on which the royal officers of justice never trod, and satisfied the needs for retribution against the worst malefactors and revenge for mere personal affronts. The officials and barons in the cities had enough problems of their own with the legal process, without concerning themselves about inland Sicily's social and economic problems.

Operating to redress local wrongs, the violent ones did not target foreigners. Their acts did keep some grain buyers from trading in Sicily. Other foreign businessmen feared less for their lives than for their sanity, as they endeavored to purchase crops and arrange contracts in the Sicilian marketplace. The system of export licenses was so complicated and so corrupt that it encouraged the traders to break the law just to fulfill some administrative requirement. A few foreigners, though, accepted the challenges.

FOREIGN ENTREPRENEURS

TEXTILES

By all the logic of economic development, Sicily should have been making clothing commercially. The big four natural fibers — cotton, linen, wool, and silk — were all produced on the island at some time. But linen was never important, and Sicily's production of cotton and wool for clothing lost importance around 1500. The departure of the Jews resulted in an abrupt decline in silk manufacture, yet Messina managed to keep exporting large quantities of raw silk. Generally speaking, Spanish efforts to revive cloth production failed because they could find no skilled Sicilians to work in the sector. In the case of silk, additional forces were at work to discourage production: the occasional fallout of ash from Etna, the chronic Messina-Catania and Messina-Palermo rivalries, the everlasting export tax, and the official prohibition against the populace wearing silk.

Sicilians' good reasons for not doing things contrasted with the eighteenth-century Englishman's urge to entrepreneurship. That brought English merchants to Sicily's port cities seeking commercial opportunities; they found Sicily an open market for clothing, and by the middle of the century were commonly exchanging English wools for Sicilian sulfur, wine, and olive oil. In the second half of the century,

England's growing uncertainty about her American market accelerated English interest in Sicily as a buyer of its manufactured cloth
and clothing.

WINE

When John Woodhouse from Liverpool went to Marsala in 1770 on
clothing business, he smelled potential in the area's grapes. England
was importing large quantities of wine from Spain and Portugal,
while Sicilians were producing wine just for local consumption. In
1773 Woodhouse and Company sent off its first seventy barrels. But
Marsala's hot summers caused wine to ferment too fast, so that it
turned sour during the month's voyage to England. Experimentation
over twenty years resulted in a wine fortified with just the right
amount of alcohol to stabilize it. The wine had a taste similar to the
popular Madeira yet could be sold more cheaply, making it a natural
for the English market.

The difficulties of marketing in England were minor compared to
those of producing in Sicily. Sicilians had little conception of investment or progress. Woodhouse had to persuade landholders in
western Sicily to grow grapes instead of cereals, and to grow grapes
for far more wine than they themselves would ever drink. To reduce
the risk to them, he paid them in advance and he provided loans.
Eventually he would have wine in casks to be loaded on ships; so
Woodhouse built a jetty. And he had to pave the street over which
his heavy product would move. Even while Woodhouse developed
the infrastructures, his wine profited him, the town of Marsala, and
the Bourbon rulers.

SULFUR

Though Sicily remained innocent of machines, the Industrial
Revolution had a quick and major impact on Sicily's economy. In
England and France from the mid-1700s industrialization was proceeding apace. Chemists in the two countries learned of Sicily's sulfur,
mined by ancient Romans but unexploited since. The Austrians'
attempt to reestablish the mines had met political opposition, and

their sovereignty was too short to permit them another go. Bourbon Sicily found compelling economic incentive to develop the mines: the nascent chemical industries needed sulfuric acid and sulfur dioxide, and the military demanded sulfur to make black gunpowder. Sicily's sulfur, just below the surface, was easy to extract, and the deposits stretching from Enna and Caltanissetta down to the south coast proved immense, sufficient to make Sicily the world's main exporter of this essential mineral.

When the Leblanc method, using sulfuric acid to make sodium carbonate, came into use in the 1790s, the ante was raised and the French-English rivalry over Sicily intensified. Soon this strife would be absorbed into a much larger war.

NAPOLEON AND NELSON

The winds of innovation that blew Frenchmen into Sicily's sulfur mines served in Paris to fan flames. The French Revolution impinged on Sicily at the end of 1793, when Queen Marie Caroline in Naples heard of the execution of her younger sister, the French queen Marie Antoinette. Sicily's Bourbon king Ferdinand, Marie Caroline's husband, saw all insurgents as enemies, then the execution of the French royal couple turned him fiercely against the French revolutionaries.

When the new French leader Napoleon Bonaparte burst into northern Italy in 1796 with his French troops and his Italian surname, most Italians believed him to be their liberator. Aristocrats correspondingly feared for their lives. As Napoleon approached Naples in the first days of 1799, Ferdinand and Marie Caroline fled to Sicily. They must have felt truly desperate — Ferdinand had ruled Sicily for forty years without visiting the island. They sailed from Naples with the British commander Horatio Nelson, on his flagship, accompanied by the British minister at Naples, Sir William Hamilton, and Lady Hamilton.*

---

* During the course of the Sicilian trip, Lady Hamilton became Nelson's lady. Thus began *the* celebrity scandal of the first years of the nineteenth century.

On January 23, 1799, shortly after the royal flight, the French occupied Naples, but Nelson's troops blockaded them. Nelson soon returned to Naples and achieved a French surrender. By the end of June, King Ferdinand again held the reins in Naples. Indebted to Nelson, the king expressed his thanks with magnanimous gifts, including a huge feudal estate near Bronte, in the western foothills of Mount Etna.*

∽

While Naples was the capital of the Two Sicilies, the mainland was the only "Sicily" that counted. On the island of Sicily, besides the few aristocrats connected with the court in Naples, no one much cared about their sovereign: he didn't rule them, the barons did.

When the royal couple first arrived in Sicily, the Sicilians greeted them with optimism. Perhaps now King Ferdinand would pay attention to Sicily, even allow it autonomy from Naples. But this was wishful thinking, for the king never indicated any such possibility, and the queen hated Sicily. The royals did their best in Palermo to maintain their lifestyle of the more cosmopolitan Naples, with costs borne by the Sicilians. The nobility, ever in conflict with the king about control, was disgusted by Ferdinand's, and even more by Marie Caroline's extravagance and absolutism. A few of the Sicilian nobles, aware of the English business interests in Sicily and of Great Britain's recent takeover of Malta, approached English officials about annexing Sicily to Britain.

The Sicilians' knowledge of the British came from various sources. For example, the poet Samuel Taylor Coleridge, on his way home to England from a job in Malta, toured Sicily in 1805. The following year Benjamin Ingham sailed down from Yorkshire to sell woolen goods; he stayed to produce wine at Marsala. Demand for the wine soon brought more Britons into the area.

Nelson's forces held Naples for only a few years before Napoleon conquered the city again and sent his brother, Joseph, to rule it. King

---

* The estate was called Maniace, a name it shares with a castle in Siracusa; they take the name from Giorgio Maniace (the Italian for Manikes), who won the area from the Muslims in 1040.

Ferdinand and Queen Marie Caroline fled to Sicily for the second time. Deprived of the mainland three-fourths of his kingdom, Ferdinand kept court at Palermo as he plotted his return to Naples. He had no interest in Sicily whatsoever and employed Neapolitans to administer his little Sicilian realm, much to the annoyance of Sicilian nobles, who coveted posts at court. As he had no hope of raising a military force in Sicily, and as the Bonapartes in Naples had designs on Sicily, King Ferdinand had to accept (in 1806) the British forces as the island's defenders.

What a boon were the eighteen thousand Britons for the Sicilian economy! As the military required barracks and roads, the builders and artisans of agricultural Sicily became acquainted with the benefits of a steady job. Sicilian purses heretofore empty now bulged with coins from the foreigners' purchases and entertainments. The farmers finally had incentive to produce more grain than needed for their own consumption, in order to feed the extra men and to export to countries hurt by Napoleon's efforts to block maritime trade. The value of agricultural land rose rapidly, and the grain producers and exporters gained as the British navy obstructed North African piracy.

The Sicilians also had reason to believe, in the first years they housed the British military, that doing so supported Sicily's relationship with the United States — specifically, that in the case of a natural disaster such as a bad harvest, the British would assure safe delivery of wheat from America. The U.S. had in fact taken sufficient interest in Sicily that from 1806 it had a British businessman, Abraham Gibbs, acting as American consul. The previous year Gibbs had hired as secretary the twenty-two-year-old Constantin Samuel Rafinesque Schmaltz, who was to remain at the Palermo consulate until 1814, then move on to U.S. citizenship and renown as a naturalist. Meanwhile in Palermo, Rafinesque Schmaltz joined Gibbs and Ingham as a significant member of the merchant community, trading of course in wine.* Also, in 1811, he established a company to export kidskin.

---

* Rafinesque Schmaltz would take his Sicily-inspired interest in wine to the United States, where his *American Manual of the Grape Vines and the Art of Making Wine* was published in 1830.

By then, war threatened again between the United States and Great Britain. The occupation of Sicily by British forces assured that Sicilians would support Britain, yet the support was authentic and enthusiastic; indeed Sicilians were so enamored of the British that one could often hear them mangling the English terms "budget," "law," and "peers."

THE CONSTITUTION OF 1812

In the upper ranks of the Sicilian nobility, a few landowners saw that if they didn't yield some of their privileges they might find themselves as completely dispossessed as their French counterparts. As an earnest of liberalization, they had a constitution drawn up and adopted by Parlamento in 1812.

The constitution declared Sicily an independent state, to be ruled by a king of its own — Sicilians gave this great weight, for (excepting the few years of Savoy) they had not had their own king for four hundred years. Parlamento was henceforth to meet annually, to make laws and levy taxes subject to veto by the king. The cities of the royal and baronial domains would send representatives to the new Camera di Comuni (House of Commons). The church would be represented, along with the nobility, in the new Camera di Pari (House of Peers).

Most radical, the constitution abolished feudalism. The barons were not divested of their domains, but now they could sell all or part of their lands if they wished (and many wanted the cash). And as the nobles were no longer even theoretically held to provide the country's military forces in lieu of paying taxes, they were going to be taxed. Landowners could no longer hold private tribunals, and the state courts would treat all men as equals. Still, no one thought of giving the peasants any political voice, voting being a concern exclusively of property holders.

Resistance came from several quarters. An independent Sicily would have to supply its own soldiers, and ordinary Sicilians complained most bitterly about a potential draft. Worse, what they'd heard about the French Revolution was Napoleonic massacres and restrictions against the Catholic Church — they weren't going to risk their lives for reforms like *that*. Sicilian nobles commonly feared land reform: their whole identity lay in their vast holdings, while the new order hoped to stabilize the economy by giving small parcels to the peasants. The yeoman farmers crucial to England's socioeconomic order would not be acceptable to Sicily's barons — who, despite this difference, wanted to align themselves to England.

Once a fait accompli, the constitution received support from the British, although they had had qualms about it from the beginning. They maintained that such a constitution might have suited one of the peoples of northern Europe, who around this time were obtaining fundamental rights for every individual, but that few Sicilians had such aspirations. The nobles hardly wanted to improve the circumstances of the vast majority. In the cities the small middle class — merchants and skilled craftsmen — depended entirely on trade with the aristocrats. Land workers in the countryside had no conception of fundamental rights, not even regarding nourishment or survival. Left to their own devices, the Sicilians would soon return courts and lands to baronial control. If the enforcement of the new laws were to depend on the British military, the Sicilians would be no more independent than before. Anyway, to provide Sicily's internal security the British were not inclined.

In the event, the Sicilian parliament of 1815 proved itself unable even to pass a tax bill. Increasingly King Ferdinand felt disgust toward the Sicilians as well as scorn toward the British. He had only needed the British until he could return to Naples and his mainland kingdom; the Austrians had just reconquered it and restored it to him. In sheer disregard of his promises to maintain Sicily as an independent kingdom and not to depart from Sicily without the consent of its parliament, the king returned to Naples and abolished Sicilian autonomy.

Sicily's Golden Age had lasted a scant decade. Until ousted by Napoleon from Naples, Ferdinand had ruled as king of the Two Sicilies. In 1816 he styled himself ruler of the Kingdom of the Two

Sicilies. It was a distinction without a difference, except to Sicilians. They had lost even that smidgen of autonomy; they were even forbidden to fly a Sicilian flag. The nobles had a practical ground too for their anger: when Palermo lost its status as capital, they lost all hope of administrative jobs.

Although Ferdinand had avoided Sicily until late in life, his visit was to have big consequences personally: a widower, at age sixty-three he married a Sicilian princess. As a result, great numbers of Sicilian nobles followed the princess to Naples. For a while Sicilians dominated the Neapolitan court, when they might have been leading Sicily.

The French no longer a military threat, the British withdrew from Sicily, ending the island's income from official Britain and from its soldiers. The continental blockade over, trade returned to the antebellum status quo, and the price of Sicily's grain dropped precipitously. In June 1816 the British consul in Messina read in a letter from Benjamin Ingham in Palermo: ". . . so much changed in so short a time. There is no trade in the shops as they sell nothing."

Two different sets of forces — the financial collapse and the confusion over the constitution — coalesced to make a very unhappy Sicily.

CONFLICT OVER CONSTITUTIONS

During the boom years of the British decade, many Sicilian storekeepers and artisans had flourished, developing into a middle class. They were beginning to make themselves heard politically and even dominated a few local councils.

That contributed to the intensified conflict over the constitution, or rather over a whole series of constitutions. The royal favorites and administrators still residing in Palermo drafted a constitution significantly more conservative than the one of 1812 and tried to impose it on the rest of Sicily. The city of Palermo called for Sicilian autonomy and more daringly for independence, but only Marsala allied itself with Palermo against Naples. Under duress King Ferdinand offered Sicily a new constitution, relatively liberal, which made feudal rights even more ambiguous. The king had some support from the three cities on Sicily's east coast; more commercial than Palermo, they desired closer ties to the continent and were ready to support the Naples constitution. The conflict escalated into civil war. When the forces of Messina and Catania approached Palermo in 1820, Benjamin Ingham was there and would report to London how "we suffered all the horrors of a siege, in conjunction with the fear of being plundered or even murdered by the rabble."

His fear was justified, for several towns suffered pillage, and Caltanissetta in central Sicily was invaded by a private army that slaughtered several residents. It took many weeks before King Ferdinand's soldiers brought an end to the warfare. The following year, 1821, the king reneged on his promise of a constitution, which gave rise to more upheavals.

The efforts to introduce a constitution brought Sicily two important changes. The deposit of grain in the government reserves was no longer required. And feudalism was dead, or at least legislated out of existence. Of course such longstanding structures and traditions would not disappear overnight. Peasants continued to call their lords "Eccellenza" and to pay fees for milling grain and pressing olives. The barons continued to take advantage of laws — and of the weakness and conflicts of the law.

The transformation of barons from holders of fiefs to private landowners with the right to sell their land did indeed result in redistribution. The idea had been to open land ownership to the middle class, and the middle class yearned to buy land. Typically, though, it was the barons who came out ahead. Regarding watercourses, for instance. Though they might sell some of their lands, barons kept those crossed by rivers and streams, or even purchased such watered lands. Given Sicily's scarcity of fresh water, the astute proprietor could now sell water at whatever price he decided, or not sell it at all, using it to maintain the peasants' dependence on him.

The king having yielded his right to reclaim feudal grants, the barons enjoyed much more freedom than previously. Lands used as common pasture were to be enclosed for agriculture, and those who lost grazing benefits thereby were to be recompensed with an appropriate sum; the lands were privatized all right, but the peasants were never compensated. The rush of legislation in the decade following the British departure did little or nothing to improve Sicily's agriculture.

KINGS FRANCESCO AND FERDINAND IV

The sojourns of the Bourbon king and queen, the occupation by British soldiers, the rancor of competing constitutions, and the abrogation of feudalism enlivened Sicily during the nineteenth century's first quarter. And then King Ferdinand died, in 1825, after sixty-five years of unexceptional rule. He personally was not the source of all the conflict — although lazy and uninspired, he was not wicked. We noted above his youthful efforts to establish schools in Sicily; later he involved himself creditably in programs against malaria and smallpox. During his reign Sicily had gained some new roads, radiating from Palermo southwest to Segesta, south to Corleone, southeast halfway to Enna, and east to Termini Imerese.

His son, Francesco, corrupt and cruel, ruled five years. Earlier he had served a long period as his father's deputy in Palermo, where in 1810 his son Ferdinand was born. Sicilians rejoiced at the first heir to the throne born on the island of Sicily since the Normans. When Ferdinand acceded in 1830, Sicilian joy was slightly marred because he was slated to rule not only their island but also, from Naples, the Kingdom of the Two Sicilies. Be that as it may, compared with earlier kings Ferdinand exhibited positive interest in Sicily, visiting the island a few times and sending his Sicilian-born brother Leopold to be governor. Like their grandfather in his younger years, these two concerned themselves particularly with education and agricultural development, even if their philanthropies touched the lives of only a tiny number of Sicilians. When they tried to reform the tax system they aroused the ire of the nobles, who made it clear that they had had their fill of Naples in any case.

Sicilians wishing to pursue careers still had to go north. An example from this period — to take a name known abroad — is Vincenzo Bellini, born in Catania in 1801, who at age eighteen went to study music at the conservatory in Naples. In the sixteen years remaining to him, he did not return to Sicily to live.

CHOLERA

In October 1836 Naples noted cases of cholera, an Asian disease not previously occurring in Western Europe. By June 1837 it had reached Palermo, whence it spread around Sicily, especially eastern Sicily. The cholera killed rapidly during the hot months of 1837; of Sicily's two million residents, some seventy thousand died of it. It was widely held, even by sober scholars of the time, that the affliction had been sent by the Bourbons.

During that horrible summer Palermo again cut itself off from the surrounding countryside and suffered a food shortage, with consequent panic and violence. Siracusani, blaming the disease first on local fishermen and then on foreigners generally, rioted, thereby facilitating the invasions of hungry peasants and of criminal gangs who looted and killed until hundreds lay dead. Catania attempted to turn the hostility to political ends, fostering alliance among its various classes in opposition to Bourbon rule and encouraging other cities to do likewise, but little came of it. This wave of rebellion, like previous ones, the Bourbons squelched easily.

CHANGES UNDER KING FERDINAND

The following year Ferdinand travelled around Sicily in an apparent effort to understand its chronic anguish. If cholera was not customary in Sicily, banditry and corruption were, undermining agriculture, commerce, and the administration. Concerned about this most backward part of the Italian lands, the king had new laws and practices introduced into Sicily. Roads were being built along the west, north, and east coasts; the Palermo-Corleone road was continued southward to Agrigento, the Palermo-Enna road eastward to Catania. These decreased the isolation wherever they passed, though huge areas of the interior were still remote. Responsibility for Sicily was daunting.

For example, Sicilian aristocrats had implored King Ferdinand to hire Sicilians for administrative posts, and he had done so; then he reneged on the grounds that Sicilians so often used their offices to favor relatives and friends that efficiency and justice were thwarted. But when he installed non-Sicilians as administrators, they couldn't communicate easily with the Sicilians and failed utterly to work with them. For the longer term, he reopened the university at Messina (closed since the 1680 riot) particularly to train non-Sicilians for administrative positions in Sicily.

Another intractable problem regarded land reform. Fundamental to the grievances of the peasants — the fieldworkers and now those toiling in the mines — was that they had never received the plots of land their fathers had been led to expect from the abolition of feudalism in 1812. The Bourbons deplored the unemployment of a third to a half of Sicily's land and anticipated increased productivity through redistribution. But to the barons the right to possess large estates was sacred and nonnegotiable. And as the barons were increasingly attracted to the idea of autonomy from Naples, the king dared not act against them.

The Bourbons vacillated inasmuch as they were caught on the horns of a dilemma, the horns being the few big landowners and the many hungry peasants. Neither group cooperated with the royal officers. Since the Normans, the Sicilians had had no government that functioned for Sicily's benefit, so that Sicilians saw any government whatsoever as inimical to their interests. Aristocrats, who among other peoples took it upon themselves to express the national will, were in Sicily defending their narrow interests against the majority. Resentful of government from Naples, the upper classes played on the universal dream of the subjugated masses to overthrow their masters — the barons persuaded the peasants that their wretchedness derived from the policies of the Bourbons. In fact, there's ample evidence in Sicily and elsewhere to indicate that, had Sicily's barons not been obstinate, the Bourbons would have introduced progressive policies on the island.

∽

Occasionally members of different classes drew into shaky alliance, but even then they lacked leaders to focus their discontent and to unite them in action. Without leaders, rebellions were doomed to fail. In many countries, then as now, uprisings against rulers occurred in the military, but Sicily never had a significant military force of its own. Intellectuals, who elsewhere fomented rebellions, were few in Sicily, where the educators lacked vigor and whence the most ambitious upper-school graduates went abroad to live.

Among the latter were young political romantics who sought the influences of the liberal north, absorbed its ideas, and applied them to Sicily, resulting in political tracts for dissemination in Sicily's cities and towns. They argued politics from different premises, but they gradually came to agree that Sicily would win autonomy only by throwing off the Bourbons and perhaps joining with the other states of the Italian peninsula. Back in Sicily a thirty-ish historian, Michele Amari, had arrived at the same conclusion. Amari knew that his views vis-à-vis the Bourbons would never pass the censors, so he wrote a long history of the Vespro (see pages 209–11), Sicily's successful uprising in 1282. The meaning of his story was not lost on literate Sicilians, and the book helped to win influential people to the anti-Bourbon cause. Shortly after its publication in 1842, Amari fled to Paris, where he gave some direction to the budding revolutionaries. Cafés in Paris were the first to resound with shouts for Sicily's *risorgimento* ("resurgence").*

ECONOMICS 1800–1848

If the Sicilians' ambitions were stimulated by the French Revolution and its underlying ideas, it's also true that the Sicilians' minds opened to those ideas largely thanks to the British in Sicily. From early in the century, when the occupying power built infrastructure, those few barons interested in progress associated it with the British. By the 1840s Sicily had experienced almost a century of economic diversification, which pushed ajar a door to the world.

---

* Giuseppe Verdi, from the Italian north, would write *Les Vêpres siciliennes* in 1855 for the Opéra in Paris. Its rousing overture notwithstanding, this opera was less than a masterpiece.

Agricultural Products

To trace the economic developments, we return to 1799, when Admiral Nelson took the fleeing Bourbon royals to Sicily. Months later, when Nelson was about to sail for Malta to fight for that island against the French, he needed hundreds of pipes of good wine for his men. In Sicily he found the Woodhouse wine to his liking, so in March 1800 he placed a large order (five hundred pipes). Subsequent orders made Nelson an important early customer for Woodhouse.

The French revolutionary wars, in fact, assured the Marsala wine sparkling success. Napoleon's continental blockade cut the British Isles and Sicily off from the rest of Europe. Even if they had wanted to, neither could buy wine from France, and Britain had those several thousand imbibers stationed in Sicily. Sicily and Britain grew ever closer.

When most of the British soldiers left Sicily in 1815, many businessmen remained. Apart from the wine, the English wanted things to eat: from Sicilian waters, salt and tunny fish; from Sicily's fields, wheat of course but also olives and olive oil, citrus fruits, honey, and almonds. They bought sumac to use in dying leather. In this period over 40 percent of all Sicily's exports went to Britain, and a third of all imports into Sicily came from Britain.

Sulfur

As the years of the 1800s passed, agricultural products declined as a share of Sicily's exports and as a share of baronial income, corresponding to the rising share of sulfur. Until the constitution of 1812, mines had been in the public domain; then in the shakeup of feudalism barons fought for absolute control of the minerals on and under their lands, and they often wound up owning the mines outright. Much of the money that land barons obtained by selling off their *feudi* went to purchase mines or mineral rights. King Ferdinand didn't gainsay the barons because he needed their support while feudalism weakened; in 1826, shortly after the accession of Francesco I, the barons obtained a law assuring that taxes on sales from mining would remain low.

Anyone who possessed land in the sulfur zone was on the road to riches. Soap and bleaches had heretofore been produced from soda ash made by burning seaweed; from the 1820s the English replaced soda ash with alkali made by the Leblanc process from Sicily's sulfur. The burgeoning chemical laboratories up north demanded sulfur to manufacture gunpowder, to treat diseases of grapevines and of human skin, and to strike matches. Within Sicily it served mostly to spark the barons. When they realized that central Sicily abounded in this mineral that foreigners would buy, they started boring holes all around their properties.

In the 1830s sulfur became Sicily's largest export both in volume and in value. The sulfur was sent out through the southern ports — Agrigento and Sciacca and Licata — which boomed. Everyone who had money to invest wanted a piece of the extraction.

But the Sicilians developed no sulfur industry. They exported it all — in the mid-1830s, 49 percent to England and 43 percent to France. The race between these two countries, and the ease with which they could obtain Sicily's sulfur, led them to mine more than their industries could use. From 1833 to 1837 the price per ton dropped by 60 percent.

To alleviate the economic crisis, the government in Naples decided to accept the offer of a French company to buy Sicilian sulfur at a guaranteed price and to build a refinery at Agrigento in return for a monopoly over Sicily's sulfur mining. The British mining companies naturally protested, prevailing upon their government to cite violation of the Anglo-Neapolitan commercial agreements of 1816, which granted Britain most favored nation status vis-à-vis Sicily. King Ferdinand, from Naples, asserted his right to absolute control of the economy of his realm. Britain, by now dependant on sulfuric acid, established a military blockade along the Tyrrhenian coast and seized Bourbon ships in those waters. This conflict of 1840, called the Sulfur War, ended with Bourbon capitulation. So much for Sicilian control over Sicily's natural resources.

Sicily's First Capitalists

Although the Napoleonic wars caused most foreign merchants to leave Sicily, Benjamin Ingham stuck it out. He expanded into world markets. Around 1810, when war threatened between Britain and the United States, he went to America to arrange exports to Boston, where his wine sold well. From New England in his own ships — brigs — he brought back oak staves, which he used for making wine casks. He involved himself in the production and trade of Sicilian commodities ranging from almonds to pumice to, naturally, sulfur. Moreover, because Sicily had just a few savings banks and no banks at all inclined to service the productive sector, Ingham lent money to other foreign merchants and industrialists, and to Sicilians as well. With his encouragement, a few of the Sicilian aristocrats and new agrarian bourgeoisie stepped gingerly onto entrepreneurship. Single-handedly Ingham raised Sicily's west into economic significance, in the process becoming the richest foreign merchant in Sicily. He was one of the world's first capitalists.

On Ingham's street in Palermo lived the family Florio, who had a flourishing business in spices, herbs, and essences. Vincenzo Florio missed being Sicilian by a few kilometers, since he was born in 1799 across from Messina on the Calabrian side of the strait. In 1814, as the French-English hostilities wound down, the Florio family sent young Vincenzo off to London, presumably to learn the trade. While still in his twenties he inherited the business, which gave him money to invest. First he bought into tobacco, then into a new maritime insurance firm with Benjamin Ingham and a few others. By 1834 he was involved with wineries at Marsala, and in 1835 he opened a sulfur mine at Racalmuto, twenty kilometers northwest of Agrigento.

Spices, always of interest to Florio, were first brought directly from the Indian Ocean to the Kingdom of the Two Sicilies in 1839, arriving from Sumatra in one of Benjamin Ingham's brigs. For Ingham's next marine adventure, he invited his younger friend Florio to participate in the purchase of Palermo's first steamboat. The steamboat would make voyages less dramatic than Ingham's brig — it would ply between Palermo and Naples and Malta. Up to this time travellers to and from the peninsula took passage on the cargo boats, which sailed irregularly, or on the postal boats, which sailed infrequently, because there was no regular passenger service; in either case, the trip from Palermo to Naples required about a week. The new steamboat would take sixteen hours, and the fare would be much cheaper too. The project was exciting not only for the improvement in transportation but also for the method of financing: Sicilian aristocrats and foreign merchants had seldom collaborated, and now both groups were buying stock.

His mind on the sea, Florio invented tuna fish, or rather the product by that name that's ubiquitous today. As far back as the Phoenicians, salted tuna had been eaten with gusto, especially by long-distance sailors. But over the centuries, as "long-distance" meant ever longer periods at sea, more and more sailors died of scurvy, which was blamed on (among other things) the salted fish. That scurvy was not caused by the fish was known before Florio's time, but he (and others as well) recognized the danger of that belief for the tuna industry, which sold the salted fish in barrels. During the 1840s Florio began to preserve tuna in olive oil (which abounded in western Sicily) and to sell the product in cans. If he had not already been a wealthy man, this would have made him one.

The export of Sicily's financial resources concerned Florio and others. Even that first steamboat, named the *Palermo,* was built in Glasgow; boatyards in Sicily were making little sailboats, nothing as demanding as a state-of-the-art steamboat. Much more fundamental, the British came to Sicily to buy raw materials for paltry sums, then they incorporated those materials into products that they sold in Sicily at high prices. England had built many great churches from the proceeds of its wool; while all over the Sicilian hills sheep bells tinkled while the shepherds died of malnutrition. Besides, Sicily was growing some cotton and could grow more.

Wine and tuna brought in money for the merchants, to be sure, and for their office staffs and agricultural suppliers around Marsala. Marsala was a commune in the province of Trapani, and Trapani had been proposing for years the establishment of a textile mill — a mill to make simple cloths for the local market, with the dual purpose of reducing the import of cloth and of providing some earnings for "all able-bodied beggars" who currently had nowhere to sell their labor. With the encouragement of government officials, Florio started a small spinning workshop in 1841 on the outskirts of Palermo; three years later, when arguments about premises had finally been resolved, the mill moved to Marsala.

An entrepreneurial genius and plutocrat, Vincenzo Florio sought to benefit the economy of Sicilians, and he did so, giving particular stimulus to western Sicily. Messina remained a principal center for foreign merchants, while significant banking and support services developed in Marsala, Trapani, Palermo, Termini Imerese, and Castelvetrano. Moreover, when the first merchants from Britain were duly succeeded by their sons raised in Sicily, more of their profits stayed in Sicily. As for the Sicilians themselves, few went into business independently; perhaps Florio's control of so many sectors scared some off. Yet thanks to Ingham and Florio and to the sulfur mining, in the first half of the nineteenth century more and more Sicilians moved up from the peasantry and began to dream about how things might be better.

REVOLUTION OF 1848

A riot broke out in Messina in September 1847 without attracting much support, and Bourbon soldiers quelled it as they had quelled previous riots. The Bourbons had come to expect such occasional disorders, more nuisance than menace because Sicilians seemed incapable of organizing themselves into wide-scale rebellion.

During the following months the political rumblings came from Palermo, still suffering consequences of its revolt twenty-seven years before. As 1848 started, Palermo experienced student demonstrations, the closing of the university, and the arrest of a dozen prominent liberals. Nonetheless arrangements continued for a party in Palermo on January 12 to celebrate King Ferdinand's birthday. Rioting throngs turned the party into the first armed conflict of the Risorgimento.

The Sicilians' immemorially local orientation meant that the cities didn't aid one another, even against a common enemy. But Palermo's lessened prestige during the preceding generation encouraged the other cities into activity and into awareness of common interests. As word of Palermo's riot spread, men from all over the island headed to Palermo to fight.

In the countryside peasants released their pent-up anger by pummeling their *gabelloti* by whatever means they had at hand, killing sheep and burning fields that were property of the *gabelloti*. The agitation spread quickly to the peninsula, with raging men starting fires south of Salerno. On the seventh day of the riots, a frightened King Ferdinand in Naples tried to placate the Sicilians by granting them greater freedom of the press as well as some administrative and judicial autonomy. That wasn't enough; the violence continued. Parts of the island went up in smoke as peasants burned forests to acquire more land for cultivation. For such an emergency the Bourbon soldiers in Palermo lacked adequate leaders and supplies; they had to capitulate. As the success of the revolt seemed increasingly likely, more Sicilians joined, and by the end of January the whole island was in rebellion.

A desperate king made more concessions, including amnesty for the rebels. On February 10 he promised Sicily a French-style constitution; such a constitution would be advanced for Europe, for it stipulated the king could not dissolve parliament, although parliament could depose the king. The rebels fought on. In March the king promised complete autonomy. For Sicilians those were heady days!*

On March 25 the new Sicilian parliament held its first session. Parliamentarians were in majority liberal aristocrats, though the middle classes were represented by intellectuals, some of whom had repatriated for the purpose. On April 13 they joined together in a formal declaration that Ferdinand was no longer their king, then burst into celebration. Grasping Sicily's three-legged symbol, the

---

* On March 16, 1848, one of the revolutionary committees approved the building of an avenue to be called "Liberty," "to give the liberated Palermo an exquisite ornament and her people, work." Via Libertà is a main thoroughfare of modern Palermo, and the words are inscribed on a monument where Via Libertà meets Piazza Mordini (across from the larger Piazza Croce).

triskelis, they erupted into the streets to dance under the *tricolore,* Italy's red-white-green striped revolutionary flag.*

∽

Leading Sicilians perceived the need for a king. This was not the first time Sicilians had sought an outsider to rule them: the Mamertines had done so (and brought about the Roman invasion), a Byzantine general invited the Arabs to take over, the victors in the 1282 Vespers gave sovereignty to Peter of Aragon, and as recently as 1812 Sicilians asked to be incorporated into the British empire. Now the victorious revolutionaries looked among northern princes for an appropriate king for the Sicilians, and in July selected Alberto Amadeo, a Savoy prince titled duke of Genoa. He responded, in effect, "Thanks but no thanks." The spurned Sicilians did not consider seriously enough the significance of his refusal. While bursting with hope, they lacked money, soldiers, and political know-how.

Rioters against the Bourbons weren't about to pay more taxes to them, and for the duration no other authority was levying taxes. Destroying royal tax records was a priority for many rioters — it would be a long time before Sicily could bring order to its finances. Vincenzo Florio contributed funds for the new government. Michele Amari took on the job of finance minister, but he proved less effective as administrator than he had as animator.

The second fundamental problem: the Sicilians refused to submit to any military draft. Volunteer troops went off to Calabria to fight against the Bourbons, and others to help Lombardy throw off its Austrian rulers — for some Sicilians felt themselves part of a germinating Italian union — but these military efforts were small and not well mounted. Sicily hired a succession of military commanders (including a Pole who spoke no Italian), then limited the commander's authority so that he couldn't possibly develop any force to defend Sicily's new independence.

∽

---

* The Italian flag is an adaptation of the French, with green substituted for blue. The green (taken from Masonic then Jacobin symbolism) represented nature and consequently natural rights, that is, equality and liberty.

Sicilians believed that now as a free people their men shouldn't be subject to military conscription. And they argued more practically that unless the peasant men worked in the fields, they would all die of starvation. That women might do the fieldwork was unthinkable — women stayed in their homes, as among orthodox Arabs. Sicilian leaders had neither the will nor the means to persuade their people to national defense.

Into the public-security vacuum marched the brigands, ready as always to impose their own authority. Some of them were or had been paid by the Bourbons, others (or maybe the same ones) had led groups against the Bourbons, but politics wasn't what drove them — under the cover of the riots they had often carried on their personal vendettas. Now with Sicily independent they went back to controlling and terrifying the villages.

Parliament showed itself powerless to address these issues. Rather than defense and finance, so basic to any nation, it was land reform about which the Sicilians most cared. The peasant could be roused to fight only by hopes of land and bread. In fact it was by promising land and bread that the nobles and intellectuals had won peasants to their anti-Bourbon rebellion. The peasants, illiterate and landless, had no representatives in parliament, no one with the authority to maintain the promise. Whether the promise should be honored or ignored became the issue that ended the parliamentarians' happy solidarity.

The Bourbons were watching; in September they sent an army against Messina. When King Ferdinand had Messina bombarded, he shocked all Europe and won himself the lasting nickname Re Bomba (King Bomb). Destroyed property included some belonging to foreigners, so Englishmen and Frenchmen prevailed upon King Ferdinand for a six-month ceasefire. Toward the end of the armistice, the Bourbons repeated their offer of autonomy for Sicily if the Sicilians would only recognize Bourbon sovereignty — as the Bourbons now held all the cards, their offer seems generous and was probably encouraged by the British. The Sicilians refused the offer, implying their willingness to fight. The Bourbons took up the challenge, this time invading Catania. Sicilian forces were not remotely equal to the

Bourbons' — Catania capitulated, and the rest of Sicily yielded without resistance.

∞

Their ouster of the Bourbons having failed, Sicilians withdrew into postmortems. It was galling to have to add 1848 to their list of ineffective revolts, after they had tasted success. Sicily's rebellion was followed by a whole series of them around Europe in 1848, which suggested that the moment had been right. But without leaders, the pundits said, uprisings don't culminate in revolutions — though that couldn't be the whole story, for the Sicilian Vespers of 1282 had no particular hero. Anyhow, the Sicilians had in fact just won their independence, only to nullify it by fighting against one another.

TRANSITION
Garibaldi (1848–1860)

When the Sicilian revolutionaries were thrashing around trying to find strong leaders, in late October 1848 they called on Giuseppe Garibaldi to serve as military chief. He applauded Sicily's anti-Bourbon insurgency and promised to come, but he got involved elsewhere.

He had lived in a world of revolutionary politics since his birth in Napoleonic Nice.* Even Garibaldi's birthday, July 4, 1807, made one think of independence. As a youth Garibaldi joined the Sardinian navy, but his republican activities soon got him into trouble. He fled to South America, where he spent a dozen years as a guerrilla in the wars of liberation, becoming known for his competence, his bravery, and his decency. He attracted further attention in Uruguay by dressing his guerrillas in red shirts, when a consignment of red wool shirts happened to become available to him cheap. The label stuck long after the shirts wore out.

When Garibaldi learned that rioting in Palermo in January 1848 had spread to the north of the peninsula, ruled by Hapsburg Austria, he led his Red Shirts (many of Italian origin) across the Atlantic to fight against Austria with the Sardinian house of Savoy. From the fierce battles Garibaldi barely escaped with his life; yet all around him he noted the desperation of the Italian peasants, similar to that of South America's poorest. The conflicts between classes would be mitigated, he assumed, in an Italy free of foreign rule, and in his mind the two objectives blended. He found glory fighting for independence in his homeland, even though the Savoy lost this war.

The Savoy Kingdom of Sardinia now comprised just that island and a mainland territory north of it, including Turin (the capital) and Nice. The kingdom's mainland teemed with refugees and activists,

---

* The French-Italian borderlands being a hotbed of republicanism, it's not just happenstance that Garibaldi started his life in this area, as had Napoleon thirty-eight years earlier.

patriots from Sicily and all the Italian states who had fled to Turin, where they could live, think, and publish freely. The Risorgimento was a child of intellectuals.

From the Savoy cities Garibaldi quickly gathered some fighting men and led them to Rome, to help defend the new Roman republic from the French. Here too the republicans met defeat, whereupon Garibaldi retreated and reconsidered his dream of an Italy free of kings. He spent nine months in 1850–51 in New York, where he thought seriously of applying for citizenship in the republican United States. But his other great love was the sea, so he took work as a naval captain and for three years sailed the world. The last months of 1853 he spent in the eastern U.S., whence he sailed for London on his way home to Nice. London then provided refuge for a host of revolutionaries, enabling Garibaldi to scheme with Mazzini and others.

The vigorous new Savoy king, Victor Emmanuel II, hoped to enlarge his realm to a Greater Italy. He made himself popular in Sardinia by implementing reforms, by supporting the constitution, and by encouraging the Risorgimento. Garibaldi while abroad maintained contact with political leaders on the peninsula and gave much thought to unifying Italy: he decided that a Greater Italy could not be formed as a republican state. The liberal policies of Victor Emmanuel made it easier for Garibaldi to relinquish his republicanism to join with those dedicated to uniting Italy under Savoy rule. The king, appreciatively, gave Garibaldi military command.

Already the symbol of unification, Victor Emmanuel named the count of Cavour premier, effectively making him Unification's architect. These two liberals envisioned the politically distinct parts of the peninsula as being annexed to the Savoy realm with its capital at Turin. The king and Cavour, recognizing that the small kingdom of Sardinia would need allies if it was to drive out Austria, inaugurated a policy of free trade that won Sardinia the support of the British and the French. Garibaldi was unaware of the particulars of the Savoy arrangements with France, and he didn't like the idea of forming an Italy that would be euphemistic for a Greater Savoy; but the immediate job was to rid the peninsula of its foreign rulers.

Garibaldi and the French each contributed to the military victory of the Savoy; by liberating Milan from the Austrians, they brought Savoy the huge region of Lombardy. It turned out that Cavour had purchased French participation at a high price, namely that the Savoy would cede their ancestral lands, including Nice, to France. Garibaldi found himself fighting for the unification of an Italy from which his hometown would be excluded. He denounced Cavour and would never forgive him, and he hated the French more than ever. Still, Garibaldi itched for an independent Italy.

The Sicilians, used to men who talk well, admired Garibaldi as a man of action. To his men he was a hero not least because of his humane valuation of lives in any army; young men arrived from throughout Europe to fight in his ranks. Garibaldi, as much as the king, had become a symbol of the unifying Italy. Inevitably he aroused jealousies. The king received him in a friendly manner, counseling "prudence and wisdom." Garibaldi resigned as general in the king's army so as to be able to act freely, then bided his time in private adventures, trying, at age fifty-two, to reassure himself that he was still vital.

The international press called Garibaldi "hero of the two worlds" as they gave front-page coverage to developments toward Italian unification. These stories made hardly a mention of Sicily. Likewise to the Savoy, busy with diplomatic and military urgencies, Sicily was simply irrelevant. Turin had a fair number of exiles from Sicily, some of whom joined in political discussions, but they were not granted much attention; there Sicilian news even of rebellions was heard with little interest, as though it regarded another continent.

Most leaders of the movement for unification were upper-class men whose experience was limited to cities: naturally they thought of Sicily as anarchic and anachronic. In contrast, Garibaldi's experience in South America had broadened him to an appreciation of peasant life in a colony, so when news arrived about the Kingdom of the Two Sicilies and its sufferings, Garibaldi listened. When another in the long series of Sicilian rebellions exploded in Palermo on April 4, 1860, Garibaldi let himself be persuaded by Sicilian revolutionaries that the Two Sicilies should be united with Italy. And that the time was *now,* for the French were threatening to overthrow Naples. By April 26, newspapers in Italy and in France reported that Garibaldi was seeking volunteers to fight in Sicily.

Volunteers, because Savoy administrators wanted no part of this expedition. If it should succeed militarily, which they doubted, the Savoy would gain Sicily, which they didn't want. This wasn't the moment for absorbing any additional region into the new Italy: after the Savoy had conquered Lombardy, the rulers of smaller principalities south of Lombardy abandoned their realms to save their lives, so that already the growing Italy covered the northwest of the peninsula down to the Papal States. Sicilians were coupling adhesion to the Savoy state with demands for a regional parliament, which the harried leaders in Turin feared as divisive for the new Italy. How much, they wondered, would their Italy benefit from inclusion of a backward, brutal region way down at the peninsular toe?

Garibaldi insisted on invading Sicily, however, and he was so famous and popular that the king and Cavour shrank from forbidding him. But they wouldn't encourage him, and they could hinder him. For one thing, they confiscated most of Garibaldi's weapons. Also, as the route from Genoa to Sicily had to cross the latitude of Sardinia, Cavour gave orders to the royal navy to capture any of Garibaldi's men who landed there. Garibaldi felt bitter about this, naturally, but he was a good captain and here sure of his course. Just before setting sail from Genoa the night of May 5, he wrote a letter of justification to Victor Emmanuel:

> Sire,
> The anguished cry from Sicily has moved my heart and that of a few hundred of my old comrades. I didn't suggest the insurrection of my Sicilian brothers, but since they have risen in the name of a unified Italy — personified by Your Majesty — against the most shameful tyranny of our times, I have not hesitated to make myself the head of the expedition. I know very well that I'm embarking on a dangerous enterprise. . . .

> If we win, I shall be proud to add this new and glittering jewel to Your Majesty's crown, on the condition however that You do not permit Your councilors to cede it to foreigners, as they have done with my native city. . . .

He was stretching things to say that the Sicilians had risen "in the name of a unified Italy (*L'Italia*)." In fact some of the men thought "La Talia" to be the name of a woman, maybe the king's wife. Most of the rioters were unaware of political developments to the north but rather were risking their lives, again, for an adequate diet. They wanted to get rid of rulers who bombed them, humiliated them, subscribed to their enslavement. The Sicilian leaders didn't place much hope in the Savoy or in Cavour, but they did in Garibaldi. They felt he understood.

Five weeks after the rebellion started, Garibaldi embarked with 1,089 men in two old steamboats purloined from a private shipping company. Staying clear of Sardinian waters, he sailed for Sicily.

∽

Just over a thousand years before, Marsala had narrowly missed being the Muslims' first point of debarkation — their leaders thought that harbor would be heavily defended and chose Mazara instead. Garibaldi redressed Marsala's loss. He first thought to land at Sciacca on the south coast, then suspected it would be heavily defended. Better would be Marsala: the British had half a dozen wineries at Marsala, with half a thousand workers; their operation was so profitable that they had reopened Marsala's port. Probably, as a consequence, the Bourbons would hesitate to engage an enemy there. In the event, when Garibaldi's forces landed the morning of May 11, two British ships lay quietly in the harbor, presumably with instructions to observe but not interfere except in particular circumstances. There wasn't a Bourbon ship in sight.

Spared battle, Garibaldi's men went ashore. When the Bourbons returned in their ships a little later, they attacked halfheartedly, but the Thousand were already beyond reach. The Bourbons did take possession of Garibaldi's two ships. Perhaps this strengthened the Red Shirts' will to fight, for they could not retreat.

The wealthier residents of Marsala, screened in their houses, stared at the ragtag men stomping off their cramped voyage. They were said to be soldiers, but how could such an ill-armed crew mount offensives against the professional troops of the Bourbons? Garibaldi promised to end rule from Naples, promised the peasants land and food, but how could he possibly accomplish this? Garibaldi and his deputies tore around Marsala, calling out for volunteers, flourishing firearms, imploring recruits to come with any kind of weapon at all. The locals remained skeptical in their houses.

The charismatic Garibaldi kept broadcasting a program that reflected the needs of the downtrodden. His experience among the South American peasants suggested how to appeal to their counterparts in Sicily, and he knew that if he was to obtain shelter and food for his men then he must gain support from Sicilians inland. They responded, cheering Garibaldi to the heavens and embracing the Thousand as having appeared in answer to millennial prayers. The country folk came forth with offers of provisions and their men enlisted, carrying scythes and stout sticks to oppose the Bourbons' firearms.

Without meeting any adversaries, the soldiers marched along the road running ten kilometers eastward from Marsala, then followed paths a further twenty kilometers, to the old hill town of Salemi. Seizing the moment hopefully, on May 14 the town council vested in Garibaldi the dictatorship of a unified Italy, which Garibaldi accepted in the name of King Victor Emmanuel. A flag was unfurled — the green, white, and red *tricolore* that during the preceding sixty years symbolized the aspirations of Italian democracy, independence, and unity. The men of Sicily and of the north together saluted as the flag began to fly from the castle tower. Salemi would be only a provisional capital, yet for now the capital of the new Italy lay in Sicily.

∾

Exercising his dictatorial power, Garibaldi responded quickly to the peasants' most urgent demands: he promised land reform, and he

MAP 15. Italy, just prior to Unification, May 1860

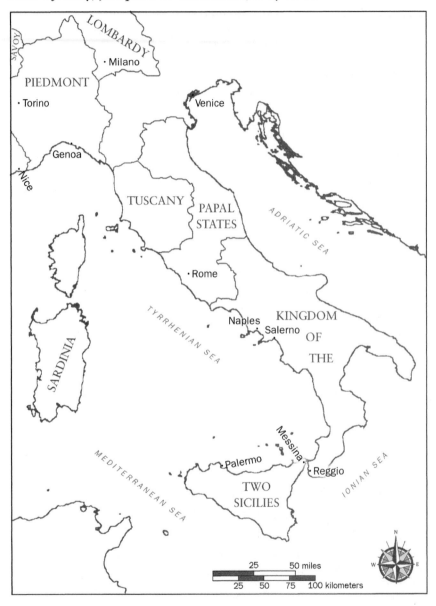

abolished the tax on milling so that the peasants could with impunity make and eat bread from the wheat they had produced. Now peasant men clamored to be part of his army, because they were eager for a new system, or because as things stood they had nothing to lose, or because they hoped for food or booty, or just for a change from their miserable routine. Really, they lacked the discipline to be good fighters, but their numbers and their ardor provided encouragement. Some city men too were attracted to Garibaldi, and they served as officers for the less able.

From Salemi the augmented Thousand turned north to follow a good road to Palermo. The next day, just southeast of the old Greek temple at Segesta, they came to Calatafimi, a village typical of the island in that it had been exploited alternately by Sicily's barons and by foreign officials. Men of Calatafimi joined Garibaldi's fighters in their first combat in Sicily. In the midst of this confused encounter Garibaldi urged his men forward by crying: "Here we'll make Italy or we'll die." When they won the battle at Calatafimi, more men rushed to join their ranks as they headed for Palermo. In several small towns along the way, including Alcamo and Partinico, they found they didn't need to fight; indeed there was hardly any enemy left, because the local people had already burned or hacked most of the Bourbon men to death.

For ten days Garibaldi led guerrilla warfare, as appropriate to his experience and his shortage of arms. He would have to change tactics at Palermo, where the Bourbons' twenty thousand professional soldiers posed a bigger challenge. When Garibaldi and his three thousand camped on a hill southeast of the city, Americans and Britons appeared with crucial supplies of guns and ammunition, while in the city the Palermitani extended welcome by ringing all their bells continuously for hours. Beyond the hearing of the camp, more practically, the Palermitani were piling their tables and mattresses into barricades. No one could doubt the overwhelming support of Palermo for Garibaldi and what he represented. In an attempt to terrorize their rebellious subjects, the Bourbons bombarded some residential quarters, the effect of which was to drive previously uncommitted Palermitani into Garibaldi's camp. Garibaldi and his men finally entered the city on May 26, to be met by a joyful pandemonium usually reserved for victors. And the fighting had not yet even begun.

They battled for three weeks — the Bourbons, after all, had a huge advantage in men and weapons. Garibaldi used his experience gained in twenty years of commanding troops and proved an excellent tactician. His strength was that his soldiers were more highly motivated than the enemy's, and his good luck was that an American ship was nearby to supply him with weapons. (Although a frigate and other ships from the cities of the new Italy were riding at anchor near Palermo's harbor all during the fighting, they sent no offer of help.)

The inflamed Palermitani harried the Bourbons, and Garibaldi knew how to stall his advances so as to profit by the civilian activity. Many of the Bourbon officers were Italian, and American and English officers approached them about the justice of Garibaldi's cause, undermining their willingness to kill Garibaldi's fighters. When the Bourbons finally capitulated, Garibaldi's men had to escort the surrendering soldiers to their ships so that they wouldn't be killed by the populace.

Garibaldi needed to conquer one more well-fortified city, Milazzo, far to the east; after that, on July 27, Messina fell easily. Three months earlier, Garibaldi had been preparing his departure from Genoa rather stealthily, denied any support at all from the men who shared his aims for a unified Italy. Since then, for that Italy, he had conquered Sicily and been acclaimed its ruler.

~ 10 ~

THE SAVOY KINGDOM
OF SICILY

GARIBALDI'S DICTATORSHIP

G aribaldi the hero! Now the journalists flocked to Sicily. The
master French novelist Alexandre Dumas arrived in his yacht
at Palermo and enrolled as writer in Garibaldi's forces. They all honored and feted Garibaldi, for his military success but even more for
his political courage.

Garibaldi the dictator was bursting with projects for modernizing
Sicily. First and essential, he had to honor his promise for land reform
— already on June 2 he had pronounced land reform official, and the
Giornale Officiale di Sicilia published the notice seven days later.
Church property would be nationalized and the land redistributed, so
as to bring unused lands into cultivation and to give peasants a stake
in agriculture. Later in June he started the wheels rolling toward
building a railway. On his agenda for the longer run: drain swamps
and dam rivers to provide more fertile land; reforest hillsides to make
better use of rainwater; prepare the people to work toward these ends
by establishing basic schools and technical schools; construct new villages and roads as links between the rural producer and his coastal
markets. Garibaldi didn't claim originality — economists had been
pleading for such improvements for a hundred years — but with his
dictatorial power and the gratitude of the people he could finally
bring them about.

Or so he believed, for a little while. Busy as he had been in his military campaign against the Bourbons, he had not considered that his

projects for Sicily might face political challenges from the Savoy. Revolutionary and liberal these men were, in regard to the north's economic progress, but they felt Garibaldi aimed too high for Sicily. Garibaldi had indeed won a short war without support from Turin, but he was a military man, not a politician; he lacked the political skills to persuade his fellow revolutionaries to accede to his wishes. Realizing that he wouldn't be able to implement major reforms in Sicily without Turin's administrative and financial support, he built bridges to the distant Savoy lands by declaring official in Sicily the tricolor flag, the metric system of weights and measures, the lira as currency, and Piedmont's laws generally.* But he still felt that it would be best for Sicily to remain an autonomous region in the new state.

Besides, for the most part Sicilians themselves wanted autonomy, even if within a new kingdom. Without autonomy, argued the historian and activist Michele Amari, they would enjoy less liberty under Savoy than they had had under the Bourbons. Amari wrote out the view of Sicily's political leaders: that the

> island at the very edge of the national territory, distant two days by steamship from the nearest ports of southern Italy[†] with slightly fewer than two and a half million residents who spoke their own dialect, accustomed for a thousand years to a free local government whether or not dominated by foreign kings . . . these conditions, we say, produce and justify the old and universal Sicilian desire.

Cavour rejected the argument. Now that Sicily was united with the Savoy kingdom, he wanted to declare it part of the realm, pure and simple. Michele Amari reported Cavour telling him:

---

* Piedmont, in Italy's northwest corner approximately where the Savoy dukedom used to be, is the region of which Turin is capital. "Savoy" no longer refers to the dukedom but to the royal House of Savoy.

† A trip between Palermo and Catania likewise took two days, and a trip between Rome and Enna took at least two weeks.

[I]f the idea of building a strong and grand nation isn't appreciated down there, the Sicilians would do well to accept the concessions of the king in Naples and not unite themselves to people who neither like them nor respect them.

The conflict, crucial for the Sicilian future, continued harshly for months. Yet, ambitious as Garibaldi was for Sicily, he felt that as long as there was a Bourbon king in Naples, he had to give higher priority to liberating the southern part of the peninsula.

❧

The peasants didn't know about such political hostilities, and they wouldn't have cared if they had known. They had learned that the *macinato* was abolished and that land reform was imminent — Garibaldi had declared it time and time again to his peasant fighters. About the end of the hated milling tax and the acquisition of their own plots of land they cared mightily.

With impatience born of hunger, while Garibaldi was still fighting to liberate northeast Sicily from the Bourbons, in mid-July peasant gangs invaded barons' lands and began to share out the crops. The agitation was entirely rural, occurring in the hinterlands of Palermo, Messina, and Catania. At Bronte, Admiral Nelson's duchy northwest of Catania, rioters demanded the division of the *latifundium*, causing a chaos in which several men and women died. On the last day of July (Messina having just fallen) the proprietors managed to send for help through the British consul to the new government. It was made clear to Garibaldi's officers that the duchy's English ownership could provoke an international incident and that Garibaldi's revolution had needed and would continue to need British support. Furthermore Garibaldi, while he strongly favored the distribution of land to the peasants, as military commander could hardly condone wildcat revolts. The National Guard arrived from Catania the morning of August 4, arrested the leading rioters, had them judged immediately in a people's court, and executed five of them that same day.

Shortly thereafter, Colonel Nino Bixio, one of Garibaldi's three deputies, published a declaration to the insurgents, to the effect that Bronte had already learned its lesson and that stealing and killing were no way to demonstrate Sicily's new freedom to a watching Europe. "In short," Bixio concluded, "either you quiet yourselves, or we, as friends of our nation, will destroy you as enemies of humanity." So *this* was Garibaldi's new Italy.

Having been lured into fighting for a new order, the peasants sank back into bitter resentment. Until then, when Garibaldi had made announcements about fighting not just for Sicily but for the unification of all the regions into a free Italy, peasants nodded in assent — they thought that Sicily would be one of the free regions. Now they heard in those words the reality that Garibaldi, having accomplished his military mission in Sicily, had new concerns. In fact, even if it was not generally known, during these very days the king and Garibaldi were conniving to enable the latter to proceed to Naples. With his troops (though most of his Sicilians had dropped out) Garibaldi crossed the strait on August 19. He thereby followed an old pattern: like the Vandals and the Arabs, Garibaldi used Sicily as a stepping-stone to the peninsula.

⚭

On the other hand, from Bixio's strong reaction at Bronte the Sicilian barons deduced that the new government wouldn't interfere with their land holding. Moreover they had grounds to hope that the government would help them protect their lands from the landless. Most barons, even if they disliked the rhetoric of the liberal, idealistic Garibaldi, liked the new state coming into being under the count of Cavour and King Victor Emmanuel. Those Sicilians who were politically aware realized that an independent Sicily would not survive; to avoid being retaken by the Bourbons, Sicily had no alternative but to join the new Italy.

Once before, from 1713 to 1720 — eons previously, before politicians even dreamed of a united Italy — Sicily had been ruled by Savoy, by King Victor Amadeus, who aroused resentment by trying to transform Sicily into something like the north. History was about to repeat itself, with a vengeance. One result of union was the transfer of power from Garibaldi to Cavour. Garibaldi had already introduced into Sicily some administrative practices, symbols, and laws of Savoy; on August 3 Cavour, abrogating all the Sicilian laws, imposed on Sicily the complete legal code of Turin, effective immediately.

Sicilians were stunned. They hadn't even been consulted by the Turin crowd. They had agreed to union, not to emasculation. They didn't intend to be subject to foreign laws. Notwithstanding the union, to Sicilians the people up in Turin were foreigners: the northerners had machines and wealth, and they spoke a different language. To the northern politicians the Sicilians were certainly foreigners — illiterate, disease-prone, criminally bent foreigners who didn't really merit Turin's generous civilizing efforts. Turin did not consider whether the Sicilians wanted the northern structures, or whether Sicilians had the resources and the ability to implement drastic reforms. It wasn't long before both parties realized that the marriage wasn't working.

To be sure, northern men of culture perceived Sicily differently, admired it for its mix of races and its mythic past, honored it as the place where Risorgimento became reality. But men of such bent weren't determining the new kingdom's policies. Among the politicians it was hard to find any who uttered public words that dignified Sicily.

Sicily having been brought under the Savoy legal code, and Sicilians screaming about it, Turin decided to have Sicilians vote on the matter, actually to ratify the fait accompli. In August the government began the legislative process of dividing Italy administratively into regions. Sicilians had every reason to believe that, once Sicily officially joined the realm, it would be a region of Italy equivalent to Piedmont, Lombardy, Tuscany, and the others. Cavour's envoys convinced Garibaldi to leave Naples and call a plebiscite in Sicily for October 21. On the same day Sicilians would elect their representatives to the assembly being constituted, at least ostensibly to arrange "the time and the manner" in which Sicily would be formally joined to Italy. Voting in private was not even considered; the majority of voters, illiterate, had to be "helped" by the functionaries. Unsurprisingly, the results endorsed annexation.

Cavour's political skills overwhelmed Garibaldi, who soon after leaving Sicily was simply signing the policy documents composed by Cavour. Cavour, with his vision of Italy as a European state, got the credit for uniting the peoples whom Garibaldi had liberated. Toward the end of October 1860, Garibaldi grumbled to a naval commander, "They treat men like oranges: they squeeze out the juice until the last drop, then they toss the peel into a corner."

SICILY IN THE KINGDOM OF ITALY

Soon, however, Garibaldi had an hour of satisfaction, on March 17, 1861, when the Kingdom of Italy was proclaimed under Victor Emmanuel II. Sicilians, for their part, took less pleasure in the birth of the Italian kingdom. Their conservatives, pining for the good old days, were represented by members of parliament from Sicily who beseeched their former Bourbon king, Francesco II, to return. Liberals, for a variety of reasons, demanded regional autonomy. It had taken just a few months for the new Savoy government to transfer to itself the hostility that the Sicilians had felt for the Bourbons.

Cavour did not live to evaluate his achievement. He died on June 6, 1861, aged fifty, from malaria. With him died Italy's program of regionalization and consequently Sicily's regional government.

IMMEDIATE IMPACT OF UNIFICATION
Of all Italians, just under 10 percent were Sicilians. Their discontents were especially three: conscription, taxation, and abuse of religion.

Religion
In its religion, Sicily remained medieval. Even though feudalism had been proscribed fifty years before, the vast majority of Sicilians remained peasants who seldom ventured beyond their lord's lands. Their only respite from mind-numbing work came on religious holidays. Churches

displayed the only manmade beauty on which a peasant ever set eyes. In the bleakest of times the only help for survival came from monks and nuns. Naturally most Sicilians felt attached to their church.

A few peasants had begun to understand the relation between, if not *their* church, at least *the* church, and their poverty. The political ferment of the last twenty years had made them aware of places up north with greater independence and literate populations and schools. They heard increasingly that their priest's lord, the bishop, had supported the Bourbon officials against the peasants, and that the church like the barons wanted to keep them ignorant. No doubt about it: ignorance equaled poverty. Occasionally a townsman would explain a dictum about religion being the opiate of the people. Maybe, as Garibaldi said, it would be good to reduce the economic power of the church.

Garibaldi as dictator expelled the Jesuits (again) and ordered a census of church lands, emphasizing that he did not intend any wholesale expulsion of the religious. Turin saw a Sicily where some two-thirds of the land belonged to the church in one way or another. Urban officials, with their economic objectives, deplored the underproductivity of this land and the parasitical nature of religious life. Starting in 1862 they legislated the closing of many monasteries in Sicily and the confiscation of their property. The lands in question, amounting to around 10 percent of Sicily's territory, were sold at auction, mostly to men who already owned great estates. Garibaldi had foreseen the redistribution of church lands as a way to get more land to the peasants and into production, but now Turin, needing quick cash, sold the land to experienced buyers and added the proceeds to the state treasury.

With this series of blows Turin deprived half the rural Sicilians of their security, both social and economic. Typically the new proprietors had spent all their money to purchase the land so that none remained to hire workers; consequently those who had labored in church vineyards and grain fields found themselves destitute. The bereft religious (many of peasant origin themselves) could no longer offer free bread. Most peasants and religious had supported Garibaldi, some had actively fought for unification, yet the new Italy starved their families and beggared their church.

Taxation

If they hoped for tax relief, they didn't get it. The new Kingdom of Italy, needing money to pay its war debts and to finance industrialization, taxed all Italians heavily. The Sicilians were enraged by the increase of their tax burden by a third over what it had been under the Bourbons. The regressive *macinato,* revoked by Garibaldi, was restored by Turin, and Sicilians found themselves taxed by various levels of government as well as by the sovereign. The Savoy made each locality responsible for facilities such as schools and roads, and while communities in the north might afford such services, those of the south could not; the Bourbons, for all their faults, had provided some infrastructure. The general Bourbon indifference had sometimes extended even to tax collection, at which Turin was efficient.

The American slogan "No taxation without representation" was well known to Sicilian intellectuals.

Conscription

The Savoy government would take not only the Sicilians' church and their food money but also the men themselves, obliging them to leave their fields and their women. True, Garibaldi had talked of military conscription (which disappointed them), but in the event he had gone around urging men to volunteer. Had only a couple of years passed since they had eagerly joined Garibaldi's troops? Those Sicilian men who could leave their families were ready volunteers in fights for good causes but ever loathe to be drafted. The Bourbons had had their own soldiers; they had not forced Sicilians into the ranks. Many Sicilians thought they could resist conscription — their forefathers had resisted without serious consequences. However, the Savoy insisted that Sicilians serve like other Italians. "We can't *vote* like other Italians," countered the illiterate peasants. (Laws from Turin made literacy a requirement for voting.) The peasants fumed as wealthy Sicilians bought exemptions. The poor could only malinger, change sons to daughters in the registry, and shoot at recruiters.

The new government reacted sharply. Turin sent General Giuseppe Govone with twenty battalions to occupy the island, to arrest "all males in the countryside who appear to be of draft age or with the look of killers." The same soldiers who actually dragged monks and nuns from their homes — the ecclesiastical property now up for sale — made war against villages where draft resisters were assumed to live. They cut off the villages' water supply, they burned houses, and they tortured men and boys. The Bourbons had never been so cruel. Men commonly fled to the mountains, and those who could fled abroad. Garibaldi had dreamed of liberty for the oppressed; now, using what liberty they had, Sicilians ran from oppression they attributed to him.

DIFFERING AMBITIONS

We, having the advantages of hindsight and two centuries of industrial production, can better understand the Savoy. Their priorities were effi- ciency and modernization, and to obligate all Italians equally toward those ends seemed only fair. After the untimely death of Cavour, the northern officials who continued his policies tended to share his goals but lack his vision, and they increased the kingdom's high-handed treat- ment of the south. Some of their functionaries posted to Sicily — exiled to Sicily? — were inevitably less civilized than the northern ideal.

Savoy transferred its capital from Turin to Florence and then, in 1864, to Rome. The officials' world was of cities proud of their cul- ture, of surrounding farms worked by their owners and for the most part commercially viable, and of producers adopting the new tech- niques and machines. They sought to industrialize the new Kingdom of Italy to the level already enjoyed by the English and the French. That was exciting — the ignorant peasants down south were not.

"Industrialization" was incomprehensible to men still plowing with oxen. "Government" was the entity that taxed them and against which they defended themselves and their families. When wrongs were done to his family and friends, a Sicilian knew what justice was and how to get it; his justice was concrete, not abstract. Sicilians took umbrage when Savoy officials kept pestering them, in some French-Italian dialect, about national defense and justice, responsibil- ities that the Bourbons had themselves assumed. The officials harangued them about academies and railways — services for which ordinary Sicilians would have to pay but that they would not be able afford to use.

What they wanted was land reform, but no land had come to them, only the shock that Garibaldi's officers had executed those struggling at Bronte to remind him of his promise. The redistribution of lands essentially shifted titles among large landowners. In the process, new groups of men presented themselves as intermediaries and took cuts from land purchases and from rental arrangements, from the sales of crops, from virtually all kinds of financial transactions. They demanded rake-offs from owners, from *gabelloti,* and from peasants. The Sicilian peasants were still at the mercy of the propertied classes. The whole Garibaldi enterprise "had changed everything without changing anything."*

THE RIOT OF 1866

Using the only means they knew to seek improvement, rural Sicilians rioted again in mid-September 1866, after six years as part of Italy. Food prices had risen by some 50 percent during the previous half year, following a dry spring; in May paper money had been introduced, of which one result was a drop in the peasants' buying power; from June Sicilians were obliged to pay a tax on tobacco, a measure to bring Sicily into accord with the rest of the republic; and funds were reduced for the July festival of Santa Rosalia. Local priests, feeling cheated by Garibaldi and angered by the Savoy treatment of their monasteries, supported the rioters.

The intention to riot was broadcast around the countryside in advance, to appeal to men just as deprived as they had been under the Bourbons. Urgent messages to Rome requesting food or funds received no effective response. The peasants, as illiterates denied the vote and scorned by government, marched some three thousand strong into Palermo, shouting for their right to survive. During the week that they tormented Palermo, their numbers increased fivefold.

---

* This statement of Sicilian perceptions is the summary line from the blockbuster novel about the Garibaldi era, Giuseppe Tomasi di Lampadusa's *The Leopard* (1958).

They focused their violence on symbols of the government, attacking police and burning public records. Most of the rioters were simply giving vent to anger about conscription and about not receiving land. Among the more politically articulate, some demanded return to Bourbon rule while others demanded the establishment of a government without any king at all. Hundreds of deaths occurred before the royal navy's bombardment brought the riot under control.

THE SAVOY SEEK MEANS OF CONTROL

The riot accomplished very little. Laws from Turin had confirmed the power of the barons and their agents over the villages. Even if Turin were to allow Sicily a vote on such matters, that would not improve the situation — the barons had acquired with their mothers' milk the practices of corruption, intimidation, and fraud. Given that the officials in elective office depended on barons for large blocs of votes, the barons controlled the officials.

Barons of some districts delegated their delicate political dealings to someone skilled in such work, often a man who had led peasants into Garibaldi's ranks or into the 1866 revolt. These more ambitious or capable among the rural men, those disposed to use violence, often the intermediaries in the land exchanges, tended to grow rich through fees in money and in kind, and wealth led quickly to respect and political power. The local power broker might well have been a mafioso. That word was coming into use as a noun, ever since the 1863 performances of a play by Giuseppe Rizzotto called *I mafiusi della Vicaria*, the Vicaria being a prison in Palermo. At that time the adjective "mafioso" had positive connotations, signifying strength or pride.

As though to promote Mafia recruitment, after the 1866 riot Italy kept a large standing army in Sicily. Soldiers are soldiers, and if some civilian officials on the spot were similarly hostile and sometimes brutal, they reflected the confusion of their leaders in the capital. The Savoy wondered why, the foreign kings gone, the Sicilians were still so contumacious; their legal Italian-speaking government in Rome had no language for communicating with ordinary Sicilians. Savoy administrators held nepotism and corruption to be common among Sicilians to the point that it was counterproductive to employ them. To meet the urgent need for Sicilian police, the northerners set up four competing forces in the hope that they might keep each other honest. Still anxious that Sicilians might gang up in an island-wide insurrection, the Savoy endeavored to foster rivalry among Sicilian leaders, and to that end divided the island administratively into seven independent provinces. The idea was to keep each province under an official with limited jurisdiction, thus restricting his spoils, though the division helped outlaws to avoid capture by fleeing to another province.

For centuries peasants had realized that the official government was against them, and the Savoy government gave the living ones no reason to change their minds. Government supported barons — how could it be otherwise? The mafiosi, on the other hand, sometimes shared booty around the village and in general shielded the villagers from government demands.

Like the outlaws, the agents of law and order used the tools of physical violence and corruption in tandem to repress the populace. Savoy officials, being of liberal persuasion and inexperienced in governing, were easier than the Bourbons to corrupt or co-opt. The Mafia embraced men of Sicily's small middle class, who easily outmaneuvered the Savoy officials in matters of Sicilian politics and economics. Whoever was running the corruption — and as a rule it wasn't clear who was running it — his or their skill made life a trial for the man serving as governor of Sicily. The deputy dictator whom Garibaldi had left in Palermo on his departure for Naples was soon followed by another, then by *prefetti* (civil governors) whose rapid turnover reflected Italy's difficulties in administering the region.

✑

Garibaldi himself was discouraged by Sicily — in 1868 he wrote to a friend:

> The outrages suffered by the southern populations are beyond comparison. I did nothing to feel guilty about; still, if I had it to do over again, I wouldn't go through southern Italy . . . as I have aroused only hatred.

Giuseppe Mazzini, unification's theorist, had problems of his own in supporting Sicily vis-à-vis Italy. He was elected in 1866 to represent Messina in parliament; but that body refused to seat him, citing an 1857 conviction for anti-Bourbon activity. How ironic! In August 1870 the lifelong republican, sixty-five years old, sailed to Palermo with plans to abet an insurrection. He was instead arrested at the port and had to spend a couple of months in prison.

By so treating the republican, the Savoy meant to dash any Sicilian hopes of self-government. The politicians' quip, "We have made Italy, now we have to make Italians," applied nowhere more than Sicily.

∞

For eight hundred years, since the apostolic legacy of the Norman rulers, the hegemony over Sicily had been complicated by the special role in Sicily of the church, and in the summer of 1870 the Savoy tied up that loose end. They weren't acting for Sicily when they set out to restrain the church in Italy — getting the church out of politics had been an aim since the start of the Risorgimento — but their 1870 treaty, which stripped the pope of temporal power, decreed the "irrevocable" end to the apostolic legacy over which popes and Sicily's rulers had fought so bitterly for centuries.

Savoy's own brief experience in governing Sicily provided only frustration. Their rule seemed scarcely better than theoretical as long as lawless men ran the island. Some of the lawless, called bandits, were small independents or small groups of independents who stole and robbed mostly for food. Other lawless, called mafiosi, had higher ambitions and operated as part of the governing apparatus but likewise resorted to violence. Bands obtained police cooperation in order to kill off other bands. So frequent was murder that it seemed almost normal — in the unexceptional year 1873 Sicily had one murder for every thirty-two hundred residents, by far the highest rate in Italy. For a trial in August 1874 it proved impossible to impanel a jury because all the locals were too afraid. The criminality reached the level of national scandal around 1875 with the kidnappings of two Sicilian barons and an Englishman.

When the party of the left won power in Rome in 1876, Prime

Minister Agostino Depretis undertook to end the banditry. The first seven months of 1877 saw strong efforts and some successes that heralded suppression. The Mafia welcomed any defeat of the bandits, considering them to be mere petty criminals who attracted unwanted attention to Sicily. But when ordinary citizens complained that their ordinary doings were being punished, and when politicians muttered fears of exposure, the government curtailed its campaign.

The Savoy had no further ideas for cleaning up the crime. They had employed military solutions in response to the social problems because the civilized system of discussion and legislation just didn't work in the south: corruption defeated the laws. Italy's parliament held back from even discussing Sicily's peculiar systems of criminality and land distribution, since all deputies to parliament from Sicily and many from other regions were allied with the landlords or the criminals, or feared retribution. In the familiar ruse of avoidance, the government established parliamentary commissions left and right; the commissions duly submitted reports superficial and circumspect, when not actually defending the status quo.

FRANCHETTI–SONNINO REPORT (1874–76)

One would have expected much the same of two scions of the baronial class from Pisa. However, both born in 1847, they had grown up in the years of resolute liberalism, and their relative youth may explain their daring. From 1874 to 1876, Leopoldo Franchetti and the half-English Sidney Sonnino, with two other men and ample firearms, rode around Sicily noting impressions and anecdotes. From their research came *Inchiesta in Sicilia*, an investigation or inquiry, which proved a tour de force.

At first, like all travellers (as they said), they loved the island, if only because "the cultured part of the population . . . is as pleasant and kind as one could imagine." Furthermore,

> . . . the beauty of the main avenues, the monumental
> aspect of the palazzi, the nighttime street lighting (one

of Europe's best), make Palermo look like the center of a rich industrious country.

[Then] going into the surrounding countryside, one is struck by signs of an advanced civilization. The perfection of the citrus gardens . . . is proverbial; every bit of land is irrigated, . . . every tree is cared for as though it were a rare plant in a botanical garden. . . . [O]ne sees grapevines and fruit trees, some olive trees . . . and everywhere, evidence that the work has been done with great care and perseverance.

The young researchers began to wonder why they'd come to Sicily. But after a few days of listening to the locals, "everything changes." They hear that

. . . a groundskeeper has been killed — shot with a rifle from behind the wall — because he had been hired instead of a man suggested by certain persons who feel themselves responsible for handing out jobs offered on the lands of others, and these certain persons take a cut of the wages. . . . Elsewhere, a young man was killed because he was setting up a refuge for children. . . . [He was] killed because certain persons, who dominated the populace thereabouts, were afraid that the young man, serving the poor, might acquire over them some of the influence that those certain persons thought belonged exclusively to themselves. The violence, the murders, take strange forms. There's the story of an ex-monk who directed criminal activity and sometimes went to provide religious comfort to people for whose injuries he was responsible.

After a certain number of such stories, the perfume of all those oranges and lemons seems to smell like cadavers.

If violence, corruption, and intimidation were taken for granted by the locals, Franchetti and Sonnino shared the dismay of northerners. The pervasive problems that had frustrated King Victor Amadeus and Viceroy Caracciolo in the eighteenth century and that had challenged economists ever since — problems that absorption into Italy was supposed to assuage — the two Tuscans described systematically.

Although the conventional wisdom attributed Sicily's problems to the bandits, Franchetti and Sonnino decided that the criminality flourished as a response to wretched local conditions. Their point of departure was the management of Sicily's lands. The few peasants who had small plots of their own could nourish themselves. But landless peasants might well starve — the lucky or more able ones would be hired perhaps 100 to 150 days a year, but they all wanted to eat 365 days. That peasants were starved and suppressed seemed in the order of nature to the fortunate few who held the land.

Although near the cities the agriculture appeared reasonably diversified — including the citrus that impressed our Tuscan friends — "what's cultivable inland is used entirely for wheat or pasture." In fact grain occupied three-fourths of Sicily's land area. Grain meant large landholdings — typically a holding covered 500 to 1,000 hectares (approximately 1,250 to 2,500 acres), but many ran between 1,000 and 2,000 hectares, and some were 6,000 hectares or more.* Large landholdings meant absentee landlords and domination by *gabelloti*. Goethe had been shocked at Sicily's feudalism; almost ninety years later Sonnino writes that "all this land is divided into latifundi called *ex-feudi*."

Franchetti's description of Sicily's criminality broke new ground. Reflecting the developments of the preceding twenty years, he distinguished the ordinary bandits from the bourgeoisie-connected Mafia. He stressed the role of the barons, explaining in detail how they benefitted from the system directly and indirectly. While capitalism flowered elsewhere in Europe, in Sicily's economic pursuits the structure was

---

* These landholdings, nothing special by American or Australian standards, are huge for Europe; 1 acre equals 0.405 hectare, 1 hectare equals 2.47 acres.

established by malefactors. Noting the hierarchy of the criminal groups, Franchetti was the first to characterize Sicily's crime as an industry.

While up north industrialization expanded the middle class, Sicily endured the expansion of the baronial system into mining. Sonnino wrote in detail, scathingly, of the work of children in the mines. (To be sure, small children were then employed in the mines of many countries, the situation in Britain being well-documented.)

The *Inchiesta* argues that since unification, the peasants' circumstances had worsened. Sonnino and Franchetti judged Sicily's barons guilty of tyranny, and the new Italian government to be an accomplice after the fact for having acquiesced in the corruption.

How to deal with Sicily's problems was the challenging crux, on which Franchetti and Sonnino disagreed. Sonnino said that, left alone, the Sicilians would work things out, even if they could only do it by emigrating from their overpopulated region. Franchetti said that leaving the power in the hands of Sicilian police and judges would only make things worse. Notwithstanding the uncertainties to which their research led them, *Inchiesta in Sicilia* was a pioneering work of socioeconomic analysis, starkly particularized. Government officials, whom Franchetti and Sonnino hoped to influence, still paid no attention to the special problems of inland Sicily, but they could no longer claim ignorance as their excuse. Unfortunately, the more the politicians learned the depth and breadth of Sicily's problems, the more they sidestepped them.

THREE SICILIANS ABROAD

Five years before the Tuscans went to Sicily to write about conditions there, Giovanni Verga (born in Catania in 1840) moved to Tuscany. From his adolescence Verga had been interested in the subjugation of the peasants and in ways of gaining independence: at age sixteen he wrote a first novel, *Amore e Patria (Love and Country)*, 672 pages with a background of the American Revolution. As an adult and emigrant, he used fiction to present the facts of Sicilian life. His stories centered on the island's poor peasants and fishermen and their struggles to improve their lives. The portrayals, simple and realistic, succeeded so well that he is considered one of the greatest Italian writers of modern times. After six months in Florence he moved to Milan, where he spent twenty years before returning to Catania. Verga was part of a massive brain drain from Sicily, that chronic condition aggravated by the tumults of Risorgimento.

An earlier "brain," Stanislao Cannizzaro, born in 1826, went in 1845 to Pisa to study chemistry. His participation in the 1848 insurrection against the Bourbons earned him a death sentence, so he fled to Paris. Through the 1850s in the Savoy cities of Alessandria and Genoa he worked on problems of atomic weights, attracting attention as a pioneer in atomic chemistry. He remained politically active. As soon as Sicily was free of the Bourbons he began working at the university of his native Palermo, where he secured his position as one of the nineteenth century's top chemists.

From the period just after unification and from a different sphere of endeavor, we have the example Ettore Ximenes, born in 1855, also in Palermo. Ximenes went in his youth to study in Naples, then in 1874 he transferred to Florence. His skill as sculptor won him prizes and important commissions; his work includes the group of *Diritto* in the monument to Vittorio Emanuele II in Piazza Venezia in Rome, statues of Dante and Giovanni da Verrazzano in New York*; and the mausoleum of General Belgrano in Buenos Aires.

Cannizzaro, Verga, and Ximenes reached the heights of their respective fields — as did other Sicilian expatriates — but legions of ordinary men too left Sicilian cities to prepare for their careers or to seek employment in the cities of the north. Often ambitious and reflective men who loved Sicily, they found themselves spending their prime years as ingredients in northern Italy's simmering pot.

PRODUCING FOR WIDER MARKETS

The Kingdom of Italy came into being in the autumn of Europe's Industrial Revolution and on the eve of the American Civil War, a

---

* Both statues are in Manhattan, Verrazzano (1909) in Battery Park just east of Castle Clinton and Dante (1921) in its own grassy triangle on West 65th Street across from Lincoln Center.

juncture favorable both for northern Italy and for Sicily's exports. American agricultural products, which had begun to enter European markets, no longer competed with Sicilian products. The virtual sulfur monopoly made Sicily an essential supplier to the new world of large machines. These forces counteracted the Italian government's disregard of Sicily as producer.

Sicily had always produced cotton in small quantities, and immediately on hearing of the American war some Sicilians expanded its cultivation. The Florio family, already involved in textiles in western Sicily, projected increases in exports of raw cotton and of cotton cloth. England, after all, was the world's major importer of raw cotton and, already Sicily's major trading partner, it might well keep on buying Sicily's cotton after the war's end. Here was a heaven-sent opportunity for Sicily's growers to collaborate with the Italian north in the drive for industrialization and international commerce. The north, however, paid little attention, providing no help whatsoever for grain producers who wanted to shift to cotton. Cotton never took root, and when the American South could again produce it, the small Sicilian cotton-growers lost heavily. Meanwhile the textile industry of Italy's north was buying cotton elsewhere.

Despite this bad experience, Sicilians who had always produced just for their families were increasingly producing for the market, which prodded Sicily into agricultural diversification not seen since the years of Muslim rule. Potatoes, rye, and rice were tried, or expanded from tiny plots, then rejected for one reason or another. Likewise flax. The growing of mulberry trees for silkworms diminished as it was found to be no longer profitable. One of the old standbys, olives, had to be cut back as olive oil gave way to gas for lighting. Each retreat signified heavy losses, because most producers farmed as monoculturists; during these years producers were just starting to experiment with new crops on a small parts of their land while keeping most in the old. Inevitably, the most enterprising growers were the first to try new ways, and when they sank back into despondency the whole sector lost.

Fortunately there were also definite successes, small (various nuts) and large (wine grapes and citrus fruits). As each of these was more profitable per unit of land than wheat — *anything* was more profitable than wheat — grain fields were rapidly transformed into vineyards and orchards. (An economist reported in 1884 in the bimonthly *Sicilia Agricola* that during the preceding thirty-five years more than a third, possibly half, of all grain fields had been so transformed.)

The planting of large orchards had only recently become economically rational; the crucial new factor was an advance not in agricultural techniques but in transportation. Just as a century before Woodhouse had had to find a way to get his wine to market in saleable condition, now the growers of citrus felt stymied. Sailboats were too slow to transport oranges and tangerines up north before they rotted; those that did make it to Europe's cities were considered a luxury. With the advent of steamships, middle-class English and Dutch could have oranges on their tables. From 1870 to 1884 the production of citrus fruit more than doubled. Like citrus, wine grapes were produced all over Sicily, but especially in the western province of Trapani. Stimulated of course by the Britons and Marsala, peasants shifted easily into grapes, which take less time than other fruits from planting to selling. Wine and citrus fruit joined grain and sulfur as products with revenues higher in Sicily than in any other Italian region.

Sicily's agriculture was modernizing, but transformation needed money. Per unit of land, wine grapes and citrus fruit require more labor than does wheat, thus offering more work for landless peasants; however an employer needed money to pay them, plus resources for his own family's sustenance until the first arboreal crop could be sold. Installing an irrigation system could eat up the lion's share of a year's profits, and using irrigation could prove very expensive where water supplies were controlled by mafiosi. Investment to maintain the productivity of land had always been worthwhile, but improvements in technology and markets meant that those who tried to farm without investing were doomed to stagnate.

Certainly money for investment became scarcer as taxes took it from rural Sicily to the industrializing north. For most peasants with their own plots, even micro-investing was out of the question. Some kinds of loan they might obtain from a *gabelloto,* but *gabelloti* weren't about to lend at reasonable rates for improving the lands of others; and a professional moneylender would charge interest of, at the very minimum, 25 percent. The banks that received remittances from emigrants weren't prepared to lend the funds to foster local development. Those who controlled rural baronies, avid as ever to transfer their rural profits to the cities rather than invest in the land, found new opportunities for investment in modern businesses such as sulfur and steamships. A shortage of money, however, doesn't suffice to explain the lack of agricultural investment in Sicily at this time, because when the immense monastic lands were offered at auction in the 1870s they quickly found buyers.

Toward 1890 economists reported that over the preceding ten or twenty years Sicily's income had increased faster than the national average. But the prosperity of a nation or region doesn't necessarily improve the conditions of its lower classes: one thinks of that in relation to England's new factory workers, though Sicily's peasants had been wretched through busts and booms for generations. During this period of expansion, the peasants faced some new problems — problems that were somewhat different in eastern and western Sicily.

PRODUCTION IN DIFFERENT PARTS OF SICILY
Agriculture
Although climate and soil are much the same in east and west, agricultural conditions were different. This may be traced back a thousand years: western agriculture was developed according to a Muslim pattern, while eastern agriculture was more influenced by the feudal pattern. We saw how Muslims tended to farm their own small properties before feudalism came, with its grants of large properties to relatively few barons. The disparity grew as the small farms were divided among the sons of successive generations, while the barons practiced primogeniture and kept their properties intact.

As the nineteenth century advanced, agriculture in the east remained grain fields, latifundia, and landless peasants. Latifundia were, if anything, getting bigger. When a year was bad (due to the difficulty of developing a new crop, or to poor weather, or to general recession) some land barons found themselves unable to maintain their properties and had to sell out. (While this applies to the west too, contemporary producers there tended to do better thanks to their wine grapes and citrus fruit.) Luckier barons could augment their holdings. It was especially in the east that fieldworkers lived in villages rather than at the fields, because wheat requires labor only about thirty-five days a year. Available for — desperate for — other work, they remained at the mercy of the barons. As the barons found themselves in increasingly competitive circumstances, they took it out on the peasants. Sonnino and (in succeeding years) others characterized the peasants as enslaved savages.

With unification came an upsurge in demand for Sicily's grain, so peasants were employed in the clearing of lands. The lands still left to be cleared were not very good. As a result of the increased demand for crops that had heretofore been luxuries, eastern Sicily was bringing poor lands into grain production while losing the best grain fields to small-scale production of nuts and fruit. Though the amount of land sown to grain rose slightly during the thirty years after unification, the yield per hectare fell. For the peasants the shift resulted in fewer days of work, lower revenues — and an increase in hunger.

The years of the 1860s and '70s brought western Sicily increased revenue, which promised improvement for the peasants. From early in the century, when Britons commercialized wine around Marsala, the western peasant enjoyed a sip of autonomy. Wine grapes required labor during five or six months of the year, so the grape growers lived near their crops. The sparser distribution of the peasants in the west hampered the land barons in repression, as did the presence of the British. Into the west's power vacuum came the organized criminals, insinuating themselves into all commercial sectors. When, in 1879, the vineyards of France were gravely damaged by disease and Sicily's wine exports soared, it was a stroke of good fortune for the Mafia. How much the peasants benefitted is another matter.

Sulfur

The western "half" of Sicily was much smaller than the eastern — the agricultural methods that distinguished the two sides overlapped along a line running from Agrigento north to Termini Imerese. Sicily's sulfur, found to the east of the line, altered Sicily's economy to the extent that it was now reasonable to think of Sicily in three parts, west, central, and east. While in the western interior the "transformation" of grain fields meant the planting of grapes and citrus, in the central interior "transformation" often referred to the digging of sulfur mines. The traditional peasant toiled as fieldworker in the fresh air, but here for a century now "peasants" also sweated underground.

Near the mines agriculture was disintegrating, literally. The area from Enna and Caltanissetta down to the south coast looked like Swiss cheese as everyone dug for sulfur in his backyard. Law after law banned the establishment of mines within (commonly) three kilometers of inhabited areas, but law after law was ignored. Residents feared for their houses as mines were dug underneath them. The sulfur was obtained by the same method used in antiquity, namely heating the ores until they melted. The emissions from the fusion process burned plant life for miles around, so much so that already in 1830 the Bourbons restricted the operations during certain seasons. For the rest of the century, nevertheless, locals complained about fumes from the sulfur polluting the waters and reducing the yields from grain fields and orchards. Even the bees showed damage from the "poisons."

As land near mines became infertile and farm work decreased, a few fieldworkers left the area. Many others had to go into the mines; in the 1880s there were some five hundred mines of all sizes. Early in the decade some twenty-two thousand men and boys were employed in them, the boys under fifteen accounting for 25 to 30 percent of the total. (In 1900, mine employment would peak at thirty-eight thousand workers.) The mines underground were very hot — around 40° centigrade (about 100° Fahrenheit) — and eternally damp, and they often collapsed. Work within them was backbreaking and soul searing. Brutalizing too, for the mineworkers preyed on each other, stealing and mugging. Men and boys exiting from the mine complex were commonly met by *padroni* demanding a percentage of their pay. Sicily's mining districts had the highest murder rates in Italy.

While mineworkers expended more physical energy than field-workers, they had less to eat. Mines subtracted land from grain fields, aggravating Sicily's perennial problem of nourishing its population. Sicily might have increased its revenue by processing the sulfur into fertilizers and insecticides (to mention products that agricultural Sicily could itself use) or even just converting it into sulfuric acid, but Sicily exported the raw sulfur.

Cheap labor costs discouraged mechanization. In a rare salute to modernity, in 1876 two rail lines were opened — from Caltanissetta to Catania and from Palermo through Lercara Friddi to Porto Empedocle (adjoining Agrigento) — to replace mules transporting sulfur. No machinery was installed to relieve the *carusi*, boys commonly aged six to eight, who for a pittance carried loads of twenty-five to thirty kilos from deep in the mine to the surface, all day long, a couple of dozen times each day.* Some of the boys were said to live in the mines and hardly ever see the sun. At the bottom of the pecking order, the children drew the lowest pay and the greatest violence. An 1886 law banned underground work for children under ten and outside work for children under nine, but the law was not enforced. The mine managers justified child labor as providing needed income for poor families, their argument intensifying during this period as other countries began to produce and transport the mineral more cheaply and the producers of Sicily's sulfur began to fear for their monopoly position.

The owners and managers of the sulfur mines, like the land barons and *gabelloti*, used private armies to exercise local control. No one dared object: Sicily's sulfur being Italy's only significant mineral export, Italy was obliged to bow to the proprietors of the large sulfur mines. The Bourbons had had to yield to the British owners in the

---

* Also around 1880 the pumice caves on Lipari employed some five-year-olds. Or maybe they were seven or eight, their growth so stunted that they seemed younger.

Sulfur War of 1840, now *Parlamento* let the sulfur barons run their mines as they saw fit.

TOURIST SICILY
The mines and the Mafia were not, of course, the face of Sicily described in literature read by people up north for diversion. These readers were shown archaeological sites and twelfth-century churches, and Sicily's sunny smiling face. Armchair travellers loved it, and some of them not scared off by reports of banditry made the actual trip. Guy de Maupassant (1850–93), the great French storyteller, toured the island extensively in 1885 and reported on *"ses beautés naturelles et ses beautés artistiques."* His writings had been praised for their realism, but de Maupassant managed not to see the realities of the Sicilians' Sicily; in fact he denied the validity of the warnings:

> The Sicilians seem to have enjoyed enlarging and multi-plying the stories of bandits in order to frighten for-eigners; and, even today, foreigners hesitate to come to this island, which is as tranquil as Switzerland.

Maupassant shouldn't have been taken in. Still, he was common among visitors to Sicily in spreading this illusory picture, allowing foreigners to think comfortable thoughts about Sicily and overlook its poverty and exploitation. A comment like his could come only from a visitor to Sicily who had not ventured off the beaten track.* Aside from Segesta and Mount Etna, de Maupassant had limited his tour to the usual cities — Palermo, Agrigento, Siracusa, and Messina — and we know that the cities appeared much more northern-European pleasant than did inland Sicily.

ITALIAN SICILY AFTER TWENTY-FIVE YEARS
In 1885 Sicily had been part of the Kingdom of Italy for a quarter century, during which its larger localities increased in population, in

---

* That phrase was already common. Patrick Brydone used it in 1770 regarding Italy.

businesses, and in standard of living. The interior increased in population but was otherwise little changed.

Enfranchisement

Legislation of 1882 extended the franchise somewhat so that the percentage of male Sicilians entitled to vote approached 10 percent. The peasant had no political voice at all — to vote, a man still had to be literate and to own property. As Italy's government worked through coalitions, an aspiring politician had to conciliate the party in power rather than oppose it; no politician benefitted by favoring the poor.

The increased suffrage, limited as it was, proved a boon for the Mafia. Mafiosi already had constituencies in villages and towns, and mafiosi with an eye to the future saw that they would be needed by politicians to deliver votes. Thus developed an alliance of property owners, political parties, and the Mafia.

Exploitation by North

That Sicily existed to supply products of the earth to people up north was no more questioned by the parliamentarians in Rome than by the ancient Romans. Logic dictated maximum investment for Italy's north if only because it lay closer to industrial Europe. In addition the north had the important resources of water power and iron. As Sicily's deputies still came overwhelmingly from the upper classes, they gave their support to policies of modernization for the north as trade-off for the assurance that Rome would not impose modernization in the south.

At this time, for instance, a continent-wide agricultural recession led Italy into a tariff war with France. In 1887, Rome legislated import tariffs on both manufactures and wheat, legislation that southern deputies supported, despite the fact that the tariffs would have serious repercussions for the south. For one thing, the tariff on wheat protected the grain producers of the south to the disadvantage of more remunerative crops. Less direct but more costly was that the tariff on manufactures protected the industries of the north. The north produced a large share of the manufactured goods it used whereas Sicily had to import all its manufactured goods, so Sicily much more than the north had to pay higher prices for manufactures or do without. Then, as one would expect in commercial warfare, other countries responded to Italy's import tariffs by refusing to purchase Italy's goods, a disaster for Sicily's export crops. And exports being a much larger share of the revenue of Sicily than of the northern regions, a drop in exports damaged Sicily more than the north. Sicily was indeed the region of Italy hardest hit.

A simpler example of how Italian politics discouraged Sicily's modernization: Although in the rest of Italy the mines were publicly owned, in Sicily the mines remained under private ownership and control.

Trains

Northern Italy had a functioning rail network by the time of unification. Improving Sicily's primitive transportation by introducing the railway was one of Garibaldi's first projects; construction actually started in 1861 and the first short line was opened in April 1863, running from Palermo thirteen kilometers east to Palermo's baronial suburb of Bagheria. Railways were planned for the whole perimeter of the island, but construction had to wait while politicians debated whether the railways should be managed from Palermo or from Rome and as large landholders pressured officials to run the rails to their estates. When the rails were finally laid, they followed some convoluted routes.

The first long line ran from Palermo to Catania, then north to Messina. Catania's agricultural hinterland, which had always had to ship through Messina, would now be served expeditiously. Then in June 1881 a line opened from Palermo to Trapani; so as to serve many localities, it ran south from Palermo to Castelvetrano and Mazara, then curved northward through Marsala. Palermo began to send goods by train to the west coast for shipment to Rome. (The direct line from Palermo to Messina wouldn't open until 1895.)

Though the trains came late, they brought a whole new world. Small towns changed dramatically when they became intermediate train stations. Heretofore some of the localities had been linked to the coast only by mule path. A suggestion of their isolation is that their men, desperately underemployed, were afraid to work at railroad construction; whether they held back because of the Mafia or because of some primitive taboo, the construction chiefs had to hire workmen from the peninsula.

Throughout this period there was serious discussion of a bridge across the strait to link the rails of Sicily and Calabria,* but instead, if only as an interim measure, the ferry service was augmented. Some fifty boats, owned by the family Florio, received subsidies from the government. Several ferries a day connected Messina with Reggio or Villa San Giovanni, and a daily ferry ran between Palermo and Naples. As ferries plied ever more frequently, the distance between Sicily and the rest of Italy effectively decreased.

THE MAFIA IN POLITICS

Modernization widened Mafia scope. The new easier, cheaper means of travel between Sicily and the peninsula facilitated Mafia connections with Rome. The extent of political corruption can hardly be exaggerated. The elections in western Sicily were inevitably won by mafiosi or their allies; eastern Sicily filled its political offices similarly, through clientelism. Sicilian politicians naturally formed alliances with politicians from other regions.

Not that mafiosi shied from local office. Holding positions in local government enabled the criminal elements to control taxation: one of the common practices was to levy a tax on mules (the peasants' only form of transport) but not on horses (which the upper classes used), or the local bigwigs simply exempted themselves from taxes. It went without saying that the mayors granted to their relatives and

---

* Starting from this period of this railway-building, plans for such a bridge have been submitted in waves, and several construction engineers became wealthy in the process. In the first years of the twenty-first century the building of the bridge has been seriously discussed again, although the population around Messina has been fighting against it.

friends posts in municipal administration as well as licenses for the *tabacchi,* the shops in each neighborhood that dispensed products of government monopolies, especially tobacco, salt, and stamps. Where courts used juries, the jurors were either mafiosi or in any case aware that an imprudent sentence invited Mafia retaliation. Judges who did not play the game found themselves isolated, threatened, or worse. Regarding all such matters, Sicily's press remained silent, as did individual Sicilians who, when pushed, usually responded that there was no such thing as a Mafia.

∾

Indeed there were no wallet-sized cards or wall-hung diplomas showing Mafia affiliation, nor were assembly-room doors labeled with the hour of Mafia meetings. A loose association existed nonetheless, of which the members were on call for one another. Like practitioners of a religion, mafiosi never forgot their duty, but few of them devoted full time to it. Those who did stood at the top of the hierarchy, whereas most mafiosi held outside jobs. The general run of Sicilians preferred to work (when they had the choice) in white-collar jobs offering security, especially government jobs, and mafiosi followed the pattern. With the help of friends and mentors, they arrived at positions of influence.

Thus, middle-level mafiosi were typically middle-class or upper-middle-class businessmen and free professionals. These are much the same men who throughout the Western world belong to clubs like Lions or Rotary or Masons, as some mafiosi did. In fact — strange as it would sound to freedom-loving Masons like Goethe and Garibaldi, and strange as it sounds to our ears — Sicily's circles of Mafia and Masons overlapped considerably. Everyone in Sicilian politics was involved in at least one of the two; otherwise a man couldn't arrive at the first rung of the political ladder. The question was who belonged to which group or groups, and the strength of the attachment.

The objectives of the Mafia were generally economic. The crucial difference between those other groups and the Mafia was, of course, the use of violence by the latter. Although Italy had tough gun-control laws, every mafioso or aspiring mafioso could obtain a gun permit through "friends of friends" and wore his gun as a badge. Like most associations, the Mafia had men to do the dirty work, and the Mafia's dirty work was to kill or to maim those who had, in a significant way, run afoul of the Mafia chieftains. The Mafia did not kill innocent bystanders: it murdered anti-Mafia fighters in public life, defecting mafiosi, and men who had reneged on their obligations to the Mafia — in short, men who in one way or another were involved with the Mafia. It did coerce men into such involvement, by threatening their families or their wallets. As long as the mafiosi could make good on their threats, they were the power structure.

Inspectors and accountants, lawyers and judges collaborated — often unwillingly, sometimes unwittingly — with those ready to use violence as a political procedure. Of course there was a Mafia, it just couldn't be distinguished from Sicilian officialdom.

THE NOTARBARTOLO CASE

Public awareness of the symbiosis rose sharply through the Notarbartolo case, because its protagonists were so prominent.

Italy's prime minister from July 1887 was Francesco Crispi, born near Agrigento and educated in Palermo. Crispi had begun his political life in Sicily conspiring against the Bourbons and then became a military officer of Garibaldi's; like Garibaldi, Crispi started as a republican but then came to favor monarchy as more likely to unite the people. In the aftermath of Cavour's death, Crispi advanced politically, and as he moved up he moved far to the political right.

Also active in politics was the Bank of Sicily. In the crucial year 1860 the bank lent funds both to the Bourbon government and to Garibaldi's dictatorship. When Sicily was absorbed into the new Kingdom of Italy, the bank suspended its operations until the sum was reimbursed by the kingdom. After the bank reopened it conducted much of its business in the north. Despite its mandate to encourage Sicily's economic development, it did nothing to stimulate Sicilian agriculture or industry. It did lend generously to politicians feathering their own nests and collaborating with the Mafia.

Raffaele Palizzolo represented the town of Caccamo (east of Palermo) in the Italian parliament. He had first come to attention beyond his district by winning an election with more votes than the district's total number of voters — not that this hindered him politically in a region known for electoral frauds. A strong partisan of Crispi, Palizzolo sat on the bank's board of directors and used that position to further Mafia interests.

Somehow the presidency of the bank fell to an honest man, Emanuele Notarbartolo. He typified his generation in having fought with Garibaldi. He distinguished himself as an officer, and in due course he became mayor of Palermo and then was appointed to the senate in Rome. As bank president, Notarbartolo wanted to inject some honesty into bank policies, and to that end, in 1889, asked Prime Minister Crispi for authority to reform the bank. Crispi didn't agree — in fact he tried to replace Notarbartolo — but Crispi's party was defeated in the May 1891 election. The losers felt threatened by a scheduled investigation of banks generally, in which Notarbartolo (though no longer bank president) was to testify. On the first day of February, 1893, in a train bound for Palermo, Notarbartolo was murdered.*

Accused of commissioning the murder was Raffaele Palizzolo. The wheels of justice turned even more slowly than usual, for Crispi was reelected in December 1893 and stayed in office until March 1896; as long as he was prime minister, there would be no movement toward trying Palizzolo. Eventually in July 1902, more than nine years after the murder, Palizzolo was pronounced guilty and sentenced to thirty years. The anti-Mafia men cheered, too soon. The appeals court overturned the sentence on a technicality. All Italy was roused to strong feelings about Palizzolo's guilt or innocence. Scholars pleaded for an independent judiciary as essential to a modern democracy. Journalists kept the Notarbartolo case on the newspapers' front pages for a decade.

A second trial, held in 1903, dismissed the case for lack of evidence.

---

* Sicily keeps alive at least the names of its anti-Mafia fighters. The most important train station in Palermo after Palermo Centrale is called Notarbartolo.

FASCI (1892—94)

A concurrent long-running Sicilian story involved many more people and had international aspects. The recovery of the United States from its civil war plus improved transport brought large quantities of American agricultural products into European markets; Europe fell into recession, and Sicily's exports of wheat and sulfur plunged. Sicily's export of wines had reached its highest point in 1879 due to disease in the French vineyards; eight years later, the French vineyards producing again, France and Italy embarked on the tariff war mentioned a few pages back. Sicily could no longer export wine and citrus fruits to what had been its major buyer. Americans seized the opportunity, by 1890 selling oranges in Europe. These developments, following upon a twenty-year boom, sank the Sicilian peasants back into hungry hopelessness.

From Italy's infant Socialist Party rose a Catania activist. Giuseppe De Felice Giuffrida started in May 1891 to unite the discouraged into Fasci dei Lavoratori (*lavoratori* are "workers" and *fasci* are "bundles," as in "in union there is strength"). Though strategy was vague, aims were explicit. First and foremost, because Italy had placed hedges around striking that peasants could scarcely traverse, the Fasci wanted the clear right to strike. Some demands addressed the peasants' continuing problems: land reform, change in contracts between peasant and employer, and reform of the tax structure so as to reduce levies on food. Other aims included freedom of assembly, freedom of speech, honest elections, and the right to worship as one wished or not to worship at all. Socialists had been spreading these ideas in cities since mid-century, ideas already developed during the Enlightenment.

Now the rural Sicilians grasped them. General military service and occasional employment abroad exposed Sicilians to new ways. Emigrants sent home letters and newspapers — not many yet, but items in each one might reach hundreds of Sicilians. Though the vast majority of rural people could not read, more could than before. Since the Garibaldi disillusionment a generation had passed, and it wasn't difficult to arouse peasants' hopes again. And this time they would embark on their own campaign.

Within two years Fasci had formed in virtually every locality on the island, drawing at least two hundred thousand people, perhaps twice that, from all classes and from most political persuasions, but predominantly and most significantly from the *contadini* (fieldworkers and mineworkers). Fasci posters were printed by the thousands and pasted on town walls, to be read aloud by a member to his eager fellows. In the villages, criers spread word about meetings and about events in other localities. It was an exciting time, noisy yet peaceful. The Fasci were part of the Western world's socialist mood; members of the Fasci were encouraged to become Socialists and many did so, but the organizations remained separate. Socialism targeted industrial workers, not peasants. The *contadini* weren't attracted by socialism as such, nor would they have been by any "-ism"; they were pushed into Fasci by growling bellies. Maybe the Fasci could *do something*. It was the strongest expression of Sicilian sentiment in six centuries.

Armed revolt wasn't on the agenda. The Fasci were a political movement, seeking economic improvement through peaceful means. They inaugurated strikes in spring '93 that proved successful. Come summer, they accepted a more difficult challenge: to better the contracts of serf-like farm workers, who rented land and thus were considered self-employed. For three months, starting in early September, peasants in the area of Corleone did no farm work, behaving with discipline and solidarity until they won their cause.*

The successes of the Fasci frightened conservatives particularly and Rome generally. Even politicians who sympathized with the Sicilian peasants felt it essential to maintain law and order. To protest the installation of Crispi on December 8, 1893, the Fasci organized street demonstrations. Near Palermo in the small town of Giardinello, where the unarmed demonstrators were proceeding peacefully in the piazza, some soldiers shot into the crowd, killing eleven and wounding scores. Of course the scene turned immediately chaotic, with looting and more killing. The riot spread to other towns, government buildings were torched, and by the end of the year the dead numbered eighty-five. As was to be expected, Rome reacted severely: Prime Minister

---

* The relevant legislation was introduced in parliament by the deputy Sidney Sonnino.

Crispi declared martial law and installed a general as governor with fifty thousand soldiers to help him. The Fasci were dissolved. How much of the strong response was justified by the events and how much it was retribution for the success of a mass socialistic movement is a question politicians and scholars still debate.*

Note that the Fasci were born in Sicily's east and were killed in Sicily's west. Peasant movements had been and would continue to be stronger in the east than in the west.

As a consequence of the Fasci movement of 1893–94, the parliament began to debate proposals for relieving Sicily's tribulations. For the first time some deputies admitted that the policies of the Kingdom of Italy vis-à-vis its south had been mistaken — they openly addressed the conditions of the latifundia and even broached the question of regional autonomy — but nothing much happened. With the next change of government in March 1896, the imprisoned Fasci leaders were amnestied by Prime Minister Antonio Di Rudini, who gave priority to Italy's "suffering workers." There were new laws, though they dealt with symptoms rather than underlying problems. In July 1896, for the benefit of Sicilians, parliament abolished export duties on sulfur, which was like locking the barn door after the horse was stolen. Unsatisfied *contadini* still rebelled occasionally — for example, in 1898 at Troina (thirty kilometers west of Mount Etna), where police put down the riot by killing eight.

Giuseppe De Felice Giuffrida, the man of the hour, was to remain a political celebrity for a quarter century. Of humble origins, he was elected and reelected deputy to parliament from 1892 until his death in 1920. It's a safe bet that he, like the Notarbartolo case, was talked about by everyone who emigrated during those years.

---

* The Fasci movement is background for the novel *I Vecchi e i Giovani (The Old and the Young*, 1913) by Luigi Pirandello, winner of the 1934 Nobel Prize for Literature. The novel's most famous lines are: "Poor island, to be treated like a conquered land! Poor islanders, to be treated as savages who need to be civilized!" Like Giuseppe Tomasi di Lampedusa, Pirandello came from a Sicilian upper-class family, some of whose recent money had come from sulfur.

POPULATION MOVEMENTS

The First Mass Emigration

Until now emigrants have been mentioned just in passing, because mass emigration from Sicily didn't start until the 1890s.

We saw, in mid-century, a number of Sicilians in Paris and in Turin, virtually all of them men from the upper classes. In all classes people were interested in moving abroad, but the absorption of Sicily into Italy did not facilitate emigration; on the contrary, the Savoy government limited it by decree. In a communication of July 1873 that would become infamous, the minister of the interior required every applicant for emigration to show he had enough money not only for the trip but also for living expenses in the new country during an indefinite period until he could become self-supporting; in addition, the prospective emigrant had to bring forward a gentleman of adequate wealth who would obligate himself to pay the emigrant's fare back to Sicily should return prove necessary. Liberals protested vociferously, among them Sidney Sonnino; it was against this background that in the 1876 *Inchiesta in Sicilia* he recommended emigration as a means of alleviating Sicilian poverty. He knew that every year thousands of Italians from other regions moved abroad. That year Sicilian emigrants totaled 1,228.

After lengthy debate, parliament did foster emigration from Sicily, southward. Tunisia, undertaking a program of public works, sought technical help from Italy. In 1878 some fifteen hundred Italian workers went to build the Tunis-Algiers train line. The country welcomed men of every occupation — excavators and accountants, shopkeepers and teachers — almost all of them Sicilian. The Italian community in Tunisia in 1871 consisting of some six thousand businessmen and professionals; in 1881 there were ten thousand. Evidently the Sicilians would emigrate, if not hampered in doing so.

∽

Bureaucracy apart, immense obstacles faced the peasant who considered emigrating. Sicilians lagged in joining this Italian movement for much the same reasons that they lagged in other Italian developments: they lacked material resources, and they lacked the experience and confidence that a man needs to venture forth from the familiar. When they did depart from the life they knew, they held on to at least one element of their security, namely their families: Through the end of the century Sicilian men were more likely to emigrate with their wives and children than were the Italian men from other regions.

They had courage, these first Sicilian emigrants, a courage born of desperation. Some of the illiterates departed with as vague an idea of "La Merica" as their fathers had held of "La Talia." Most of Sicily's emigrants were field hands and miners, of whom the vast majority went to the Americas, where they could expect to find unskilled work. (This contrasts with the emigrants from northern Italy, fewer in number, more highly educated and skilled, who had reasonable expectations of finding work in the industrialized countries of Europe.)

Through 1880, some 800 to 1,250 Sicilians migrated each year to other countries, then their number rose gradually, reaching eleven thousand in 1889. Emigration remained at that level in 1890, 1891, and 1892, during which years those considering the move found their prospects improving. At the Sicilian end, the church, fearful of socialism and then of the Fasci, encouraged the faithful to depart, while the Fasci movement taught peasants about their potential. At the American end, as the emigrants established communities, they beckoned relatives and friends, extending reassurance about the daunting life change. In 1893 more than 14,600 emigrated, a substantial jump, though still less than 1 percent of Sicilians.

Although the emigrants were few, their impact was enormous. In Sicily's interior, where life had long been stagnant, movement abroad was opening eyes to the wider world. Old people who had never left their lord's lands and never seen as much as a pond (for Sicily has few bodies of water) now heard sons and grandsons comparing visions of crossing the ocean. Men who talked endlessly about the military adventure of their lives, who still hummed the tunes they had sung while marching with Garibaldi, now heard young people singing of New York and Buenos Aires. Girls who dreamed of getting married to a man with a piece of land were replaced by girls wanting to know if *her* young man intended to emigrate, and if so — crucially — whether he would take her with him. Literacy courses began so that *contadini* could read letters from abroad, letters often written by scribes.

Macroeconomic Influences

Letters home noted advantages of living in America, even when America had financial problems. A grave depression afflicted the capitalist world in 1893 (with disastrous results for Sicily's exports, from sulfur to sumac); recessions followed in 1896 and 1900. The American condition, though, was reckoned to be temporary, whereas the poverty of Sicily was known to be eternal. As a result of the 1887 tariff that subsidized wheat (at the expense of Sicily's crops requiring intensive labor), land was returned to grain fields and many peasants to their former extreme underemployment. Italy was taxing wine production so heavily that quality was threatened. In Palermo, industrial workers were striking. Back in the 1850s, Horace Greeley had popularized the phrase "Go west, young man" as a spur to ambitious young Americans. Its Sicilian version was: go west, go north, go anywhere; here you have no chance.

Americans even reduced the number of Sicilian mineworkers laboring wretchedly for a pittance. Around the turn of the century a new method of sulfur extraction came into use — the Frasch process, which obtained sulfur of high purity by pumping it from salt domes. Sicily's sulfur lies not in salt domes but in sedimentary deposits, where the Frasch process can't be used. Within a few years the customers for Sicily's sulfur had transferred 90 percent of their business to Louisiana, so that most of Sicily's sulfur workers lost their jobs.

Again Sicilians subsisted on grain and fruit, now with their thoughts — bitter thoughts, hopeful thoughts — turned toward America. From the mid-1890s emigration from Sicily increased rapidly.

Sicily Grows More Urban

Much of the western world was urbanizing around this time to serve the new factories. In Sicily, where factories were insignificant, urbanization was largely the result of emigration. A simple, partial explanation is that the smaller the locality, the higher the proportion of residents who moved abroad: at the extremes, from communities of less than two thousand inhabitants, 15 percent emigrated, while from the three big cities only 3 percent emigrated.

Another influence on the urbanization was emigrant remittances. Emigrants, who had left as young peasants but grown citified in their lives abroad, wanted to provide homes for their relatives, or for themselves someday, in a place with more friends and more facilities than the villages they had left, especially as the villages were now emptying out. This increased the flow of money from village to town. When transactions were rural, the corresponding funds remained in the villages to buy food and to repair or replace housing. When transactions moved to the towns, the sellers of food and construction materials moved with them. The village usurer himself often became a moneylender in the town. As transportation improved, these movements accelerated.

Between 1861 and 1911, the share of Sicily's population living in villages decreased significantly, while the share of the total population living in towns and cities correspondingly increased, with the towns of thirty thousand to a hundred thousand showing the greatest increase. A young emigrant of the 1870s returning forty years later to retire would have found the village life he remembered to have been largely replaced by town life.

SICILY'S POPULATION DISTRIBUTION BY SIZE OF LOCALITY

Size of locality	1861	1911
Villages (fewer than 10,000 pop.)	48%	28%
Small towns (10,000–30,000)	32%	40%
Larger towns (30,000–100,000)	8%	16%
Catania, Messina, Palermo	12%	18%
All Sicily	100%	100%

Source: The raw data are from Vanelli, *Sicilia*, extract from the *Atti della Commissione Parlamentare d'Inchiesta sulla disoccupazione*, vol. III, tomo 4, pp. 418–19. Quoted in Francesco Renda, *L'Emigrazione in Sicilia, 1652–1961*. (Caltanissetta and Roma: S. Sciascia, 1989), pp. 54–56. I calculated the percentages.

∽

Urbanization meant increase not only in size but also in facilities, including the theaters of which the barons were especially proud. Palermo, a theater town since the thirteenth century, opened the Politeama Garibaldi in 1874; immediately afterward started building the Massimo, which opened in 1897 as the third-largest theater in Europe; and opened the Biondo in 1903. Small towns already had conspicuous theaters — notably Vittoria, Noto, and Castelvetrano (which flaunts a visit from Goethe).

Long famous among European elite for her production of operas and plays, Palermo attracted many foreign musicians and dramatists. The dean of lyric theater, Richard Wagner, finished his orchestration of *Parsifal* in Palermo in early 1882, then sojourned in Sicily for a few months. The German composer Richard Strauss stopped in Siracusa briefly in spring 1893 and returned thirty years later for two weeks in Taormina. The bad boy of the English theater, Oscar Wilde, spent two months in Sicily in 1897 and returned in 1899. Aristocratic foreigners arrived in such large numbers that in 1900 Palermo opened the ultra-luxury Villa Igiea on the outskirts.

Sicilian patrons of such theaters generally went up north for medical treatment and sent their sons up north to study, for they were not as willing to finance secondary schools or hospitals. Even Palermo still lacked a modern hospital. As for schools, in the first years of the century only about 60 percent of the residents of the city of Palermo knew how to read, and in Palermo's hinterland and everywhere else on the island the literacy rate was 30 to 40 percent. Though there was no discussion yet about making schooling obligatory, primary schools were increasingly common in the towns. In rural areas Sicily didn't build schools; upward mobility of peasants was still blocked by the barons.

THE YEARS OF PEAK EMIGRATION TO WORLD WAR I

Sonnino had theorized that emigration would relieve rural Sicily's poverty; he lived to see vast emigration, though not much improvement in the lives of peasants relative to other Sicilians. Land ownership in these years became even more concentrated, because while many migrants from inland Sicily had possessed no land at all, some had small plots, and these generally fell to the larger landholders. This did not bode well for the remaining peasants, nor for agricultural advance.

The twentieth century dawned during a general prosperity, of which Sicily enjoyed some benefits. It provided peasant families with cash to send one or more of their members abroad: Sicilian emigrants numbered 106,200 in 1905, 127,600 in 1906. This was not just a reflection of emigration trends in Italy generally, for statistics for the preceding dozen years indicated that, when emigration increased, the emigration from Sicily increased substantially as a proportion of all Italy. Forces causing Sicilians to emigrate were peculiar to Sicily, or at least stronger in Sicily. (Emigrants from Sicily in absolute numbers and as a percentage of emigrants from Italy, for each year from 1876 to 1925, are given in table A of the appendix.)

As conditions in Sicily improved, emigration dropped sharply from 1906 for the next five years. But even when the push of dire poverty slackened, the pull of America continued strong. Between 1880 and 1914, Sicilians spread themselves all over the Americas in one of the greatest population movements the world has ever known.

∽

The first emigrants were pioneers, whereas the later ones naturally had an easier time. For example, those considering emigration in the first years of the twentieth century had an additional source of information in the newspapers and magazines that had proliferated, reflecting the sharp rise in literacy. Even more important was personal contact. Letters kept arriving to foster dreams, and some, eventually, came with money to pay for a relative's voyage. On a daily basis the dream was kept alive by "Americani" — emigrants returned to Sicily from the Americas. They included men more or less established in their new country who proudly visited their families of origin once for a few weeks or months, virtual commuters to South America who worked six months each year there and spent the rest of the year in

Sicily, younger men working in the States who went back to Sicily to fetch a bride, older people who had worked for years in the New World and had returned to their hometowns to die.

Only a small percentage of those who had emigrated succeeded in reaching high rungs on the economic ladder, but among those who returned to Sicily for whatever reason the percentage of "success" was higher. The Americani and those who had remained in Sicily compared themselves with one another, and, even when the Americani disliked life in their new land, they knew themselves to be proof that the New World offered incomparably greater economic opportunity.

MAFIA MOVEMENTS

Mafiosi were naturally among those attracted, though they had their own concept of "opportunity." Sicilian criminals wanted by the Italian police fled in the emigrant throng. Besides, in the cities of the eastern United States the conditions in which new immigrants lived fostered criminal activity. Early in the century New York police and academics began to concern themselves with the connections between the American Black Hand and the Sicilian Mafia; from 1907 Italians too began to study the Mafia and its causes.

One of the few New York detectives with an Italian surname, Joe Petrosino, had achieved respect and local renown by coupling his stance against crime in the immigrant community with his sympathy for immigrant aspirations. He embarked on a trip to Sicily to investigate the American-Sicilian criminal links, sailing covertly and arriving in Palermo February 28, 1909. On March 12 in the early evening, in a major piazza in central Palermo, Joe Petrosino was murdered, apparently by individuals he trusted.

Some mafiosi returned from the States to Sicily bringing modern techniques of gangsterism. In America, where most immigrants from most countries had been miserable peasants and were now scrambling for better lives, every immigrant community harbored a small class of delinquents. The Sicilians were unusual, however, in taking state-of-the-art criminality back to their homeland and infusing it into every sector of a society well adapted to accept it.

Mafiosi were just a small current in one of history's major population flows. All in all, around a third of Sicilians emigrated.* The people who left were not necessarily from the most comfortable peasant families, but they were from the most ambitious. It was a great loss to rural Sicily. Northern patriots lamented the loss to Italy of these emigrants.

THE ECONOMY BEFORE WORLD WAR I

Curiously, during this period of mass emigration the number of Sicily's inhabitants did not decrease. In fact Sicily's population, which was counted as 2,408,500 in the census of 1861, rose in every census thereafter through 1921. As Sicily experienced virtually no immigration, the population grew because of a high birth rate and an increasing life expectancy. The revenues coming to the island due to technological advance had to be distributed among a larger population.

LACK OF ECONOMIC DEVELOPMENT
In the first decade of the new century, Sicily acquired many of the appurtenances of modern life. That is the good news; the bad news is that Sicily received them passively.

From the 1890s the Kingdom of Italy experienced rapid economic growth. Through most of this period the prime minister was the left-leaning Giovanni Giolitti, who was more sympathetic to the south than his predecessors. In Sicily his government financed railways, port facilities, and rural roads; it constructed or modernized hospitals so that they could deal with the age-old epidemics of cholera and typhoid fever, which broke out all too often among the poor, and with acute cases of malaria.

As people moved from villages to towns, they had more access to

---

* That is, the number of emigrants during the period 1876–1915 (1,352,930) was more than a third of people counted in the 1911 census of Sicily (3,695,493).

schools. Attendance at schools for children through age fourteen was about the Italian average, and the same was true for trade schools and universities. These high levels relative to regional income reflect Sicily's high unemployment: the schools absorbed young men who couldn't find work. Yet Sicily lacked a technical school for agriculture; the young men wishing to work for improvements in Sicily's primary sector had to study in the periphery of Naples or in cities farther north.

Industry, seen universally as the engine of growth, in Sicily never gained momentum. Obviously, Sicily was distant from markets up north. Probably more important, Sicily had nothing for fueling industrialization equivalent to the north's vast capacity for hydroelectric power. The north being so industrially advantaged, northern politicians could hardly have been expected to foster industrialization in the south. When wagons were needed for Sicily's trains, the northerners asked for bids and chose a factory outside Italy to build them. When the government arranged big contracts for ships, they assigned none to the Florio plants in Sicily.

THE SINGULARITY OF FLORIO

The Florio empire survived into the twentieth century, barely. Son of the founder Vincenzo, Ignazio Florio added substantially to the family fortunes: he owned a bank; factories for textiles, ceramics, and tuna canning; a navigation company with a hundred ships; the Oretea steel foundry (where he produced the machinery and boilers for his ships); and the thriving original wineries, selling under the name "Marsala Florio." Certainly a vast empire, but each Florio operation was small in European terms, and, with the coming of trains and expansion of markets, unprofitable, so Ignazio merged with northern interests. The Florio industries would now function with different priorities, after Florio's name had personified big-business Sicily for sixty years. Around 1910 began the sale, piece by piece, of the Florio companies, and although it had been awhile since Palermo had played in the big industrial leagues, the city recoiled. Labor leaders howled about recession for the island.

The significant question for Sicily's economy is why the pioneering Florio remained unique. Why, in an era of great economic expansion, didn't Sicily engender other major entrepreneurs? True, Vincenzo Florio was born into a family with a successful medium-sized business, but his wasn't the only such family. His family had the vision to send him to England for an apprenticeship, yet there were many Englishmen in Messina and on the west coast from whom ambitious young Sicilians might have learned. Vincenzo Florio didn't have models to follow for his career. Woodhouse and a few other Englishmen put together large wineries in Sicily, but they did so to serve an existing English market and they had the backing of the British government, thus they ran no great risks. Ingham did advance toward vertical integration and toward diversification, but not nearly so far as Florio. The generation of John D. Rockefeller and Andrew Carnegie was in diapers when Florio seized opportunities in tuna and transport, heading into unknown waters. As he established his big businesses, Florio did develop relationships with leading politicians who then subsidized him, but there's nothing to indicate that Florio was ever involved in ruthless blocking of competition.

SICILIANS DO LITTLE FOR THEMSELVES

Business venturers were rare, in any case. Midlevel merchants in Sicily tended to be foreigners who kept their ambitions in the orbit of foreign trade. *Gabelloti* and mafiosi, enterprising though they were, lacked interest and discipline for urban-based, long-run, competitive businesses. This left barons as potential entrepreneurs; up north it was common for members of the nobility to invest their resources in some kind of business. But Sicily's barons, as we have seen, always lacked the inclination, and therefore the skills, to employ themselves in any useful manner. Barons didn't care to produce because producing had little value in their social realm — it "wasn't the thing to do." Their ancestors had learned from the Spanish that advancement comes as a favor from officials, and from the church that economic concern militates against salvation.

In fact, success and social mobility made Sicilians suspicious; rich as the Florios were, the family was never accepted into Sicilian high society. In all classes the suspicion of anyone or anything unfamiliar overwhelmed any drive for gain. To be sure, the suspicion of strangers had a good rationale in an arena of bandits, and the proliferation of bandits provided economic rationale for not entering business. Men joined their relatives and neighbors in what they perceived as common defense of their locality, against the government or any outsider; even in this they bound themselves with blood oaths to be loyal to their new "family."

The same men would not collaborate in efforts to improve the infrastructures of their community. Peasant men with lots of time on their hands did not get together to build the roads that would have connected them to markets and schools. Along Sicily's coasts, malaria still enfeebled many people, but no baron ever organized local men in a project to drain the swamps. Speaking of water, a maxim of the time advised: "When your neighbor's house is on fire, fetch water for your own house." The idea of a man investing his meager resources with others' or depending on the commerce of others in the hope of some later profit was not seriously considered.

Opportunities there were: Even if the Sicilians lacked resources for large-scale industrialization, they could certainly have developed larger markets for their agricultural products. Without the wealth and the entrepreneurial genius of a Florio, however, they would have had to work as a team or get organized by some foreigner. The English were still thriving with their wine, a competitive business demanding the use of modern technology. The smaller wine producers, unable as individuals to mechanize, resisted learning and buying through cooperatives, and by 1900 they could sell their grapes only for blending with those of northern regions. Sicilians liked to attribute their poverty to the government — earlier to the foreign kings, now to Rome — and while the government could have done far more than it did to develop Sicily's productive capacity, it's also true that the Sicilians could have done more for themselves.

∽

Sicilians continued to petition Rome for improvements. The elderly Sidney Sonnino, in parliament from 1880 (shortly after his *Inchiesta*), maintained his fight on behalf of the Sicilian peasant. In recent years he had allies in Luigi Luzzati and a few other deputies. The Sicilian cry for agricultural reform finally brought more northerners, concerned about the economic development of the kingdom, to support a strong agricultural sector in Sicily, and thus the more efficient and more humane use of Sicily's land. They met resistance from southern deputies, even of the left, who risked personal loss should the system become less exploitive. The best promise toward ending the blockage was Italy's introduction, in June 1912, of universal (male) suffrage. But any immediate effect of voting rights for peasants was buried in the eruption of a major European war.

WORLD WAR I

Although the Great War broke out as reaction to the shooting of an Austrian archduke in June 1914, a rising fever of European nationalism had augured the war during the preceding few years. In 1912 and 1913 Sicilians in increasing numbers rushed to leave Italy for America. When the war began in August 1914 the Kingdom of Italy declared neutrality, but it entered the war in May 1915 as ally of the British and the French.

For Sicily this proved a "revolutionary" war, in a social sense: it changed the peasants' inland mentality. Sent off to war in the Dolomite mountains of northeast Italy and in the highlands of Turkey, common soldiers from Sicily not only fought beside soldiers from the rest of Italy but also ate and drank, sang and prayed with them. The Sicilians learned to speak Italian and learned something about life on the continent. Men whose emotions had always centered on their families perceived, in the shared trenches, that near-strangers could be their brothers too. *Contadini* entrusted their lives to city men, and found the trust reciprocal.

Prewar legislation had enfranchised the peasants; the Great War emancipated them. Before the war, *contadini* had marveled when

their visiting "Americani" cousins didn't treat the landed rich obse-
quiously; now the *contadini* understood, and they would never again
kowtow. The mobilized men learned the strength of their numbers,
developed ambitions, and determined that (if they survived the carnage) they were not going back to latifundia to be treated like slaves.
Men of the world now, they found they received some sympathy
from the baronial sons who led their regiments. An understanding
grew between the young peasants and the young barons that by
fighting the war the peasants were earning a right to fields of their
own once they returned home.

But there was another side to the military medal. Allied efforts
depended not only on foot soldiers but also on war matériel — guns
and bullets, trucks and ships. In Italy the factories producing such
goods were located in the northern half of the peninsula. The men
working in those factories (expanded during wartime) were needed
right where they were and so received exemption from service as soldiers. Southerners in northern Italy saw cities full of civilian men and
cried discrimination. Sicilians had a new excuse to bolster their traditional unwillingness to fight as draftees. Draft evaders and deserting
soldiers joined outlaws hiding from recruiters in the mountains.
Under the tutelage of criminal gangs, they looted and rustled animals
for food. They carried on their own warfare, against Sicilian towns.

Meanwhile, the military demanded wheat, wheat, and more
wheat. Orchards and vineyards, labor-intensive, were uprooted (as
in Roman times) in order to plant as much land as possible with
wheat. Specialized workers came to Sicily from the north to expand
the chemical and metallurgical industries and manage them. Peasants
previously producing crops other than wheat could easily be drafted
as unskilled labor for the factories. So Sicily industrialized — not to
any great extent when compared with regions up north, but far more
than had ever been anticipated for this grain land.

With the end of the war came the inevitable slowdown of the
economy. Northern factories returned to peacetime production,
withdrawing industrial work from Sicily. Sicily had lost its markets
for fruit and wine. The need for agricultural labor having lessened,

Map 16. Sicily and Italy, 1860–present

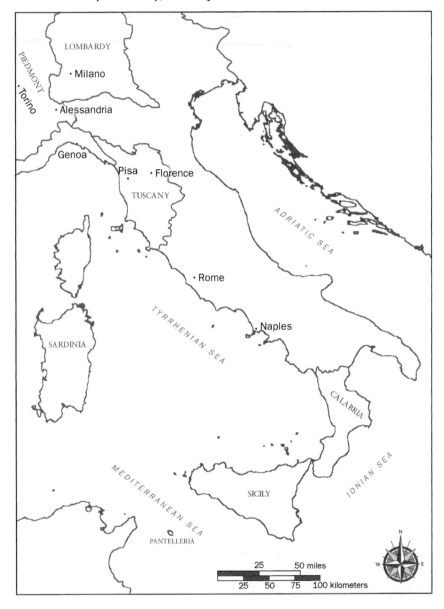

the returned soldiers found that they were not only without land of their own but without any work at all.

They had an advocate in a young priest from Caltagirone, Luigi Sturzo. Caltagirone was center of a province that functioned relatively well, and Sturzo knew how to engage the different social classes in his Christian endeavor of putting the poor to work. He spread his message widely through the newspaper of the Christian Democratic Party, *L'Ora*, of which he became editor. In the chaotic postwar period, he worked with peasants and artisans in cooperatives, prevailing upon men with more education to provide leadership and to expand organization. Sturzo arranged loans for good Christian men whose employers would stand surety. It was his sense of Christian morality that underlay both his ambition to improve his people's economic lives and his dissatisfaction with the prelates' conservatism; he envisaged a political party based on "the Catholic conscience" but free of the church hierarchy. In 1919 he joined with a few likeminded laymen to establish the Partito Popolare Italiano, the first organized expression of the Catholic Left. In the 1919 elections the PPI won 14 percent of the votes cast in Sicily.

Even before the war's end, parliament had decided to improve the lot of war veterans returning to the fields. The Visocchi-Falcioni edicts of 1919 and 1920 would give to such men, and to cooperatives, temporary possession of land being cultivated poorly or not at all. But the legislative process is slow, and Sicily's landless had heard too many promises that remained unfulfilled. Starting in October 1919, large groups of ex-soldiers invaded former *feudi*, hundreds of them all around the island, for demonstrations and for seizure. This time, along with the day laborers and tenant farmers, small landowners participated. As had happened in the past, some of their protests turned violent. Eventually, in the summer of '22, one of the parliamentary proposals for improving land use actually became a law, the Micheli law, enabling the state to expropriate any uncultivated part of a latifundium that could be improved to the benefit of agriculture. Italy's political Right, terrified by this interference with private property, hurled anathema at the socialist and Catholic reform deputies who had voted it. Benito Mussolini, seeking support from the Right, stretched out his hand to help.

FASCISTS CONTROL THE KINGDOM

The rise to power of Mussolini was a northern movement of little interest to Sicilians. Mussolini called his followers Fascists, though the connection between them and the Sicilians' own popular Fasci of 1893–94 is tenuous: both groups employed the word *fasci* to stress the importance of working together, and the publicity-conscious Mussolini liked the cachet of the old name. The Fasci had been Sicilian politics; Fascism was not.

EARLY INVOLVEMENT OF SICILIANS
Scarcely any Sicilians participated in Mussolini's culminating March on Rome on October 28, 1922, but Mussolini would take his seat as prime minister three days later, and some Sicilians nibbled at the bait of power. Aware that fascism had less following in Sicily than in the other regions, Mussolini invited Sicilians of good liberal credentials to join his cabinet. In the highly personalized world of Sicilian politics, these ministers just by being there would attract Sicilians to the Fascist Party, and their unquestioned respectability would help to enhance the Fascists' reputation.

Of his four ministers from Sicily, one with an international reputation was Giovanni Gentile. The renowned philosopher, born in 1875 in the backwater Castelvetrano, long held that Sicily was too isolated from European culture, and he believed that fascism would draw Sicily into the main currents. During the twenty months (until July 1924) that Gentile served Mussolini as Minister of Public Instruction, he ardently increased the number of schools* and instituted a much-needed (and long-lasting) reform of curricula, and he established a

---

* Sicilians today like to point out the schools ("the town's *first* school") built by the Fascists.

Ministry of Labor that developed social welfare plans (though these remained on paper).

Mussolini was skilled at propaganda, and liberal Sicilians listened hopefully to the Fascist promises of a social welfare state, although the Fascist authoritarianism was contrary to Sicilian values. These two aspects of Fascist pronouncements caused ambivalence among the educated classes. On the other hand Sicilian landowners, threatened by the postwar demands of *contadini* for their own land and the decrees of 1919–20, were relieved in 1922 when the Fascists annulled the decrees and chased the peasants from the uncultivated land.

For most Sicilians, whose distrust of state ran high, Mussolini's exaltation of party and state over the individual was reason enough for wariness. His imperialistic designs put off men who would be forced into his armies. What repelled most people though was Mussolini's brutishness. The Fascists were roughnecks, using violence even gratuitously to impose control. A case in point is Catania, upon which *squadristi* (members of the Fascist militia) descended a few days after the March on Rome. Catania's communal council, dominated by the political heirs of the 1893–94 Fasci leader De Felice Giuffrida, had given its support to the Fascists and accepted Mussolini's government without any resistance at all; yet the Fascists carried out a *coup de commune*. The Fascist squadrons routinely destroyed public offices and workers' councils, not only to inflict damage but also to intimidate others who might doubt Mussolini's omnipotence.

At the highest levels of Italian politics stood Vittorio Emanuele Orlando of Palermo, like Gentile known internationally. A deputy to the Italian parliament from 1897 and a minister of public instruction under Giolitti, Orlando sponsored a 1904 law providing funds to raise teachers' salaries, to cut the number of pupils per class, and to establish public instruction in the evenings. Orlando held ministerial positions throughout World War I and then, as prime minister, represented his country as one of the Big Four negotiators for peace (gaining a certain notoriety when he stormed out of one session). During the Fascists' postwar ascendance he supported them, though not enthusiastically. Because Orlando had the respect of Sicilian leaders, Mussolini wanted him on his side for the next elections; and Orlando acquiesced.

A yearlong campaign showed the Fascists' utter intolerance of any views differing from the party line and their determination to bully dissenters into silence. In a political speech on the last day of March 1924, Giovanni Gentile declared,

> Fascism must be served. The governing [of Italy], all the governing, must remain in the hands of those who, because they have always obeyed, are the only ones who have the right to command.

In April's national election the Fascists won nationally and even triumphed in Sicily, to the satisfaction of Sicily's upper classes. Having been confirmed in office, Mussolini abolished all non-Fascist political parties. He called himself dictator, effective January 3, 1925. Now the Kingdom of Italy was a Savoy kingdom in name only.

FASCISM AND THE MAFIA

Though Mussolini wasn't going to bother with elections anymore, local elections to be held in Palermo on August 2, 1925, gave Orlando another opportunity to oppose Mussolini's Fascists. Orlando, having earned his epaulets west of Palermo in Mafia-dominated Partinico, was quite at home in rough politics. Supporting Orlando were all the city's democratic groups, that is, all the anti-Fascists except the Communists. Orlando welcomed Mafia support, too. In a speech the week before the election he avowed:

> [I]f by Mafia you mean a sense of honor . . . an intolerance of bullying and abuse . . . a generosity that confronts the strong but indulges the weak, a loyalty to friends . . . if by Mafia you mean these sentiments . . . even with their excesses, then in that sense you're dealing with qualities inseparable from the Sicilian soul, and I declare myself mafioso and happy to be so!

Whatever the elder statesman hoped to accomplish by such a controversial statement, the Fascists won the votes of the Mafia and then won the election. At this tug-of-war between liberty and totalitarianism the local press stood quiet on the sidelines. Media silence during an important political contest: it was an eerie expression of fear.

Some ordinary Sicilians showed their distaste for fascism by emigrating. Thanks to increased literacy and improved communications, emigration was not as definitive an experience as before the Great War — it could be undertaken as a temporary move for political security. Many *persone non grate* to the Fascists departed, among them Luigi Sturzo, founder of the Partito Popolare Italiano, who fled to London, then spent several years in the States. Emigration would never again reach the high levels of 1901–10, but in the first Fascist years, 1921–26, emigrants from Sicily averaged 25,000 to 30,000 annually. (See table A in the appendix.) Of course the migrants included mafiosi, who went back and forth across the ocean to profit from the economic and political differences between the two countries.

Sicily's political lines were drawn. The Fascists kept the support of the upper classes, an alliance soldered by the Mafia. The Mafia, like the barons, traditionally sided with the ruling group so as to maintain their control of the lower classes. Anti-Fascists were the democrats, including those liberals who at first favored the Fascist program then defected because of Fascist brutality. The most militant opponents of fascism were Socialists and Communists, whose leaders quickly perceived the Fascists' social welfare projects to be mere empty promises. The Socialist representative in parliament, Giacomo Matteotti, criticized their brutality; in 1924 they murdered him.

In a country where political rationales were often confusing, the Fascists' underlying philosophy was quite simple: they needed to control everything. Mussolini's early rhetoric had courted the masses, but before long his party was demanding adherence.

∽

The Fascists knew the Mafia to be strong and pervasive not only through their reading of history but also because they had used the Mafia to win elections; and the Fascists would tolerate no other strongmen. Having canceled all voting at the national level, the Fascists didn't need the Mafia anymore. The start of 1925, as soon as Mussolini made himself dictator, was the right moment, and he had the right man.

He named Cesare Mori as Sicily's *prefetto* (civil governor), charging him particularly to destroy the Mafia. A professional policeman, Mori had already spent twenty years in Sicily and had aligned himself with the latifundisti. Back in 1913, when several hundred field-workers had demonstrated in Trapani, he suppressed them and arrested seventy of the leaders. It followed that in the April 1924 elections Trapani province gave the Fascists the lowest percentage of votes of all Sicily's provinces. Pursuing the Mafia, Mori could have kept himself busy just in Trapani, where all the towns supported Mafia business and all the villagers subsisted on Mafia sufferance. But the alliance of landowners and *gabelloti* with the Mafia constrained Mori locally, since his connections and sympathies were with the landowners. So he acted elsewhere.

He first targeted an area thirty kilometers south of Cefalù, around the town of Gangi, high in the mountains honeycombed with bandits' tunnels. Resistance to invaders through the years had produced hiding places of great density and ingenuity. To hinder the outlaws from fleeing to another locality, Mori spread his net over a wide area throughout which he installed his forces on hilltops. The first arrests, of seventy-two people, took place November 28, and operations continued during December. The first evening of January 1926 he sent out word that all outlaws were to surrender themselves within twelve hours or face the consequences. He had timed his siege for the holiday season, and the heavens supported him by sending snow; these conditions favored finding the wanted men at home.

Few outlaws gave themselves up, although all knew that "the consequences" could prove fatal for their families. Some fled the area; others preferred to wait for the shootout. When it came, Mori's men captured several dozen outlaws, held mass trials, and executed them. A couple of Mafia leaders were taken and jailed. No such serious action against organized crime had been mounted since the aftermath of unification. Mussolini sent Mori a telegram telling him to keep up the good work.

The siege of Gangi would become the symbol of Mori's *modus operandi*, though the prefect also commanded operations in several other districts. For example, he had some 150 men arrested near Piazza Armerina. Mori bore down most heavily on poor rural areas, but he intended to end Mafia activity in the cities as well. One ruse peculiar to cities was frequenting train and carriage stations to meet arrivals who were known to have come for medical consultation or who seemed ill, and directing them to accomplices who were either corrupted physicians or fakes; once the patients were undressed, making off with their belongings was child's play. To counter this Mori assigned men to watch all stations and bar suspicious-looking individuals from entering. Also, Palermo, like any big city, had coteries of young men who dressed extravagantly and lived the high life; Mori thought that they could not have come by their resources honestly and, during the week before Christmas, he had large groups of them arrested. Mori vaunted his quick successes in catching criminals — he wondered why this had not been done decades ago — but others wondered if he wasn't needlessly disrupting the activities of law-abiding citizens.

∽

Traditionally the Mafia placed its associates in government jobs, and once the Fascists were in power mafiosi penetrated the Fascist bureaucracy. Administrators, Fascist or otherwise, squandered and embezzled public funds routinely. Those services northern Italians obtained on request from government agencies were in Sicily available only by bribing officials. In this climate, criminals had little difficulty arranging acquittal by judges or release from prison. It was partly to make punishment more certain for criminals whom his men had arrested that Mori set about cleansing the bureaucracy through mass firings of employees.

It got worse. In rural areas, Mori's subalterns imposed their own dictatorships. In every locality ordinary people were subject to knocks on the door during the wee hours and to arrests on trumped-up grounds. The *squadroni* of thugs purported to be seeking mafiosi or (because Mafia association in itself wasn't a crime) criminals, or Communists, or Socialists, but they weren't fussy about whom they arrested. Where their prey wasn't at hand they seized relatives, sometimes female. They went clumping through entire neighborhoods and arrested en masse. They didn't bother with niceties like basing an arrest on a crime having been committed. Given that an accused could be declared guilty on the basis of his or her confession alone, the *squadristi* obtained confessions through torture. Then, often, this effort proved to have been unnecessary, for Fascist judges started trials presuming guilt, paying little attention to evidence as they sent large groups of people to prison. To be sure, Sicily had suffered from criminality, and the Fascists caught many criminals, but, as the liberals maintained, the cure was worse than the disease.

TOTALITARIAN TARGETS

To imprison and execute powerless individuals was one thing, but to restrain prestigious organizations the Fascists needed other strategies. The Masons, associated with the political dirty tricks of the Mafia, fell with it. For a long time, Masons had fostered Sicily's agricultural development, and when the new Fascist Party urged programs for social advance it gained the Masons' support. But when the Fascists seized power the Masons had second thoughts — and the Masons were influential. The Fascists, feeling threatened by any rival political influence, certainly by secretive influential associations, banned them in 1925. Then legislation of late 1926 banned all parties and movements opposed to fascism, driving their members into hiding or into exile.

The Fascists could hardly ban the most influential and pervasive association of all, the Catholic Church, yet they feared church control over Italians. To increase church support, the Fascists in 1929 arranged the Accords of Lateran, which made Catholicism the official religion of Italy. Nonetheless, in Sicily a fair percentage of priests sided with the peasants against the state. The loss of the monasteries had fostered monks' empathy for the landless peasants. Priests developed the early agricultural cooperatives, the first of them at the turn of the century, and the Great War brought about intense contact between religious and laymen. While some prelates did side with the Fascists, men in religious garb could no longer be presumed to support the establishment.

Sicily's "establishment" wasn't as stable as it had been. Industrialization up north widened the barons' horizons. They saw the world of the future, into which they would not fit. They looked at Britain, where aristocrats involved themselves substantially in democratic government, but the Sicilian barons didn't see how they could use their own feudalistic prerogatives to that end. Since the occupation by the British over a century before, Sicily's barons had had to battle continually to protect their privileges and property, and they were tired. Northern Italy's aristocrats were experiencing a similar if less severe confusion, which accounts for their support of Fascists, who could solve all problems through organization. Sicily's barons were ready to compromise their own rule of the island, but they balked at accepting a political system from Italy's north.

To the extent that priests associated themselves with the populace, the traditional ties between local churches and barons weakened. To the extent that barons wished to participate in the industrial world, religious practices lost the fundamental place in their lives. Barons had bought monasteries' lands; now they missed having monks at their service. Recent laws had forced the church out of the Middle Ages, where the barons still wanted to live. For the conservative baronial class, conservative fascism seemed to offer spiritual haven. And then the Fascists drove the Mafia underground — the Mafia to whom the barons had looked for protection. The barons were up the creek without a paddle, since at the helm of government the Fascists had installed an entirely different class of men. The position of these new officials depended first on party loyalty, incidentally on qualifications, and not at all on land ownership.

AGRICULTURE

Ironically, the large landowners were the major beneficiaries of the Fascists' defeat of the Mafia. Theft of cattle and other animals dropped significantly. In consequence, the latifundisti no longer needed the Mafia to protect them, and, the Mafia having left the scene anyway, the latifundisti could loosen their bonds to *gabelloti*. The *gabelloti* didn't have to terrorize the peasants any more; the Fascist *squadroni* were doing that. With lessened demand for their services, *gabelloti* felt less free to fight against other *gabelloti* at the landowners' expense. The baronial ledgers of a few years back had their pages covered with expenses for new animals and for protection fees; now these items seldom appeared. Some barons even thought about increasing their revenue by improving their lands. A hasty few switched from wheat to fruit and nuts, crops that employed more labor and promised higher returns.

But another aspect of Fascist policy militated against that change. In the face of agronomists and economists who argued with one voice for the diversification of Sicily's agriculture, Mussolini insisted on wheat. Nature gave him a good excuse: the 1924 harvest was so inadequate that Italy had to import the staple. The next summer, anxious parliamentarians imposed a tariff on wheat, which — this is common to protective tariffs — made it unnecessary to produce wheat competitively; it encouraged the producers' inefficiency, an encouragement the Sicilian producers scarcely needed. Although half of Sicily's arable land was already given to grain, they expanded the grain fields. The new grain land, unavoidably of poorer quality than that already in cultivation, came in the main from pasture, portending a decrease in the number of animals, which in turn would cancel out the benefits from the decline in animal theft. The Fascist officials, realizing some of this, wanted to discourage the enlargement of grain fields and reward the increase in yields per hectare. The subsequent prizes and subsidies heartened the latifundisti.

All this "battle of wheat" (as it was called) was fought out in parliament, where the deputies lent their ears to those men who made representations. Although the barons no longer had much voice in national government, Rome still favored them over the peasants.

THE FASCIST SOCIOECONOMIC SYSTEM

The old hierarchies of dependence intrinsic to feudalism were finally abolished in Sicily by the Fascists, who created an entirely new system for organizing a population. Their "corporative state" operated through government agencies and government-sponsored associations that controlled all social and economic activity, from nourishment to health care to schooling. They even relieved people of the chore of thinking for themselves. This bureaucrat's paradise prevailed in northern Italy from fascism's first years but entered into Sicily more slowly: Sicilians weren't running to take part in some northern scheme that smelled like military organization. Mussolini himself, in January 1925, lamented that "southern Italy completely lacks faith in the Fascist regime." He should have known that Sicilians, at least, lacked faith in *any* regime.

Everyone was to work for a "corporation," under contract to the state. The big landowners were assigned to a corporation of agricultural employers and held to humane treatment of the peasants. Eventually, persuaded or coerced, a scant third of Sicily's agricultural workers joined corporations, even though promised decent pay and assistance for those who became ill or old. A few peasants were given plots of their own, although even those had little more hope than the others of farming above subsistence level on their unimproved land. That had not changed, but working for the state rather than for the baron proved not to be so bad after all.

Likewise corporatism reached Sicily's towns and cities without changing them. Fascism's prohibition of strikes troubled the industrial workers up north, but in Sicily strikes had been small and infrequent anyhow. The workers in the island's few factories were happy to be working there, with or without collective contracts. The Fascists eventually succeeded in arranging scores of collective contracts around the island, though almost all with firms serving just their local communities. The only major change the Fascists made in Sicily's economic organization was to take over the badly weakened sulfur industry in 1927.

MAP 17. Sicily as divided administratively in 1927

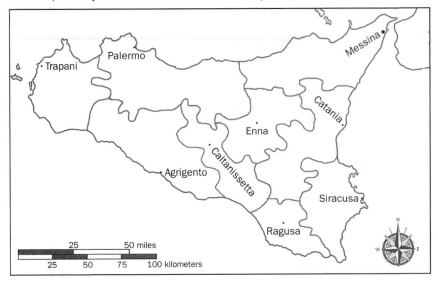

The Fascists didn't accomplish much else in 1920s Sicily. Mussolini and his officials made more promises than their predecessors, but they made little more than institutional changes. They modified Sicily's provincial borders. Sicily's agriculture, stagnant when the Fascists arrived, remained stagnant. In the rural areas as in the urban, the Fascists succeeded only in creating a climate of fear that Europe had not experienced since the Inquisition. The Fascist police state controlled the minute details of ordinary lives, censoring newspapers, using building concierges as spies, issuing political directives through musical "corporations." Overshadowing everything was the thuggery.

THE YEARS OF THE GREAT DEPRESSION

Economics came to the fore with the Wall Street crash of October 1929. The liberals had long sought ways to reduce the socioeconomic gap between Sicily and the industrialized world; now the gap diminished as large sections of the industrialized world sank toward the level of Sicily.

Sagging world markets hurt Sicily badly, because of its dependence on exports. The strong recommendations of the experts had persuaded Sicilians to grow fruit, to the extent that on the eve of the Depression citrus fruit accounted for half of Sicily's income from exports. Suddenly fruit became a luxury that former customers could no longer afford, and during the first five years of the Depression those exports dropped by half.

Again Sicily shifted its land and efforts back into grain. Mussolini's earlier call for higher yields had not led the government to finance much in the way of land improvements, so landowners felt constrained to invest their own money. While smaller landowners could not afford to do so, the larger landowners introduced machinery and chemical fertilizer. In consequence, the fraction of Sicilian land held as latifundia increased slightly during the Fascist period, from 22.6 percent in 1927 to 26 percent in 1934. The Depression years that saw an increase in yield of grain per hectare also saw an increase in the percentage of peasants who were landless.

Fertilizer, at least, was now being produced in Sicily, as part of a small chemical industry. Asphalt to make Sicily's roads was being dug near Ragusa, inland halfway between Siracusa and Gela. The presence of mineral oil in the area, extending into the sea, had been known for a long time; now some chemists thought it worthwhile to explore for petroleum. But drilling for oil is risky, just the sort of activity Sicilians don't like; and as long as the locals weren't interested, Italy's big chemical companies saw no reason to leave the north.

Mussolini had made belligerent movements around the Mediterranean, and one would have thought minerals quite important to a ruler with plans to expand his empire. After nationalizing Sicily's sulfur mines in 1927, however, the Fascists hardly tried to increase output from them. The government preferred to develop smaller reserves up north. Diminished as Sicily's sulfur industry was since the advent of the new process in America, in the years before the First World War Sicily produced over 325,000 tons annually, about seven-eighths of Italy's output. But in the early 1930s Sicily produced only 265,000 tons annually, about two-thirds of Italy's output. This provided Sicilians with an additional reason to move north; some 325,000 of them did so in the years 1931 to 1936.

⁓

As indicated above, the Fascists targeted all groups with a philosophy different from their own. That extended to religious nonconformists. Sicilians had not given vent to racial hatred since the Inquisition, but the Fascist climate of brutality made violence acceptable. Moreover, from the 1929 Lateran Accords the Catholic Church found itself the Fascists' partner in ridding Italy of non-Catholics.

Following the model of Hitler's Germany, in 1938 Italy imposed racial laws with Jews as particular targets. Sicily had only a few Jews, who were duly expelled from their positions in medicine and education. The main impact of Italy's racial persecution on Sicily was indirect and economic.

For foreigners were watching. Whether due to philosophy or to fear, after Mussolini took power the tourists avoided Italy, including Sicily, which was much less Fascist. The British particularly stayed away, and the British had been the mainstay of Sicily's tourism. They were so incensed by religious persecutions that when Mussolini imposed the racial laws, the British boycotted Italian goods, likewise disproportionately Sicilian goods. Another, contrary, wind also hurt Sicily: when Italy went to war, the Sicilians' special relationship to England aggravated Mussolini's suspicions toward them.

The Sicilians' special relationship to the United States grew out of the migration, but the emigrants and their progeny became less interested in Sicily during the '30s, or at least decreased the money they sent to their home country. It was little compensation that from America arrived Sicilian-American gangsters, threatened by the anti-crime investigations of the Prohibition era and seeing potential in the Mafia's abasement.

As Italy's economic situation worsened, Mussolini's grandstanding increased. He promised another resurgence of Italy, this time by foreign conquest. The ancient Romans had started their empire with

Sicily's grain, and Mussolini envisioned something similar for himself. To implement his imperialistic designs he would need soldiers and the grain to feed them. Sicilians perked up at the prospect of work. Still, when Sicilians learned of the roads being built by the Fascists in Ethiopia, they were incensed that the Italian government had done nothing toward improving Sicily's inadequate road network.

Earlier Mussolini had shown himself against Hitler, but when England and France opposed Mussolini's move into Africa, he drew closer to Nazi Germany, making the alliance official in May 1939. The previous month, the Fascists invaded and occupied Albania. Libya, governed by Italy since 1912, was in 1939 declared part of Italian territory. Italy now ruled three poor countries. Furthermore, Mussolini sided with Hitler to support Franco in the Spanish Civil War. All these interests around the Mediterranean renewed Sicily's strategic importance.

Mussolini liked to point out to Sicilians that their region lay at the geographic center of the empire. Needing to send grain out from that center to support his military forces in lands barely self-sufficient, he would have to increase as much as possible the product of Sicily's grain land. The production of grain was so inadequate that in 1937 the Fascists imposed a lower quality of bread, an echo of the suffering Sicilians had experienced during Spanish rule. Mussolini had rejected a proposal for land reform in 1922, but in 1937 he declared that the latifundia would end, although it still took him three years to approve the relevant law.

The Sicilians dragged their heels too; they had never warmed up to Mussolini. When Fascist officials commanded Sicilians to support the war effort by delivering their crops to central stores, the order was pretty much ignored. Attempts at coercion failed, as fieldworkers left the land. Urban Sicilians' resentments were aroused when the Fascists tried to impose on local bureaucrats a work schedule that would preclude their returning home for the traditional midday meal. Mutual mistrust reached such a level that in August 1941, with the war well under way, Mussolini transferred the entire Sicilian bureaucracy to the peninsula. Not that all the bureaucrats went.

TRANSITION
World War II and Its Aftermath (1943–1948)

THE BRIEF WAR IN SICILY

Italian aggrandizement contributed to the outbreak of the Second World War in late 1939. In due course the Allies chose Sicily for their first major campaign against the Axis: a major campaign in that the world's two greatest military powers met in direct combat, and in that the American and British forces numbered 450,000 men while the German and Italian forces numbered 405,000. In the wee hours of July 10, 1943, American forces landed near Gela, whence they easily occupied western Sicily. Eastern Sicily was another story, for there the British and Canadians had to do fierce battle against Germans. The Sicilians themselves lacked military weapons because the Fascists had not dared to arm the recalcitrant.

Thousands of Sicilians were killed and thousands more maimed when the Allies, targeting Germans and their supply lines, dropped their bombs. The badly damaged cities included Messina, Catania, and Augusta on the east coast, Palermo and Trapani in the west. The warfare of course reduced the fields to shambles. For most Sicilians now hot meals were only a memory. Likewise the things they used to buy — pre-war Sicily had obtained virtually all its manufactured goods from up north, and now no goods at all were brought in, not even matches. Destitute, hungry, and ill, defenseless and terrified, Sicilians longed to be rid of the Germans and of their Italian Fascist supporters. Someone wrote his bitterness in rhyme on the wall of Catania's municipal cemetery: *"Evviva il Duce — che qui ci conduce!"* ("Long live our Leader, who leads us here.") After thirty-eight days of horror, on August 17 Sicily fell to the Allies, the surrender formalized in the Treaty of Siracusa, signed September 3.

THE AMGOT MONTHS

As so many times in the past, Sicily was under foreign rule, this time shared by the Americans and the British. The Allied Powers, though, saw themselves only as a provisional government, there until the Germans were driven from the rest of Italy. Meanwhile Sicily was cut off from the peninsula. Under AMGOT — the Allied Military Government of Occupied Territory — Sicily experienced seven months of constant internecine strife. It would prove consequential for Sicily's political evolution.

The American and British occupiers, together some four hundred military men, divided the island administratively. The British took control of the eastern part (the provinces of Messina, Catania, Siracusa, and Ragusa), the Americans controlled the rest. The Allies' division of the island took account of political differences between eastern and western Sicily that happened to correspond with political aspects of Britain and the United States.

Western Sicily had been the Mafia stronghold until the Fascists subdued it in 1925; here now, as the Fascists fell, the mafiosi surfaced again. Indeed they received a boost from the Americans, who, even before invading Gela, were gathering information from the adversaries of the Fascists. The American military made a point of using Sicilian-Americans who spoke local dialect, and some of those most effective at ingratiating themselves with the Sicilians were American mafiosi. Those Sicilian mafiosi still in jail from the Mori cleanup were freed, along with other political prisoners, to be acclaimed by the Americans as anti-Fascists.

In eastern Sicily the British found few mafiosi but plenty of separatists. Ambition for Sicily as an independent state was nothing new, in modern times the idea having floated around from the British occupation in the early 1800s until unification in 1860. The idea revived when disgust with Fascist-run Italy brought forth partisans of separation. As writers chronicled the exploitation of Sicily under Savoy, the movement grew. By the time the Allies arrived in July 1943, the advocates of independence were well organized.

The Allied military government decided first and foremost not to rule the Sicilians directly but rather through Sicilian functionaries. That choice was an important one, they knew, and it obliged them to exercise great care in appointing the officials. Accordingly the Allies sought locals without Fascist taint, but finding them was easier said than done. The political parties of the early 1920s had been destroyed by the Fascists, no other parties started up during the war, nor had the Sicilians formed any significant guerrilla force. Sicilians weren't necessarily honest about their wartime sympathies, thus the foreigners were dependent for recommendations on local respectables such as priests, lawyers, and policemen.

In western Sicily mafiosi tended to have, along with anti-Fascist credentials, the respect of their communities; consequently, many men appointed to prominent positions in western Sicilian towns were mafiosi or collaborators. It may well have been that some American government officials had ties to the Mafia; some Americans then in AMGOT acknowledged later that they couldn't have cared less about the Mafia, its presence or its practices. Americans (and Britons) in AMGOT had been instructed about Italian society and government; nonetheless occupiers often took at face value those Sicilians who presented themselves as anti-Fascist landowner politicos. It was urgent to clean up the physical mess of war and to make the fields productive again: the Americans wanted men who could get things done.

Eastern Sicily cared less about material cleanup and more about political change. The British military, whose country was then in a socialist mood, had jurisdiction over the part of Sicily with the separatists, whose policies were mainly socialist. Never beyond view of the detritus of Fascist Italy's war, the separatists envisioned an independent, economically viable Sicily with industries and a rationalized agriculture beneficial also for peasants. These *indipendentisti* thought that the war on the Italian peninsula would continue for a while, and they believed that Italy's king, Victor Emmanuel III, had compromised himself by cooperating with the Fascists. Therefore, the *indipendentisti* argued, the Allies would benefit militarily and politically by making Sicily a separate state. For a couple of months they persuaded themselves that the military government's administrative dealings with separatists signified Allied support of separatism.

But within days of the Allied occupation of Sicily the war on the Italian peninsula changed course. Mussolini lost power. The king and the new prime minister, Pietro Badoglio, signaled their willingness to surrender to the Allies. Three months of negotiations culminated in Italy's switching sides: on October 13, 1943, Italy declared war against the Germans. The Allies, though seeking military bases in the Mediterranean, weren't eager to abet secession from Italy.

The separatists, with a few hundred thousand adherents from all classes of society, had the only political voice in Sicily. It was pervasive and shrill. Large landowners (and thus the Mafia) joined the separatists because they thought they could maintain their privileges better in an independent Sicily than in a democratizing Italy. The threat of separation was serious enough so that in December 1943 the Soviet foreign minister, Andrei Vishinsky, visited Palermo to emphasize his opposition to a Sicily nominally independent but under the control of the Americans. Furthermore, the Russians demanded a speedy end to AMGOT. In any case, once the Fascists were gone from power in Italy, the Allies had no use for an independent Sicily. Their return of Sicily's administration to the Italian government in February 1944 seemed to end any possibility of Sicilian independence.

TO WHOM SHALL SICILY BELONG?

Now aligned with the Allies, Italy was still at war; and in war as in peace, Sicilians complained, Italy exploited Sicily. While mines on the peninsula were allowed to sell their sulfur at the market price, those in Sicily had to adhere to a (lower) price fixed by the government. Because much of the peninsula was unable to grow its own food, Badoglio's government called upon Sicilians to deliver set amounts of wheat to government storehouses. For Sicilians themselves, food rationing was instituted: two hundred grams of bread and a hundred grams of pasta per person per day. The new prime minister also instituted a draft. Many of the Sicilian men had spent the war years unsure even to which belligerent they owed allegiance, and they had escaped to the mountains. The survivors who struggled back to their homes and fields after the American liberation were now being ordered to distant Italian fronts. Draft evaders returned to the mountains, fugitives from Italian justice. Everyone was incensed at this latest exploitation by the Savoy government, and it provided new wind for the separatists.

GRAIN CRISIS

Of the various economic and political demands fueling each other, the grain crisis was fundamental and focal. Previous grain harvests had perforce been shared with the Italians on the peninsula. Then, in 1943, the summertime warfare intensified food scarcity and therefore speculation. The grains that were harvested were almost entirely put aside for later sale by the large landowners. So much the better for the black market; almost all wars give rise to a black market, and Sicily's proved especially remunerative for its mafiosi managers thanks to the artificial curtailment of grain supply for local consumers. Grain producers and Mafia had long been associates anyway, and the black marketeers were often *gabelloti*.

The grain crisis aroused primarily the populace, the form of government aroused primarily the intellectuals. Innumerable political and social groups, active and interacting, articulated the different views. Even the politically alert found it difficult to follow the action.

At first ordinary Sicilians demonstrated without incident, sometimes under separatist auspices, about the food shortages and high prices. The Communist Federation of Sicily was established early in '44 to organize some of the discontent, and Communists supported regionalism rather than separatism. In an unconnected activity, in the second half of '44, Mafia leaders were talking seriously with American officials about making Sicily an American protectorate.

On October 19, 1944, while Palermitani were demonstrating peacefully, Italian soldiers shot into the parade with fatal results for about twenty-five people. That very day, by coincidence, Rome legislated new conditions for agricultural labor. Under the law sponsored by the Communist deputy Fausto Gullo, contracts could allow the landowner one-fifth to one-half of the product, depending on how active he was in the production. Though for the peasants this was a definite improvement over existing contracts, many on the Left objected because the law did not address the fundamental issue of landownership. The Right, of course, complained about interference with private property.

Tension grew, manifesting itself in big organized protests, especially in southeastern towns. At a few nearby latifundia peasants still denied access to uncultivated lands occupied them anyway — peasants' occupation of lands was their activism, equivalent to factory workers' strikes. The government denied university students the military exemption they had received in earlier years, giving students their motive to join the urban fray; in the three big cities they assumed positions of leadership. The students at Catania set fire to the city hall on December 14. Southwest of Catania, as the Christmas season continued, a few towns turned themselves into military camps and "republics," claiming powers of law enforcement and justice. Insurrections claimed lives. The Italian government made its response at the "republic" of Comiso in mid-January 1945, gunning down dozens.

Disregarding the misery of the ordinary Sicilian, Rome blamed the rebellion on the separatists. The latifundisti and the Mafia (both of whom cherished order, as in "the established order") moved away little by little from the separatist camp. Antiseparatists now included the political right on the one hand and the Communists on the other; they sought to slow the separatists by promising autonomy. The grand leader of the separatists, the former parliamentarian Andrea Finocchiaro Aprile, would unhappily begin to work toward compromise, while younger and more stubborn separatists turned to violence, forming a Voluntary Army for Sicilian Independence (Esercito volontario per l'indipendenza siciliana, or EVIS).

By the time the Allies knew themselves victorious over the Axis, in the first weeks of 1945, the Italian government and Sicily were engaged in something terribly close to war. To buy time, at the end of January the government in Rome set up a committee to plan special regional status.

BANDIT INVOLVEMENT

Finocchiaro Aprile rejected the alternative of autonomy within Italy. As early as September 1943 he wrote to leaders of the United States and Great Britain, and on February 1, 1945, he proposed to the new United Nations that Sicily be granted independence under the tutelage of Allied powers. But the Allies weren't interested, and that closed the political road to separatism. Shortly afterward, in June, the militant wing suffered a reverse when one of its leaders was killed in an ambush. Deciding that they were too weak to fight alone, the separatists called upon the bandits in the western hills. It's doubtful that Sicily's separatism could have been attained through violent means at any time, but now it was certainly too late; this desperate separatist move only encouraged the bandits by giving them a political excuse for their actions.

Although they added significantly to an alliance against government that was becoming ever more complex, the bandits generally didn't know or care what the separatists were trying to achieve, nor did they have political pretensions of their own. Coming entirely from inland villages and hamlets, working (if at all) as day labor in the grain fields, mostly illiterate, bewildered by political rhetoric and by the recent changes of Sicily's government from Italian to German to AMGOT to Italian again, they targeted any representative of civilization they could find. They upgraded their arsenal with weapons left behind by the Germans, and they killed as a supplement to looting, larceny, extortion, or kidnapping. The banditry of this postwar period was probably as bad as it had ever been, and by 1945 there was scarcely a village in Sicily — certainly there was none in western Sicily — without its band of outlaws.

Their leaders were local men from the lowest levels of government employment and shop-keeping; a few bands consisted of such men with slightly more education and organizational ability. Among them was a promising fellow named Salvatore Giuliano, born in 1922 in the hills southwest of Palermo, at Montelepre, barely literate but bright and clever. He had worked at smuggling grain, until in September 1943 at a police blockade he killed a policeman. Taking to the hills, he formed his own band, living on plunder. He took upon himself the protection of other smugglers, thereby winning the admiration of bandits in nearby hills. They started calling him the "king of Montelepre." He came into contact with the separatists, and an alliance was formed; EVIS designated him "colonel."

More Law, Protest, and Banditry

Further legislation about tenant farming triggered another wave of protests starting in May 1945, this time between Gela, Licata, and Caltanissetta in the heartland of feudalistic estates. The time had come, the demonstrators shouted, to implement the Gullo law of the previous October, without any ifs, ands, or buts: the distribution of grain must take place right after harvest, right on the threshing room floor. This time they had a law behind them, they had the support of persons of greater standing in the rural communities than the peasants themselves, and they had the support of the organized Socialists and Communists — even they were determined that the law be respected. Too often the government had passed laws without providing any means to implement the legislated change, which was a mockery of the principle of law — a mockery that must end.

The protest escalated into a movement for improving the lot of the peasant. The call to action echoed even up north. Participants represented the whole spectrum of political thought, from Catholics to Communists. They played down their doctrinal differences in order to accomplish something definite, and they agreed that their agreement on rules wouldn't suffice — they needed a law with teeth. The result was the government accord of June 23–25. (To have arrived at it in just three days was itself a victory.) The accord set definite percentages for division between landowner and tenant farmer, depending on crop and on yield; these criteria were less open to dispute than how "active" the landlord had been. Sicily's peasants now worked under as good conditions as in any region of Italy. Joy of achievement nourished the developing social conscience. The episode was a ray of sunshine in a Sicily still somber from the war.

To be sure, the improvement for the peasants did not satisfy all rural Sicilians. Innately resentful, the bandits were carrying on as ever, in fact they had extended their operations beyond their traditional districts into the hinterlands of Messina and Gela. Like the peasant movement, Sicilian banditry attracted wide political attention. The Mafia moved in and soon exercised control; mafiosi loved to lord over ordinary bandits. The Communists, employing a variety of tactics to destabilize Western governments, introduced a few men into bandit ranks. Not that the bands in the remote Sicilian hills needed foreign drummers, as they marched to their own music.

Among the bandit leaders, Giuliano had risen to unprecedented fame. He made known that he had written to President Truman of his need for weapons to fight the Communists so that he might bring Sicily into the United States. It's unclear how much Giuliano actually worked with EVIS and how much with his own band on his own account. Whatever motivated him, police records attest to the constancy of his work at the end of 1945 and the start of 1946. Each week his band made three or four serious assaults in the highlands around Palermo, against army barracks, police cars, passenger trains, communications depots, and factories. He burned and despoiled and shot in cold blood, on a regular basis. When the sum of two million lire was offered for his capture, "dead or alive," he took it as an honor.

From the AMGOT days, the Mafia had resented the separatists because of their large following; then separatists had trespassed on Mafia turf to make alliance with the western bandits, commissioning Giuliano. Hence the Mafia watched Giuliano with particular interest. In any case, if Giuliano's animation had come from EVIS, he would need to find new patrons, for the long-ailing separatist movement died in the spring of 1946. Its heirs: strengthened outlaws and excited peasants.

These two groups would be the bane of Sicilian officials when the region became responsible for its own internal affairs: On May 15, Sicily was granted special autonomous status within Italy.

—◦ 11 ◦—
AUTONOMOUS REGION

I n the postwar shakeup, Italy changed governmental form, when in the referendum of June 2, 1946, Italians chose a republican state over the monarchy, 54 percent to 46 percent. The newly autonomous Sicily voted to retain the monarchy. Once again Sicilians expressed a view contrary to that of Italians generally. Those Italians most in favor of monarchy were the latifundisti of the Mezzogiorno, but Sicily's latifundisti hardly campaigned. Their quiescence, due in part to their traditional lack of leadership, now suggested that they were giving up their fight for privilege.

Italy's change from kingdom to republic and Sicily's to an autonomous region were too consequential to be achieved overnight. Almost two years would be needed to write Italy's new constitution in its final form and enact it, with Article 116 certifying Sicily's autonomy.* Only after enactment would elections be held for the new parliament in Rome. One knew in advance that the time between the pro-republic vote and enactment of the constitution would be fraught with politics.

---

* Officially, therefore, Sicily became an autonomous region in 1948 — one hundred years after Sicilians fought for and won their independence from the Bourbons.

COLD WAR POLITICS

Some of Sicily's politics reflected international politics in these first years of the Cold War. The Mafia had always aligned itself with money and power, which heretofore had been seen as controlled by the latifundisti; now both were held by the Americans. Mafiosi loved the United States for its openness and its stress on expedience, while they disdained the Left for its support of the peasants, that is, of the weak. Traditionally allied to the political right, the Mafia was happy to follow America in its opposition to communism.

AMERICAN CONNECTIONS
Before starting the Cold War, we'll back up for a moment to the earlier relations of the Mafia with the States. We have noted the connections between the Sicilian Mafia and the American Mafia at the time of heavy emigration from 1890 to 1910. One emigrant from Sicily in 1907 was the ten-year-old Salvatore Lucania, who settled with his family in New York's Lower East Side. In the 1920s American Prohibition stimulated the criminal transport and sale of alcohol, giving the Mafia an opportunity to expand. Lucania took the name Lucky Luciano and in the 1930s he became head of the American Mafia's international division, where he developed the business and introduced the name "Cosa Nostra." The Sicilian Mafia, even when pushed underground by the Fascists, took note of Cosa Nostra practices for an eventual revival as an American-style "trust" of illegal business.

Luciano was jailed in New York in 1936. Nonetheless, with war coming on he cooperated with the American intelligence services in their protection of the New York waterfront. Later he provided information for the 1943 landing in Sicily. As reward, the Americans released him in 1946 and deported him to Italy. Lots of stories are told about Luciano, especially about how the Sicilians treated him badly; in any case in 1947 he moved to Cuba to direct American drug traffic. Soon forced to return to Italy, he flitted around the Sicilian Mafia circles, and as a handsome *capo* and admired teacher he became the personification of the era's Sicilian-American

Mafia, just as Giuliano became the personification of the era's Sicilian bandits.

In contrast to the cosmopolitan Luciano, Giuliano was home-grown and spent his entire life in Sicily's poor hill country. Young Giuliano carefully tended his image as king of Montelepre, sovereign and invincible. As he had earlier responded to the flattery of sepa-ratists, now he associated with the owners and managers of the large estates. These reactionaries, wishing to suppress anything that smacked of social advance, presumably did not have to give Giuliano detailed instructions about how to use his skills. The vaunted Americans too were aligned against the Left. The Left was gaining adherents — in fact it won handily the election of April 20, 1947, for members of Sicily's first Regional Assembly. Ten days later, on May Day, in a cel-ebratory mood, some three thousand people went into the country-side at Portella della Ginestra (near Piana degli Albanesi) for a Communist-sponsored holiday picnic. At 10:30, as the secretary of the local Socialists (a shoemaker) started his welcoming speech, shots from nearby hills startled the crowd. In several minutes of contin-uous fire, Giuliano and his band killed eleven and gravely wounded about thirty.

The grief and fury in most of Sicily were matched by the fury and frustration of the Italian police. They had endeavored to capture Giuliano since his first raids and now added a huge sum of money to the effort, but his military organization was better than theirs, his intelligence was better, and he had protectors in high places. Blame flew around officialdom, intensifying the usual discord between Left and Right, between Sicily and the Italian government.

ELECTIONS OF APRIL 1948

So our narrative on outlaw personalities leads back to politics (which it too often does in Sicily). Was Sicily's regional election of 1947 an augury for the all-Italy election to be held the following year, when Italians would vote for the first parliament of the new republic? Not only did Sicily's peasants have the support of the Left, the defense of the peasants had moved far beyond Sicily. The Italian rightists and

America generally feared that Italy would go Communist.* The Italian election of April 18, 1948, thus became a contest between democratic capitalism and communism.

It shouldn't have been much of a contest: The Italians were grateful to the American liberators; many Italians had relatives in America and themselves had gone there or dreamed of going there (whereas they had nothing relating them to Russia); moreover, Italy was the cradle of Western civilization, the protection of which had been assumed by the Americans. But to make sure, the Americans pressured Italian-Americans to write to "the old country" with reminders of these points and with advice to vote Right.[†] The Americans also stationed warships around Italy (and made plans to occupy Sicily militarily should the Left win). More delicately, they sent ships with foodstuffs, still scarce in parts of Italy. The Marshall Plan had been announced in June 1947 and developed over several months that coincided with Italy's electoral campaign, but before this vast aid for Europe's reconstruction could actually be delivered, the Americans thought it wise to send Italy some ready-to-eat assistance.

The church stepped up its political activity to favor the Christian Democrats, preaching to the faithful about Communist atheism and cowing those Catholics who supported the Left with the risk of losing paradise. Along with the Mafia and America, the church contributed significantly to the rightist cause. In the year between the regional and the national elections, the intensity of violence against union members and leftist politicians increased dramatically.

Threatened with the loss of material benefits by the Americans, the loss of a heavenly hereafter by the church, and the loss of life by the Mafia, Italians chose mostly Christian Democrats (Democristiani,

---

* About the southern Italians' leanings, Americans received a word of reassurance from the Mezzogiorno-experienced Carlo Levi, who told how "in their barren provinces the peasants dream of the U.S. as an enchanted land." *Life*, America's most widely circulated weekly magazine, published this several-page article, "Italy's Myth of America," on July 7, 1947.

† In effect, to vote for the Christian Democrats, who were the political descendants of the Fascists. The Americans, certainly, had just fought a war against fascism — "politics makes strange bedfellows."

called DC) to represent them in parliament. So did Sicilians, especially in the urban areas.

THE PASSAGE TO REGIONAL AUTONOMY

About the significance of the 1948 elections Sicilians wondered, often skeptically. Government had always been imposed on them by non-Sicilians, and it had kept them poor while favoring the rich. The political activity of ordinary Sicilians, especially rural Sicilians, remained direct: They participated in the banditry and admired Giuliano, paraded with the separatists, indulged the mafiosi, and followed the Communists — any concept appealed, so long as it was antigovernment.

Nonetheless, the threat of separatism had forced the government in Rome to give Sicily a local government with authority to change fundamentals.* The Sicilian region now had responsibility for the island's agriculture, fishing, industry, and commerce; public works and mines; protection of artworks and landscapes; religious works; museums and libraries; tourism; and primary instruction. (The national government retained responsibility for money and banking, transport and communications, conditions of employment, health, and secondary and higher education.)

In the years 1848 to 1948, probably more than in any previous century, Sicily had experienced momentous episodes. Sicilians united in political action, for the first time in six hundred years, to win their freedom from the Bourbons. Then they proved incapable of holding it. Later they witnessed the birth on their soil of the Kingdom of Italy. They saw the demise of the baronial class and the curtailing of the property rights and temporal power of their church. They watched as a third of their countrymen departed forever. They fought in two world wars. Now, finally, they had been granted the right to control

---

* Sicily is one of five regions within Italy to have autonomous status. Sicily has more autonomy than the others.

their own internal affairs. The Sicilians were very poor; only time would tell if the new regional government would improve their lot.

SOME CHALLENGES

If men who had fought for Garibaldi could have tramped through inland Sicily in 1946, they would have found little changed from their own time. The fields in summer were still dry, few of them irrigated; Sicily had not a single reservoir. Tradition and economics still bound the majority of peasants to a large patron, in conditions that northerners considered barbarous. Although by now electricity and indoor plumbing reached virtually everywhere, roads adequate for vehicular traffic were still few and far between, certainly in comparison with the Italy's north: in 1947 for every thousand square kilometers, Italy as a whole had 359 kilometers of communal roads, Sicily had only 84.

In the grain lands, illiteracy still prevailed. The poverty of the rural areas hindered the building of schools and the employment of teachers, and illiteracy greatly reduced access to information from the wider world, including information about modern agriculture and about how one might acquire schooling. At the end of World War II, of every five Sicilian residents, two were illiterate.

Working-class men in the cities and towns could generally read but still lived in poverty. Manual workers and artisans without their own shops could not expect steady work, and when they found work their employers tended to treat them shamefully. Machines and organization were as primitive as they'd been up north during the first period of the Industrial Revolution, and salaries hardly sufficed to feed a family. Strife was common, strikes less so, as demonstrators ran a high risk of jail and a higher risk of permanent unemployment.

Catholic religious, in Sicily as elsewhere, provided ad hoc relief to the poor, and an occasional priest even operated programs to bring more wealth into a community. But until the Kingdom of Italy came into being and deprived them of their lands, bishops and abbots had commonly been feudal lords, and lordly habits die hard: the church as institution still bolstered the structures of poverty. In the late 1940s, land reform and labor strikes were supported by Communists, and as Communists were "enemies of God," then the church must oppose land reform and labor strikes. Bishops expressed their obligation to persecute leftists, denying them the sacraments and threatening excommunication. The church furthered its political aim of maintaining its superiority over communism by treating peasant movements and labor movements as "sin" and readers of leftist publications as "sinners." Cardinal Ernesto Ruffini, archbishop of Palermo from March 1946, led prelates in denying the existence of the Mafia, saying it was a crazy idea of those who wanted to defame Sicily.

AMERICAN INFLUENCES

The United States government considered land reform and labor strikes in much the same way as the church, although the Americans used different rhetoric. Sicily would receive money from the Americans' Marshall Plan, a Europe-wide program of postwar reconstruction with the overlapping motives of deflecting movements toward communism and fostering markets for American producers. The Marshall Plan wasn't designed to further economic justice within any country.

Americans and Italians decided jointly on the allocation of Italy's Marshall Plan funds. Sicily, with some 10 percent of Italy's population, received 10 percent of the Italian funds for agriculture but only 2.2 percent of the Italian funds for industry. The assistance thereby reinforced the status quo in Sicily's economic sectors, although the island would have benefitted from more industry. Nor would the assistance bring the peasants closer to having plots of their own: To avoid land reform, the Americans gave priority to land improvements (in effect, on the big landholdings). The Americans did bring in the DDT that finally conquered the island's malaria, and they gave impetus to railway transportation and to schools.

∞

There was another side to the American coin, as seen by ordinary Sicilians. Before their own memories of World War II had faded and as they learned about the atomic bomb and Hiroshima, they were caught up in an American war against communism. Every political speech in Sicily reiterated the positions of these adversaries and every church sermon referred to them, while the majority of Sicilians knew that their ambitions as peasants and workers were supported by the political Left. International calls for peace demonstrations brought many Sicilians into the streets. When General Eisenhower visited Italy in January 1950, half the cities and towns of Sicily were scenes of anti-American protest.

Many countries around this time underwent demonstrations against nuclear war and against the Americans, but never before had Sicily participated in a multinational political activity, expressing concern as a member of the family of nations. The peace movement around 1950 had a second significance, evident to the eye: the protesters in the piazzas included large numbers of women. During the recent war, women had been obliged to leave their houses for activities necessary for survival, and Italy's 1946 constitution extended suffrage to women, but Sicilian men really began to notice only in the peace movement of 1950.

GIULIANO'S DEATH AND ITS SIGNIFICANCE

A dramatic event shifted the priorities of discourse. In the southwestern town of Castelvetrano, three hours into July 5, 1950, Salvatore Giuliano was killed. He had been on Italy's "most wanted" list for over three years, the object of massive police and military attention — never before had Europe seen several police forces devoting so much energy for so long to the hunt for a single criminal.

If Giuliano's death closed one chapter in the story of Sicily's underworld, it opened another. The first reports told of his death in a shootout with the carabinieri; and as a subtitle, that in their satisfaction the carabinieri promoted the leader of the successful team from captain to colonel. It soon transpired though that Giuliano had been killed by his lieutenant and cousin, Gaspare Pisciotta, acting on orders of the Mafia and with the promise of immunity from the police. But due to some mixup Pisciotta was arrested, and from jail, feeling betrayed, he told all. Essentially, Giuliano had attracted too much attention to Sicily's underworld by his banditry and then by his politically inspired May Day massacre, so the Mafia was better off without him. While even these sketchy details are less than certain, there's no doubt whatever that the government forces proved unable to capture Giuliano, whereas the Mafia brought him down.

The Mafia had already rendered an important service to the political Right by delivering crucial votes for the April 1948 election. By disposing of Giuliano, the Mafia secured its link to the governing Christian Democrats.

AGRICULTURE

The Democristiani, in power, get credit for an agricultural reform long proposed by the Left. Taking the name of deputy Silvio Milazzo and passed on December 27, 1950, the law decreed expropriation of land from the latifundisti (and compensation for them) and its distribution among peasants by lot. Moreover, the Milazzo law limited landholdings to a maximum 150 hectares and imposed norms for land improvement for all holdings exceeding 20 hectares.* To oversee the land improvements and carry them out itself in cases of nonperforming landholders, the law created an Agency for Agrarian Reform (Ente per la Riforma Agraria in Sicilia, or ERAS). An advanced law, it seemed to be an adequate response to the peasants' repeated demands.

Unfortunately, most of the peasants who were to benefit from the law were still peasants, able to read barely if at all and unprepared to exert their rights against tricksters. ERAS was another Sicilian agency, quick to grow to several hundred bureaucrats and to include mafiosi among its employees and executives. *Gabelloti*, skilled in making Sicilian agriculture remunerative for themselves, took prime ERAS jobs. Back on their rural holdings, they sloughed off their worst lands on the peasants while retaining the water sources. Peasants coming into possession of lands were burdened with all kinds of fees, often for services they didn't receive; they were duped into contracts requiring them to provide labor; they sometimes even lost their new

---

* 150 hectares equals about 370 acres; 20 hectares equals about 50 acres.

lands to old latifundisti. Needless to say, many of the old latifundisti managed to save their family lands from expropriation.

⚘

The duchy-latifundium at Maniace, passed down through Admiral Nelson's descendants, still had peasants mired in medieval grain lands. Sicilians knew this ex-*feudo* near Bronte as the site where Garibaldi's officers executed peasants claiming lands he had promised them. The Fascists expropriated the property in 1940, but with war's end its English owners reclaimed it. The then duke of Bronte successfully requested the Italians to exempt this English enclave from nationwide social legislation. Forced to wait for an adequate diet and for their own plots of land, the local peasants would not wait patiently: in the clamor of land reform during the postwar years, the peasants occupied the duchy, again.

The noted author Carlo Levi, who in the 1930s lived as an exile in the rural Mezzogiorno, visited Maniace in 1952:

> We walked around the fields talking with the peasants, who told us that, to avoid the [Milazzo] expropriation, the duchy had forced the peasants to buy the lands where they were working. "Forced" with the threat of selling them to others and throwing these peasants out of work. . . .
>
> Peasants who lacked money were told to borrow it, and the lenders of [the nearby towns] Tortorici and Randazzo charged interest of 35, 40, and even 50 percent. The price of the land, set by the duke, was double its value. The peasants sold their cows and their tools to pay the first installment so that they wouldn't be evicted. The land had to be paid for within five years, but if a payment was missed the land reverted to the duchy.

To keep the large landowners from avoiding expropriation by distributing their lands among relatives and heirs, the Milazzo law included a date beyond which the landowners could not validly transfer their lands.

> The forced sale of the Maniace land took place, for the most part, after the established date of 27 December 1950. . . . Thus the peasants forced to buy found themselves indebted and ruined, owners of land subject to expropriation under the Land Reform Act.*
>
> While the peasants were telling me these facts, the duchy's armed strongmen passed by, watching us diffidently. In the air was feudal terror. A short thin desperate peasant told me: "We are abandoned dogs like at the time of the Muslims."

The vagueness of the Milazzo law led to further struggles by the peasants in the fields and by the lawyers in the courts. Some of the battles were won by mafiosi. Land still being the main source of power in Sicily, the new owners of medium-sized parcels skipped up the Mafia's ladder to leadership.

The politics of landownership played against a background of the modernizing agricultural sector. This is not to say that Sicily's monoculture changed into mixed farming — that was precluded by Sicily's dry summers and lack of grasslands. The island's few plains were still seeded to grain and the hills to fruit. Nevertheless, around 1950 chemical fertilizer came into common use, and so did agricultural machinery, especially tractors. Then the Regione, through the 1950s, invested in land clearance and reforestation. It constructed several lakes as reservoirs, facilitating irrigation. These improvements raised yields and total production. The augmented crops reached markets

---

* With the reforms of the 1950s and '60s, some of the Maniace duchy was expropriated, but on the land under the control of the English, the peasants would continue in their ragged clothing and ramshackle windowless huts for another generation. Finally in 1981, after intellectuals took up the cause, the town bought the ex-*feudo* and turned it into a *borgo* (a village for the peasants). So ended Sicily's feudalism in the computer age.

faster as mule paths were upgraded to roads, sixteen hundred kilometers of them in the period from 1947 to 1958.

One consequence of all this was a technological unemployment
that drove peasants into towns and sometimes out of Sicily.* The
census of 1951 reported that 51 percent of Sicily's labor force
worked in agriculture; ten years later it would be 41 percent. As conditions on latifundia improved and jobs became scarcer, peasants'
rebellions petered out.

MINING

The sulfur mines during this period continued their decline. Once
they had introduced the Frasch process of extraction around 1900,
the Americans picked up Sicily's sulfur customers, and it proved
definitive: Even when Italy and America were on different sides
during World War II, Sicily's sulfur sales didn't increase. Under the
circumstances, the government would not improve conditions for the
workforce, now reduced to ten thousand miners at 119 active mines.†

At the northwestern corner of Sicily's sulfur zone, forty kilometers
south of Termini Imerese, is Lercara Friddi, an unexceptionally primitive agricultural village until unexceptionally primitive sulfur mining
began there. Lercara was distinguished only as the hometown of
Lucky Luciano. Among the resigned miners working on June 18,
1951, was the seventeen-year-old Michele Felice, whom the adults
considered not really a miner but just a *caruso* (a boy who carries the
excavated mineral to the surface). Then a tunnel roof caved in,
crushing the youth. An occupational hazard, rued the men who went
to help him but had to remove his remains. In their next pay packet
those men found they had been docked for the hour during which
they occupied themselves with Michele, and the boy's survivors found
that his pay had been calculated to the time of his death, because after

---

* Emigrants in the 1950s went especially to Switzerland, France, and Germany. Of
the decade's emigrants fewer than 30 percent went to the Americas, in contrast to
the emigrants of 1890–1913, of whom 90 percent crossed the Atlantic.
† This compares with twenty-two thousand employed in sulfur mines around 1880
and thirty-eight thousand at the peak in 1900.

all he had not worked the entire day. These details attracted journalistic attention to an otherwise ordinary incident.

It was in this environment that postwar miners battled for economic justice, their impact far outweighing their numbers. Their strikes against the state as mine owner followed a track parallel to that of the peasants occupying the lands of their private owners. The Korean War starting June 1950 caused a slight rise in the sulfur production and a corresponding rise in the miners' hopes. At the start of 1952, at every one of Sicily's sulfur mines, the workers joined in a general strike for higher salaries, decent pensions, and safer working conditions. The skinny ailing men and their withered women, withstanding police brutality, held out for seventy days. Despite 3,185 arrests, the strike failed and workers returned to the mines planning bitterly for their next conflicts.

As the war wound down in early 1953, the employment of miners dropped off. The miners protested intermittently yet violently. The Regione financed exploration of new sulfur sites and found and developed a few, but could maintain them only with subsidies.

〰

The miners apart, the northern Italians and non-Italians interested in Sicily's mining sector paid little attention to sulfur's death rattles; instead they watched the spurting petroleum. The Americans had undertaken their first explorations before the war, and Gulf Oil was drilling near Ragusa within weeks of the American landing at Gela. Under Italian law the state controlled mineral deposits, the agency for oil being the Azienda petrolifera di Stato, known as AGIP. Sicily, as an autonomous region, passed its own law in March 1950 giving greater rights to whatever companies found oil, so that foreign and private companies gained relative to AGIP. Concessions to explore for oil were won by AGIP, Gulf Oil, British Petroleum, the northern Italian Montecatini, and others. The first oil gushed on October 27, 1953, and over the next few years the petrochemical industry grew rapidly along Sicily's southeastern coasts.

This development in Sicily made Italy an oil producer, like the OPEC countries. Basking in increasing attention from world economic powers, Italy offered to serve as intermediary between the Middle East (with its Communist ties) and the West. In the atmosphere of the Cold War, the United States and its oil-importing European allies feared that Italy would position itself between the Western world and the Communist. The Soviet Union was always maneuvering for influence in the Mediterranean, and although the USSR had ample oil of its own, Sicily's production of this fundamental resource enhanced its value in the East-West conflict.

THE BOOM OF THE 1950S

The oil boom brought in money. Concurrently, as lands changed hands with the agricultural reforms, land prices rose rapidly and the circulation of money accelerated. More money arrived as economic assistance. The Marshall Plan, though returning southern Italy to its status quo ante bellum, injected some capital. The more important impact of the Marshall Plan on Sicily was as model. Fearing communism, Rome decided that integrating the Mezzogiorno into the thriving Italian economy would be a lesser evil. What the Americans had done through the Tennessee Valley Authority, the Italians would do through the Cassa (meaning "fund") per il Mezzogiorno. This decision to pour money into the area was made in 1950, though significant sums of money would not reach Sicily for years.

INDUSTRIALIZATION?
The projected Cassa per il Mezzogiorno occasioned a surge in the long-running arguments about industrializing Sicily. Liberals saw how countries up north had rebuilt with Marshall Plan funds and wanted that modernity on the island. Regardless of what might be modernized in Sicily, though, one could not neglect agriculture. The hitch was that increasing the island's agricultural exports would require large companies to cultivate huge properties efficiently — in other words, agribusiness techniques would need to be implemented — yet Sicily was having to reduce its large holdings because their

owners had proved so wasteful and reactionary. The oranges grown by the millions in Sicily were processed into juice and jellies on the peninsula; most tuna, since Florio had departed, was canned up north. Except for fresh food, Sicily imported virtually everything; would be better off to the extent that it processed its crops and manufactured the goods it used.

Over the years Sicily had received many grants to improve its economy, but projects had fizzled when they came up against opposition from the land barons. One example: the dam for the Belice River in Sicily's southwest, long projected but never started because of such opposition. But if money was invested in new industries that weren't already entangled with vested interests, it would prove less threatening.

Unfortunately, industrialization for Sicily was less a matter of processing and manufacturing than of extracting minerals. From the end of the war a small group of small industrialists, under the name Sicindustria (and led by Domenico La Cavera), argued that Sicily would never reach its economic potential without heavy industry. Unable itself to finance industrialization, Sicindustria developed instruments that would distribute the investments of interested northerners among several industries and would guarantee investors to return the amount invested plus a bit of interest. Also important to Sicindustria was that new industrial companies receive technical and marketing aid. The Regional Assembly, persuaded by Sicindustria, passed enabling legislation in 1957. But the big northern industrialists saw no advantage in fostering southern industries that would become their competitors. In the rhetoric of the times, the big industrialists called the Sicindustria scheme Communistic and made sure that the law would remain a dead letter.

Investors had to maximize their profits while they could; they were indifferent to modernization of Sicilian life. Already in the mid-1950s, just a couple of years into the oil boom, the talk was of the poor quality of Sicilian petroleum deposits, which meant high production costs, and of the small quantity, which would not attract big buyers. The sulfur days were over, and it looked like petroleum production would last an even shorter time.* All through the 1950s government bodies hugely subsidized Sicily's mining sector. The mines were controlled by the north, and northern industrialists were disinclined to industrialize Sicily because of its distance from the markets up north and its lack of other natural resources essential to heavy manufacturing.

RESURGENCE OF THE CATHOLIC LEFT

How national resources should be divided among the classes is a continuing issue in most countries; in Sicily the question had intermittently exploded with regard to the grain lands. Now the focus expanded to the oilfields. The Right (represented by the Christian Democratic Party, the DC) took it for granted that oil revenue should be divided among Italian and foreign big businesses. The Left (represented in this context particularly by the Communist Party, the PCI) argued that this new wealth from Sicilian soil should be shared by Sicilian workers. Except for the Communists, the peasants had no voice (and, despite living near the oilfields, no fuel other than straw or wood). The church still lined up with the Right, if only because it opposed anything favored by the Communists. While Sicilian prosperity increased, political dialogue reached new levels of rancor.

In October 1958, Sicilians elected as regional president Silvio Milazzo, who as deputy in Rome had sponsored the 1950 agricultural reform act. Milazzo was Democristiano, with qualms about it. Having grown up in a political family in Caltagirone and become a disciple of Luigi Sturzo, Milazzo felt that politics should be based on Christian values but independent of the church. As Milazzo through the 1950s sought reconciliation between the church and those who fought for the peasants, he gained wide support that extended into the ranks of Catholic religious as well as Communists. The Communist Party saw in Milazzo a good opportunity to lure Catholics away from the DC into a new party of Catholics open to dialogue with the Left.

---

* Sicily's petroleum industry survived the century. In early 2002 the threatened closure of a refinery at Gela, after complaints about pollution, gave rise to days of strikes.

A month after his election, the DC forced Milazzo's hand by expelling him and his deputies from the party. Because they collaborated with Communists, Cardinal Ruffini excommunicated them. Milazzo continued to argue that Sicily's desperate situation called for aid from any and all sources, and that Sicily's autonomy could too easily be exploited by a single governing party — it needed nourishment from democratic opposition. Turning his politico-religious isolation to good account, Milazzo formed a rainbow coalition, notably nudging Catholics and Communists into a heretofore unthinkable alliance. His new political party, founded at the end of 1958 as the Christian Social Union of Sicily (Unione siciliana cristiano sociale, the USCS), used the slogan *unitas in varietate* (union in variety).

In the first year of USCS power, 1959, a law granted the mining sector a huge low-interest loan, to pay salaries to its workers and to revitalize the industry.* In another law, for land reform, the USCS gave the Agency for Agrarian Reform (ERAS) new powers, to obtain land for peasants and to supply them with free technical assistance. This was social legislation in line with Christian values, and it pleased the Left. The Right vilified Milazzo as a Trojan horse for carrying Communists into a Western government, and the Americans shunned him.

The USCS lacked the huge financial base needed to maintain a social movement, so it had to scrounge for funds. That was an invitation to the Mafia, which insinuated itself easily into a wide-based coalition. When inevitable conflicts between different wings of the party resulted in vacant posts or uncertain policies, the Mafia resolved the matter to its own advantage. Then too, the USCS welcomed aristocrats (and their money), and by August 1959 they were prominent enough among the elected officials so that the press criticized the "government of barons." In brief, the old elements of the Right co-opted the new party of the Catholic Left. Corruption rose to new highs, while legislation fell off.

---

* The subsidies proved ineffective. Sulfur mines closed so rapidly that in 1969 there remained just fifteen active mines with scarcely three thousand miners.

Another financial scandal, this one about the management of the sulfur mines, brought the short life of the USCS to an end in 1961.

THE NEW SICILIAN PROSPERITY

Milazzo's endeavor — autonomous Sicily's grand experiment in representative government — lasted scarcely a moment in the course of centuries of fighting for a more equal distribution of wealth. It happened to be the moment when Sicily had more money than ever before.

During Sicily's first dozen years of autonomy, virtually every economic feature assumed a modern look. The commercial fishing industry replaced rowboats and sailboats with motorized craft. When Sicily gave shipbuilders a ten-year tax holiday, some 120 of them went to Palermo and Messina; their ships eventually employed several thousand sailors, and Messina exported recently developed hydrofoils. At a time when tourism was expanding universally, the Regione gave it high priority, building new roads to archaeological sites and facilitating hotels and other accommodations for tourists, even establishing a hotel school. Just between 1953 and 1957 the number of foreign tourists almost doubled, from 8,545 to 16,136, and tourism from other regions of Italy also increased.

Rural Sicilians celebrated the prosperity by flicking switches: in the period from 1947 to 1957, the production of electricity quadrupled, and wiring was gradually extended to the villages. Indoor plumbing also became the norm. All these new facilities created a boom in commerce. And as the disposable time and income of Sicilians increased, they could attend more cultural and sporting events, so, with financial help from the Regione, those sectors expanded. Once Sicily was supporting pop singers and soccer players who lived like Midas, fewer non-Sicilians thought of the region as primitive.

∾

Yet the intervention of the Cassa per il Mezzogiorno had barely started. Several years of discussions culminated in the decision against funding Sicily's industrial sector, and to provide money instead for infrastructure and touristic development — that is, for massive public works.

Sicilians stood with arms outstretched all during the 1960s to catch the manna pouring down from the Eternal City. Half the funds were earmarked for school buildings, the rest for hospitals and sanitariums, aqueducts, roads, fishing ports, and reforestation. Grants for construction projects proved very lucrative when the actual construction work could be delayed indefinitely or performed shoddily. Not only did speculators crowd 'round to lobby for specific projects, but they also placed their own people in decision-making positions. As plans were drawn up and subsidiary agencies created, the bureaucracy grew, and the bureaucrats had their own channels for routing some of the funds into their private bank accounts. Rare was the person who acted beyond private interests for the public benefit.

A case in point: water. Through a century and a half of laws to raise the productivity of agricultural land and to provide some for the peasants, the largest landowners had maneuvered to retain the supplies of water. Peasants cultivating their own small plots had no alternative to buying water at high prices. The water barons certainly didn't want reservoirs and irrigation systems under public control, as projected by the Cassa per il Mezzogiorno; nonetheless, they claimed money earmarked for such improvements. A wry comment at the time, with wider application, was, "The reservoir won't supply drinking water, but it will put bread on your table."

The Regional Institute for the Financing of Medium and Small Businesses was established to funnel money from Palermo, Rome, and abroad, with the one aim of fostering entrepreneurs. The lack of entrepreneurs, it's often said, is one of Sicily's fundamental economic problems. But that needs qualification, for it applies to businesses legally constituted. An entrepreneur is one who organizes, manages, and assumes the risks of a business or enterprise; Sicilians involved in illegal activity often do just that in their quest for kickbacks or rake-offs, notably in their development of the alcohol business in the 1920s and then of the weapons and drug trades. One of Sicily's fundamental economic problems is, rather, that the Mafia monopolizes the island's entrepreneurial talent.

Since vested interests — the big landowners, the Mafia — threatened to vitiate any program of assistance, the Cassa would have to placate them. So the Cassa proved amenable when the old barons and *gabelloti* presented themselves as construction magnates. Evidence of their success stood in virtually every Sicilian community, in the form of a large building never completed. Other buildings, with frameworks of cheap materials, collapsed. Some, still in use, are far too grandiose for the populations they serve; they are called "cathedrals in the desert."

Corruption was hardly peculiar to Sicily, but in Sicily it was pervasive and deadly. Murders were infrequent — the threat was enough — whereas the Mafia used the political machinery constantly. As Sicily's elections were procedurally honest, the members of the assembly had to find ways to obtain votes in order to remain in power, and the Mafia could deliver the votes; voters knew that as long as they remained in Sicily, they were dependent on the Mafia for their livelihood. Then too, the church instructed its adherents to vote DC, especially throughout the Cold War. Prelates used their patronage opportunities to fill posts in government administration and financial institutions. The mafiosi advised on legislation and received protection from prosecution; they shared the loot with politicians. From autonomy in 1948 to the 1990s, with partial exception only during the short Milazzo period, this alliance of politicians, Mafia, and church held all Sicily's political and economic power.

A FIGHTER FOR ECONOMIC JUSTICE

Danilo Dolci, age sixteen, chanced to visit a Mafia stronghold when his father was sent to manage the train station at Trappeto, a poor fishing village thirty kilometers west of Palermo.* Dolci's month there impressed him so deeply that he returned a dozen years later to spend the rest of his life as a social activist. Unaffiliated with any religious group or political party, he set out independently to raise the living standards in one small area. To succeed he would have to beard the Mafia.

---

* The train follows the coastal route rather than the much shorter, but hilly, direct route passing Giuliano's Montelepre.

Dolci came from northeast Italy, so his first challenge was to make himself understood to Sicilian peasants and to gain their confidence. In October 1952, seven months after his arrival in Trappeto, at the bed of a baby dead from starvation he began a fast. Within a week the authorities got his message and arranged jobs for the local men — Dolci had found an effective vehicle. He wrote, too. His first book, *Banditi a Partinico,* published in October 1955, won acclaim for developing the thesis that "banditry is born from desperation." While he deplored the violence that deprived "his" peasants of income and hope, he saw that among the wretched peasants the strongest were the bandits, who were ready to "resist, while the others succumbed."

In *Inchiesta a Palermo,* published in December 1956, he wrote about the struggle to survive without remunerative work. Meanwhile, having learned how illegalities in commercial fishing were depriving locals of income, in the first weeks of 1956 Dolci attracted a thousand of the local poor to the beaches of Trappeto to fast in protest. And there he planned with them a "strike in reverse," in which hundreds of unemployed came together to rebuild a country road that had deteriorated to uselessness; in Sicily it was a great novelty for men to cooperate in a community project.

This time the authorities reacted by sending him and four of his lieutenants to jail, refusing to grant bail because Dolci had "every likelihood of offending again." But in his August trial the judge recognized his behavior as "a movement of particular moral value," and he was sent forth, in effect, to continue his offenses. The church, though, considered him a troublemaker and anathematized him when he won the Lenin Peace Prize in 1958. Dolci declared himself to be no Communist but intent on improving local conditions through nonviolent means.

His accomplishment lay in arousing Sicilian peasants to constructive action, peasants who previously had been roused on occasion, but only to make demands on government. By 1955 Dolci was inciting peasants to do something about their limited access to fresh water by building dams and removing control of the water supply from the Mafia. Unable to obtain funds in Italy, he developed support groups in other European countries and in the United States. Money flowed in, as did hundreds of foreign notables and students. A fast in September 1962 pushed the Cassa per il Mezzogiorno to agree to construct a dam across the nearby river Iato; despite political obstructions, the dam was eventually built (and the reservoir is still in use). Dolci created educational centers for peasants and encouraged them to speak out, to determine their aims, to publicize them at conferences, to protest locally and in Rome against the Mafia, which kept them poor. He continued to fast, to write, and to cope with arrests, trials, and jail terms.

Dolci's books reported the life experiences of the local peasants. He titled his 1960 book *Spreco* ("Waste") and focused it on that particular aspect of western Sicily's underdevelopment. Examples include manure, which the peasants burned because they were unaware of its value as fertilizer; the topsoil carried away by landslides because no one anchored it with trees; the houses of emigrants, allowed to disintegrate. "There's work for everyone; I would say indeed that there are not enough arms or heads to do what's needed. And for this [lack of jobs] we can't forget how much of the responsibility is national." The finger he pointed could have been that of Sidney Sonnino, coauthor of the *Inchiesta* of eighty-five years before.

ᥞᴏ

Dolci was nominated more than once for the Nobel Prize, but he never received it. In 1959, however, a Nobel Prize was awarded to a Sicilian, the poet Salvatore Quasimodo. Born in Modica in 1901, Quasimodo, like Dolci, was the son of a frequently moved stationmaster (not quite a coincidence, for railway men and their families were among the most cosmopolitan of Italians). In contrast to Dolci, Quasimodo followed the usual route of moving from Sicily to the north; he left at nineteen to study in Rome, taught for many years in Milan.

His five volumes of poetry published in the 1930s abounded in verbal complexities. He wrote as a disciple of contemporary Italy's "hermetic" school, using literary symbolism to oppose Mussolini discreetly. Nonetheless his anti-fascist activities led to his imprisonment during World War II. Afterward he couched his humanism in more accessible language, and it was for his poetic concern for man in a violent world that he won the Nobel. Although his writings allude to his Sicilian experience, he never returned to Sicily to live. *Spreco.*

MODERNIZATION IN THE MAFIA MANNER

THE END OF RURAL MISERY

For as far back as the time of Spanish rule in the sixteenth century, Sicily's peasants had been disadvantaged compared to peasants up north, so when Danilo Dolci set out to bring them into an easier modern world, it seemed he was tilting at windmills.* As it happened, much of what Dolci sought for the peasants of the Trappeto area became reality during the 1960s for most Sicilian peasants.

For one thing, the peasants were a far smaller percentage of Sicilians than they had been in their fathers' generation. Feudal estates had disintegrated due to the war and to the postwar land reform, so that agriculture provided jobs for fewer peasants, and the erstwhile peasants shuffled off to the cities. Moreover, the peasant class of the 1960s was a cut above that of earlier generations because, from the period of land reform, those who left the rural areas were the day laborers, while many who stayed behind possessed some land. Result: fewer *contadini* (peasants), more *agricoltori*. At the same time, peasants benefitted from the general prosperity: Italy's industry grew so fast during the 1960s that journalists wrote of an "economic miracle." Italy's augmented income permitted the introduction of social legislation, including health insurance, unemployment insurance, and old-age pensions, covering rural Sicilians like other Italians.

Directed specifically at the poor south was the Cassa per il Mezzogiorno. Any huge government program has its delays and its mistakes, its cheats and its interests to satisfy, though perhaps more of them in Sicily than up north. Critics of the Cassa per il Mezzogiorno were

---

* Miguel Cervantes (1547–1616), who wrote of Don Quixote tilting at windmills, spent a couple of months in Messina starting mid-September 1570.

legion, and their criticisms often justified. Nevertheless the Cassa set up cooperatives for wine producers and made loans at low interest for buying land and for buying animals, fertilizer, and agricultural machinery. Now every village had a primary school, and buses carried rural children to secondary schools. Virtually all children born during or after World War II learned to read, so that the rate of illiteracy is approaching zero as those in the older generation die off.* And they do not die off as early as their ancestors, for the Cassa built hospitals around the island.

"THE MORE THINGS CHANGE . . ."

Sicilians marveling at their island's transformation were soon jarred back to reality. Just before daybreak on July 19, 1966, in Agrigento a landslide crashed into several twelve-story apartment houses. City officials knew that the hilly site was composed of porous tufa rock, very crumbly, but they had given the building permits to the mafiosi speculators anyway. The residents, fortunately warned in time to evacuate, lost everything they had in their homes, including the money invested. As no one was held accountable, speculators had a green light for more abusive building. The most egregious example was probably Gela.

There's an old maxim, "the more things change, the more they remain the same." The expansion of the bureaucracy brought into the cities people who needed housing. The construction industry has characteristics from which the Mafia could easily profit: it employs many unskilled laborers, and most of the material used in construction ends up hidden within the walls. Shoddy building practices and corrupt officials would cause, as in Agrigento, dozens of personal catastrophes during the 1960s and '70s. As the *contadini* shed their rural ways for those of the city, so did the mafiosi.

For a few centuries the vested interests had secured their privileges by terrorizing peasants; now they were learning to do so by manip-

---

* As a fraction of residents aged six years and older, the illiterates dropped from 28.4 percent in 1951 to 2.8 percent in 2001. The rate of illiteracy remains a little higher in the rural areas than in the urban and a trifle higher among females than among males. (Census data are from ISTAT.)

ulating urban financiers. One catalytic event: a major earthquake on January 15, 1968, that killed about 230 people and made thousands homeless in the Belice Valley, wine country east of Salemi, already poor and Mafia-infested. The earthquake rumbling had hardly stopped before the region's politicians claimed vast amounts of money from the Cassa per il Mezzogiorno, from ministries in Rome, and from abroad. Inevitably some of the arriving grant money went into the politicians' own houses or pockets, but apart from that the politicians used the funds to rebuild in the newest and most elegant manner with their personal stamp, constructing modern highways and viaducts and commissioning modern sculptures, while they deliberated over rebuilding small towns in geometric urban layouts or in the style of Levittown. A few of the more able victims got tired of waiting and built houses for themselves, but most of the destitute peasants lived in army tents and barracks for a dozen years and more before their new housing was ready.

Across the island, twenty kilometers southwest of Siracusa at Avola, riots broke out on December 2, 1968, when the day laborers of the grain fields struck for higher pay. Backed by trade unions of the Left, they blocked the Avola-Siracusa road. Two peasants were killed, in what was to prove the last of the peasant tumults.

The Mafia Moves into the Cities and into Drugs

Earlier analysts of Sicily's criminality erred in explaining the Mafia as a rural phenomenon, a function of the latifundia. As soon as mafiosi had a whiff of the money to be injected into the Sicilian economy, they went where the money was (Rome and Palermo) and where it would be spent. The governments were making public expenditures primarily to pump money into the economy; their aim of improving public services was secondary. The situation was made to order for the Mafia, which could feed at the trough with impunity.

There's no way to sketch a picture of Sicily's prosperity during the 1960s and '70s without putting the Mafia in the foreground. It goes without saying that the urban Mafia engaged in illegal activities;

everyone knew about the cigarette smuggling and the drug trafficking and the gun running, and about the loan sharks (of whom most Sicilians stayed clear) and the protection racket (which extorted money from those otherwise unbothered by Mafia affairs). Disconcerting was how the Mafia wove itself into the Sicilians' newly urban life. Sicilians arriving in the city moved into houses built by Mafia speculators. They took work, overwhelmingly, in the public sector, which meant they had to be in the Mafia's good graces. Whoever operated a business had to pay taxes to the government and another "tax" (the *pizzo*) to the Mafia. Mafiosi ran most of the bigger businesses directly. Sicily's "economic miracle" involved a lot of illegal commerce.*

Sicily's urbanization shifted the causes and venues of violence. Banditry was no longer a problem. Mafia strife erupted sporadically during the middle and late 1960s between rural bands (the conservative "old Mafia") and urban bands (the venturesome, drug-trafficking "new Mafia"), likewise between groups settling turf disputes as they moved into the cities. In one case, Palermo's mayor allotted certain plots on Lazio Avenue to mafiosi friends of his for development, but they quarreled so seriously that, in December 1969, there was a rash of murders, which gained fame as the "massacre on viale Lazio." One hundred fourteen of the principals in the massacre were brought to trial; one result was the 1971 murder of the judge, Pietro Scaglione, the first judge killed by the Mafia.

Palermo's population, 434,500 in 1951, grew to 698,500 by 1981.† The construction sector grew apace. The Mafia used a few front men to acquire building permits. The profits from construction put money into so many pockets that the Mafia directed funds into further building so as to extend the boom. It seems that Sicilians barely abandoned the rural areas before they, as new urbanites, were having second homes built outside the towns to demonstrate their

---

* Illegal activity, untaxed and unreported, is such a large share of the region's economy as to compromise Sicily's economic statistics.

† This proved to be the high point. Census figures show the city's population as 699,000 in 1991 and 687,000 in 2001. Catania and Messina show similar rise and decline.

middle-class status. As if that weren't enough, mafiosi desiring an urban building lot would force owners to sell or would "undevelop" the plot by tearing down whatever was sitting on it. Developers of such sensibilities didn't much care about the aesthetics of new buildings; they razed many of Palermo's beautiful villas and parks to replace them with shoddily built, unadorned, concrete cubes of apartment houses. The Mafia violence eventually abated, but the unsightly new structures remained to dominate the landscape. Local residents refer to this building spree as "the Sack of Palermo."

Mafiosi took a bite from every slice of the urban pie. Newcomers typically rented, and the Mafia typically took a fraction of their rents and all other contracts. Palermitani in the 1970s couldn't even avoid contributing to Mafia coffers by getting sick or dying: the Mafia had arrangements with doctors, nurses, and funeral directors, and it controlled the cemeteries. Yet the city was thriving. A Palermo judge denouncing the Mafia octopus remarked, at the time of the 1973 oil crisis, that Palermo "may be the only Italian city in which there are hundreds of building sites, and in which, despite the economic crisis . . . luxury-goods stores are starting up."

Actually, Palermo wasn't unique. During the 1960s the Mafia developed Catania into a major port for receiving morphine base and refined heroin. Messina too became a significant Mafia transfer point between Sicily and the north, while in the mountainous hinterland some traditional-minded mafiosi gained control of animals and pastures. In the past the Mafia had flourished in western Sicily and limited its activities in eastern Sicily, but by now mafiosi were commingled with other wealthy residents of the east coast. Sicilians familiar with the island as a whole perceived not a single Mafia but several, for targeted sectors and ways of operating differed from province to province. All over Sicily the rise in living standards coincided with the proliferation of the Mafia.

∽

The city life and attendant consumerism new to Sicily already characterized the United States, tempting the Mafia to develop America as a drug-selling market. It was a logical step in modernization, for the

Sicilian Mafia had been trafficking in illegal drugs since Lucky Luciano organized the business. Since then drugs had burgeoned as a quintessential international business, with producers, suppliers, and customers worldwide. By 1970 the Sicilians were actively seeking a larger share of the market and working toward vertical integration, that is, increasing not only their shipping but also manufacture and sales.

Trafficking already brought into Sicily "hundreds of millions of dollars in payment of heroin." So reckoned Judge Rocco Chinnici of Sicily's Court of Appeals, who was investigating the effects of the Mafia on politics and economics. "To a large extent," he averred, "the Sicilian economy is based on drugs. . . . Huge amounts of money [are] laundered through all kinds of financial institutions (some operated by mafiosi)." Chinnici elaborated that the criminally obtained funds "are invested in construction, in agricultural processing, in commercial and industrial activities which are completely legal."

THE SINDONA AFFAIR

One enormous laundering operation came to light as part of a bank scandal that erupted in New York City. It nonetheless involved the three impediments to Sicily's economic development: the church, the Mafia, and the DC party.

The protagonist was Michele Sindona, born in 1920 in Messina to a modest family. The local bishop spotted Michele as a bright boy and arranged for his education. He grew into a young man during the war, when he came under the tutelage of black-marketing mafiosi. Sindona started his career in 1948 as a corporate lawyer in Milan. His timely contributions to the DC gave him political clout. By 1970 he was a business magnate presiding over an empire that included six banks in four countries and several hundred other corporations; his net worth was estimated at $450 million. Right-wing politicians facilitated his American dealings: his corporations included the newspaper *The Rome Daily American* and the real estate conglomerate that owned the Watergate residential complex in Washington, D.C. He spoke highly of the financial dynamism in the United States and disparagingly of Italian economists and bankers as he siphoned large sums out of Italy and transferred them to the U.S. As a major player in world finance, Sindona could, and did, control Italy's financial establishment and its stock market. He wanted an American showpiece for his portfolio, and so in July 1972, for forty million dollars, he obtained a 22 percent share in the Franklin New York Corporation, parent of the Long Island-based Franklin National Bank, a very large bank of excellent reputation. As its biggest shareholder and primary decision-maker, Sindona managed through foreign-currency speculations and various frauds to sink the bank in just two years. In May 1974 Franklin made its first announcement of loss, of fourteen million dollars, but the losses would turn out to be much greater. Sindona and Franklin were in the media almost daily over the next few years, in what was to be the largest bank failure in United States history to date.

Foreign-currency speculation and fraud were central to Sindona's preeminence. In the mid-1960s he had established a brokerage firm for large clients, a firm able and willing to convert the jumbo earnings of Sicily's drug lords into foreign currencies and deposit them in foreign (often Swiss) banks. Other wealthy, powerful depositors came from Italy's political and financial worlds, even from the Vatican*; they too appreciated the secrecy of these deposits.

A bank failure has a domino effect, as frightened patrons withdraw their money not only from the troubled bank but also from associated banks and investments. Sindona's empire crumbled in a matter of months, destroying banks in the United States, Italy, and Switzerland. Concurrently, alarm spread among Sindona's clients, who feared the loss of both their money and their good name. Mafiosi in particular wouldn't take such losses lying down.

Sindona appreciated that. While criminal charges were being prepared against him on both sides of the Atlantic, he considered how

---

* Sindona was put in charge of the Vatican's foreign investments in the mid-1960s, and from that time he had been working closely with the Vatican bank, the Istituto per le Opere di Religione (Institute for Religious Works), or IOR. Some Vatican funds were naturally used in Sindona's dubious activities. The loss to the Vatican due to the Sindona collapse is estimated at seventy million dollars.

he might get his clients to rescue him. He was living in New York to avoid criminal prosecution in Italy, fighting against Italy's attempts to extradite him. In Italy he appeared dramatically on April 6, 1975, across five columns on the front page of Turin's *La Stampa*. He had given this major Italian newspaper an interview in which he said he was writing a book with details about his foreign transactions, including the names of those on whose behalf he had carried them out. Suddenly some leading Italians wanted to gratify Sindona.

In March 1979, in Manhattan, Sindona was indicted on ninety-nine federal charges of fraud, conspiracy, and misapplication of bank funds. It appeared that Sindona bought his controlling shares of the Franklin National Bank with millions that weren't even his, that he had diverted them from Italian banks he controlled. In response to that accusation, as to the others, Sindona pleaded not guilty and returned to his freedom on bail. He was scheduled to return to court for trial in September, but early in August his lawyer reported that he had disappeared.

Amid a lot of other speculation, the authorities suggested that Sindona had been abducted or was being protected by the Mafia to keep him from talking during his trial about his alleged Mafia connections; the latter theory was to prove correct. The disappearance did result in the indefinite postponement of Sindona's trial. He reappeared in New York ten weeks later with a bullet wound in his thigh, which he had had inflicted in Sicily to bolster his claim of being kidnapped by Sicilian leftists. His adventures weren't yet finished. He was jailed, his trial finally got under way, and in March 1980 he was duly convicted. The night before his scheduled sentencing, in jail, he slit his wrist and was taken to hospital in critical condition. He was finally sentenced a month later, on June 14, to twenty-five years in prison and a fine of $207,000. Four years into his sentence he was temporarily extradited to Italy to face charges of fraud and of murder. Convicted of both, he could no longer doubt that he would spend the rest of his life behind bars. Anyhow, the rest of his life would be short — a few days after his conviction he died of cyanide poisoning. Whether he killed himself or was killed by the Mafia to shut him up absolutely will probably never be known.

∽

Business on Sindona's scale would not have been possible without collaboration, or at least toleration, at the highest levels. Although the scams of the Sindona affair revolved around banks outside Sicily, the affair had great significance for Sicily in that it spotlighted relationships between the Sicilian Mafia and some respected leaders of Italian business and politics.

Anti-Mafia investigations regularly signal "a breakthrough." One breakthrough grew out of Sindona's fake abduction and his attempt to blackmail men who had used him as launderer. During Sindona's stay in Sicily, he and his Mafia associates were arranging a meeting to collect the blackmail money. Such a delicate matter could only be handled, needless to say, by top-ranking mafiosi. They sent a letter to the victims by trusted courier, but thanks to a phone tap, the courier was intercepted. He proved to be a certain Vincenzo Spatola, one of the wealthiest men in Sicily and indeed in Italy. His family's money came from construction (with no scent of dishonesty). He gave generously to political, religious, and public causes. Now it came to light that he had provided several weeks' hospitality to the "abducted" Sindona, after having personally done the "abducting" in New York. Spatola's many relatives lived around Palermo and around New York, and in due course the investigators proved that Spatola's was a Mafia family, deeply involved in heroin trafficking. When the *New York Times* headlined a late-1977 article "Italy Shaken by Banking Scandals," it was no longer reporting on the Sindona-Franklin swindle, but on activities of several Italian banks. The executives of these were charged primarily with misapplying bank funds and exporting capital illegally, capital in the millions of dollars. (Some of the money had been transmitted through Sindona, but that wasn't the point.) Accusations reached as high as to the general director of the country's central bank for savings institutions. The same article reported on a huge chemical company, whose chairman had sought a low-interest loan for investing in Italy's poor south, only to spend the money elsewhere and cook the balance sheets.*

The complexity and breadth of such financial operations indicate that their perpetrators were men of intelligence and diligence. For the most part already wealthy from legal sources, in these years of the Cold War they typically excused their behavior as acceptable capitalism and complementarily anti-Communist. In a minute, we'll see how these points apply to Sicily.

But first there's a loose end to tie up — what about the charge against Sindona for murder? Investigators in the United States and in Italy had been collaborating to unravel the strands of Sindona's colorful tapestry. Palermo's deputy superintendent of police, Boris Giuliano, had noticed at the Palermo airport cash-filled suitcases directed to New York, and he went on to track ill-gotten money to Sindona's banks. An industrious lawyer in Milan, Giorgio Ambrosoli, was appointed by the courts to arrange the liquidation of a Sindona bank there. Both Giuliano and Ambrosoli were murdered in July 1979, and Sindona was suspected of commissioning the killings. He was formally accused of the murder of Ambrosoli, whom he had tried hard to intimidate.

THE 1970S MAFIA AND ITS OPPONENTS

Like Ambrosoli, a few politicians dared to fight against the Mafia, knowing they were risking their lives. They brought forth the first parliamentary commission of inquiry in the early 1970s, though it accomplished little. Too often the zealous efforts of anti-Mafia investigators were thwarted by directives from higher up. Partly as a result, while the new Mafia was shifting into higher technology and finance, anti-Mafia efforts tended to focus on gang wars. Still, mafiosi murderers were regularly arrested and tried. A series of arrests caused enough havoc among Mafia leaders that they reorganized in the mid-1970s, with their base at Corleone.

---

* This is a history of Sicily, not of the United States, but it's only fair to remind ourselves here that greed can impel American men of influence just as it does Italian. David Kennedy, a secretary of the treasury under Richard Nixon, got sucked into the Sindona maelstrom; he admitted accepting two hundred thousand dollars.

By that time Sicily was enjoying nationwide programs as well as supplemental ones that together provided a decent standard of living for the average family and ample opportunities (even if not all at home) to advance legally into higher spheres of income. Yet in Sicily, apparently more than in most regions of the industrialized world, the illegal still beckoned. To some extent this was tradition, following in the footsteps of one's father. We have seen that the highest steps of Sicily's social pyramid had long been occupied by land-barons, living parasitically in Palermo or at the royal court abroad; when the social order changed in the postwar period, the barons did not. Pushed from their lands and unprepared for any high-paying respectable occupation, more than ever they needed position based not on what they knew but on whom they knew. We have already noted the earlier close connection between the Mafia and the governing party. As cash became more important and more available, some politicians who at first had been induced just to turn a blind eye to illegal activities gradually became active collaborators.

Some of them were Masons. Sicily's influential Masons had their own lodge in Palermo, of which the membership and activities were kept secret even from other Masons. One member in the Masonic upper reaches was the physician who had supervised Sindona's bullet wound. These Masons were instrumental in placing each other in high-level government jobs where their loyalty to their friends overrode any concern for welfare of Sicilians generally. (The overall Masonic organization has since disowned this lodge.)

Just as "Masons" in Sicily assumed different characteristics from those in other Western countries, so did "Communists." In Sicily the Communist Party offered the only political home to those working against the Mafia.

Well-Being without Development
The Mafia higher-ups used the drug money, like the Cassa money, for its own luxurious living. Few seemed to care. The pie, miraculously, had gotten big enough that there were pieces for everyone. Sicilians were eating better than ever before, if "better" means more

meat and dairy products. Their peasant fathers had obtained tractors after years of striving, but the new urbanities quickly purchased cars and motor scooters. Families came to consider a regular salary as a right, and second jobs and women working for pay became common ways of supplementing the men's salary. Non-earners had new, easy access to government pensions of one kind or another. Few Sicilians still faced a daily struggle to stay alive; most juggled their budgets to buy conveniences and diversions and advancement. Why condemn mafiosi when you could emulate them?

Some observers condemned the Mafia because it had the economy in a stranglehold. As Franchetti and Sonnino had observed a hundred years before, the Mafia brooked no competition in controlling jobs. The public sector was the bailiwick of the new mafiosi as the latifundia had been of the *gabelloti,* and those employed in the public sector feared, as had the peasants, to lose their income for displeasing the capo. The possibilities of being hired outside the public sector were few. The Mafia permitted small stores to sell food and the usual range of urban necessities — mafiosi too buy these items — but each store was a family affair, discouraged from employing outsiders. When modern life required larger businesses, such as supermarkets and hotels, the Mafia involved itself in their operation. Anyone outside Mafia circles who endeavored to start a factory, for instance, would find no functionaries to process his permits and no suppliers to sell him materials; he would be "taxed" exorbitantly, and if that didn't defeat him, he would be threatened with bodily harm. The Mafia, in short, decided which work was to be done.*

Sicilians who wanted to work generally had two alternatives: either play the Mafia game or leave Sicily. During the years of heightened prosperity and of the Cassa's promise to increase prosperity further, the number of Sicilian emigrants reached its postwar peak. Far more Sicilians left Italy during the years 1966 to 1971 than at any other time in the second half of the twentieth century. (See the

---

* The Mafia, although anti-Communist, coerced a business structure like that under contemporary communism: you can work for the state, you can run a mom-and-pop business, but you can't hire more than a couple of people.

appendix table "Sicilian Emigrants from Italy," page 459.) In these years the Western world was enjoying an economic boom, so that Sicilians had their choice of countries to work in. Whatever other forces were involved, the fact remains that the emigrants were people who preferred to work abroad rather than remain in Sicily.

Again, Sicily was losing ambitious people, among whom were certainly some who might have established small businesses. Sicily was still importing virtually all its manufactured goods. From the 1950s through the 1970s, the world's social scientists argued indefatigably for economic development to help poor peoples toward self-sufficiency. The idea was to grant funds — "seed money" — for starting up factories and businesses or buying equipment and learning techniques to make production more efficient. In due course the subsidized venture should be able to survive on its own, perhaps earn profits, by getting more goods and services to more people at lower prices. Public bodies granted Sicily substantial sums, but very little went to produce goods for Sicilians to buy. The Mafia directed the funds toward the public sector, which was easier to control, or else funneled the public money to entrepreneurs who were Mafia associates. Sicily's improved standard of living in this period did not come about through economic development.*

∽

The economic structure was based not on selling products or worthy services but on selling power. As the Mafia limited and controlled the jobs, getting a job had to be arranged either through a mafioso or through some influential friend, a system known as *clientelismo*. In this, Mafia monopolization of power blends with the Mediterranean inclination to turn every dealing into a personal relationship, however ephemeral. Calling on friends for help is universal, but where inefficiency and indifference prevail, a stranger wishing to accomplish any business at all must transact it through go-betweens. The agents who

---

* Sicily's oil boom, coinciding with the arrival of public funds, did not stimulate economic development. Petroleum production is capital intensive, and those Sicilians who were employed generally worked in low-level jobs; furthermore, the profits were taken from Sicily.

are most effective gain respect and power. In Sicily it's an old story, but formerly, in villages and the then-smaller cities, people depended on their extended families and on genuine friendships, and needs were simpler. With urbanization, people's needs grew more complex and their lives more anonymous, so that *clientelismo* became a series of ad hoc relationships.

Like many governments, Sicily fills most of its jobs in public administration through competitive exams and fills high-level jobs politically. Sicily's political appointees include competent and caring public servants, but in the hiring process their subject expertise has no more importance than the color of their hair. Rating connections over competence inevitably leads to inefficiency and misuse of government funds. Within any organization the powerbroker and his clients form a clique to perpetrate and shield embezzlement, favoritism, and the like. Everyone was held in thrall by the obligation of *omertà*, terrified of consequences for reporting any Mafia activity.

Those wishing to work without Mafia-imposed constraints are likely to leave the island. This contributes, for one thing, to the general weakness of the professional preparation provided within Sicily. Unable to get good jobs locally, young Sicilians throng Sicily's three universities, knowing that even on graduation they will find few opportunities on their island. Accordingly, few professors can feel excited about preparing students to move away. The system offers professors no rewards for energizing students or a broader public. In this context, too, the Mafia milieu discourages initiative.

EXERCISING POLITICAL WILL

The Regional Assembly

Although the institution of the Regional Assembly from 1946 to 1948 gave an appearance of greater democracy, it didn't signal much substantive change. Perpetually ruled by outsiders who had their own priorities, most Sicilians thought "representative government" to be gibberish. When given the vote, they used it to legitimate the power of someone they thought already strong enough to defend them rather than to bestow power on someone who might articulate their desires. So the center of control remained pretty much where it had been under the Bourbons. While the term "ex-*feudo*" had disappeared from Sicilians' everyday vocabulary, *"baroni"* was (and still is) regularly used to indicate the regional politicians.*

Its mandate stranded the Regional Assembly between two economic worlds. Sicily had most of the aspects of an underdeveloped country but, not being a country, couldn't make basic economic policies for itself. Another difficulty was that the assembly provided little scope for the individual assemblyman to win attention through spirited legislation. For a while after the end of the Second World War, when Sicily was in dire straits and the economic-development clarion began to sound universally, the Regional Assembly responded with allotments to encourage production. But as funds came to Sicily more and more from Rome, assemblymen lost interest in economic policy.

In the 1950s and '60s Sicilians perceived that the men they elected had less influence over their lives than did the men in Rome — in other words, that Sicily was still under foreign rule. They saw the Mafia strengthening itself by distributing the favors that Rome granted. By the time Cassa funds flowed into Sicily during the 1970s, it was a foregone conclusion that they would be channeled through mafiosi and their friends. The funds from Rome were a windfall for the assemblymen, too; to get their share they had only not to interfere with the Mafia.

Regional autonomy had been granted, at least in part, to meet Sicilians' complaints that they were always exploited by foreign governments. Against the Mafia, which was exploiting Sicily from within, the assembly never even tried to struggle. Importantly, when public funds became available, the assembly might have assumed major responsibility for setting spending priorities to benefit the commonweal or for minimizing the corruption inevitable in any large government program,

* As the assembly had ninety seats, an alternative nickname for the body was *"i novanta ladroni"* ("the ninety thieves").

but it didn't. Nor were assemblymen above compromising the region's autonomy in the context of jobs. While Sicily was receiving Cassa funds, industries up north were clamoring for Sicilian workers, thus the north was less than eager to increase the region's self-sufficiency. The assembly just accepted northern policies, in a replay of the 1870s.

Ordinary Sicilians viewed autonomy as a symbol of their distinct character as a people. They didn't really expect the assembly to do much, and they watched passively as their elected representatives discoursed on their problems but balked at trying remedies. As in 1282 and 1848, Sicily in the 1970s muffed a chance for representative government.

∽

The Italian Parliament in Rome tried now and again to curb Sicilian corruption, but (as illustrated in the Sindona case) it sometimes appeared that the Mafia had more success in corrupting Rome.

Sicilians as a whole were caught up in the system, as Judge Chinnici made plain:

> . . . precisely because [the Mafia businesses] create jobs and produce wealth, [they] cut into the fabric of the regional society, economy, and politics by influencing elections.

"You've never had it so good," trumpeted the DC, accurately. Sicilians were not about to jeopardize their prosperity.

THE PEACE MOVEMENT AT COMISO
In its campaigns the DC also reminded the voters that it was aligned with the church against communism, manipulating Sicily's devoted Catholics to blanch at godlessness. Nonetheless, many Sicilians objected to the role assigned to their island should the Cold War turn hot.

The southeastern province of Ragusa, besides benefitting from the oil boom, developed Sicily's most modern agriculture (especially fruits and vegetables). In August 1981 Sicilians learned that NATO had chosen the old airfield at Comiso, in the center of Ragusa province, for the installation of Europe's largest missile base. When Comiso administrators had learned of the plan a few months earlier, they rejected it, but NATO pushed ahead anyway to expand the airport to accommodate 112 cruise missiles. Sicilians, their island once again important in world politics for its central Mediterranean location, shrank from becoming a prime target for nuclear bombs. They responded not through their assembly but in their traditional way.

The size and the vehemence of the protests surprised the NATO people and the Italian government. As quickly as October 11 some thirty thousand people gathered in Comiso, and that was just the beginning of years of continual fasts, marches, and demonstrations. Although the Italian media chose to downplay these, Comiso turned into a center of the international movement for disarmament. English pacifists came to teach the Sicilians how to respond nonviolently to the Italian government repression. At the end of 1982 a large group led by Italian intellectuals marched to Comiso from Milan. Delegations arrived from every Western country, and a Japanese delegation in 1983 signed a friendship pact between Comiso and Hiroshima. Despite the agitation, the first sixteen missiles were brought to Comiso in March 1984. Shortly thereafter the Cold War tensions eased, making moot the Comiso conflict.*

MAFIA TARGETS POLITICAL VIPs
Traditionally, the Mafia didn't target any non-mafiosi establishment figures for violence — it preferred to co-opt them. We noted above, though, the first Mafia murder of a judge in 1971 and the murder of two anti-Mafia investigators in July 1979. As the Mafia adapted itself to modern party politics, its internal strife over spoils gave way occasionally to its actions against the Left. The Christian Democratic Party always had its Left and Right, the right wing, supportive of the Mafia, generally dominant. In the mid-1970s the left-leaning group

---

* During the Serbian war of the early 1990s, the NATO base housed hundreds of refugees from Kosovo. The base finally reverted to Italy in January 2002.

elected one of its men, Michele Reina, secretary of the DC for Palermo province. Cardinal Ruffini spoke out against these leftists and scorned their call for dialogue. The reactionary Mafia felt encouraged to rid Sicilian politics of the leftist Reina and murdered him in March 1979. Six months later they killed a judge, Cesare Terranova, who was a member of the Communist Party. The president of the region,* Piersanti Mattarella, belonged to the DC left and endeavored to express Christian values in his government; in January 1980 he became another Mafia victim. In August 1980 the Mafia successfully targeted judge Gaetano Costa, who had issued arrest warrants for certain members of the Mafia's leading families.

In 1981, when NATO chose Comiso for its missile base, one of the organizers of the protest against it was Pio La Torre, head of the Communist Party in Sicily and one of its deputies to parliament in Rome. For thirty-five years La Torre had been active in the fight against the Mafia, and now he was preparing a law against association with the Mafia. He was murdered on April 30, 1982.

These murders of dignitaries hardly distracted mafiosi from their internecine wars, which in 1981–82 killed over three hundred people just in Palermo. But it was the Mafia's targeting of dignitaries that caused national scandal. A few years previously mainland Italy had suffered bouts of terrorism that caused Italy to tighten its laws and to treat as a hero the antiterrorism chief, the effective general Carlo Alberto Dalla Chiesa. Named to deal with Palermo's slaughter, he took up the post on May 1, 1982. Ordinary Sicilians hailed his arrival, but Rome denied him the powers he thought necessary to bring the Mafia to heel. For example, he recognized the importance of digging into Mafia finances (such as the work being done by Judge Chinnici); when asked what ought to be done that wasn't being done, the general responded:

> We should begin with an investigation, an analysis, of
> how the Mafia gets its money. An analysis that leads to the
> confiscation of profits from illicit or dubious businesses.

---

* President of the Sicilian Region is equivalent to an American state governor.

Nonetheless, he started immediately to tighten the laws in Sicily and to enforce them. Four months after his arrival, on September 3, the Mafia killed him.

In this Sicilian climate of disgust and fear, Judge Chinnici prevailed upon the office of Palermo's public prosecutor to set up a unit to prosecute Mafia activities in their political and economic aspects. The new focus evidently raised apprehensions, for on July 29, 1983, the Mafia assassinated Judge Chinnici.*

Since entering into drug trafficking, the Sicilian Mafia maintained a level of violence much higher than in the preceding centuries. The high incidence of murders and the insolence in killing men of probity was entirely an urban phenomenon. Palermo, the usual venue, was stimulated to erect a monument to "victims of the Mafia." A more significant monument was a new law: heretofore mafiosi had been arrested for criminal conspiracy, but the speedily enacted Rognoni–La Torre law made a crime of *"associazione mafiosa."*†

The anti-Mafia colleagues of the assassinated La Torre applied the new law with vengeance. Most of the targeted supporters and protectors of the murderers were Democristiani, to be sure, but the several thousands implicated included politicians of all political stripes as well as from most of Italy's regions. Although the relevant arrests would continue for a few years, as early as the campaign for the 1983 elections Sicily's DC found that most of those who might have been considered for candidacy were in jail or in danger of being arrested.

---

* Those named above are only a few of the Mafia's victims in this period. Among the other victims were several policemen. Mafia violence reached its high point in 1981–83.

Sicily's homicides per 100,000 population, 1979–85 average: 8.3. For the same years, the U.S. had a rate of around 9.0 for "arrests . . . for murder and nonnegligent homicide." Although the figures aren't exactly comparable, the American statistic reminds us that there's no grounds for thinking Sicily uniquely violent. (Giorgio Chinnici and Umberto Santino, *Violenza programmata: Omicidi e guerre di mafia a Palermo dagli anni '60 ad oggi.* [Milan: Franco Angeli, 1989], p. 53. The U.S. data are from the U.S. Department of Justice, *Sourcebook of Criminal Justice Statistics,* figure 4.9.)

† ". . . association . . . when those who take part use . . . intimidation and . . . subjugation and *omertà* . . . to commit crimes, to acquire (directly or indirectly) the management or in any case the control of economic activities . . ."

Much the same applied in regard to the position of mayor, not yet directly elective. One DC stalwart in Palermo was herself an anti-Mafia fighter, the pediatrician Elda Pucci. She had been instrumental in getting the city of Palermo to act as plaintiff against Judge Chinnici's murderers, so the mayor-makers thought she would safely represent DC respectability. Once installed as mayor, Dr. Pucci set out to improve the city's infrastructure, overall in very poor condition. Roads were badly potholed, running water was a sometime thing, and sewers and public transport had grown theoretical. Yet all of them were priced exorbitantly because mafiosi contractors assured first of all their cut. Palermo's street lighting, so state-of-the-art when Sonnino and Franchetti had admired it 110 years previously, had given way by the 1980s to lighting uncomfortably and dangerously dim. Pucci wanted to introduce an open system of bidding for contracts, but the Mafia-controlled city council would have none of that. And someone blew up Pucci's country house. Seeing the handwriting on the wall, she resigned in April 1984.

WOMEN POLITICALLY EMANCIPATED

By that time Dr. Pucci entered office as mayor, her sex was hardly a factor, which is noteworthy in a region where women traditionally remained at home. Her mayoralty is a good impetus though for us to catch up with this 50 percent of Sicilians. Women as a political group, we already noted, first gained attention in the peace movement of 1950, then urbanization led to women working increasingly outside the home, in schoolrooms, offices, and shops. Once schooling became accessible, it was provided for girls as for boys, and the reluctance of some rural families to educate their daughters was soon overcome.

Rural traditions subjugating girls survived as glaring vestiges. For example, a young man wishing to take a particular girl as a wife but running into difficulty of some kind might kidnap her. Although even for this purpose kidnapping was a crime, the charge would be dropped on the couple's marriage. In 1966, in Alcamo (a good-sized town, conservative and a Mafia stronghold), Franca Viola was desired by a young man who didn't interest her. With the help of friends, he abducted her and sequestered her for a few days. So far so good. But when he released Franca and she returned home, she absolutely refused to marry him. She withstood pressures from her family and friends to "do the right thing," while the media spread this story of primitive Sicily throughout the Western world. In due course her abductor was given a sentence of eleven years.

Even in the mid-1960s Sicilian girls attended university in great numbers, and it followed that over the next decade women became unexceptional participants in Sicily's economic and political life. Today, in Sicily as in much of the Western world, women in politics are a small minority but no longer a rarity: women have been mayors of several towns, including Partinico (between Alcamo and Palermo), Cefalù, and Caltagirone. But no more in Sicily than elsewhere have the public activities of women brought about change in a benign direction.

CHARACTERISTICS OF SICILIAN EMPLOYMENT

EMPLOYMENT IN THE PUBLIC SECTOR
The inpouring of public funds during the 1960s and '70s changed Sicily extensively, not least in the way Sicilians support themselves. Just a few statistics will highlight the narrative of the last several pages and also bring us up to the year 2000.

No change was more consequential than the emergence of women. Traditionally women never worked outside the home because Sicily's biggest problem was its shortage of paid employment. Always employment in Sicily had been overwhelmingly in the agricultural sector and seen as the responsibility of males, with small numbers of men working in the industrial sector (essentially mining) and commerce.

Partly because Sicily offered more jobs for men than for women, by the 1970s more Sicilian girls than boys attended university, and of the enrolled students a higher percentage of girls than boys remained to graduate. As the educational level of women increased they had fewer children and entered the labor force in greater numbers. From 1971 to 1981, the employment of women ages twenty to forty doubled. Women's entrance into paid employment took place concurrently with the growing employment in public administration, and those new jobs went overwhelmingly to women.

The mass employment of women and the shift from agriculture and industry into services had started earlier up north, but Sicily quickly caught up. Over the last generation, agriculture's share of Sicily's total employment dropped from 28.5 percent in 1971 to 9.1 percent in 2001, while industry's share of total employment dropped, not so dramatically, from 33.7 percent in 1971 to 20.5 percent in 2001. (See the appendix table "Employment by Sector," page 459.)

Though the statistics do not permit exact comparisons, there's no doubt that a much larger proportion of employees in Sicily work in public administration than is the case up north. Shifting to money values shows us that in 1999, as a percentage of gross internal product, in Sicily public administration accounted for 10.0 percent of the total, while in throughout Italy public administration accounted for only 5.3 percent of the total. That is, in Sicily public administration had twice as large a share in the economy as it did in Italy as a whole.*

Another salient point regarding Sicily's employment in the public sector: While much of the industrialized world's shift into services was occasioned by information technology, of this Sicily remained almost innocent. Public administration and commerce hardly modernized.[†]

⤬

---

* Sicilians have a general disposition for employment in public administration. In the north of Italy many of the jobs in public service and in schools are held by Sicilians.

[†] The proposition that mentality has not caught up with technology is complicated to prove but is exemplified in ways easily seen by any visitor to Sicily. One example appears on every business street. Photocopiers are ubiquitous. At any given time, in offices and in copy shops, fewer than half the photocopiers function. Most operators are unable or unwilling to use the reduce/enlarge button, and only near universities is the customer allowed to do her own photocopying. So the customer stands there while the operator takes half an hour to do a two-minute job. The little copy shops where the entire business depends on one machine, which is manned and fussed over by five or six people, particularly stimulate reflection on underemployment.

In Italy's economic statistics, public administration (including defense) accounts for virtually all of a category called "services not destined for sale." Where no value is set on work, people lose motivation to work. In Sicily, where half the labor force is employed at "services not destined for sale," the lack of motivation is reinforced as societal norm. Sicilian skeptics say "the work of the Sicilians is to seek grants."

But even in that search, the performance leaves much to be desired. For years the European Union has designated funds for unemployment relief and economic development in Europe's least-developed regions, to be given to the region on its request for the funding of a particular project. For years Sicily has neglected to take full advantage of the offer, sometimes not even bothering to respond to letters from Brussels advising that the availability of a particular grant for Sicily was about to expire. Uncollected by Sicily, the funds are then reallocated to other poor regions that applied with project outlines, so that Sicilian taxpayers are contributing funds to unemployment relief in Portugal and Greece. Sicilians explain that their lack of organization hinders their writing of grant proposals.

MISONEISM: THE WORD AND THE ATTITUDE

Indolence depresses the Sicilian economy in general. Giovanni Falcone, a judge who devoted his life to understanding the Sicilian character, tried to explain:

> The invaders arrived from many countries, and every time [the Sicilians] had to adapt themselves, or pretend to adapt themselves, waiting for them to go away. At the end they did go away, leaving us as legacy a temperament that I would define as misoneist, made up of apparent submission and loyalty to tradition, together with a raving pride.

Although the English "misoneism" is scarcely used, educated Sicilians often attribute to *misoneismo* a given lack of organization or of initiative or of response. The word literally means a hatred or intolerance for something new or changed. In the case of inaction when a formal request would bring money, it may actually be that officials view the grant with disfavor as they view modernization generally with disfavor. The Mafia has always seen modernization as a threat, which is significant given the direct participation of the Mafia in the economy generally and the public sector particularly.

EXAMPLES: LIBRARIES AND TOURISM

When Sicilians moved, en masse, from village to town and city, they brought the inefficiency and politicization of agriculture with them to the public administration and to virtually every aspect of urban Sicilians' daily lives. Reporting from every sector being impractical, I will illustrate with two examples, choosing activities with which the reader is familiar.

Sicily's library system is "autonomous" from that of Italy. Like library systems everywhere, Sicily's operates under financial constraints, but here the crucial lack is of management. Sicily has some of the Western world's earliest documents on paper (see chapter six) and archival material from half the peoples of Europe, which makes the poor functioning of the library system especially regrettable.

As Palermo's libraries possess millions of books and documents, a researcher is resigned to slow going; it's eye-opening, though, how much the search for particular information is expedited for a researcher who "knows someone." Normally the researcher is disappointed, given modern technology, that the regional library can't locate a catalogued book in its own stacks nor say if the requested material is available through another library. Many of the cards in the catalogs were written in the 1800s and are illegible to patrons without specialized training. Personnel assert that some day soon the catalog will be computerized, but these are institutions that never got around to using typewriters, available to them for a century.

Palermo's municipal library is repairing one of its buildings, making many of its books inaccessible for a few years. And while the city's regional library is generally "open," frequently it cannot distribute material to patrons because of absent employees or problems with water or electricity. Library personnel meet laments and questions with hosannas to the city's great patrimony of books and documents, seemingly unaware that the patrimony loses value to the extent that it can't be used.

~

The tourism sector, like public administration, is a good vehicle for job creation because it is highly labor-intensive. Even better, while workers in agriculture have been replaced by machinery and Sicily's mines have proved uncompetitive, Sicily will not soon lose its gentle beaches and sunshine. Nor are beaches and sunshine greatly vulnerable to mismanagement. Sicily's fresh food and folk festivals appeal to northern city dwellers. During the universal tourist boom of 1981–2000, Sicily's revenue from tourism increased considerably, though it appears that Sicily was carried along on the wave rather than doing much to encourage growth.

Oodles of public money have been spent to develop Sicily's tourism, which is now a major source of revenue for the island. But one sees everywhere how Sicily could do much more.

Sicily strongly favors tourists in large groups over small ones. This may be justified by the revenue, even though much of the profit from large groups remains with the organizers abroad. In any case, Sicily could improve its earnings, and its image, by encouraging independent travellers and retirees inclined to spend winter in this mild climate. But they are discouraged by the Mafia wars and by the Mafia disinclination to have strangers around.

Although few people on Sicily's streets speak English (or French or German), the tourist offices are generally unhelpful: they'll give you a city map and a list of hotels but can only rarely answer your question about a train strike or even a local event. Using modern communications could overcome this difficulty at little cost. A few localities do indeed advertise telephonic tourist help in the major languages. However, phone calls in the three languages for help in finding a hotel or a doctor or an intercity bus are answered by someone who says, in Italian, "Sorry, I don't speak English."

As in the days of the latifundia, travel around the coast is much easier than travel to the interior. The train system is run by Italy: timetables are accessible, comprehensive, clear, and dependable except when service is interrupted by strikes. Of particular interest to tourists is that the railway doesn't circle the island; the missing piece is along the south coast, precisely between the primary archaeological sites of Agrigento and Selinunte. City buses in Palermo and the other big cities work reasonably well, but bus travel between cities is less satisfactory. The privately owned intercity buses don't coordinate their schedules; their only stop in a town may be at Giuseppe's Bar on the periphery; posted timetables often are out of date; and even for Italian-speakers phoning to get such information is complicated.

Sicily prepares some splendid exhibits, many of them in Palermo. Up north exhibits serve as magnets to attract out-of-towners, who then spend at the city's hotels, restaurants, and shops. But Sicily seldom "markets" its exhibits; in fact the dates of an exhibit may be announced so close to its opening that interested out-of-towners can't schedule attendance. The main complaint of travellers to Italy is that Sicily's hotels are too few and far between and (correspondingly) overpriced.

Public employees, for lack of much else to do, block initiatives. In a certain small town, a public-spirited private citizen of moderate wealth spearheaded the development of an annual nonreligious festival. Each summer the festival attracted people from a wide area and brought revenue into the town. After a few years the local administration told him to stop; the town itself would run the festival. As no one in the town administration was inclined to work at it, the festival lost élan and after three years ceased.

Another example, from Sicily's major archaeological site at Selinunte: Tourists would show up in twos and threes throughout the day wanting to employ a guide, but guides were available only for a half day at a cost of about a hundred dollars. The visitors, finding the price exorbitant compared with other tourist sites, wouldn't buy and left disappointed, often complaining to a particular information officer. She in turn suggested to her superiors that the site change to a system common elsewhere: a guide would be available to start a tour at a particular hour of each morning and afternoon, and tourists could assemble at that hour and share the expense. The information officer's suggestion was met with a directive to mind her own business and a warning that any further initiative on her part would result in her transfer to a site far from her home.

During the early months of each year Sicilian newspapers run articles and ads about summer employment for Sicilians in tourist accommodations outside of Sicily, especially for jobs as animators — tour guides or entertainers — in resorts. Typically the item quotes an employer to the effect, "We're looking especially for Sicilians because Sicilians are the best in this field." Those who speak a second language are of course most in demand, but even just in Italian, Sicilians' volubility and their talent for expressing interest in others combine into a saleable resource, another resource from which northerners profit. Sicily underutilizes these young people as it underutilizes its patrimony of books.

Inertia and sabotage: both can be praiseworthy when employed against a government imposed from outside. They are counterproductive in the context of a democracy where the aim is job creation.

THE "MENTALITÀ MAFIOSA"

Blockage is central to the Sicilian experience. It's the cause of the massive emigration, both because individuals become tired of constant frustration and because blockage reduces opportunities for employment. The restrictions of Sicily's economy have ever hindered individuals from outshining others in production. Misery not only loves company, it resents those who advance out of it. Persons who "rise above themselves" meet roadblocks, if not car bombs.

This lengthy discussion of indolence and blockage is meant to show where Sicilian history has led and to provide some understanding of how the Mafia mentality impinges on Sicilian life in ways that have nothing to do with crime. In fact Judge Falcone warned against the confusion of the *mentalità mafiosa* with the *organizzazione mafiosa*.

When Prime Minister Vittorio Emanuele Orlando, in 1925, proudly declared himself mafioso, he mentioned Mafia virtues of generosity and loyalty (see chapter ten). Clearly, in his public pronouncement, he was referring to the mentality. As he said, it is this characteristic, or blend of characteristics, that makes Sicilians Sicilians.

Among the peoples of the Western world, the Sicilians, it's probably fair to say, are among the most pleasant and hospitable. They have had this reputation among tourists since there have been tourists. And at least since cinema has been cinema, the Sicilians have been the people most notorious for their violent crime. This dichotomy of character is complex, but if one were forced to explain it in a single word, that word would be "tolerance."

In Sicily, more than elsewhere, the tolerance of inconvenience slides into a generalized tolerance of criminality. Again I'll make the point through examples, picking (from a book-length list) two at opposite corners of the island. At Messina, the bridge across the strait (see chapter ten) in all probability will never be built — though a very long series of engineering firms has been paid from public funds to design it. At Mazara, one of Italy's main fishing ports, fishing is a Mafia business. Buyers come in their trucks and take the tuna directly from the pier. To accommodate the traders, an enclosed wholesale fish market has long been planned. But, as the current arrangement facilitates tax evasion, Mazara's commercial fishermen strenuously oppose the market, and the government relents. After all, goes the common refrain, those guys have to earn a living too.

Let's move from work activities out to Palermo's streets. Although Palermo's central streets are perhaps cleaner now than they were in Goethe's time, they still present a hazard for those on foot: Every sidewalk, along broad avenues as well as narrow medieval streets, is blocked by cars and motor scooters, so that pedestrians must maneuver back and forth between sidewalk and roadway. This example of the private use of public property may be petty, but it's clear and common, tolerated by pedestrians and police alike.

The private use of public property is a fundamental charge against the Mafia. Most blatantly, they have used the Cassa funds and the government apparatus as resources in their private, venal business affairs. While Sicily has no monopoly on crime and corruption, it is extraordinary in the Western world in that the crime and corruption are part and parcel of government.

Sicilians resent their notoriety — why do they tolerate the cause of it? We can appreciate that the Sicilian barons, sensitive to their inferiority under foreign rule, developed a touchiness about status and an inclination to disregard the foreigners' law. But the Bourbons were ousted by the middle of the nineteenth century, and Sicilians gained the right to control their internal affairs by the middle of the twentieth. They have the apparatus of a Western democracy and by now they understand that, for effective democracy, laws have to be painstakingly legislated and equitably enforced. Sicilians brag that they lack the patience for such work.

"A government of laws and not of men," so appealing to Anglo-Saxons, is less so to Sicilians, who demur that it's abstract and inflexible. They don't want laws that they can't get around, laws that give them little chance to exhibit their superiority by evasion. Zero tolerance, the current Anglo-Saxon curative for criminality, would never work in Sicily.

The Mafia is so pervasive in the island's political economy that it's tempting to attribute every case of wrongdoing to mafiosi. But sometimes blockage, corruption, and violence occur in Sicily without any Mafia participation, just as they occur outside of Sicily and Italy. In Sicily in a given case it may be difficult to determine if or how much the Mafia was involved, just as in a given case it can be difficult to distinguish victim from accomplice.

CRACKS IN THE MAFIA WALL

With ordinary Sicilians remaining passive and with money in hand to buy politicians, the Mafia could operate its drug businesses smoothly. However, there was a fly in the Mafia's ointment. The drug business became so huge and so global that the Mafia, in running it, had to work closely with non-mafiosi — greedy people of several nations and no loyalties. When arrested, these people sometimes gave details about their associates. And mafiosi themselves broke their code. The first was an American: around 1960, a mafioso hit man and drug pusher, Joe Valachi, named names in the hierarchy of the American organization; his assertions provoked a public outcry, which led in turn to a police roundup. In Palermo, in 1973, the mafioso Leonardo Vitale turned himself in and confessed in detail, giving names of other mafiosi and particulars of organization and activities, but he spoke with a mystic air and behaved crazily — it probably *was* crazy at that time to speak out about the Mafia — so the police wrote him off as a nutcase. (Vitale was confined to an insane asylum for ten years; upon his release in 1984 he was killed by the Mafia.) In 1978 the boss of the town of Riesi, Giuseppe Di Cristina, started to open up, but before he could say much he was murdered. Still, *omertà* wasn't what it used to be.

A new chapter in the *omertà* story opened in June 1984 in Brazil, with the meeting of two distinguished men born and raised in central Palermo. We have already met Giovanni Falcone, the anti-Mafia investigator. He had made the long trip to Brazil to question Tommaso Buscetta, a prisoner being held for running the drug-trade in Italy and the Americas. The Brazilian judge put the questions to Buscetta, and the dapper, articulate, cosmopolitan fifty-six-year-old replied succinctly, impressing Falcone. The reaction was mutual. Buscetta eyed Falcone in a way that suggested, "With *you* I'll talk."

A protégé and friend of Lucky Luciano, Buscetta had the skills at finance and organization that one would expect in a high-level executive of an international conglomerate. His quick rise in the ranks got him into jail and into hot water with other Mafia bosses. In fact, after a former employee of Buscetta's failed at a murder attempt in Palermo during an early 1980s Mafia war, the target of the hit smelled a plot. As a consequence, in the second half of 1982 Buscetta had to stand by forsaken as his brother-in-law vanished in Brazil. Two weeks later his two sons (who were innocent of Mafia dealings) vanished in Palermo. Then in December his son-in-law was shot dead in Palermo. Within a few days Buscetta's brother was shot dead in his small factory, together with the brother's son.*

Buscetta knew himself to be a walking corpse until American investigators offered him a new face and financial security in return for information about his American connections. Sicilian lawmen took the role of collaborators, partly because Italy had no program of witness protection. Extradited from Brazil to Italy and imprisoned in Rome, Buscetta told his story through the autumn of 1984. Judge Falcone skillfully encouraged him to reveal the master players on the drug-trafficking scene. To be sure, a lot of what Buscetta said was already known to Falcone and his colleagues. Throughout the talks, moreover, Buscetta refused to divulge the names of corrupted politicians. But Buscetta's flouting of *omertà* prompted many other mafiosi to come forward, and these *pentiti* filled in some gaps. (*Pentiti* means "the repentant ones," though many of them acted from motives other than repentance.)

Buscetta's revelations gave the Sicilian investigators the specifics they needed to make indictments for almost a hundred murders, among them the 1982 murder of General Dalla Chiesa. Palermo's Ucciardone prison was fitted out with multi-man cages to hold the 470 defendants; this maxitrial (as it came to be called in both Italian and English) marked the first time that the Mafia, as a unified organization, was accused of responsibility for crimes. It was for this purpose that La Torre and Rognoni had been determined to get a law criminalizing Mafia association; now charges could be entered against the malefactors of whom Leonardo Vitale had spoken to the police a dozen years before. The defendants were mafiosi who had directly caused mayhem and murder; no politicians were on trial. At the end of the trial, which lasted almost two years, the jury declared guilty 344 defendants, sentencing nineteen Mafia bosses to life in prison and also sentencing lesser mafiosi heavily. In addition, imposed were fines approaching ten million dollars.

---

* Threatening a foe with the death of his relatives was a common Mafia tactic, but in the Buscetta murders the Mafia outdid itself.

Many Sicilians cheered, but others were displeased by the whole idea of a maxitrial. One has to think of the thousands of Sicilians directly associated with the Mafia and the hundreds of thousands whose incomes depended directly or indirectly on the Mafia. As the trial got underway, demonstrators carried through the streets signs saying, in effect, "Don't rock the boat." Residents of the zone where the new fortress-courtroom was being built, and neighbors of judges and prosecutors continuously protected by armored vehicles, resented the noise: perhaps the anti-Mafia activities were okay but, please, not in my backyard. Palermo's principal newspaper, *Il Giornale di Sicilia,* continually editorialized against holding the trial. The anti-Mafia investigators were hardly surprised: having dedicated their lives to changing the Mafia-dominated system, they had suffered for years from isolation and even from sabotage by their superiors in government.

SOME ANTI-MAFIA FIGHTERS
AND THEIR VICTORIES

No one thought the maxitrial would extinguish the Mafia or end its domination over Sicily; at best the long sentences might reduce the criminality. Among the realists were the anti-Mafia investigators who had worked so hard to produce the maxitrial and who could be gratified by its results.

Falcone was successful in drawing out not only Buscetta but also other mafiosi. Untiring in his efforts to bring Mafia malefactors to justice, Falcone nonetheless treated them with respect; he understood the pride in being mafioso in a region that provides a man with few occupational opportunities to hold his head high. Having worked with and learned from Judge Rocco Chinnici, the mature Falcone sought evidence of mafiosi crimes in their bank records (a task for which many other investigators were unsuited).

Falcone's knowledge of the lives and connections in Sicily's underworld was matched (maybe even surpassed) by his longtime friend and colleague Paolo Borsellino. Early in his career, Borsellino had been deeply affected by the murders of civil officers who were his friends, but as he went about his investigations, though revolted by the brutality, he always sought some spark of humanity in the depraved killers. If he could identify with them, he could also reach them. Both Falcone and Borsellino dedicated themselves to building a state strong enough to suppress the Mafia — as youths, Borsellino had been attracted by fascism, Falcone by communism — and that lay behind their choice of becoming magistrates. They wanted more muscle in the law. Neither would join a political party; both felt it might compromise integrity (or seem to compromise integrity) when investigating politicians.

On the other hand, another young man wanting to use his career to suppress the Mafia chose the political route. Leoluca Orlando, son of a Palermo lawyer (and no kin of the World War I prime minister), had begun a career in administrative law, in Sicily a common springboard to politics. He was teaching at the University of Palermo when his mentor, Piersanti Mattarella, the Democristiano president of the region, was murdered in January 1980. The murder in September 1982 of General Dalla Chiesa further aggravated the disarray of the DC occasioned by the arrest of many of its leaders. In 1983 (as noted above) the DC chose Elda Pucci for Palermo's mayor, but when she realized she wasn't going to be able to accomplish anything she resigned after just a few months. In 1984 the DC appointed Giuseppe Insalco as mayor, but he too disappointed his party by expressing his own will to clean up the bidding for city contracts; he didn't last long. The populace was finally crying for politicians who would take action against the Mafia. In spring 1985 the DC named as mayor Leoluca Orlando.

Orlando worked with Falcone to get Palermo's city government to appear on the side of the prosecution in the maxitrial. From then on he lived like Falcone, with death threats and bodyguard. Orlando's detractors complained that he was devoting too much time to useless anti-Mafia efforts and not enough time to their city. Actually, Orlando did more than his predecessors to clean up Palermo physically, including districts still badly damaged from the 1943 bombing. Amid the clutter of scaffolding, the locals could be heard sharing their amazement that something was finally being done. On Saturday evenings Palermo's central streets were closed to vehicles, shops had the option of staying open late, and as a result Palermo reanimated the dying tradition of the *passeggiata* (the evening stroll). Nearby stood Palermo's *municipio* (city hall), built about the time of Columbus's voyages; strollers were encouraged to enter and view the priceless paintings and brocades. During this Orlando administration, lots of young people sported T-shirts emblazoned with "Io ♥ PA" (I love Palermo). All around Sicily, from the time of the maxitrials, mush-roomed placards and bumper stickers stating, *"Il governo siamo noi"* ("the government is us" — in Italian the grammar is correct). Orlando was extremely popular with the people of Palermo, but he was pro-viding too much reform for the party leaders, who forced his resigna-tion at the end of his five-year term.

As the maxitrial in Palermo progressed, proceedings got under way for another trial (dubbed maxi-2, with eighty defendants) that would focus on Mafia crimes in the area surrounding the capital. The vil-lages of Sicily, with their unskilled youth and high unemployment rates, supply much of the Mafia manpower, so it was essential to raise the anti-Mafia flag there too. In the province of Trapani, a Mafia stronghold, no broad investigations had been made in recent times. As soon as the verdicts were handed down from the maxitrial, Paolo Borsellino was offered a post as chief prosecutor in Marsala, the second city of the province of Trapani; he seized the opportunity.

With the closure of the maxitrial, the politicians who controlled the purse strings weren't inclined to support further anti-Mafia investigations; and now the anti-Mafia teams felt more free to indulge themselves in infighting. Of course there was still anti-Mafia work to be done in Palermo, as the investigators were reminded in mid-January 1988 by the murder of Giuseppe Insalco, who had spent a short time in 1984 as Palermo's mayor. He had meanwhile occupied himself in political and welfare activities, and had talked of exposing continuing irregularities in city contracts. Perhaps the maxitrial hadn't affected the Mafia after all. It figured — of the 114 defendants at the maxitrial who were acquitted, in short order the Mafia killed eighteen. In this environment it's no surprise that virtually all of those declared guilty and imprisoned were by 1991 free again.

MAFIA MURDERS MORE SHOCKING THAN EVER

Living with only rare breaks from continuous extreme tension, the anti-Mafia investigators bantered constantly about their imminent deaths. Attempts had been made on Falcone's life from the days of the Buscetta confessions, and he knew it was just a matter of time before the Mafia liquidated him. Like other top-level investigators, Falcone reduced the risk by restricting his social life to close relatives and a very few trusted friends, by never announcing his plans, and by moving around in armored cars. Supercautious and superprotected as Falcone was, killing him would demand organizational skill that included collaboration from within his tiny circle. The Mafia achieved its aim on May 23, 1992, with a car explosion that echoed all over Italy.

For more than seven years, starting with the Buscetta confessions, Falcone had been a celebrity. Regarding his professional activities every Sicilian had an opinion, though the opinions differed widely. Falcone's assassination brought most Sicilians together, to grieve. They felt bereaved of a close friend who was also their advocate. From their windows they hung banners made from bedsheets, on which they proclaimed "Falcone lives!" and implored "We're tired of leaving Sicily — get the *mafiosi* out of Sicily!" His funeral was one befitting royalty, with thousands standing outside the church in the rain and the service broadcast live on television. Stores were shuttered; strangers wept everywhere you looked. A month after Falcone's death, Italian trade unions sponsored a rally in Palermo. About forty thousand people came, from all over Sicily and beyond. It was the largest protest ever against the Mafia. Some of those present spoke of their lifelong resentment of the Mafia but said that they had felt it too dangerous to report to the authorities the corruption that came their way; they'd felt cowed into *omertà*. Falcone's courageous life had given them the courage to stand up against the Mafia and be counted (at least in the safety of numbers). Likewise, storekeepers who had been paying the *pizzo* for years this day hung anti-Mafia slogans in their front windows. An essential ingredient in the Mafia's domination of the island for generations was their success in intimidating the populace. Now fewer were intimidated.

The more analytical among the bereaved wondered why, if Falcone had long been on the Mafia's execution list, it chose this moment to murder him. His success in the maxitrial and its spinoffs aggrieved the mafiosi, to be sure, but that was five years in the past, and by now virtually all the convicted were freed. While the Mafia held its grudges for a long time, payoff for Falcone's past deeds would be only a partial explanation of the timing. More important was Falcone's imminent increase in authority and resources, for anti-Mafia operations were being reorganized with Falcone at the head.

It's useful to digress for a moment to the broad political picture. The 1986–87 maxitrial convulsed the DC Party at the national level. The DC lingered, however, because the crumbling of Soviet communism shook the political Left. Italy's Communist Party, already in decline, now splintered; the Communists, traditionally the anti-Mafia voters, no longer provided effective opposition to the DC. But this created a big challenge for the Democristiani, who had always presented their party as the only protection against communism. If the Communists had no more political force, then why should anyone vote DC? The Democristiani had to find another raison d'etre. Still mindful of its losses ten years before in the hunt for corrupted establishment figures, the DC set out to establish anti-Mafia credentials.

Like run-of-the-mill political organizations, the Mafia responds to wider political forces. The effectiveness of the anti-Mafia unit, the murders of Falcone, and others in the early 1990s, and the arrest of ringleader Totò Riina and his successors over the next few years, took place as the Mafia assimilated the end of the Cold War. For decades the Mafia tried to justify itself as a bulwark against communism in Mediterranean Italy, but it no longer had even that flimsy raison d'être. Mafiosi in increasing numbers cooperated with the forces of law.

This political circumstance underlay the decision, at the national level, to expand anti-Mafia operations. A green light had already been given to a new elite force, drawn from Italy's various police branches, to occupy itself exclusively with organized crime. It was this force that Falcone was to have headed, as a super-prosecutor. Borsellino would inherit the post.

If not Falcone's murder itself, then the continuing post-murder demonstrations changed moods everywhere. For example, the anti-Mafia investigators in Palermo, long treated poorly or at best ambivalently by Rome, felt new hope that someone up there might be listening to their requests. Thinking back nine years to the murder of Judge Rocco Chinnici, who had been murdered by a bomb set off in a car parked in front of his building, those responsible for the protection of Borsellino asked that a no-parking zone be created in front of his mother's house, where Borsellino visited each week. The request hadn't yet worked its way through the bureaucracy, and would never need to be considered, for Paolo Borsellino was killed at that exact spot on July 19, 1992, eight weeks after the murder of Falcone. The means was a remote-control car bomb, the blast from which could be heard for miles around. An even louder explosion burst all across Sicily, as the demonstrators' grief gave way to fury. Shouts and banners are best summarized as "Why the fuck don't you protect us?"

∽

Finally came some changes. Beyond the rhetoric, Rome realized that Sicily was in a critical state. She sent Sicily seven thousand soldiers, mostly young and untrained, but able at least to relieve Sicily's trained policemen from the task of guarding magistrates and judges. Traditionally, imprisoned Mafia leaders ran their businesses from jail with impunity, but now these bosses would be transferred and isolated. To get more disillusioned mafiosi to testify in court, the state offered reduction of sentences and relative security through Italy's new witness-protection program. Suddenly *pentiti* were coming out of the woodwork — not crawling but jumping — to talk. They were disgusted by all the murders, and they were just exhausted by the brutality of being mafiosi. They told investigators of their crimes and of their colleagues and of the high-level politicians with whom they had dealt —of dealings with politicians as high as former prime minister Giulio Andreotti.*

Aroused Sicilians continued to show their feelings. From the nineteenth of each month (Borsellino was murdered on July 19) to the twenty-third (Falcone was murdered on May 23) the bedsheet banners fluttered from windows. Going back to an hour after Falcone's death, the large ficus tree in front of Falcone's apartment house had become the focal point for expressions of sympathy — flowers, holy cards, scrawled poems — and for resistance.†

✑

The public thought of Mafia wars as an internal matter, as indeed they generally had been. The murders of Falcone and Borsellino indicated that the Mafia had declared war on authority. (That was just what the Mafia had disparaged Salvatore Giuliano for at the time of the Second World War.) The Mafia had grown inordinately rich, thanks to its drug dealings, and now investigators were poking into its bank accounts. Mafiosi were being brought into court, found guilty, and jailed for long terms, and — this was something really new — the Mafia couldn't get the verdicts overturned. Politicians who had grown rich and powerful through bribes for ignoring crimes now proved unwilling or unable to help criminals. Those who let the Mafia down had to be punished with death. So did the judges who imposed definitive sentences, and the investigators who knew most about Mafia activities.

Spurred to action, Italy's law officers had arrested hundreds of mafiosi and their business and political associates, and they were

---

* Andreotti was indicted in 1995 for (among other charges) selling political favors to the Mafia. He was found guilty, but in 1999 the verdicts were overturned.

† Fifteen years after the murders it remains so. Soldiers no longer keep vigil at the spot, but officers continue to guard dozens of judges and anti-Mafia fighters. Sometimes along the beach, for instance, one sees a judge at his early-morning jogging being followed closely by a squad car.

conducting Europe-wide searches. A sting on November 17, 1992, picked up seventy-five individuals suspected of smuggling, extortion, bribery, and electoral fraud. But the authorities were seeking especially the men behind the murders of Falcone and Borsellino. Particular suspicion fell on Salvatore ("Totò") Riina, believed to be a chief in the industry of heroin and cocaine, as well as killer of over one hundred persons. With the help of information from a *pentito*, police arrested Riina on January 15, 1993.

Riina, nicknamed "The Beast," was the capo di capi of Cosa Nostra and had been in its inner circle from the early 1970s. For all that time he had been on the police wanted list. He lived with bodyguards, much as Falcone and Borsellino had been obliged to do, though Riina's guards were mafiosi. Apart from that, Riina led an apparently ordinary life, mostly in Corleone and Palermo and at his summer home in Mazara. He received guests, sent his kids to the city school, attended church, and was treated at the city hospital. Yet the locals seldom saw him socially, he didn't bother them in any way, and if any neighbors had suspicions, they seem not to have acted on them. It goes without saying that Riina enjoyed political protection, twenty years of it.

Totò Riina and a long list of his colleagues were accused of involvement in the murders of Falcone and Borsellino and brought to trial in 1995, at Caltanissetta. Two years later, on September 26, 1997, the proceedings ended with life sentences for Riina and twenty-three of his deputies (though most of the twenty-three were already in jail). Eight years on, the convicted are still in prison, which, in Sicilian affairs, indicates a breakthrough.

LIVING WITH THE MAFIA

Mafia murders are dramatic moments in Sicily's recent history, examples of what makes the island notorious throughout the world. That view of Sicily doesn't take into account the vast majority of Sicilians, who (like Europeans generally) live far removed from criminal violence and deplore it. It's important to realize that wars between Mafia factions hardly touched ordinary Sicilians directly. The main impact of the Mafia has always been on economic life.

By now everyone who shops in Sicily realizes that built into Sicily's price structure are the Mafia's cut and the cost of importing virtually all goods. And everyone who works for a salary can see that filling jobs with political cronies rather than by merit creates inefficiency, the economic and social costs of which are pervasive. Many young job-seekers leave the island without even applying for employment at home, persons of entrepreneurial bent don't start businesses there, and the lazy use the Mafia as rationalization. Official income statistics show Sicily having a significantly higher percentage of residents living in poverty than the Italian average, though Sicily's high level of unreported income would lessen the gap.

Sicily perceives the Mafia much as the Western world perceives big business: it's a fact of life. You can, with effort, avoid direct dealings with it; you can write against it and demonstrate against it; but willy-nilly you contribute to it. In its pursuit of money it does some deplorable things — even killing — for which its leaders are occasionally jailed, but that's a risk one takes to exert economic control. As the locus of money and power, the Mafia naturally attracts some ambitious and respectable people to work with it.

Sicilians don't barricade themselves. They tend to be suspicious, but they show themselves to be talkative, friendly, and hospitable. By and large they see the Mafia (that is, the organization) as a caste of outlaws in times gone by, like in Hollywood Westerns; today's mafiosi are "our little brothers gone astray."

This attitude goes a long way toward explaining why anti-Mafia efforts have proved ineffective and why, more concretely, jailed mafiosi have served only short terms. On the other hand, as Sicilians grew more cosmopolitan with increased schooling and increased travel, they increased also their understanding of how the Mafia was hurting them. But many people still don't realize that their indulging the Mafia mentality on little things eases the way for the Mafia organization to terrorize and kill.

∾

Earlier drives against Sicily's peculiar politico-criminality had political motives (1876–77 to "Italianize" the Sicilians, 1925 to suppress a power block hostile to the Fascists); now Sicilians themselves want the Mafia tamed for economic and moral reasons. Though the anti-Mafia manifestations are too sparse to be called a movement, it's significant that they sprout in the grass roots. The need for leaders goes largely unfulfilled, since many who might fill such roles have left the island to work, like other ambitious Sicilians.

Anti-Mafia drives of previous eras succeeded in impairing the Mafia for years, but it always made a comeback. Evidently the Mafia has filled a need in Sicilian society. As recently as the Second World War the Sicilian populace was poor, ignorant, and socially passive, a pushover for Mafia control. But Sicily has experienced a marked change in condition, and one wonders to what extent Sicilians have undergone a corresponding change in character. The Christian Democratic Party no longer exists; it fell in Italy's battle for "clean hands," the country's wiping away of political corruption. The party's demise might have stimulated political rethinking in Sicily, yet in elections at the end of the century Sicilian voters favored newly named parties of the Right. Sicilians have never used periods of Mafia weakness to implant honest government or to encourage entrepreneurs to diversify the island's economy. Consequently, and unfortunately, the Mafia is still Sicily's characteristic institution.

Over the last generation the Mafia has lost much of its spirit as blood brotherhood and is fragmenting into groups of gangsters. Nonetheless, Italy continues to use mafiosi to do the state's dirty work, such as trading in weapons and controlling the flow of migrants. The Mafia, whatever its modern incarnation, won't go away any time soon.

The Mafia's hegemony is the complement to Sicily's political stagnancy. Sicily has candidates who promise to clean up the mess and who sometimes win elections. There would doubtless be more if Sicilians called for them. Sicilians know whom they are voting for; they know and bewail the Regional Assembly's thirty-year irrelevance to Sicily's problems.

Only when their good guys, their innocent guys, their courageous

guys, were being killed did Sicilians en masse cry *"Basta!"*
("Enough!") The assassinations of police-protected judges and police
officials receive the most attention, but just since the time of the maxitrial the Mafia has murdered dozens of others. In August 1991 the
Mafia killed a businessman, Libero Grassi, who had scorned attempts
at extortion. In September 1993 the Mafia killed a priest, Giuseppe
Puglisi, who had been trying to show young people of a Mafia neighborhood that life offered better paths. Once in a while the Mafia per-
forms its carnage outside Sicily: five people lost their lives in May
1993 when the Mafia bombed the celebrated Uffizi art museum in
Florence.

During February and March of 2000, Mount Etna erupted every
two or three days. Sicilians consider Mafia violence with much the
same fatalism as they consider volcanic violence. In recent years, it's
worth noting, judicious fires and bombs have successfully controlled
lava streams.

SOURCES OF HOPE FOR THE FUTURE

At the start of the new millennium, what forces in Sicily might
foment change?

LEOLUCA ORLANDO
A popular mayor thrown aside by the party leaders, Orlando established his own party called "Rete" ("Network"). In 1992 the procedure of choosing mayors changed, so that candidates for the office
submitted themselves to direct ballot, and voters sent Orlando to
City Hall again from 1995 to 2000. Having served as mayor for as
long as the law allows, he left office with his honor intact. He campaigned for president of the Sicilian region but was defeated and had
to content himself with a seat in the assembly. The pundits say he
lost because anti-Mafia sentiment was weaker in rural areas than in
Palermo.

Ever the reformer, at one point he said, "Our goal is normality.

What is normal here now is the extraordinary." It will be interesting to see how and where he surfaces again.

RITA BORSELLINO AND "LIBERA"
When the judge Paolo Borsellino fell victim to the Mafia in July 1992, his sister Rita, a pharmacist, resolved to work toward his goals. She joined with a few like-minded people to unite some small anti-Mafia associations. Under the name "Libera" they have established programs for kids who might otherwise have no hope of ever securing honest employment. In particular, Libera uses land expropriated from convicted Mafiosi to prepare youngsters for work in agriculture and wine-making.

THE CHURCH
In traditional Sicily, each village was run by a triumvirate: the mayor, the Mafia boss, and the priest. For a quarter century after World War II, Sicily's prelates were so out of touch with modern life that even devout Catholics ignored their political pronouncements. As Archbishop Ruffini of Palermo was proclaiming the nonexistence of the Mafia, few parish priests dared to speak to the suffering the Mafia caused their flock. "For many years," one priest commented later, "the church hid in the sacristy."

With Ruffini gone, in the early 1970s the church shifted its position to recognize Mafia activities and deplore them. The milestone document was issued under the auspices of the Sicilian bishops in 1973, and the following years heard similar condemnations. The Catholic Left started publishing again. When the Mafia killed General Dalla Chiesa in September 1982, speakers at his funeral included Ruffini's successor, Cardinal Pappalardo, who declared a spiritual war against the Mafia. For many priests and nuns this was a license to participate in anti-Mafia manifestations. Exhaustion from internecine wars and then the maxitrial kept Mafia operations in check during the rest of the 1980s, during which time many parish priests, freed to follow their consciences, undertook social activities such as facilitating honest occupations for youngsters of risky neighborhoods. We recall

Father Giuseppe Puglisi, who paid with his life for speaking out to youth against the Mafia.

Pope John Paul II also spoke out. Shortly after the arrest of Totò Riina, the pope visited Sicily in May 1993 and made a point of speaking in Trapani, in order to pay public honor to those who had died in the anti-Mafia struggles. The Mafia responded by exploding bombs in Rome to damage major churches. In a situation reminiscent of the Sindona scandal, there's speculation that churches have been involved in the laundering of Mafia money, and that would be one good reason to keep prelates from sermonizing against the Mafia. However strong or weak it may have been, the bond between the Mafia and the church has been loosened. Although a significant proportion of priests in Sicily still avoid doing anything that might raise the hackles of a mafioso, it's undeniable that the church has taken a strong anti-Mafia stance. This can only encourage Sicilians in their protests.

TOURISM

The tourist industry doesn't make speeches about it, but as a labor-intensive field it provides jobs for people who otherwise would have no source of honest income in Sicily. This is not to say that tourism is innocent of Mafia involvement, for many of the hotels and bigger restaurants are involved in Mafia dealings in one way or another. Still, it's a sector providing employment, especially jobs for young people and for the unskilled, and Sicily would benefit by creating more such employment.

Although the entertainment industry likes to depict Sicily as a land of nonstop Mafia shootouts, the loudest noises in Sicilian tourist spots come from discotheques. Different countries have different kinds of violence: nobody here shoots at strangers, nor has there yet been a serial killer targeting women. Sicily's malefactors have always left foreign visitors alone; statistics are tenable since 1950, and in these fifty-plus years the number of tourists in Sicily physically harmed by the Mafia is zero.

Tourists may still be apprehensive about visiting Sicily, but Sicily's tourism has greatly increased over the last quarter century. In 1999 Sicily received 3,616,000 tourists who slept in the region for twelve million nights, generally without being awakened by gunfire. It's no longer a secret that Sicily is an agreeable vacationland: during the 1990s tourism in Sicily increased by 3 percent each year, a bit more rapidly than the Italian average. As in much of the world in our time, the vast majority came on organized tours.

For the inadequacies of tourist infrastructure mentioned earlier, the independent traveller has compensations. Certainly the active traveller can find adventure — nondangerous adventure — just in getting around. As in Goethe's time, independent travellers find the locals eager for conversation and skilled at expressing themselves with hand movements: one of the satisfactions of Sicily is communicating across the language barrier. The same people who shirk in their jobs will on their own time go to great lengths to help visitors. Sicily's attractions are many and varied: several archaeological sites are just steps from good beaches. It rains only in winter; visitors from April to November are guaranteed warmth and sun. The food is fresh and tasty, the prices are reasonable. Tourists go home with good memories of a fascinating island. The potential for economic development is here.

IMMIGRATION

If mass tourism is recent, immigration and emigration have always been salient points of Sicilian history.

It's sometimes not clear in the statistics and on the streets who is an immigrant and who is a tourist, but there's no question that the immigrants come overwhelmingly from the Third World. Immigrant problems are newer in Sicily than elsewhere; the census of 1981 counted only fourteen thousand resident foreigners on the island, of whom a mere two thousand were from Africa and Asia. At the end of the year 2000, Sicily's foreign residents numbered fifty thousand, of whom thirty-four thousand were from Africa and Asia. Being just 1 percent of the total population, immigrants in Sicily are few compared with other parts of the Western world, but they are many for a region lacking jobs for its own people.

The figures relate only to those foreigners legally in Sicily. Illegal immigrants have settled into the agendas of most Western governments, and Sicily, being easily reached by fishing boat from Third World countries, doubtless has more than its proportionate share. The illegals commonly arrive at Sicily's minor islands of Lampedusa and Pantelleria, between Sicily proper and North Africa. In each recent year the coastal police have caught one to two thousand North Africans attempting illegal landings.

Given Sicily's proximity to North Africa, it's no surprise that half its immigrants are Muslims, mostly nationals of Tunisia and Morocco. Though residing all over Sicily, they concentrate in the south of Trapani province where they labor in the vineyards and occupy most positions in Mazara's fishing industry. After Tunisia, the country with the greatest number of nationals in Sicily is Sri Lanka; Sri Lankans and Filipinos of both sexes work as domestics and perform menial jobs in restaurants and hotels. Ragusa province's flourishing agriculture employs a few thousand Africans; Ghana, especially, has a large settled community here. Commonly seen in Sicily's coastal areas too, black Africans are a reminder both of Sicily's complex peopling and of Sicily's sharing in European conditions.

Arrivals from the Third World are birds of passage, hoping to move north. Most do so. Increasingly, though, the migrants who stay in Sicily awhile would like to remain there — if only they could get work — as they find Sicily pleasant. Sicily is peaceful, not only free of war but relatively free of stress. The bureaucrats aren't mean: Sicilians have a strong folk memory of emigration, and many of the bureaucrats grew up in the north or spent a few years working there. Sicilians tell me, though, that the ethnic tolerance here is high because Sicilians are naturally hospitable, and that accords with my experience. Besides, the Third World nationals are doing work that Sicilians don't want to do.

EMIGRATION

Work that Sicilians don't want to do — what a change from a hundred years ago! Sicily no longer has groups of people who suffer from hunger. Sicilians no longer earn a plate of pasta by grueling work and gruesome subservience. Emigration is no longer seen as a question of physical survival but as one of the roads that today's families might follow. Emigration still indicates, in large measure, dissatisfaction with opportunities for earning a living, but despite unemployment and underemployment, Sicily is much closer to satisfying Sicilians' needs than it was before World War II.

During the peak decade of emigration from Sicily, that is 1901 to 1910, the emigrants averaged about a hundred thousand annually. In the period 1972 to 2000, they averaged about ten thousand annually. Emigration has declined even more when it is considered as a proportion of Sicily's population, because of Sicily's population increase.*

Sicily's emigration is still high, reflecting the shortfall of jobs in Sicily relative to the other regions of Italy. Of all emigrants from Italy, in 1901–1910 Sicilians accounted for some 15 percent; in 1986–1997 Sicilians accounted for 27 percent. Up north people can change jobs in the same city; as this is much harder to do in Sicily, Sicilians change countries instead.

Partly, but only partly, because English-speaking countries have discouraged immigration, Sicilians go overwhelmingly to countries on the European continent, especially Germany, France, and Belgium. This has transformed the migration experience, for those living abroad can return to Sicily often.

And they do return. Sicilians *like* Sicily. Up north is associated with work, and few Sicilians consider work anything other than a necessity to get money. To Sicilians what's important are family and friends, and in Sicily one has more time to spend with them. Most urbanities or their close relatives have a country home, so that they still have ties to a traditional culture. Sicilian tolerance (or inertia) means that nobody hassles you. Sicilians possess all the modern conveniences — Internet, microwaves, pacemakers — but they don't obsess about them.

---

* Sicily's population 1901 was 3,529,800; in 2000 it was 5,076,700.

∽

As I was finishing my research for this book, I asked around — in Italian, naturally — "What do you think is the most important change in Sicily since the Second World War?" Almost everyone responded: the proceedings against the Mafia. Thinking that might reflect the recentness of the trials, I would move the discussion to the Mafia's role in the prosperity to which Sicilians became accustomed during these years, only to hear that just as the high standard of living is taken for granted, so is the Mafia's bolstering of it. And when conversation turned, as it often does, to the way their grandparents had lived, to emigration, to America, I was surprised by how many people declared, sometimes shifting into English, "Now America is *here*."

STATISTICAL TABLES

TABLE A
SICILIAN EMIGRANTS FROM ITALY, 1876–1925

	Emigrants to other countries from Sicily	Emigrants from Sicily as percentage of emigrants from Italy
1876	1,228	1.1
1877	767	0.8
1878	1,065	1.1
1879	888	0.7
1880	884	0.7
1881	1,143	0.8
1882	3,215	2.0
1883	4,040	2.4
1884	2,420	1.6
1885	2,186	1.4
1886	4,270	2.5
1887	4,653	2.2
1888	7,015	2.4
1889	11,308	5.2
1890	10,705	5.0
1891	10,130	3.4
1892	11,912	5.3
1893	14,626	5.9
1894	9,125	4.0
1895	11,307	3.9
1896	15,432	5.0
1897	19,109	6.4
1898	25,579	9.0

1899	24,604	8.0
1900	28,838	8.2
1901	36,718	6.9
1902	54,466	10.3
1903	58,820	11.6
1904	50,662	10.8
1905	106,208	14.6
1906	127,603	16.2
1907	97,620	13.9
1908	50,453	10.4
1909	94,833	15.2
1910	96,713	14.8
1911	50,789	9.5
1912	92,788	13.0
1913	146,061	16.7
1914	46,610	9.7
1915	16,169	11.1
1916	20,073	14.1
1917	6,004	12.9
1918	2,087	7.4
1919	36,476	14.4
1920	108,718	17.7
1921	23,082	11.5
192	22,367	8.0
1923	36,070	9.2
1924	28,956	7.9
1925	23,760	8.5

Source: The figures are from the *Annuario statistico dell'emigrazione italiana dal 1876 al 1925* (Rome, 1925). Quoted in Renda, *L'Emigrazione in Sicilia, 1652-1961.* (Caltanissetta and Rome: S. Sciascia, 1989), pp. 74–75. I calculated the percentages.

TABLE B
SICILIAN EMIGRANTS FROM ITALY, 1963–74

1963	4,744
1964	6,809
1965	8,221
1966	25,234
1967	33,028
1968	40,744
1969	26,532
1970	22,104
1971	36,943
1972	6,642
1973	8,175
1974	8,447

Source: ISTAT (Italy's Institute of Statistics): *Movimento anagrafico del comune*

TABLE C
EMPLOYMENT BY SECTOR (NUMBER/PERCENT)

	1971	1981	1991	2001
Agriculture	377,644/28.5	267,350/19.9	209,000/14.1	128,000/9.1
Industry	446,279/33.7	384,443/28.7	309,000/20.9	287,000/20.5
Other activities	500,176/37.7	689,336/51.4	960,000/65.0	988,000/69.4
TOTAL	1,324,099	1,341,129	1,478,000	1,403,000

Sources: Data for 1971 and 1981 in Giuseppe Giarrizzo, "Sicilia oggi (1950-86)," p. 673, in Maurice Aymard and Giuseppe Giarrizzo, *Storia d'Italia: Le regioni dall'Unità a oggi: La Sicilia*. Data for 1991: directly from ISTAT. Data for 2001: ISTAT, "Occupati per settore di attività." I calculated the percentages.

GLOSSARY AND NOTES
ON ITALIAN WORD ENDINGS

In the Italian language, nouns take on the plural form by changing a final letter, always a vowel to –i (for nouns whose singular forms end in –o or -e) or –e (for nouns whose singular forms end in -a).

In English the residents of a city are indicated by suffixes, as in Boston*ian* and London*ers*. The equivalent endings in Italian are *-ano*, *-ana*, and *-ese* (singular) and *-ani* and *-esi* (plural).

All words below are Italian unless otherwise indicated.

ager publicus (Latin) — land obtained for or set aside for the public purpose.

agricoltore — small farmer who owns some land and uses some modern methods; a level above a peasant.

barone — traditionally, member of the aristocracy, the English baron; now, a powerful person in any field, especially administrative, able and willing to dispense patronage.

capo — chief, boss.

Carabinieri — one of Italy's several police forces, with particularly wide-ranging powers and with a reputation for smartness and efficiency. A *carabiniere* is a member of the force.

caruso — in Sicily's sulfur mines, a boy at the bottom of the pecking order who carries the excavated mineral to the surface.

contadino — rural resident, peasant.

Democristiano — member of Italy's right-wing Christian Democratic Party (DC), operational from the end of the Second World War to the 1990s.

dhimmi (Arabic) — Muslim designation for Christians and Jews.

feudo — a landed estate held and controlled (but not owned) by a man of lesser rank on grant from a lord, in return for service, especially military; fief.

gabelloto — estate manager; Sicily's *gabelloti* gained economic and political importance in the seventeenth century and maintained it for more than two centuries.

latifundisti — owners of latifundia.

latifundium, -ia (Latin) — vast tract of land, worked by slaves and in Sicily producing wheat.

macinato — tax on the milling of grain, first imposed by the Spanish and continuing off and on for centuries.

mattanza (Arabic) — procedure for catching tuna, introduced by the Muslims and still in use.

metropolis (Greek) — at the time of the Greek colonization of Sicily, used in the sense of "mother country."

Mezzogiorno — Italy's southern "half," roughly, including Sicily. Naples, at its northern end, is considered its capital. The Mezzogiorno is poorer than Italy's north.

municipio — city hall, town hall.

oecist (Greek) — leader of group colonizing a site in a new land.

omertà — obligation of silence in regard to Mafia association and activities.

padrone — master, owner, employer.

passeggiata — late-afternoon promenade traditional in Sicilian towns, in which many residents take part.

piazza — square, as an element of urban layout.

pizzo — a regular payment demanded by the Mafia, generally of businessmen.

praetor (Latin) — ancient Roman magistrate ranking below a consul and having chiefly judicial functions.

prefetto — civil governor (for Sicily, appointed in Rome).

quaestor (Latin) — ancient Roman official concerned chiefly with financial administration.

squadristi — members of a squadrone, which, under Fascist government, is a corps of thugs authorized to impose order.

GLOSSARY OF NAMES

This list does not include Greek gods, nor popes or foreign kings whose individuality had no importance in Sicilian history. A "?" indicates that date is approximate.

Adelaide: third wife of Count Roger, mother of King Roger

Aeschylus (525–456 B.C.): Greek poet, migrated to Sicily

Agathocles (361–289 B.C.): ruler of Siracusa 317–289 B.C.

Alagona: family of barons important in Sicily from 1300s

Alcibiades (450–404 B.C.): Greek politician who deprecated Sicilians and incited Athens to invade Sicily in 415

Alfonso X (1221–84): king of Castile; ca. 1252 considered by pope for kingship of Sicily

Alfonso ("the Magnanimous"; 1396–1458): king of Aragon and Sicily 1416–58

Amalasuntha: heiress to the kingdom of the Ostrogoths, murdered in 535 with political repercussions

Amari, Michele (1806–89): historian, politically active during Risorgimento

Anacletus II: anti-pope who invested Roger II as Sicily's king

Anassila: tyrant of Reggio ca. 390 B.C.

Andromacos: founder of Taormenion, 358 B.C.

Aprile: see Finocchiaro Aprile

Archestratus (ca. 300 B.C.): Gelan who wrote cookery book

Archimedes (287?–212 B.C.): Greek man of science who spent his life in Siracusa

Aristotle (384–322 B.C.): Greek man of science who spent his life in Siracusa

Augustus: see Octavian

Baldwin (d. 1118): king of Jerusalem, stepfather of Sicily's King Roger

Barbarossa: see Frederick I

Becket, Thomas: see Thomas à Becket

Belisarius (494–565): Byzantine general under Justinian

Bellini, Vincenzo (1801–35): Catania-born composer of opera

Bixio, Gerolamo ("Nino"; 1821–73): Italian sailor and general, lieutenant of Garibaldi in Sicily in 1860

Bonaparte: see Napoleon

Borsellino, Paolo: Sicilian judge and anti-Mafia investigator murdered by Mafia in July 1992

Brydone, Patrick (1736–1818): Briton who wrote a travel journal about his visit to Sicily in 1770

Bufalino, Gesualdo (1920–96): writer about Sicily

Buscetta, Tommaso (1928–2000): mafioso who in mid-1980s spoke out against Mafia organization and practices

Caecilius (first century B.C.): Sicily-raised Jew, literary critic in Rome

Caesar, Julius (102?–44 B.C.): Roman general, dictator of Rome from 47 B.C.

Cannizzaro, Stanislao (1826–1910): Palermo-born chemist of renown

Caracciolo, Dominico (1715–89): viceroy in Sicily 1781–86?

Carlo II (1500–58): king of Sicily 1516–56; Holy Roman Emperor as Charles V

Carlo V (Charles, Carlos; 1716–88): king of Sicily 1735–59

Carondas (end of seventh century B.C.): law-giver in Catania

Cavour, Camillo Benso, Count of (1810–61): Italian politician, leader of Risorgimento

Cervantes, Miguel (1547–1616): Spanish writer who visited Sicily in 1570

Charles of Anjou (1226–85): king of Sicily 1266–82; maintained title until his death although Sicilians had given it to Peter of Aragon

Charles of Salerno ("the Lame"; 1248–1309): son of Charles of Anjou; pope-supported king of Sicily 1285–1309, rivaling Peter of Aragon and his heirs

Charles V, Holy Roman Emperor (b. 1500): see Carlo II

Chiaramonte: family of barons important in Sicily from 1300s

Chinnici, Rocco (1925–83): Sicilian judge murdered by Mafia in 1983

Cicero, Marcus Tullius (106–43 B.C.): Roman lawyer and politician, midlevel official in Sicily ca. 76 B.C.

Clement IV (end twelfth century): French pope, enemy of Hohenstaufens

Cleon: important figure in major slave revolt in Sicily 135–132 B.C.

Coleridge, Samuel Taylor (1772–1834): English writer who visited Sicily in 1805

Columbus, Christopher (1451–1506): Italian navigator who discovered New World for Spain

Conrad (1228–54): king of Sicily 1250–54

Conradin (1252–68): titular king of Sicily 1254–68

Consolo, Vincenzo (b. 1933): Sicilian writer of fiction focused on Sicily

Constance de Hauteville (1154–98): posthumous daughter of King Roger; queen of Sicily 1194–98; mother of future Holy Roman Emperor Frederick II

Constance II (1247–1392): daughter of Sicily's king Manfred; wife of Peter of Aragon; queen of Sicily 1282–1302

Constans II (630–668): Byzantine emperor 641–668

Constantine IV (654–685): Byzantine emperor 668–685

Crispi, Francesco (1818–1901): b. Ribera (Sicily); Italian politician at peak 1859–96

Daedalus: hero of Greek mythology, father of art and technique

Dalla Chiesa, Carlo Alberto (1920–82): Italian general and antiterrorist fighter murdered by Mafia in 1982

Damocles (early fourth century b.c.): courtier of Dionysius the Elder

De Felice Giuffrida, Giuseppe (1859–1920): politician in Catania who led Fasci political group early 1890s

Diodorus (b. 90? B.C. in eastern Sicily): traveler and historian

Dion (409–354 B.C.): Siracusa-born politician of royal blood

Dionysius the Elder (430?–367 B.C.): b. Siracusa, tyrant of Siracusa 405–367 B.C.

Dionysius the Younger (397?–344 B.C.): b. Siracusa, tyrant of Siracusa but abandoned power to his uncle Dion

Dolci, Danilo (1924–97): social activist and writer

Domitian (51–96): Roman emperor A.D. 81–96

Ducetius (mid-fifth century B.C.): Sicel leader of rebellion ca. 450 B.C.

Dumas, Alexandre (1802–70): French writer who joined Garibaldi in Sicily

Edmund (b. 1245): the English king Henry III's younger son, named by pope as king of Sicily

Edrisi: see Idrisi

Eisenhower, Dwight (1890–1969): American general in Second World War and then president, who visited Sicily in 1950

Empedocles (fifth century B.C.): b. Agrigento; Greek philosopher

Epicarmus (525?–440? B.C.): b. Megara Hyblea, Greek dramatist

Eufemius: Byzantine general instrumental in Muslims' invasion of Sicily 827

Eunus: Syrian-born leader of major slave revolt in Sicily 135–132 B.C.

Falcone, Giovanni (1939–92): Sicilian judge and anti-Mafia investigator murdered by Mafia in May 1992

Ferdinand I (1380–1416): king of Aragon; king of Sicily 1412–1416

Ferdinand II of Aragon ("the Catholic"; 1452–1516): king of Sicily 1479–1516

Ferdinand III (1751–1825): king of the Two Sicilies 1759–1825: ruling from Naples, fled twice to Sicily for short periods

Ferdinand IV (1810–59): king of the Two Sicilies 1830–1859

Finocchiaro Aprile, Andrea (1878–1964): leader of Sicily's separatists at end of Second World War

Florio, Ignazio (1838–96): director of Florio enterprises after the death of his father, Vincenzo

Florio, Vincenzo (1799–1868): Sicilian entrepreneur in various fields, extremely successful

Francesco I (1777–1830): king of the Two Sicilies 1825–1830

Francesco II (1836–94): last king of the Two Sicilies (1859–1860)

Franchetti, Leopoldo (1847–1917) — northern politician, co-author of major study on Sicily, 1876

Franco, Francisco (1892–1975): Spanish general who won Spanish Civil War (1936–39), then ruler of Spain until his death

Frederick I (Barbarossa) (1122–90): Holy Roman Emperor; king of Germany, important in foreign policy of Sicily's King William II

Frederick I as king of Sicily, **Frederick II** as Holy Roman Emperor (1194–1250) an outstanding figure in European politics

Frederick II (1272–1337): king of "Trinacria" (i.e., Sicily) 1296–1337

Frederick III ("the Simple"; 1342–77): king of Sicily 1355–77

Gaiseric (d. 477): king of the Vandals, ruled Sicily from 468

Garibaldi, Giuseppe (1807–82): Italian general and leader of Risorgimento; conquered Sicily 1860

Gelon (540–478 B.C.): tyrant of Gela and then of Siracusa

Gentile, Giovanni (1875–1944): philosopher and Fascist politician

Giacomo of Aragon: see James II

Giolitti, Giovanni (1842–1928): Italian politician at peak 1890s–1921

Giuffrida: see De Felice

Giuliano, Salvatore (1922–50): Sicilian bandit involved in politics

Goethe, Johann Wolfgang von (1749–1832): German man of letters who wrote travel journal about his visit to Sicily in 1787

Gorgias (487?–380? B.C.): b. Leontinoi, Greek philosopher

Greeley, Horace (1811–72): American newspaper editor

Hamilcar (d. 480 B.C.): Carthaginian general beaten by the Greeks at Battle of Himera

Hamilcar Barca (Thunderbolt) (290?–229 B.C.): Carthaginian leader in first Punic War, in western Sicily fought against Romans; father of Hannibal

Hannibal (d. 406 B.C.): Carthaginian general who took Selinunte and razed Himera 409 B.C.

Hannibal (247–183 B.C.) — son of Hamilcar Barca; Carthaginian general, famous for crossing the Alps. Active in Carthage during Second Punic War, never involved in Sicily.

Harald Hardrada (1015?–1066): king of Norway, participated in invasion of Sicily 1038

Henry III of England (1207–72): sought crown of Sicily for his son Edmund

Henry VI of Germany ("the Cruel"; 1165–97): son of Frederick I (Barbarossa); husband of Constance de Hauteville and on that account ruler of Sicily from 1194

Herodotus (484?–420? B.C.): Greek historian

Hesiod (ca. 800 B.C.): Greek poet

Hiero (or Hieron) I: tyrant of Siracusa 478–466 B.C.

Hiero (or Hieron) II (306?–215 B.C.): king of Siracusa

Hippocrates (d. 491 B.C.): tyrant of Gela 498–491 B.C.

Hitler, Adolf (1899–1945) — dictator of Germany from 1933, ally of Mussolini during Second World War

Homer (eighth century B.C.): born in Asia Minor, first of the world's major poets

Ibn Hamdis, Abu Mohammed (1055–1133): poet who fled Sicily at Norman conquest

Ibn Hawkal, Abu 'l-Qasim Muhammad: merchant from Baghdad who visited Palermo ca. 970; wrote travel journal

Ibn Jubair: Muslim traveler in Sicily late 1180s

Idrisi, Ash-Sharif al (1099–1165): geographer at court of King Roger

Ingham, Benjamin: English businessman who from 1806 was in wine business in Marsala, then expanded commercial interests widely

Isabella of Castille ("the Catholic"; 1451–1504): queen of Sicily 1479–1504

Isabella of England: married Holy Roman Emperor Frederick in 1235 (she was his third wife), therefore queen of Sicily

Isabelle (Yolande) of Brienne (d. 1228): queen of the Latin Kingdom of Jerusalem; married Holy Roman Emperor Frederick in 1225 (she was his second wife), therefore queen of Sicily

James II (1264?–1327): king of Aragon; king of Sicily 1285–96

Joan (b. 1166?): daughter of King Henry II of England; wife of Sicily's King William II

John (1397–1479): king of Navarre and Aragon; king of Sicily 1458–79

Justinian (482–565) — Byzantine emperor; ruler of Sicily from 535

La Torre, Pio: Sicilian politician murdered by Mafia in 1982

Lampedusa: see Tomasi

Leopoldo: brother of Sicily's king Ferdinand IV; governor of Sicily

Levi, Carlo (1902–75): Italian anti-Fascist and writer about the Mezzogiorno, including Sicily

Louis IX (later Saint Louis; 1214–70): king of France and brother of Charles of Anjou

Luciano, "Lucky" Salvatore Lucania (1897–1962): American Mafia leader, born in Sicily and raised in New York City

Manfred (1232–66): king of Sicily 1258–66

Manices (or Maniace), George: Byzantine general who invaded Sicily ca. 1040

Maqueda, Bernardino Cardenas, duke of (d. 1601): Spain's viceroy in Sicily 1598–1601

Margaret of Navarre: queen of Sicily 1154–66, King William I's wife and collaborator; regent 1166–71 for King William II

Maria of Aragon (1367–1402): daughter of king Frederick III, queen of Sicily 1377–1402

Marie Caroline (1752–1814): wife of King Ferdinand III

Martin the Elder (1356–1410): co-king of Sicily 1392–95; king of Sicily 1409–10 as Martin II

Martin the Younger (1374–1409): co-king of Sicily 1392–98; king of Sicily 1398–1409 as Martin I

Mattarella, Piersanti (1935–80): Sicilian politician murdered by Mafia

de Maupassant, Guy (1850–93): French writer, especially of fiction, who visited Sicily in 1885

Mazzini, Giuseppe (1805–72): Italian leader of Risorgimento; in 1866 Messina elected him to Parliament

Milazzo, Silvio (1903–82): Sicilian politician who supported the peasants and founded short-lived political party

Mithaecus (fifth century B.C.): Siracusan who wrote cookery book

Mori, Cesare (1872–1929): Fascist civil governor of Sicily who acted strongly against Mafia in mid-1920s

Mussolini, Benito (1883–1945): Italian Fascist leader and dictator

Mustansir: king of Tunisia ca. 1270

Napoleon Bonaparte (1769–1821): French revolutionary who invaded Italy 1796

Nelson, Horatio (1758–1805): English admiral and supporter of Bourbons who spent time in Sicily from 1799

Notarbartolo, Emanuele (1834–93): president of the Bank of Sicily; murdered in 1893, probably by a lieutenant of Prime Minister Crispi

Octavian (63 B.C.–A.D. 14): often called simply by his title "Augustus"; first Roman emperor, from 29 B.C.

Odoacer (435?–493): king of the Heruli, a Germanic tribe; ruled on Italian peninsula; ruled most of Sicily from 476

Orlando, Leoluca (b. 1947 in Palermo): politician, mayor of Palermo, two terms between 1985 and 2001

Orlando, Vittorio Emanuele (1860–1952): Italian statesman from Palermo

Palizzolo, Rafaele: Sicilian politician and supporter of prime minister Crispi, accused of murdering Notarbartolo in 1893

Panatius (fifth century B.C.): leader of aristocrats in Leontinoi

Pappalardo, Salvatore (Cardinal): from Catania, archbishop of Palermo from March 1973 to June 1996

Peralta: family of barons important in Sicily from 1300s

Peter I (1239–1285): king of Aragon, then, when Sicilians installed him, also king of Sicily 1282–85

Peter II (1305–42): king of Sicily from 1337

Petrosino, Joe (1860–1909): New York City detective, anti-Mafia investigator, murdered in Palermo 1909

Phalaris: tyrant of Agrigento 570–554 B.C.

Philip Augustus (1165–1223): king of France; sojourned in Sicily 1190–91

Philip II (1527–98): king of Sicily 1556–98

Philip IV, duke of Anjou (1683–1746): king of Sicily 1700–13

Phintias of Akragas: tyrant of Akragas, founded Licata in 280 B.C.

Pindar (518?–438? B.C.): Greek poet at court of Hiero I

Pirandello, Luigi (1867–1936): born near Agrigento; man of letters, won Nobel Prize in 1934

Pisciotta, Gaspare: killer of Salvatore Giuliano, at behest of Mafia

Plato (427–348 B.C.): Greek philosopher; visited Sicily ca. 387 and again 367

Polybius (203?–120 B.C.): Greek historian living in Rome

Pompey, Gnaeus ("the Great"; 106–48 B.C.): Roman general and consul, defeated Julius Caesar in battle at Messina ca. 49 B.C.

Pompey, Sextus (75–35 B.C.): son of Gnaeus Pompey; republican opponent of Octavian in battles off northeast Sicily ca. 37–35 B.C.

Pucci, Elda: physician and politician who served as Palermo's mayor 1983

Ptolemy (third century B.C.): the king Ptolemy, contemporary of Hiero II (not the great Ptolemy of science, second century A.D., who wrote the Almagest)

Pyrrhus (318?–272 B.C.): king of Epirus (Greece) who vainly beseiged Marsala in 277 B.C.; named as king of Sicily

Quasimodo, Salvatore (1901–68): b. Modica; poet, won Nobel Prize in 1959

Reina, Michele: Sicilian politician murdered by Mafia in 1979

Richard, earl of Cornwall: brother of England's King Henry III, offered kingship of Sicily ca. 1252

Riina, Salvatore ("Totò"): head of Sicilian Mafia arrested in January 1993 and jailed

Rizzotto, Giuseppe (1828–95): actor, author of play of which performances, from 1863, popularized the word "mafiosi"

Robert Guiscard (1015?–85): first Norman count of Sicily, from 1057; older brother of Count Roger

Roger de Hauteville (Count; 1031–1101) count and ruler of Sicily from 1062

Roger (1095–1154): ruled Sicily as count from 1101, invested as king 1130 and 1139; son of Count Roger, therefore this younger king is sometimes referred to as Roger II, though there was never a King Roger I

Ruffini, Ernesto (Cardinal): from Italian north, archbishop of Palermo from early 1946 to June 1967

Salvio: leader of major slave revolt in Sicily ca. 103–99 B.C.

Scarlatti, Alessandro (1660–1725): Palermo-born composer

Sciascia, Leonardo (1921–89): wrote novels about Sicily

Scipio, Publius Cornelius (234?–183 B.C.): Roman general in the Punic Wars, who trained a volunteer army in Sicily

Shakespeare, William (1564–1616): English dramatist who set two plays in Sicily

Simonides (556?–467 B.C.): Greek poet, immigrant to Sicily

Sindona, Michele (b. 1920): Sicilian mafioso, active also in New York, major participant in a financial scandal in mid-1970s

Sonnino, Sidney (1847–1922): northern politician, co-author of major study on Sicily 1876, life-long supporter of Sicilian peasants

Spartacus (d. 71 B.C.): leader of major slave revolt on Italian peninsula 70s B.C.

Stenius: man of wealth in Termini Imerese in 70s B.C.

Stesichorus (640?–550? B.C.): Greek poet who spent his life in Sicily

Strabo (63 B.C.– after A.D. 21): Greek geographer and historian

Strauss, Richard (1864–1949): German composer who visited Sicily

Sturzo, Luigi (1871–1959): priest and politician in period between First and Second World Wars; developed Sicily's Catholic Left

Tancred (d. 1194): king of Sicily, 1189–94

Terillus: tyrant of Himera deposed by Theron; this was proximate cause of the consequential Battle of Himera (480 B.C.)

Theodoric (454?–526): king of Ostrogoths, conqueror of Italy, ruler of Sicily

Theron: tyrant of Agrigento 488–473 B.C.

Thomas à Becket (1118–70): English archbishop, murdered December 29, 1170

Thucycides (460?–400? B.C.): Greek historian

Timeaus (b. 356 B.C.): Greek historian

Timoleon (410?–336? B.C.): tyrant of Siracusa 344–337 B.C.

Tomasi di Lampedusa, Giuseppe (1896–1957): author of major novel about Garibaldi's war in Sicily

Trasibulo: tyrant of Siracusa 467–466 B.C.; brother and heir of Heron I

Trasidio: tyrant of Agrigento 473–472 B.C.; son of Theron

Urban IV (1200–64): pope, worked to enthrone Charles of Anjou in Sicily

Ventimiglia: family of barons important in Sicily from 1300s

Verdi, Giuseppe (1813–1901): Italian composer

Verga, Giovanni (1840–1922): master novelist who wrote particularly about Sicilians

Verres, Caius: Roman administrator, governor of Sicily 74–71 B.C.

Victor Amadeus, Duke of Savoy (1666–1732): king of Sicily 1713–20

Victor Emmanuel II (1820–78): king of Sardinia, then from 1860 king of the Italy that he helped to create

Victor Emmanuel III (1869–1947): last Savoy king of Sicily

Viola, Franca: young woman of Alcamo who rejected traditional forced marriage in 1966

Vishinsky, Andrei (1883–1954): Soviet foreign minister who visited Sicily 1943 to oppose separatism

Vittorini, Elio (1908–66): b. Siracusa, major writer about Sicilians

Vittorio Emanuele: see Victor Emmanuel

Wagner, Richard (1813–83): German composer who visited Sicily

Walter of the Mill: bishop from England who became power-broker in Sicily under the two kings William

Wilde, Oscar (1854–1900): English man of letters who visited Sicily

William I ("the Bad") (1120-66): king of Sicily from 1154

William II ("the Good") (1154–89): king of Sicily from 1172

William of Holland: installed by pope ca. 1247 as king of Sicily in opposition to H.R.E. Frederick

Winckelmann, Johann Joachim (1717–68): early archaeologist who attracted attention to Greek ruins in southern Italy

Woodhouse, John: English businessman, the first to commercialize wine from Marsala, starting 1770s

Xenophon (430?–355? B.C.): Greek historian

Ximenes, Ettore (1855–1926): Palermo-born sculptor

NOTES

For classical works cited, I have generally not given a publisher, as each has been published in numerous editions with the same numeration of sections and paragraphs. All translations are by me unless otherwise stated.

CHAPTER 1: LIPARI
> page 1 "On the western side" — Homer, *The Odyssey*, XII, 100–25.
> page 3 the story of the Ithacan king Odysseus — Homer, *The Odyssey*, X, 14.

CHAPTER 2: THE GREEK PERIOD
> page 29 "Tuna in abundance" — Strabo, *Geography*, I.2.15–16, describes the habits of swordfish and tuna, and the hunting of them. He cites Polybius. (To allay any confusion, tuna get eaten by swordfish even though tuna tend to be the larger.)
> page 30 "Charybdis spews forth water 'thrice' . . . 'twice.'" — Strabo, *Geography*, I.2.16.
> page 54 "money among Selinuntans" — Thucydides, *History of the Peloponnesian War*, VI, 20.
> page 60 "Where happiness derives" — Plato, *Epistles*, letter # VII.
> page 62 "live every day" — Plato, *Epistles*, letter # VII.
> page 63 "Sicily, Greek Sicily" — Plato, *Epistles*, letter # VIII.
> page 67 Archestratus, *Hedypatheia: Greek Culture and Cuisine in the Fourth Century B.C.E: Text, Translation, and Commentary*. Edited by S. Douglas Olson and Alexander Sens. (New York: Oxford University Press, 2000).

CHAPTER 3: ROMANS
> page 80 "they treated well . . . Elymi too were of Trojan descent." — Cicero, *The Verrine Orations*, Second Speech, Book IV, 32 § 71; Second Speech, Book V, 31 § 83. *The Verrine Orations* can be found, for example, in two volumes of the Loeb Classical Library (Harvard University Press, 1928; reprinted several times).

page 81 "explained . . . descent from the ancient Trojans." — Cicero, Verrine, Second Speech, Book V, 32 § 33.

page 83 "around June of each year" — Cicero, *Letters to Atticus*, V.13; V.14; VI.1.16. The letters are of early summer, 51 B.C.

page 87 "many of the large landowners in Sicily came from Rome" — Diodorus Siculus, *Biblioteca historica*, xxxiv–xxxv, 2, § 34.

page 92 "a personal pilgrimage . . . brambles." — Cicero, *Tusculan Disputations*, 5.64–66.

page 93 "no well-crafted gods at all . . . 'taken away.'" — Cicero, *The Verrine Orations*, Second speech, Book IV, 21 § 46–47.

page 95 "defending the entire province of Sicily." — Cicero, *Verrine*, Against Q. Caecilius, 2 § 5.

page 95 "the first place . . . harbor for our ships." — Cicero, *Verrine*, Second speech, Book II, 1 § 3.

page 95 "some women . . . lust" — Ibid., Book V, 10 § 28.

page 95 "Countless sums . . . banished" — Cicero, *Verrine*, First speech, Book V, § 13.

page 96 "Strongly fortified harbors . . . which they conquered" — Cicero, *Verrine*, First speech, Book V, §§ 13–14.

CHAPTER 5: MUSLIMS

page 141 "schoolteachers" — Ibn Hawkal, Abu al-Kasim, *Description de Palerme au milieu du Xe siècle de l'ère vulgaire*, translated from the Arab by Michel Amari. (Paris: Imprimerie royale, 1845), p. 30.

page 149 This is the gist of Ibn Hamdis' poem found, in Italian, in Melo Freni, *Il Giardino di Hamdis* (Palermo: Sellerio, 1992), p. 13.

CHAPTER 6: NORMANS

page 164 "so splendid . . . originality." — *L'Italia descritta nel "Libro del re Ruggero,"* compiled by Edrisi (Rome: Coi tipi del Saliucci, 1883), § 20 (p. 23).

page 166 "A baptized sultan" — Michele Amari, *Storia dei Musulmani di Sicilia. Seconda edizione modificata e accresciuta dall'autore . . .* (Catania: R. Prampolini, 1933–39), vol. III, p.372.

page 169 The Idrisi quotations are from *L'Italia descritta, op cit.,* §§ 21–22 (pp. 24–25).

CHAPTER 9: BOURBONS

page 277 "criminal they may be" — P(atrick) Brydone, *A Tour through Sicily and Malta, in a Series of Letters to William Bickford* (London, 1773) letter dated 21 May 1770.

page 278 He arrived at the port of Palermo — Johann Wolfgang von Goethe, *Italienische Reise* (Travels in Italy). 1816–29 (in parts), journal date 3 April 1787.

page 278 the anecdote starting "How can your city" — Goethe, op.cit., journal date 5 April.

page 279 "mass of uninterrupted fertility" — Goethe, op.cit., journal date 27 April.

page 279 "wishing for a winged horse" — Goethe, op.cit., journal date 28 April.

page 280 "serious people . . . eating thistles" — Goethe, op.cit., journal date 30 April.

page 280 "without equal for whiteness and softness" — Goethe, op.cit., journal date 24 April.

page 281 the women of Caltanissetta — Goethe, op.cit., journal date 28 April.

page 291 "There is no trade" — quoted in Raleigh Trevelyan, *La Storia dei Whitaker* (Palermo: Sellerio, 1988), p. 132.

page 309 The excerpts from Garibaldi's letter can be found in G. Sacerdote, *La Vita di Giuseppe Garibaldi* (Milano: Rizzoli, 1933), pp. 519–20.

CHAPTER 10: THE SAVOY KINGDOM OF SICILY

page 316 "island at the very edge . . . universal Sicilian desire." — Quoted in Francesco Renda, *Storia della Sicilia dal 1860 al 1970,* vol. I (Palermo: Sellerio, 1984), p. 167. The idea was widely propagated in these months; the specific quotation is from a report of 19 October 1860, of which one of the authors was Stanislao Cannizzaro.

page 317 "the idea . . . nor respect them." — Quoted in Francesco
Renda, *Storia della Sicilia dal 1860 al 1970*, vol. I (Palermo:
Sellerio, 1984), p.170. Cavour said this on 7 July 1860.

page 320 "They treat men like oranges" — Quoted in Max Gallo,
Garibaldi: la force d'un destin. (Paris: Fayard, 1982), pp.
280–81.

page 323 "all males in the countryside" — Quoted in Rosario Romeo,
ed., *Storia della Sicilia* (Naples: Società editrice Storia di
Napoli e della Sicilia, 1970), IX, 380.

page 326 "The outrages" — Giuseppe Garibaldi, *Lettere ad Anita e ad
Altre Donne*, compiled by G. E. Curatulo (Rome: A. F.
Formiggini, 1926), p. 115.

page 328 "the cultured part of the population" — Leopoldo Franchetti
and Sidney Sonnino, *Inchiesta in Sicilia* (Florence: Vallecchi,
1974), Vol. I, p. 3–4.

page 330 "what's cultivable inland" — Ibid., Vol. II, p. 17.

page 330 "three-fourths of Sicily's land area." — Ibid., Vol. II, p. 113.

page 330 "Grain meant large landholdings" — Ibid., Vol. II, p. 17.

page 331 ". . . left alone . . . overpopulated region." — Ibid., Vol. II, pp.
252ff.

page 339 Guy de Maupassant, *La Vie errante* (1890).

page 366 "Fascism must be served." — Quoted in Francesco Renda,
Storia della Sicilia dal 1860 al 1970, vol. II. (Palermo: Sellerio,
1984), p.371.

page 366 "if by Mafia you mean" — Quoted in Giuseppe Carlo Marino,
Storia della Mafia; dall'onorata società a Cosa nostra (Rome:
Newton & Compton, 1998), p. 128.

page 373 "southern Italy" — Quoted in Christopher Duggan, *La Mafia
durante il Fascism* (Soveria Manelli [Italy]: Rubbettino, 1986),
p. 1. Translated from the English in *Fascism and the Mafia*
(New Haven: Yale University Press, 1989).

CHAPTER 11: AUTONOMOUS REGION

page 390 Americans . . . stationed warships — according to the then
head of the CIA, William Colby, reported in Giuseppe Carlo

Marino, *Storia della Mafia; dall'onorata società a Cosa nostra* (Rome: Newton & Compton, 1998), p. 180.

page 396 "We walked around the fields" and the immediately following quotations ending "at the time of the Muslims" — Carlo Levi, *Le Parole sono pietre: tre giornate in Sicilia* (Turin: Einaudi, 1956), pp. 113–114.

page 398 the incident in the Lercara mine — Ibid., pp. 66ff.

page 407 "every likelihood of offending again" in "Cronologia essenziale," edited by Franco Alasia e José Martinetti, in Dolci, *Comunicare, Legge della Vita* (Manduria: P. Lacaita, 1993).

page 408 "1960 book *Spreco* . . ." Dolci, *Spreco; documenti e inchieste su alcuni aspetti dello spreco nella Sicilia occidentale.* (Turin: Einaudi, 1960). The examples and the citation in this paragraph are from *Spreco*, p. 23. Translated into English by R. Monroe as *Waste: An Eye-witness Report on Some Aspects of Waste in Western Sicily* (New York: Monthly Review Press, 1964).

page 413 "may be the only Italian city" — Rocco Chinnici, *L'Illegalità protetta* (Palermo: La Zisa, 1990), pp. 27–28.

page 414 "hundreds of millions of dollars" — Ibid., p. 50.

page 414 "huge amounts of money" — Ibid., p. 27.

page 424 "precisely because [the Mafia businesses]" — Ibid., p. 32.

page 429 "The invaders arrived" — Giovanni Falcone, *Cose di Cosa Nostra*, (Milan: Rizzoli, 1991), p. 81. Translated into English by Edward Farrelly as *Men of Honor: The Truth about the Mafia* (London: Fourth Estate, 1992).

page 453 "In 1999 Sicily received" — ISTAT (Italy's Institute of Statistics), "Il turismo in Sicilia negli anni novanta," 3 October 2000, unpaged.

page 453 "during the 1990s tourism . . . increased" — Ibid.

page 453 "census of 1981" — Rome: Caritas, Immigrazione, 2001, p. 422.

page 453 "At the end of the year 2000" — Ibid., p. 431.

SUGGESTIONS FOR FURTHER
READING IN ENGLISH

Bibliographical Note

Most of my raw material comes from works published only in Italian, so I am not giving the complete list here. I would be happy to send the list to any interested reader who mails me, care of the publisher, a stamped, self-addressed envelope large enough for twenty sheets. As the subject is history, many of the factual details can be found in an English-language encyclopedia such as the Britannica.

In Italian, I have made most use of the ten-volume *Storia della Sicilia,* edited by Rosario Romeo (Naples: Società editrice Storia di Napoli e della Sicilia, 1970). For material regarding the Muslims and the Normans, I have read with pleasure two books by Michele Amari, *Studi medievistici* (Palermo: Flaccovio, 1970) and *Storia dei Musulmani di Sicilia, Seconda edizione modificata e accresciuta dall'autore . . .* (Catania: R. Prampolini, 1933–39). For the modern history, especially political, I have obtained many particulars from the books of Professor Francesco Renda and of Dott. Romolo Menighetti, and for modern economic history from the monographs of Dott. Rosario Lentini at the Banca di Sicilia.

Forty years ago Professors Moses I. Finley and Denis Mack Smith walked the paths of Sicily with notebooks in hand, and while my purpose and my focus are different from theirs and I don't always agree with their interpretations, I found their books useful. The abridged edition is *A History of Sicily* (London: Chatto & Windus, 1986).

THE GREEK PERIOD

Sjöqvist, Erik. *Sicily and the Greeks.* (Ann Arbor: University of Michigan Press, 1973).
"When Ancient Greeks Went West" in *National Geographic* 146:2 [Aug 1974], pp.149–89.
"The Phoenicians: Sea Lords of Antiquity" in *National Geographic* 186:3 [Nov 1994], pp. 2–37.

NORMANS

Norwich, John Julius. *The Normans in Sicily: The Normans in the South 1016–1130 and The Kingdom in the Sun 1130–1194.* (New York: Harper & Row, 1967).

HOHENSTAUFEN PERIOD

Abulafia, David. *Frederick II: A Medieval Emperor.* (Oxford University Press, 1988).

———. *Commerce and Conquest in the Mediterranean, 1100–1500.* (Brookfield, Vt.: Variorum, 1993).

Runciman, Steven. *The Sicilian Vespers: A History of the Mediterranean World in the Later Thirteenth Century.* (Cambridge University Press, 1958).

EARLY TOURISM IN SICILY

Brydone, Patrick. *A Tour through Sicily and Malta in a Series of Letters to William Beckford* . . . 2 vols. (London, 1773).

Goethe, Johann Wolfgang von. *Italian Journey.* One excellent translation of the *Italienische Reise* into English is by Robert R. Heitner (New York: Suhrkamp Publishers, 1989).

SICILY BECOMES PART OF ITALY

Tomasi di Lampedusa, Giuseppe. *The Leopard* (New York: Pantheon, 1960). This novel gives a romanticized view of Sicily during the period of Unification.

Trevelyan, George Macauley. *Garibaldi and the Thousand* (New York: Longmans, Green, 1911) is probably the best of the many biographies of Garibaldi.

It seems that Garibaldi's every political idea and every romantic encounter were recorded somewhere, and he himself was an assiduous letter-writer, so the reader can find a plethora of material for particulars about Garibaldi's Sicilian experiences. The Garibaldi-Muecci museum on New York's Staten Island includes a dedicated reference library.

SICILY NEWLY PART OF ITALY

Dickie, John. *Darkest Italy: The Nation and Stereotypes of the Mezzogiorno, 1860–1900.* (New York: St. Martin's Press, 1999.)

EMIGRATION

Foerster, Robert F. *The Italian Emigration of Our Times.* (Cambridge: Harvard University Press, 1919.) This is the basic scholarly work on Italian emigration to all parts of the world.

Vittorini, Elio. *Conversations in Sicily*, with an introduction by Ernest Hemingway. (New York: New Directions, 1949). This is the translation of the short novel *Conversazione in Sicilia*, 1937.

FASCISM

Lyttelton, Adrian. *The Seizure of Power: Fascism in Italy 1919–1929.* (Princeton University Press, 1973, 1987).

THE MAFIA

Arlacchi, Pino. *Mafia Business: the Mafia ethic and the spirit of capitalism.* (London: Verso [distributed in the United States by Schocken Books], 1986.) There are hundreds of books of varying quality on the Mafia; I recommend those of the sociologist Arlacchi as combining serious scholarship with a readable style.

Duggan, Christopher. *Fascism and the Mafia.* (New Haven: Yale University Press, 1989).

SOCIOECONOMIC CONDITIONS FROM THE MID-TWENTIETH CENTURY

Dolci, Danilo. *Outlaws.* (New York: Orion Press, 1961). This is the translation of *Banditi a Partinico*, 1955.

———. *Poverty in Sicily: A Study of the Province of Palermo*, with an introduction by Aldous Huxley. (Penguin Books, 1966). This is the translation of *Inchieta a Palermo*, 1957.

———. *Waste: An Eye-witness Report on Some Aspects of Waste in Western Sicily* (New York: Monthly Review Press, 1964). This is the translation of *Spreco; documenti e inchieste su alcuni aspetti dello spreco nella Sicilia occidentale*, 1960.

Levi, Carlo. *Words Are Stones: Impressions of Sicily.* (New York: Farrar, Strauss & Cudahy, 1958). This is the translation of *Le parole sono pietre; tre giornate in Sicilia*, 1956.

Mangione, Jerre. *A Passion for Sicilians: The World around Danilo Dolci.* (New York: Morrow, 1968).

Maxwell, Gavin. *The Ten Pains of Death*. (Dursely, England: Alan Sutton, 1959.) Essay on Sicilian small-town life and poverty, and sympathetic portraits of traditional festivals and characters.

Sciascia, Leonardo. *The Day of the Owl* (London: Paladin, 1987, 1984); this is the translation of *Il giorno della civetta*. Sciascia's other works of fiction include *Sicilian Uncles* (Manchester, England: Carcanet, 1986), and *Open Doors and Three Novellas* (New York: Knopf, 1992).

Simeti, Mary Taylor. *On Persephone's Island*. (New York: Knopf, 1986). Life and food in Sicily's wine country, by an American long living there.

INDEX